Kinship in Europe

For
Effie Emmeline
and Bastian Luc,
and to the
memory of
Nesa

Kinship in Europe

Approaches to Long-Term Developments (1300-1900)

Edited By

David Warren Sabean

Simon Teuscher

Jon Mathieu

Berghahn Books
New York • Oxford

First published in 2007 by
Berghahn Books

www.berghahnbooks.com

©2007

Library of Congress Cataloging-in-Publication Data

Kinship in Europe : approaches to long-term development (1300-1900) /
edited by David Warren Sabean, Simon Teuscher, Jon Mathieu.
    p. cm.
Includes bibliographical references and index.
ISBN 978-1-84545-288-9 (hardcover : alk. paper)
  1. Kinship--Europe--History. 2. Europe--Social life and customs. I.
Sabean, David Warren. II. Teuscher, Simon. III. Mathieu, Jon.

GN575.K56 2007
306.83094--dc22

                                2007021131

British Library Cataloguing in Publication Data

A catalogue record for this book is available from the British Library

ISBN-10: 1-84545-288-7   ISBN-13: 978-1-84545-288-9   hardback

Printed in the United States on acid-free paper

Contents

Glossary

affinal	related by marriage
agnatic	kinship traced through males
clan	group of people of common descent
consanguineal	related by blood
cross cousins	a cousin through a mother's brother or a father's sister
dot	dowry
dower	portion of real property allowed to a widow for her lifetime
endogamy	marriage within a group, such as with consanguineal kin
exogamy	marriage outside a group, such as outside a kingroup
fidei commissum	contract regulating the use from undivided estate
heterogamy	marriage of unequals
homogamy	marriage of equals
hypergamy	marriage upwards into a higher social group, especially of women
isonymy	having the same name

kindred	the group of kin related to a particular person
lineage	line of descendants from a particular ancestor
matrifocal	kinship focused on a particular (usually older) woman
matrilateral	related through the mother
matriline	line of descent through females, or uterine kin
neolocality	residence not determined by origins of either spouse
parallel cousin	a cousin through the father's brother or the mother's sister
patrilateral	related through the father
patriline	the line of descent through males, or agnatic kin
patrilocality	residence determined by the husband's origins
uterine	kinship traced through females
uxorilocality	residence determined by the wife's origins

Preface

The development of kinship in Europe between the Middle Ages and Modernity has frequently been discussed in terms of a decline or contraction towards the modern nuclear family. During the last two decades, a number of critical studies on the history of kinship in specific social and geographic settings have appeared, many of which have—on the basis of both empirical evidence and of methodological reflection—called into question the assumption that the importance of kinship decreased steadily between the Middle Ages and the twentieth century. Indeed, recent historical research has demonstrated that kinship constituted a dynamic and highly constructive element in many specific social and geographic contexts during the modern era. Still, widely held assumptions about the decline of kinship prevent the results of such studies from receiving the attention they deserve in more general discussion about Western history.

This book presents contributions by a number of historians who have conducted case studies into kinship relationships and kinship organization between 1300 and 1900 and uses their work to discuss the long-term transformations of kinship in Europe. Rather than a linear development, we suggest a succession of at least two distinct major transitions. The first leads from the late Middle Ages into the early modern period and is connected to local variations of the process of state formation and reconfigurations in property holding. The second begins in the mid eighteenth century and sheds new light on the process of class formation, political modernization, and the dynamics of capitalist productive relations. Each of these transitions brought significant changes in the ways in which kinship mattered, and it is quite possible to contend that it gained significance in important new ways without suggesting that "kinship" occupies a quantifiable domain that rises and falls.

Our concern is with kinship in particular. Of course, marriage, the nuclear family, or the household, all of which have become topics of specialized historical research in recent decades, are directly related topics. But they shall only be drawn into our discussions to the extent that they affect relationships that reach beyond domestic units. The attempt to single out kinship does not assume that any particular relationships are primary, biological, or dominant. Throughout the entire period we are examining, other forms of personal relationships, such as friendship, clientage, and voluntary associations undoubtedly played equally important roles in many fields of cooperation. And it has always been the case that in many situations, kin and non-kin could assume very similar functions. We also understand that the notion of kinship—as it has been conceptualized in anthropological and historical research during the nineteenth and twentieth centuries—has always been informed by contemporary cultural presumptions. Yet, while kinship is a category that can only be used with critical caution for the investigation of past societies, in order to grasp its contours empirically, we ought not to begin by blurring distinctions between kin and non-kin.

Like most other relationships that matter in an individual's life, kinship in the sense of relationships that are largely defined by marriage and descent has, since the Middle Ages, been connected to the devolution and distribution of property and associated with relatively well-established claims to rights, as well as obligations and duties. Kinship is a phenomenon that throughout this entire period, although in varying terms and contexts, has continuously been a distinct topic of religious, legal, and other debates. Examining kinship provides insight into connections between general structures and everyday behavior, between class formation and gender divisions, and between the micro and macro levels of historical research, and challenges the antagonism between approaches to society focusing on interest and those based on the analysis of emotion, sociability, or culture.

Methods to cope with the difficulties of comparing kinship systems in the past were first developed by social anthropologists, whose main focus was on cultural differences between Western and non-Western societies. In recent years, historians have widened the discussion to include regional and social differences within Western society and raised doubts about the assumption of a fundamental dichotomy between the West and the "rest." Historians established that even the apparently structureless kinship systems of the West were highly structured—and that structures varied considerably from period to period and from place to place. More so than anthropologists, historians came to compare variations of kinship phenomena related to changes of institutional frameworks and economic practices. The recent endeavors towards comparison have contributed to clarifying differences in terminology and methodology, which allows approaching the long-term development of European kinship in more organized form.

The two transitions we propose, one from the Middle Ages into the early modern period and another from the latter into the modern period, also serve as organizing principles for the book, dividing it into two main sections. Each of them is preceded by a brief outline that gives an overview of the subsequent contributions and relates them to each other. This allows us to dedicate an introductory section to the wider context of research into kinship. David Sabean and Simon Teuscher discuss results of recent historical case studies about kinship in particular regional and social settings that open up questions for the two transitions. While we are fully aware that we are dealing with research that largely owes its questions and methods to the work of anthropologists and sociologists, we have made a deliberate choice to highlight the breadth of current historical research into kinship and to limit the volume to contributions by historians. The one exception is a second preliminary article by Sylvia Yanagisako who discusses why new historical approaches to the development of European kinship matter for debates in the field of social anthropology.

The contributions in this volume have grown out of papers held at three conferences. The first involved a round table session on "Family, Marriage, and Property" at the August 2000 meeting of the International Historical Congress in Oslo, Norway, where we first adumbrated the possibility of discussing systematic shifts in European kinship since the late Middle Ages. A second gathering developed some of the issues in a series of sessions at the European Social Science History Conference in The Hague, the Netherlands, in February 2002. These two conferences were followed by a major conference in Ascona-Monte Verità, Switzerland, in the fall of 2002. The present volume does not represent proceedings of these meetings, during which many more papers were presented than we could possibly fit into one book. While the conferences were part of an ongoing effort to intensify historical debates about kinship and will hopefully lead to additional publications, the contributions to this volume were chosen in order to present disparate perspectives on the long-term development that, while not agreeing amongst themselves, are committed to a common debate.

The introduction by Sabean and Teuscher does not attempt to bring together the different themes and issues considered in the chapters that follow. Rather, it offers a synthetic argument about a chronology for kinship *in* Europe, with the individual contributions in one way or another offering comparative reflections on its principles, suggestions, and observations. We have expressly tried to avoid a schematic approach in order to emphasize the fruitfulness of the challenge to long-term assumptions about kinship and modernization, which have almost always been understood as stories about freeing the individual from commitments to ascribed relations. Along the way, we talk about property regimes, ecclesiastical rules, state institutions, gender, and class relationships, but our focus is on kinship over the long term, and we have not offered a systematic treatment of any of these issues. We expect that each of them will offer ample opportunity for future conferences and collections of papers.

This book and the cycle of conferences on European kinship it grew out of would not have been possible without the generous support of several institutions on both sides of the Atlantic, each with a wonderful staff: The Swiss National Science Foundation, the Centro Stefano Franciscini, the Istituto di Storia delle Alpi at the Università della Svizzera italiana, the Henry J. Bruman Chair of German History, and the Center for Medieval and Renaissance Studies at the University of California, Los Angeles. Finally, we would like to thank the numerous participants in our conferences, the translators, and the authors of the chapters who have demonstrated great patience with the many revisions we had to ask for in order put together a book that bridges gaps between diverse traditions of scholarship.

Chapter 1

Kinship in Europe

A New Approach to Long Term Development

David Warren Sabean and
Simon Teuscher

Kinship has been said to be in decline at almost every moment during Western history. Historians have viewed the appearance of the most diverse new social structures—guilds and brotherhoods in the Middle Ages, the state in the early modern period, the market and voluntary associations in the eighteenth and nineteenth centuries, or social security in the twentieth—as either displacing kinship or replacing its lost functions. Western self-identity has a heavy investment in understanding the long-term development of its kinship practices as successive contractions toward the modern nuclear family. Within this framework, kinship is the functional predecessor of almost everything, but never a constructive factor in the emergence of anything. In what follows, we will suggest that a growing number of studies not only contradict widely held assumptions about the declining importance of kinship, but also point to broad, common, structural shifts in the configurations of kin across Europe between the Middle Ages and the early modern period and again at the turn of the modern era. In this introduction and in this book, we do not bring the story of kinship into the twentieth century, which would require considerations of a third transition and new structural features that demand treatment in their own right.

The different national and methodological traditions of historical scholarship into European kinship present quite diverse approaches, levels of interest, and progress. While we cannot attempt to synthesize the considerable and disparate debates on the subject, we do aim to provoke discussion between different schools of thought by highlighting what we see as broad historical shifts in the articulations and dynamics of kinship. The heterogeneity of research debates is, of course, in part due to the heterogeneity of the subject matter itself. How kin groups organized themselves in different time periods and places, in the town or the countryside, on the noble estate and the peasant farm, among office holders, courtiers, workers, and industrial entrepreneurs presents great differences in both the goals they attempted to realize and in the materials with which they had to work.

Kin relations depend on a wide array of exchange and communication. A sketch of long-term developments is necessarily selective, and we will have to concentrate on those articulations of kinship that lend themselves to comparison and have been addressed by numerous case studies: patterns of inheritance and succession, systems of marriage alliance, the circulation of goods, and the patterned practices of relationship, among blood relations and allied families, as well as developments in the terminology and in the cultural representations of kinship. A great deal of comparative discussion about kinship has been focused on the level of explicit rules in codifications of law and custom. The analysis of legal doctrines, judicial decisions, and innovations in legal instruments certainly remain a crucial task of analyzing kin organization. Nonetheless, some of the most important new research shows that law can be a very flexible instrument for quite different ways of doing things and that practice cannot be deduced from legal norms.[1] In contrast to older research, which implicitly expected kinship systems to have been uniform within broad regions, we expect to find tensions between diverging patterns of organizing kinship. Examining such tensions, for instance, between the conceptions of kinship that regulated the distribution of property and the ones that were highlighted for purposes of political representation, allows for a more specific picture of the driving forces of transformation.

In what follows, we will suggest two major transitions in the development of European kinship that many recent case studies from different regions and social settings call attention to. The first leads from the late Middle Ages into the early modern period, and the second can be traced from the mid eighteenth century. The fifteenth and sixteenth centuries witnessed a new stress on familial coherence, a growing inclination to formalize patron-client ties through marriage alliance or godparentage, and a tendency to develop and maintain structured hierarchies within lineages, descent groups, and clans and among allied families.[2] These developments were closely connected to processes of state formation and the formalization of social hierarchies as well as to innovations in patterns of succession and inheritance, new forms of delineating and mobilizing property, and novel claims to privileged rights in office, corporations, and monopolies. While the first transition can be associated with an increasing stress on vertically organized relationships, the second one brought about a stronger stress on horizontally ordered interactions. Beginning around the middle of the eighteenth century, alliance and affinity, rather more than descent and heritage, came to organize interactions among kin. During the early modern period, marriage alliances were sought with "strangers," frequently cemented long-term clientage relations, and created complex patterns of circulation among different political and corporate groups (*Stände, ceti, ordres*) and wealth strata. From the mid eighteenth century onwards, marriages became more endogamous, both in terms of class and milieu and among consanguineal kin: marriage partners sought out the "familiar." These innovations are intimately related to the formation of social classes and a differentiation of new gender roles within property-holding groups from the late eighteenth century onwards. And they also reflect reconfigurations in political institutions, state service, property rights, and the circulation of capital. If anything, the nineteenth century can be thought of as a "kinship-hot" society, one where enormous energy was invested in maintaining and developing extensive, reliable, and well-articulated structures of exchange among connected families over many generations. Even though we are trying to understand systems and structures as well as general transitions and unidirectional shifts, we do not intend to replace a master narrative about the constant decline of kinship by another one that is similarly simple. But even less do we want to fail to go beyond the uncontested generality that kinship at all times was diverse, situational, and unsystematically interconnected with other relationships. Our hypotheses aim at stimulating comparative discussions that are both specific enough to relate kinship phenomena to a wider context of social change and sufficiently open to include variations, alternative logics, and innovations.

First Transition: Middle Ages to the Early Modern Period

How Much of a Transformation Was There in the Eleventh Century?

Historical research has long been building on the notion of an antagonism between state organization and kinship, which assumed that as formal institutions of government grew, kinship lost its relevance. Lawrence Stone characterized the state as "the natural enemy" of kinship, and Jacques Heers argued that early state organizations attempted to "break all the ties of kinship."[3] Searching for a period when the state was particularly weak, historians zeroed in on the eleventh century, expecting to find vigorous kinship forms. Between the 1950s and the 1970s, Gerd Tellenbach, Karl Schmid, and Georges Duby gathered evidence of a shift in aristocratic kin organization around the year 1000 that has since been considered one of the most significant ruptures in the development of European kinship.[4]

In the preceding Carolingian period, the kinship system was adapted to a geographically mobile aristocracy in which wealth and prestige were largely based on service in a comparatively strong royal administration. In general, representations of kinship were less oriented towards generational depth than towards establishing horizontal links to living members of extended and overlapping networks that modern research often refers to as *Sippen* in German or *cousinages* in French. Hierarchies within these groups were not defined by specific genealogical constellations, but by individual members' positions outside their kin group, such as their closeness to rulers (*Königsnähe*). Kinship reckoning was bilateral, inheritance devolved on all the children, and women transmitted property and could perpetuate kinship identity. After the year 1000, the organization of kinship changed as the administrative structures of the Carolinigan Empire disintegrated. Royal rights of taxation and jurisdiction were appropriated by local counts or seigneurs, who considered themselves no longer accountable to a central authority. Aristocrats consolidated property on a particular place, which they frequently fortified and exploited as an autonomous lordship. They became sedentary, tied to their land, and concerned with preventing partition of their estates.

In this context, there emerged new conceptions of kinship that stressed patrilineal descent and the exclusion of family members who earlier would have participated in the wealth and prestige of the *Sippe*. Both daughters and younger sons were increasingly excluded from succession to local lordship that could thus be passed on unchanged from fathers to their oldest sons (primogeniture). New forms of representing

kin groups through coats of arms and surnames highlighted the continuity of agnatic groups over the course of generations. Some scholars
even observed traces of a spread of this dynastic family model down to
the social group of peasants.[5] Georges Duby stressed that hierarchies
within the new patrilineal dynasties came to be defined by gender, birth
order, and descent, emphasizing vertical structural patterns. Excluded
younger sons tended to continue a non-sedentary lifestyle by seeking
service in warfare with other lords and became the stock of recruitment
for the new social group of knights. The sisters of the successor were
frequently married off to his socially inferior vassals, and such alliances
hierarchically interlinked dynasties of different status.

While there is broad agreement about a trend towards stronger
agnatic relationships being *initiated* during the Middle Ages, the model
developed by Tellenbach, Schmid, and Duby has been whittled away at
for some time now. Recent scholarship has pointed to kin terminology,
theological discourses, and patterns of inheritance to show that kinship
in Europe throughout the Middle Ages and the early modern period, in
many respects, remained fundamentally bilateral despite changes in the
transmission of property. Indeed, medieval Latin and most Western ver-
naculars abandoned the elaborate Roman kinship distinctions between
paternal and maternal kin. Both in the high and the late Middle Ages,
the most frequently used terms to describe and address kin, such as
Latin *consanguineus* or *amicus*, French *lignage, ami* or *ami charnel*, or
German *fründe*, were not only used indiscriminately for paternal and
maternal (blood) relatives, but also often even for in-laws. Only at the
end of the Middle Ages did terms that singled out the patriline become
more prominent.[6] Also, ecclesiastical legal principles of the Roman
Catholic Church stressed bilateral conceptions of kinship through prohibitions of marriage within a quite extensive range of kin. One had to
marry outside, with someone who was "un-familiar," external to the
group descended from great-great-great-great-grandparents and
beyond. This is a negative way of describing those to whom one had
recognized positive links and ties of obligation; theological representation (largely preserved by later Protestant communities on the continent) recognized relatives on the agnatic and uterine sides as equal,
with shared substance diminishing only with generational distance.[7]

Moreover, recent research into high medieval regimes of property
transmission shows that many segments of society were not committed
to consistent systems of property transmission at all—certainly not in
the rigid sense that can be found in more densely regulated early modern societies. Inheritance arrangements could vary from family to family, and even within the same royal or noble family, the principal estate

could go undivided from a father to his firstborn son in one generation, while an equal division could take place in the next.[8] Some studies have argued that to the extent that property transmission during the High Middle Ages turned patrilineal at all, it did so in restricted ways. Patrilineal succession to specific rights did not necessarily entail a fully fledged dynastic family organization nor inhibit dividing property in many different ways.[9] It is useful to distinguish between inheritance and succession.[10] While the oldest son might "succeed" to his family's main estate and to his father's political position, all of the children might inherit property equally both immovable and movable. Patrilineal and primogeniture patterns applied primarily for succession to those lordly rights and titles that had to be passed unchanged from one generation to the other in order to preserve a family's social or political status. The shift toward patrilineal systems was, on the one hand, less general than earlier research had assumed, but on the other, more specifically related to modes of linking political power to the possession of certain goods such as castles, titles, and offices that remained stable over the course of generations. The elements of patrilineal kin organization that can be traced in the eleventh century were thus less due to a stateless stage of Western history than to attempts to institutionalize power. Accordingly, recent studies show that the patrilineal penchant of kin organization was reinforced in the course of the later Middle Ages and the early modern period as more institutionalized forms of organizing political power developed. Thus, both the chronology and the causality of the patrilineal turn of European kinship need to be reconsidered.

Changes at the End of the Middle Ages

The strong focus in older research on inheritance, which emphasizes issues of bilateral and unilineal systems of property devolution, has overshadowed the importance of marital property regimes, how spouses bring together, manage, and pass on their wealth.[11] In this respect, Martha Howell's in-depth study of the northern French city of Douhai is particularly thought provoking.[12] There, between the fourteenth and sixteenth centuries, a gradual, but at least for the upper classes, general transition of property regimes took place. In the older system, the property spouses brought into marriage and acquired throughout its duration was completely merged. Each of the spouses was the sole inheritor to the other, while their children only inherited whatever was left after the second spouse's death. The husband could freely dispose of the entirety of the marital funds, but at his death, his widow stepped into the exact same "male" rights he had previously held. This included the right to merge possessions from the first marriage into a second one. In the new regime, the property each spouse had brought into marriage remained separated. Parents provided their marrying daughters with a dowry that their husbands could not dispose of, nor did spouses inherit from each other, and children could claim inheritance immediately upon the death of each parent. Under both systems, marital property was frequently regulated in the form of written contracts, but whereas the contracts of the older system were between just two people, the wife and her husband, the new system required the participation of large numbers of kin who also came to acquire lasting responsibilities. Members of the wife's family of origin would protect her property both while her husband was alive and thereafter. After the husband's death, members of his family of origin would be in charge of defending the property interest of his children against the completely separate ones of their mother.

It seems that several regional societies developed similar commitments to the non-merging of lineal property, together with institutional guarantees for and by the lineal kin.[13] If future research should show that this corresponds to one general trend, the most diverse regimes of property transmission would represent innovations of the late Middle Ages. In Douhai's older inheritance pattern, property was primarily passed on within the same generation. As opposed to this, early modern partible and impartible inheritance systems alike tend to stress the devolution of property downwards in the chain of generations, along lines of descent that were construed as unaffected by marriage alliances. This shaped perceptions of property as something that belongs to lines of descent and entails lasting legal obligations of the members of the family of origin towards each other. While this is more obvious in patrilineal systems of inheritance, we should not fail to see that partible inheritance systems were also constructed as coherent practices at the turn of the early modern period.

There are additional reasons to reconsider the age of both the partible and unilineal inheritance patterns as we encounter them in the early modern period. Such systems are mainly known from regional and local statutes or customals (such as German *Weistümer* or French *coutumiers*) that, with few exceptions, were written down no earlier than the fourteenth to sixteenth centuries. Today, researchers largely agree that references in these texts to age-old law mainly served to legitimate attempts by central authorities to impose innovative rules in areas that had previously been characterized by different or altogether less regular practices.[14] Uniformity of norms, the training of personnel to administer and interpret the law, and the homogenization of practices, all were part of the development of regional cultures of both partible and impartible devolution in the transition to the early modern state apparatus.[15]

A number of recent case studies demonstrate how group specific patterns of property devolution underwent profound changes at the end of the Middle Ages, some of which occurred rapidly, within a few generations. So far, there have been few studies into the medieval developments that led to the consistently partible inheritance that in some regions emerged at the beginning of the early modern period.[16] But a number of recent examinations stress that thoroughgoing patrilineal systems of property devolution only developed at the passage to the early modern period. We would like to illustrate this with results of studies on groups as diverse as the English, German, and Sicilian elites.

Eileen Spring has recently studied the practices associated with entail and strict settlement in the English nobility and gentry between 1300 and 1800. Although a common law rule favoring primogeniture was in place from the beginning, families often provided well for younger children, including daughters, and rules concerning the inheritance by females in the absence of a male heir allowed for an estimated 40 percent of property to fall into the hands of women.[17] From the late Middle Ages onwards, the history of property law and familial practice was in the direction of excluding female succession and imposing strict primogeniture, patrilineality, and patriarchal rule, with the process only coming to final form at the beginning of the eighteenth century.[18]

As in many other systems of inheritance with a stress on patrilineality and primogeniture, the crucial means of dividing property rights in the English aristocracy were neither the testament nor legal and customary rules, but contracts at marriage. Those spelled out the charges to which the estate that the eldest son inherited would be liable for his younger siblings and regulated the contributions families of origin made to the marital funds of their daughters and sons.[19] In the early stages, grooms provided for the widowhood of their brides by giving them a dower which amounted to a third of the husband's estate. But successively, the dower was replaced by a practice whereby the family of the bride provided a portion, to which the groom answered with a jointure, a sum to be drawn upon in the case of his earlier death. By the sixteenth century, the ratio of portion to jointure was 5:1, and by the end of the seventeenth century, it had fallen to 10:1.[20] All during the marriage, the husband held the wife's portion and received the income from it. The upshot of this system was to throw the entire costs of maintaining a wife and settling a widow back onto her own family. Thus, throughout the late Middle Ages and the early modern period, both male and female properties were ever more strongly tied to their respective patrilines of origin.

In his investigation into kinship in the late medieval high nobility of western Germany, Karl-Heinz Spiess detected expressions of a patrilineal consciousness as early as the thirteenth century. Nevertheless, noble territories kept being divided equally among both daughters and sons well into the fourteenth century. In this period, daughters began to be excluded from rights to the main territories, but continued to receive substantial compensations at least up to the sixteenth century. Equal division among sons persisted until the fifteenth century, when territories came to be more consistently passed on undivided from fathers to their oldest sons, with younger sons increasingly excluded from inheritance and marriage. In the course of the fifteenth century, daughters came to be excluded from inheritance even in the absence of sons, with the next relative in the male line (for instance, the father's brother's son) succeeding to the estate.[21]

The stronger agnatic stress indicates a change of emphasis in the understanding of the material and immaterial goods that the high nobility passed on from generation to generation. In the older system, each son could marry and found a new line. The risk of a lineage's extinction was thus minimized, or—as in a contemporary formula—the dynastic name and reputation were preserved, while its property was divided through inheritance and merged through marriage with portions provided by other dynasties. In contrast, primogeniture reflected a change in the nature of noble property, which increasingly formed into stable territories with extensive administrative bodies. While the older inheritance system maintained the honor and prestige of all the branches of a dynasty, the new one aimed at preserving the integrity of state-like entities. Indeed, Cordula Nolte demonstrated that preventing the division of the noble territory was as much, if not more, of a concern of the officers who served the administration than of the members of a territorial lord's own family.[22] Joseph Morsel's case studies suggest that the kin conceptions and inheritance patterns of the lower German nobility changed at the same time and in a similar way. Here, patrilineal conceptions of *geschlecht* not only inhibited the divisions of estates, but also defined collectives with enduring obligations and privileges to hierarchical positions within the new, territorial political systems.[23]

A recent study of the Sicilian social elites by E. Igor Mineo presents a social group that was also late to develop consistently patrilineal patterns of inheritance. This group continued to divide property equally among all daughters and sons until the late fifteenth century, when consistent patterns of patrilineal inheritance spread rapidly. Along with this came a change in cultural representations of kinship. While memories of past generations had previously been shallow, the fifteenth century witnessed a rising interest in tracing paternal kin back over several generations. The political landscape of Sicily had long been characterized by a strong royal administration. Rural seigneuries had not been direct sources of political power, and urban social hierarchies depended on individual family member's relationships to the crown. The patterns of inheritance changed in close connection with the emergence of new institutional mechanisms of distributing power: the emergence of a parliament, noble status for its members, and new rules for inheritable rights to sit on city councils. These institutional mechanisms defined social and political positions less by personal relationship to the crown than by affiliation to specific groups. The stress on patrilineal conceptions of the family evolved around mechanisms of passing on such affiliations from one generation to the other.[24]

The upshot of recent historical work suggests that in the most diverse social groups, patrilineal forms of property devolution and of representing kin groups did not develop as the result of a sudden rupture during the eleventh century and disintegrate thereafter, but emerged and were gradually reinforced over centuries, with the crucial period of transition being much later than the consensus emerging in the 1970s suggested; namely, between 1400 and 1700. Patrilineal patterns repeatedly came into place to transmit goods that entailed political privileges and a specific position within social hierarchies. Throughout the Middle Ages and the early modern period, ever more goods adopted similar qualities—territories with a state-like character, titles, and certain properties that served as carriers of permanent, indivisible entitlements. Succession to these things came to be undivided, even when wealth and landed property could continue to be partitioned among the heirs. Still, it is important to see that titles and political position always had to be supported by significant amounts of property, which implied that unigeniture practices worked to establish a core of property and rights that differentiated sharply among the potential heirs.

Similarities and Variations in Early Modern Systems of Exclusion

Social groups of the early modern period provide evidence of a great variety of alternative systems to preserve the integrity of goods "carrying" political and social rights, not all of which entailed primogeniture or an exclusion of women. Examples are provided by what Bernard Derouet, Elisabeth Lamaison, and Pierre Claverie call "patrimonial lines" among farm holders in France. Here, the patrimony itself, not a particular heir, needed to be at the center of practices of succession, and the patrimony sometimes, even in the presence of a male heir, could fall to a daughter.[25] But—and this is the important point—succession to a patrimony was "closed," even when parents exercised judgment about the most suitable heir. As Derouet points out, in some French impartible inheritance systems, *maisons* gave the names to their members and ascribed obligations and exchanges between different houses carried along through time, irrespective of the particular kinship relationships and alliances of the moment.[26]

A comparative study of all the ways that families concentrated succession in Europe awaits its historian, but attention should be called to other forms by which families restricted entrance to goods in order to preserve the substance of specific estates and, where necessary, to keep the bulk of the property under the governance of one male heir. The instrument of choice on the continent was the entail or the *fidei commissum*, which Habakkuk compared to the English strict settlement.[27] It allowed the organization of families around a property that descended intact over many generations, while its yield was distributed to family members according to patterns that varied strongly from one group to another. In some ways, the practice was most rigorous in Spain, where it goes back essentially to the beginning of the sixteenth century. Originating with the great houses in Castile, it spread downwards to the minor nobility and across the different provinces, and it seems to have played an important role in the development of large landed agglomerations. The *fidei commissum* made its way to Austria around 1600 and to Hungary in the course of the seventeenth century.[28]

Noble and patrician families organized a great deal of their social exchanges around goods that they controlled through their relationship to the state or to the Church.[29] For urban communes in Southern Europe, Gérard Delille has found elaborate forms of organizing kin that defined succession to offices, the dividing lines of social inequality, and the patron client relationships that crisscrossed them. As patriciates closed off, the division of the population into *nobili* and *popolari* was institutionalized in the form of hereditary orders, each of which had access to particular offices. The emergence of these dual constitutions went along with divisions of noble patrilineages into several branches. While at least one branch remained noble, others could sink to the order of *popolari*. The reinstatement of the latter, however, could step in as soon as the chain of succession in the superior branch was interrupted. Delille's most recent work is the most ambitious study to date

of the institutionalizing of kinship structures consonant with developments in political organization during the early modern period.[30]

At the passage from the late Middle Ages into the early modern
period, groups of families came to treat public goods as a kind of shared
property. Particularly striking examples are provided by Heinz Reif and
Christoph Duhamelle, who have studied noble families in German
ecclesiastic territories.[31] Although offices in these territories were distributed by co-optation into the cathedral chapters and not directly
passed on by inheritance, narrow groups of related families came to
monopolize them through patterns of marriage and inheritance. Eligibility to the offices became ever more severely restricted to members
of families that had held them before. At the height of the system, any
individual acceding to office had to demonstrate sixteen quarterings,
that is, all of his great-great-great-grandparents had to have belonged to
qualified families. Primogeniture never became an element of these systems. The canons had to remain celibate, so that the ones who made
fortunes as officeholders could not be the ones who transmitted these
fortunes to their offspring. Offices and wealth were passed on along
separate routes from uncles to nephews. The families systematically
reduced the number of marrying children both male and female, and
established contracts that guaranteed that the property of the ones who
pursued ecclesiastic careers would fall back to the offspring of the sibling who was designated to marry and have children.

We still know far too little about how new property arrangements
affected patterns of cooperation and conflict within kin groups. A number of studies suggest that regimes of property devolution with a stress
on patrilineality and other mechanisms of exclusion developed along
with intrafamilial hierarchies, house discipline, and claims to authority
that were less structured through individuals' positions outside their
families than along the division of familial assets. Here, it largely
depended on the main inheritor's authority whether his excluded siblings and children could marry, establish their own households, or invest
into their own careers.[32] There are indications that the trend towards
more exclusive systems of inheritance also changed the manners in
which kinship and other types of relationship interacted. Examinations
into clientage in urban societies with bilateral inheritance in the late
Middle Ages found ample evidence of patron-client relationships
between people who were not related through kinship and often only
cooperated for a limited amount of time.[33] As opposed to this, studies
into early modern clientage have detected patterns of patron-client relationships that were kept alive over several generations and reinforced by
marriage alliances.[34] Against this background, new exclusive systems of

intergenerational transmission can be understood as elements in broader attempts to stabilize patterns of cooperation and to perpetuate relationships over several generations. A very important mechanism to maintain patron-client relations over several generations was offered by god-parentage as the village study of Neckarhausen found for the period up through the mid eighteenth century.[35]

Tensions between Representations and Practices

The traditional story is that emerging state institutions had to compete with older, kin-based forms of social organization. However, some recent studies have demonstrated that state organization systematically had recourse to normative concepts of kinship and reinforced their significance. Simon Teuscher's study on the city of Bern in the fifteenth and sixteenth century found that patterns of mutual support and cooperation in most fields presented little evidence of a preference for kin. Informal cooperation was often characterized by situational constellations, in which neighbors and changing constellations of friends, patrons, and clients played a more important role. Yet, in normative statements, contemporaries often postulated far-reaching solidarity among kin. A marked pressure to act—or to appear to be acting—in accordance with these norms of kin-solidarity was only felt in situations that called for strongly formalized legitimization, such as decision making in the city council. Private letters reveal that a main concern of informal preparations for official decision making in the council was to legitimize alliances between various people by providing them with an appearance of being based on kinship.[36]

Larger kin groups could be mobilized for political purposes through their representation as descent groups, even though they did not share in property and were so internally differentiated that they had little everyday interaction. This is a point that both Christian Maurel and Joseph Morsel made in their respective studies on Marseillais citizens and the German lower nobility during the late Middle Ages. As in many other contemporary settings, the affiliation that was stressed in political contexts was the large patrilineal group of kin that shared the same surname and had a remote common ancestor. Maurel showed how such groups comprised very distinct families of different social and economic status who rarely had much to do with each other. Inheritance took place within, rather than between, such families. Nevertheless, these larger agnatic and patronymic groups did cooperate intensively to gain access to city-office, claims to which were thought of as residing with such groups as a whole.[37] In Morsel's study, the patrilineal *geschlechter* were less grounded in intensive cooperation than in categories that were construed for the specific purposes of political classification and public representation.[38]

Particularly interesting in this respect are groups that highlighted patrilineal concepts of kinship despite the fact that they followed consistently bilateral patterns of inheritance. This is the case in the elites of the city of Bern in the period around 1500 or in the Swabian village of Neckarhausen during the eighteenth century.[39] There, David Sabean observed that practices of naming children singled out patrilineal lines within a completely bilateral system of kin-reckoning and property devolution. Boys almost always received their names from their paternal kin, from their fathers or their paternal uncles. And girls received their names from their mothers and their paternal aunts. Sabean relates this to village politics where, in spite of an electoral system, there emerged a trend for sons to succeed their fathers in offices.[40] In such cases, patrilineal concepts served as informal additions to the rules that shaped political constitutions.

*   *   *

To sum up, between the High Middle Ages and the early modern period, we can observe varied but comparable trends toward more well-established family strategies as well as more consistent patterns of property devolution, succession to office, and political power. In the course of these developments, many social groups showed indications of a greater stress on either patrilineality or other modes of passing goods undivided from one generation to the other. The last few examples show that patrilineal orientations varied considerably and did not necessarily imply fully fledged dynastic forms of organizing kin. The exclusion of daughters and of younger sons often initially applied to those goods, the possession of which granted access to political privileges and to positions in formalized hierarchies. Which goods acquired such characteristics as core property was just as varied as the early modern political systems themselves. Some noble families rapidly went over to excluding daughters and younger sons from almost all of their assets. For others, patrilineal transmission continued to concern mainly intangible goods, such as names and affiliations to privileged groups, while the large remainder of a family's assets had no such implications and could be merged, converted, and evenly divided among multiple heirs. In both cases, transformations in the modes of property devolution were coordinated with changes in the political meaning of possessing certain goods. In the general, overall trend during the early modern period, we can discern an ever increasing organization of kinship relations structured vertically and hierarchically around restricted succession to office, rank, and privilege and around ever more clearly regulated—and often more narrowly defined—inheritance practices. An individual's fate as well as his or her orientation within domestic space and within the network of related households, dynasties, lineages, and kindreds was largely established within the process of downwards devolution—whether through partible or impartible inheritance practices.

The research we have referred to does not support the common assumption that there was a general passage from rigidly structured kin-cooperation and vaguely structured state institutions to rigidly structured state institutions and weakened kingroups. On the contrary, the most diverse examples indicate a particular affinity between the stress on tight conceptions of kin organization and the formation of stable, highly formalized, and ultimately bureaucratic and state-like institutions. Both bureaucratic patterns and patrilinear or related forms of kin organization operate with stable hierarchies of functional roles (the heir, those admitted to and excluded from marriage, on the one side, the ruler, the holders of clearly defined offices, on the other) that can be filled according to predictable mechanisms by a succession of individuals. And both define relationships between roles along general criteria that can be verified without regard to subjective dispositions or agreements of the moment. Under this perspective, state formation and the realignment among kin and family appear as strongly interrelated developments at the passage from the Middle Ages to the early modern period.

At the passage to the early modern period, patrilineal and similarly exclusive conceptions of kin organization acquired an almost constitutional status. Although this in itself indicates a very significant social change, we should not overlook the normative character of kin conceptions that were "good to think with," that lent themselves to describe the order of society and that therefore appear prominently in the sources. Such concepts stress the axis between fathers and sons, the exclusion of women from wealth and power, and the continuity of entities such as lordships, states, and offices that circulated according to rules that were unaffected by the logic of markets and considerations of the moment. Thus, focusing on patrilineality without asking about the practices by which it was brought about can reinforce overly simplistic images of the late Middle Ages and the early modern period as characterized by static, hierarchical, and patriarchal societies. A closer look reveals that even the perpetuation of radically patrilineal patterns of devolution seem, in reality, to have depended on complicated settlements among husbands and wives or sisters and brothers, and on sales or mortgages that allowed for paying dowries and compensations. It was part of the transition we described that such aspects of the family organization were downplayed for purposes of representation, while the order of society was legitimized as the outcome of highly predictable mechanisms of succession and inheritance.

Second Transition: At the Turn of the Modern Era

Capital, Credit, and Kin Cooperation

During the eighteenth century, in places, from the early decades, but almost everywhere by around 1750, the structures stressing descent, inheritance, and succession, patrilines, agnatic lineages, and clans, paternal authority, house discipline, and exogamy gradually gave way to patterns centered around alliance, sentiment, interlocking networks of kindred, and social and familial endogamy. By no means did notions of agnatic lines disappear, and there are many indications of new practices among the middle classes to gather together family archives, publish the letters of this or that aunt, and to celebrate family memory through elaborate genealogies, publication of memoirs, and festive gatherings.[41] In Germany, many families in the decades after 1870 went so far as to found legally registered societies (*eingetragene Vereine*), restricting membership to all the male descendants of a particular ancestor—almost always born in the early decades of the eighteenth century—and creating an organization complete with president, treasurer, secretary, and archivist.[42] There seems to have been a need to memorialize and periodically assemble agnatic cousins to the fourth, fifth, and sixth degrees, a matter that still awaits its historian.[43] Many of the practices of property devolution continued into the nineteenth century, such as the strict entail in England and the *fidei commissum* in Prussia, but nevertheless, there are several indicators of a transition—progressing in uneven fits and starts throughout Europe, and not carried out everywhere, even by the end of the nineteenth century—towards systems of inheritance that partitioned property and distributed wealth more equitably among the heirs.[44] The adoption of partible inheritance rules in the *code civile* put pressure on systems of closed succession throughout France and in territories far across the Rhine. Beginning in Spain after 1820, the *fidei commissum* was abolished in law, and throughout Europe during the nineteenth century, in legal discussion, political tracts, and novels, entails were attacked as economically, socially, and morally bankrupt.[45] In German states, like the newly constituted kingdom of Württemberg, bureaucrats thought that the forms of closed inheritance found in the freshly acquired territories inhibited development and a healthy economy.

The progressive dissolution of patrilineal systems of property devolution was probably mostly prompted by bourgeois concerns, by people whose wealth came to be centered more directly on money, credit, and exchange than on land, monopolies, and birthright. There was, of course, the problem of middle-class creditors face-to-face with systems of landed property tied up in legal complexities and not easily mobilized. But more importantly, the century between 1750 and 1850 witnessed a burgeoning of trade and industrial enterprise. Wealth flowed through different channels, and the issue for those undertaking risky adventures in mining, metallurgy, textile production, and international trade was not how to manage and capitalize on a property that had descended over several generations, but how to bring together investment capital through credit and assemble reliable staff or correspondents.[46] This necessitated skills of persuasion, networks of friends and allies willing to commit resources to new ventures, and the kind of intimate relations necessary to train the new generation, circulate information, provide advice and advocacy, and fulfill positions of trust. It was, of course, not just a matter of middle-class economic dynamics that led to the mobilization of wealth. Many landlords of the period needed capital in order to invest in agricultural improvement, became subject to land, credit, and commodity markets, and cultivated mechanisms to survive bankruptcy socially.

There was no single response on the part of family and kin to the new dangers and opportunities that came in the wake of the capitalization of agriculture, the expansion of industry, and the intensification of regional, interregional, and international exchange. Kinship structures are not dependant variables, but innovative and creative responses to newly configured relationships between people and institutions and around the circulation of goods and services. Therefore, there could be many different ways of developing patterns of interaction, cultivating networks, and evolving systems of reciprocity. "Kinship and the alliance system of the nineteenth century were crucial for concentrating and distributing capital; providing strategic support over the life of individuals; structuring dynasties and recognizable patrilineal groupings; maintaining access points, entrances, and exits to social milieus through marriage, godparentage, and guardianship; creating cultural and social boundaries by extensive festive, ludic, competitive, and charitative transactions; configuring and reconfiguring possible alliances between subpopulations; developing a training ground for character formation; shaping desire and offering practice in code and symbol recognition ... training rules and practices into bodies; and integrating networks of culturally similar people."[47]

There are many examples of how this worked, but we can take one English instance of a nineteenth-century entrepreneurial family—the Courtaulds—studied in a classic work by D. C. Coleman.[48] The development of the family textile industry was based on a supply of cash and credit provided by a fairly extensive network of family and friends.[49] Capital was accumulated through such connections throughout Europe, and it is not until very late in the century when access to finance capital began no longer to be found primarily among family and friends.[50] Coleman's study demonstrates the reliance on family, not only for the many management positions, but also for a range of other positions in the expanding firm. The intense familial intercourse went well beyond business, however, as members attended the same Unitarian chapels and carried on a vigorous correspondence full of religious ideas. And of course, the cultural foundation of familial exchange was also expressed in considerable political activity. In short, the family was embedded in a particular milieu of radical dissent, which they also actively maintained and helped construct.[51] It was from within this milieu that they married, that they found their creditors, and that they recruited the personnel to direct and manage their business enterprise. In all of this, kinship played a central role. The generation senior to the founding of the firm (1828) made multiple alliances between a few families (all Unitarian) in the later decades of the eighteenth century, with some of the first connections going back to an earlier period of apprenticeship of the men. Their children intermarried, creating a series of ever repeated alliances that lasted through the century. Brothers, brothers-in-law, cousins, fathers and sons, uncles and nephews cooperated in religion, politics, and business. Sisters, aunts, mothers, and female cousins provided capital (they received equal inheritances in each generation), and, although Coleman does not go into their lives in any detail, it is clear that they were not at all passive in family politics, and we suspect that they were central figures in constructing the alliances that determined the flow of resources, the promotion of individuals, and the coherence of their particular milieu. Certainly they were active correspondents with their male family members. In any event, the history of the family offers a fine example of the way in which social endogamy closely articulated with familial endogamy.

Similar dynamics can be found throughout property-holding classes across Europe from the mid eighteenth century to the eve of World War I. Many different strategies of kinship interaction can be found, but we are barely at the stage of describing and analyzing any of them, let alone being able to map the different possibilities by region, class, or occupation. We already know that a particular region could employ several different strategies of alliance according to occupation and property.[52] In separate studies of a south German village and the rural Neapolitan hinterland, the authors argued that the development of rapidly expanding land markets and reconfigurations in political dynamics from the mid eighteenth century were closely tied up with new forms of familial alliance, which not only made for ever tighter endogamy within kingroups but also ever more controlled marriage within wealth strata.[53]

New Elite and Cousin Marriage

The articulation of kinship structures with the destabilizing conditions of the market, economic and class differentiation, and entrepreneurial opportunity is only part of the story. We have suggested that the "property" around which family hierarchies were constructed, life chances allocated, and patrilines crystallized from the late Middle Ages onward could take many forms, from peasant farms and noble estates to ecclesiastical prebends, royal offices, and membership in urban patriciates, gilds, and noble caste structures. The complex state reforms associated with the turn of the nineteenth century brought an end to almost all these forms of familial privilege. The French Revolution, by putting an end to the sale of office, necessitated new forms of recruitment, promotion, and tenure, and encouraged a new political culture throughout the regions and urban centers of France. In Württemberg, to give a German example, while there was no expectation in the eighteenth century for any particular office to descend along a patriline, a small number of families controlled access to office—even the Protestant pastorate became a closed hereditary caste—and critique of "old corruption" was already strong by the mid eighteenth century.[54] After the reconfiguration of the realm in 1815, constitutional battles surged around the issue of the relation of private interest to the public exercise of office, with the champions of a revised administrative monarchy winning the battle in the post-1815 decade. An administrative apparatus divorced in principle from private familial interests was constructed under King Wilhelm I. We have already discussed the noble families that controlled the cathedral chapters in the extensive ecclesiastical territories in northwest Germany and the Rhineland. As these territories were integrated in the newly constructed secular states during and after the Napoleonic era, the older rights to office were abolished.[55] As in France, one can speak here of a shift to a system of "careers open to talent." In 1811, the aristocratic control of accession to office in municipal governments in Spain was abrogated.[56] Or, for another example, after 1765, the Austrian authorities reorganized the government in Lombardy, ending the formal predominance of the patricians.[57] Thus, in all of these states, the older, closed, caste-like structures gave way to reconfigured regional elites whose kinship dynamics relied less on the devolution of specific goods and titles than on the maintenance of well-integrated networks and multiple exchanges between allied families. Wherever we look, the class of bureaucrats and officials reproduced itself, no longer through devolution, but through an open system of exchange, with allied families building a culture from within which each generation succeeded the other. The new order did indeed require talent, which in turn was channeled through connection and networking. Describing the change here as a shift from vertically structured to horizontally structured familial dynamics is a loose but effective way to characterize the nature of the reconfiguration.[58]

The changes we have delineated in the economy and state have most often been brought under the general concept of "modernization." And the story of modernization has included the rise of the nuclear family and the cutting off of extensive kinship ties. What we are suggesting, however, is just the opposite. The transition to the nineteenth century is characterized by the construction of systematic, repeated alliances between families, patrilines, or agnatically constructed groups, recognized by a common surname—however one wants to describe them—who, over many generations, contracted repeated marriages, circulated godparents, and took over offices of guardianship, tutelage, and legal representation, creating tight bonds of reciprocity, extensive overlapping kindreds, and networks of kin recognition well beyond what most of us can imagine for ourselves today. At the heart of the system was cousin marriage, and cousins were repeatedly turned into brothers- and sisters-in-law and spouses.

Coincidental with the shifting nature of political and economic relations of elites, landholders (from noble to peasant), merchants (from capitalist entrepreneur to petit bourgeois), and officeholders, there was a fundamental alteration in the ways that families could connect with each other. Ecclesiastical and state law in continental Europe had forbidden marriage between quite extended relatives. In Catholic countries, according to canon law, a person could not marry within the circle bounded by third cousins without a dispensation. Nor could one marry into the same kingroup a second time; one could not marry up to and including a third cousin of a deceased spouse. Most Protestant states (except England) kept the same formal system, but stepped the prohibition back one notch to second cousins, and until late in the seventeenth century, did not allow dispensations on a regular basis. The system of prohibitions made it impossible for families to continue alliances between themselves in the following two or three generations, and what little detailed study of genealogies there is shows that families did not continue alliances in the fourth or fifth generation either. There was no impulse to construct alliances over many generations at all.[59] In England, too, there is little evidence through the seventeenth century of repeated consanguineal marriages.

Throughout Europe, the typical alliance between two families had to be one of "strangers." There were indeed various strategies for linking families together, and in French scholarship one such strategy has come to be called "rechaining."[60] Some of the patterns that have been found include a marriage that closes a circle of three or four sets of in-laws, a marriage between a father/son pair and a mother/daughter pair (or uncle/nephew with an aunt/niece pair), or two cousins with two siblings.[61] Nonetheless, such forms of alliance can be understood as reinforcing certain intragenerational connections, but they do not and cannot lead to continuous solidarities over several generations utilizing the same forms. Indeed, most studies so far suggest that these kinds of marriages are often to be understood in terms of patron/client relations, linking households of unequal status together.[62]

From around the middle of the eighteenth century, pushed from below, the older prohibitions became subject to pro forma dispensations or were abrogated altogether. From that period onwards throughout Europe and in all property holding groups, endogamous marriages were part of the reconfiguration of kinship. Forms of alliance that had previously been considered as incestuous, such as marriage with the deceased wife's sister or with a niece, or were simply prohibited, such as first and second (or third) cousins, became fully acceptable and made up part of the overall strategies of noble, middle class, and peasant families.[63] First cousin marriages reiterate an alliance from the previous generation, while second cousin marriages repeat an alliance first struck by grandparents. Yet, when one looks at a genealogy as a whole, one finds that in any particular generation, both first and second cousin marriages can be found; two siblings might marry two siblings, and various other connections might occur that link two patrilines that are not directly consanguineal. That is, families frequently put together several marriages in each generation, linking them through varied paths, but all with the same intention to draw the bonds between them ever tighter. And also, very important were remarriages that repeated the same alliance (with the deceased spouse's sibling, sibling's child, or cousin). All these marriages created a dense set of exchanges linking families over several generations, reinforced by godparentage, guardianship, capital transfers, religious and political activity, family festivals, exchanges

of children for education, socialization, or care, and many more transactions that are amply documented in the literature.[64] Along with this
closeness based on familiarity came a stronger appreciation of romantic
love, emotional accord, and similarity of personality as the basis of legitimate marriage. This was by no means contrary to economic considerations: the flow of sentiment and the flow of money operated in the
same channels.[65] We have already seen how the Courtauld family
entered into alliances within tightly knit religious association and a circle of political fellows. But they also allied themselves with the same
families over many generations. George Courtauld and William Taylor
were apprentices together in the 1770s. They married one another's sisters: "From these two marriages came most of the partners or directors
for a century."[66] The next generation found several first cousin marriages, and two Taylor/Courtauld cousins married with a new family
(Bromley siblings), with a subsequent marriage to a deceased wife's sister. After some Courtaulds or their allied family members made new
marriages with other families, such as the Bromleys, the following generation found either fresh cousin marriages or other exchanges among
the newly allied lines. In more than one case, a man marrying a cousin
found he was also doubly her brother-in-law. The political, religious,
social, and business milieu was fostered by intense traffic for well over
a century within a set of allied families.[67]

Tensions between representation and practice

We are arguing that a tight, endogamous pattern of alliance can be seen
as modern, not archaic, certainly in the sense of being developed during
a period of capitalized agriculture and wage -labor, protoindustrialized
and industrialized production, and state rationalization. It was also tied to
the transformation of class relations throughout Western society: class *differentiation* went hand in hand with kin *integration*. In a period of rapid
population increase, undergoing capitalization and intensification of agricultural and industrial labor; where class differentiation was increasing
and the pains of harsh economic cycles and subsistence crises were
sharply felt; where regional mobility was increasing and the villages, small
towns, and cities were becoming economically more integrated into
wider markets; where property holdings were becoming decimated and
subject to rapid turnover or landholders becoming subject to credit and
commodity markets; and where pauperization came to characterize large
swathes of the population and affect the pattern of social relations—with
all this going on, property holders of all scales, officials, and petits bourgeois consolidated and extended the system of marriage alliances developed in the fifth, sixth, and seventh decades of the eighteenth century.

The question arises, why, since there was considerable knowledge and discussion about close, consanguineal marriages—increasingly during the nineteenth century—among medical practitioners, biologists, and geneticists, there was practically no notice taken of the phenomenon among sociologists. Novelists showed no hesitation to understand social milieus in terms of the close interaction of kindreds and frequently pointed to the strategic importance of marriages among such social groups linking families together that already had many such links from earlier generations. Perhaps the explanation lies in a triple distortion of perception derived from the dominant binaries of public and private, male and female, and culture and savagery (or civilized and primitive). With everything relegated to the private, familial, domestic sphere coded as female, male sociologists were not very much interested in investigating that area of secondary importance. But they also designed sociology as a science of the civilized, cultured, and modern societies (the West) and developed anthropology for the natural, primitive, or savage peoples (the rest). Sociology might deal with the "family," the relationships, sentiments, and moral dimensions of the stripped down, paternal, nuclear unit thought to be central to European/American advanced societies, leaving anthropology to deal with "kinship," the strange marriage practices of the estranged other world. With kinship coded as private, female, and primitive, it could only be a residual category of the West's past.

The old story of the rise of the nuclear family and the decline of the importance of kinship is not simply innocent. It has been used as the model that all modernizing economies and societies are held up to. Their present has been understood to be our past. The history of the family is part of the history of the rise of the Western individual, cut loose from the responsibilities of kin, and cut out for the heroic task of building the self-generating economy. In the story that Western sociologists told themselves, kinship became the property of primitive societies and part of the specialization of the disciplines; anthropology for them and history for us. Lewis Henry Morgan was the first prophet, inventing the system of kinship calculations of primitives for both socialists (Marx and Engels) and sociologists, all the time being married to his first cousin and watching his son make a similar alliance. And Weber contracted a "conventional" cousin marriage after turning down two other cousins.[68] The hidden past of Western arguments about the necessary connection between development and rational family configurations lies in repressed consciousness about self and curious projection about the other.

Our argument here is that European kinship systems were reconfigured in the half century after circa 1750. Even though we are well aware that the mapping of kinship systems in Europe is just at its inception, it is hard to overlook the central importance of cousin marriages and repeated consanguineal endogamy, homogamy, and familial-centered construction of cultural and social milieus. This in itself contradicts the traditional story of European modernization—the new kinship dynamics were crucial for the construction of local milieus and thereby contributed to the formation of classes in the nineteenth century, they were the fundamental resource for capital accumulation and business enterprise, and they were the mechanism for political elites and officials to reproduce themselves.

Conclusion

In this introduction, we have pointed to the importance of understanding kinship for analyzing some of the salient features of European history since the late Middle Ages. With all due caution and with as much complexity as possible in the space available to us, we have suggested a broad, but coordinated periodization for a phenomenon that has so far been described in terms of decline rather then of qualitative change. The process of modernization in Europe had a first phase (the "early" modern), which saw the birth of modern fiscal regimes, bureaucracies, armies, legal codes, political theory, and dogmatic theology, to name some of the most important forces that together shaped the new, emerging state forms of "absolutism," sometimes "enlightened" and sometimes not. Historians have understood that property regimes were implicated in all of the crucial changes. Derouet has shown how quite different political regimes at the village level were coordinated with different forms of property devolution, and most recently, Delille has shown how across Southern European estate systems, practices of property devolution, state governance, officeholding, and violence in their often kaleidoscopic interactions with each other in regional and local complexes can be examined to revise our understanding of the fundamental historical processes thoroughly. Kinship is central to the project, and in this first phase, it resonated closely with "property," practiced and thought of as something that continued down along the generations and around which families, lineages, and dynasties constructed their hierarchies and alliances. States, economies, and societies entered into a second metamorphosis around the middle of the eighteenth century, with wealth, credit, and capital channeled in new ways, and states emerging that could no longer tolerate the colonization of their "public" institutions by private families. As a result, alliances came to be redrawn, and the private life of coordinated families became the fertile ground for constructing classes, reproducing the grasp of elites on the levers of the emerging nation states, and providing the funds, material, and personnel for improving landlords, capitalist merchants, and industrial producers.

We are well aware that we are providing here only the first crude maps of the terrain of kinship, and it seems to us that there are four tasks that lie ahead for research into this promising area. (1) There needs to be more research that specifies the different ways in which kin could operate or be mobilized by region, class, and occupation. Some time ago, Martine Segalen already dealt with a region of leaseholders in the west of France that, during the nineteenth century, did not construct consanguineal alliances, as we have talked about here, but constant overlapping linkages, creating chains of in-laws, constituting dense, regional "kindreds" crucial for access to information, land, marriage partners, and labor opportunities. Or to give another example, Werner Mosse suggested that among Central European Jewish banking families, two or three basic patterns of kinship emerged that both set the groups of allied families off from each other and created close ties of cooperation within them—with each kinship network being constructed on different principles.[69] We also need to look more into the links between the nature of material and immaterial goods (lordship, offices, education, capital assets) and the patterns of their distribution and devolution among kin. (2) Kinship, whether studied by anthropologists or by historians, is subject to quite different national traditions of analysis. Despite all the criticism by Foucault and Bourdieu, among others, the French tradition seeks out structures and concentrates most centrally upon marriage and marital exchange. The British tradition was always concerned with behavior and with the "web" of relations among kin. There were many attempts among anthropologists to combine alliance theory of the French with the understanding of group recruitment among the English, but a great deal more needs to be done to think through the two traditions for historical research. Marriage in Europe, especially where there is no divorce, shapes lasting relations and provides a long-term element for attaching and detaching individuals, houses, and kindreds. One way to get at the dynamics of kin would be to examine crucial dyads in the various societies, looking at the interaction of brothers, brothers and sisters, fathers and daughters, and so forth, in a systematic and comparative way. We cannot leave the analysis of primogeniture simply to the privileging of the eldest son without looking at the lives of the cadets/cadettes. There needs to be considerable more research into the resources available to women and younger sons. Here, the British tradition in anthropology of stressing "jural" relations could lead to the fruitful examination of rights and duties, claims and obligations, of the different kinds of kin. (3) Another important matter to consider is the role of the state in the shaping of kin and the role of kin in the shaping of the state. We have already made a great deal out of the way landed property in the early modern period was intimately related to and frequently hardly distinguished from public property. In regimes where the sale of office developed, such as Spain and parts of France, quite different familial dynamics were available than in southern Italy, where access to office was related to closed "castes." In the nineteenth century, sharper distinctions between the private sphere and public state function were made, and yet the class of bureaucrats reproduced itself through the same families. Exploring how this was possible will probably lead us to local, regional, and national kin structures and patterns of alliance as complex as those in Renaissance and Baroque Europe. A related topic is the relation between kinship organization and changes in ecclesiastic and secular law. The period we have covered is one of the formalization, uniformization, and codification of legal systems, which went along with the emergence of new concepts of normativity that also must have affected the manner in which obligations to kin, inheritance rules, and incest regulations were understood. (4) One of the most promising areas of research is the way kinship and gender interact with each other. As a result of the exclusion of woman from landed property in many areas of Europe, women tend to disappear from the historical picture. Yet, we know increasingly from the consideration of aristocratic and ruling families that women were active participants in government and in the construction of alliances. In the nineteenth century, it appears that the construction of alliances among property holding groups from the petite bourgeoisie to the new regional aristocracies was largely in the hands of women, who carried on vast correspondences and labored at the integration of allied families, looking out for the educational and professional interests of the youth, and helping with the accumulation of the necessary capital for all kinds of enterprises. Mapping kinship from the perspective of women will probably open up a new understanding of what constitutes the political and lead to another way of breaking up the clean line between public and private.

Notes

1. Cf. Bernard Derouet, "Les pratiques familiales, le droit et la construction des différences (15e-19e siècles)," *Annales HSS* 52 (1997): pp. 369–91; Eileen Spring, *Law, Land, and Family: Aristocratic Inheritance in England, 1300 to 1800* (Chapel Hill and London, 1993), pp. 3–4.
2. For the latest and most stimulating introduction to this for all of southern Europe, see Gérard Delille, *Le maire et le prieur: Pouvoir central et pouvoir local en Méditerranée occidentale (xve-xviiie siècle)* (Paris, 2003).
3. Lawrence Stone, *The Family, Sex and Marriage in England 1500–1800* (London, 1977), pp. 132–35; Jacques Heers, *Le clan familial* (Paris, 1974), pp. 129–35, 265. This argument has been made again, although, in a less apodictic form, by David Gaunt, "Kinship: Thin Red Lines of Thick Blue Blood," in *The History of the European Family*, ed. David I. Kertzer and Marzio Barbagli (New Haven, 2001), vol. 1, pp. 257–87.
4. Karl Schmid, "Zur Problematik von Familie, Sippe und Geschlecht, Haus und Dynastie beim mittelalterlichen Adel. Vorfragen zum Thema 'Adel und Herrschaft im Mittelalter',"*Zeitschrift für Geschichte des Oberrheins* 105 (1957): pp. 1–62; Gerd Tellenbach, "Vom karolinigischen Reichsadel zum deutschen Reichsfürstenstand," in *Herrschaft und Staat im Mittelalter*, ed. Hellmut Kämpf (Darmstadt, 1956), pp. 190–242; Georges Duby, "La noblesse dans la France médiévale: une enquête à poursuivre," *Revue historique* 226 (1961): pp. 1–22; Georges Duby, "Lignage, noblesse et chevallererie au XIIe siècle dans la Région maconnaise. Une révision," *Annales ESC* 27 (1972): pp. 803–23. For overviews on recent contributions to the debate: Martin Aurell, "La parenté en l'an mil," *Cahiers de civilisation médiévale* 43 (2000): pp. 125–42; Dieter Mertens and Thomas Zotz, "Einleitung der Herausgeber," in *Karl Schmid. Geblüt, Herrschaft, Geschlechterbewusstsein: Grundfragen zum Verständnis des Adels im Mittelalter. Aus dem Nachlass herausgegeben*, ed. Dieter Mertens and Thomas Zotz (Sigmaringen, 1998), pp. IX–XXXIII, here pp. XVIII–XXVIII; Janet Nelson, "Family, Gender and Sexuality in the Middle Ages," in *Companion to Historiography*, ed. Michael Bentley (London, New York, 1997), pp. 153–76, here pp. 160–64.
5. Aurell, "Parenté," p. 135.
6. Anita Guerreau-Jalabert, Régine Le Jean, and Joseph Morsel, "Familles et parents. De l'historie de la famille à l'anthropologie de la parenté," in *Les tendances actuelles de l'historie du Moyen Âge en France et en Allemagne*, ed. Jean-Claude Schmidt and Otto Gerhard Oexle (Paris, 2002), pp. 433–46; Anita Guerreau-Jalabert, "La designation des relations et des groupes de parenté en latin médiéval," *Archivum Latinitatis Medii Aevii* 46/7 (1988): p. 92f; Anita Guerreau-Jalabert, "Sur les structures de parenté dans l'Europe médiévale (Note critique)," *Annales ESC* (1981): pp. 1028–49, here pp. 1030–31, 1043–44; Simon Teuscher, *Bekannte—Klienten—Verwandte. Sozialität und Politik in der Stadt Bern um 1500* (Cologne, Weimar, Vienna, 1998), pp. 75–84; Joseph Morsel, "Geschlecht als Repräsentation. Beobachtungen zur Verwandtschaftskonstruktion im fränkischen Adel des späten Mittelalters," in Otto Gerhard Oexle and Andrea von Hülsen-Esch, eds., *Die Repräsentation der Gruppen. Texte—Bilder—Objekte* (Göttingen, 1998), pp. 259–325, here pp. 263–70, 308–10; Juliette M. Turlan, "Amis et amis charnels. D'après les actes du parlement au XIVe siècle," *Revue historique du droit français et etranger* 47 (1969): pp. 645–98.

7. On the issues of marriage prohibitions and the reckoning of kinship, David Warren Sabean, *Kinship in Neckarhausen* (New York, 1998), pp. 63–89; Guerreau-Jalabert, "Sur les structures," pp. 1033–38.

8. Joanna H. Drell, *Kinship and Conquest: Family Strategies in the Principality of Salerno during the Norman Period 1077–1194* (Ithaca, 2002), pp. 90–121; Aurell, "Parenté," p. 133; Teofilio Ruiz, *From Heaven to Earth: The Reordering of Castilian Society, 1150–1350* (Princeton, 2003), pp. 87–109.

9. Anita Guerreau-Jalabert, "Parenté," in *Dictionnaire raisonné de l'Occident medieval*, ed. Jacques Le Goff and Jean-Claude Schmitt (Paris, 1999), pp. 861–76, here pp. 862–66; Guerreau-Jalabert, "Familles et parents," pp. 438–40.

10. On this distinction compare Guerreau-Jalabert, "sur les structures"; Derouet, "Pratiques familiales."

11. David Warren Sabean, "Aspects of Kinship Behaviour and Property in Rural Western Europe Before 1800," in *Family and Inheritance: Rural Society in Western Europe 1200–1800*, ed. Jack Goody, Joan Thirsk, and E. P. Thompson (Cambridge, 1976), pp. 96–111.

12. Martha C. Howell, *The Marriage Exchange: Property, Social Place, and Gender in Cities of the Low Countries 1300–1550* (Chicago, 1998).

13. Howell found some indicators that similar shifts of marital property regimes took place in several places of contemporary Northern Europe; Howell, *Marriage*, pp. 234–35.

14. Simon Teuscher, "Kompilation und Mündlichkeit. Herrschaftskultur und Gebrauch von Weistümern im Raum Zürich (14-15. Jh.)," *Historische Zeitschrift* 273 (2001): pp. 261–78; Martine Grinberg, "La rédaction des coutumes et les droits seigneuriaux: nommer, classer, exclure," *Annales HSS* 52 (1997): pp. 1017–38; Derouet, "Pratiques familiales," pp. 370–72; Rolf-Dieter Hess, *Familien- und Erbrecht im württembergischen Landrecht von 1555 unter besonderer Berücksichtigung des älteren württembergischen Rechts* (Stuttgart, 1968).

15. Early modern systems of partible inheritance have been discussed for the southern German village of Neckarhausen by Sabean, *Kinship*, and in comparative perspective with France by Derouet, "Pratiques familiales," pp. 370–72.

16. Derouet, "Pratiques familiales," pp. 370–72.

17. Spring, *Law, Land, and Family*, p. 93.

18. Spring, *Law, Land, and Family*, p. 144.

19. Spring, *Law, Land, and Family*, chap. 5.

20. Spring, *Law, Land, and Family*, pp. 50–52.

21. Karl-Heinz Spiess, *Familie und Verwandtschaft im deutschen Hochadel des Spätmittelalters. 13. bis Anfang des 16. Jahrhunderts* (Stuttgart, 1993).

22. Cordula Nolte, "Der kranke Fürst. Vergleichende Beobachtungen zu Dynastie- und Herrschaftskrisen um 1500, ausgehend von den Landgrafen von Hessen," *Zeitschrift für historische Forschung* 27 (2000): pp. 1–36.

23. Morsel, "Geschlecht," pp. 259–325.

24. E. Igor Mineo, *Nobilità di Stato: Famiglie e identità aristocratiche nel tardo meioevo: La Sicilia* (Roma, 2001).

25. Elisabeth Claverie and Pierre Lamaison, *L'impossible mariage. Violence et parenté en Gévaudan, xviie, xviiie, xixe siècle* (Paris, 1982). See the detailed analysis of their material in Sabean, *Kinship*, pp. 407–16. Bernard Derouet, "Parenté et marché foncier à l'époque moderne: une réinterprétation," *Annales HSS* 56 (2001): pp. 337–68, here pp. 350–59; Bernard Derouet, "La transmission égalitaire du patrimoine dans la France rurale (xvie-xixe siècles): Nouvelles perspectives de recherche,"

in *Familia, casa y trabajo: Historia de la Familia*, 3 vols., ed. F. Chacón Jiménez (Murcia, 1997), vol. 3, pp. 73–92, here pp. 89–90; Bernard Derouet, "Territoire et parenté. Pour une mise en perspective de la communauté rurale et les formes de reproduction familiale," *Annales HSS* 50 (1995): pp. 645–86, here p. 685; Bernard Derouet, "Le partage des frères: Héritage masculin et reproduction sociale en Franche-Comté aux xviiie et xixe siècles," *Annales ESC* 48 (1993): pp. 453–74; Bernard Derouet, "Pratiques successorales et rapport à la terre: Les sociétés paysannes d'ancien régime," *Annales ESC* 44 (1989): pp. 173–206, here pp. 174–75, 176–77, 191–96; Bernard Derouet and Joseph Goy, "Transmettre la terre: Les inflexions d'une problématique de la différence," *Mélanges de l'école française de Rome. Italie et Méditerranée (MEFRIM)* 110 (1998): pp. 117–53.

26. Derouet, "Pratiques successorales," pp. 176, 191–92; Derouet, "Parenté et marché foncier," pp. 352–53; Bernard Derouet and Joseph Goy, "Transmettre la terre," pp. 119–20.

27. H. J. Habakkuk, "England," in *The European Nobility in the Eighteenth Century. Studies of the Nobilities of the Major European States in the Pre-Reform Era*, ed., Albert Goodwin (London, 1953), pp. 1–21, here p. 3.

28. Raymond Carr, "Spain," in Goodwin, *The European Nobility*, pp. 43–59; H. G. Schenk, "Austria" in ibid., pp. 102–25; C. A. Macartney, "Hungary" in ibid., pp. 126–39.

29. J. M. Roberts, "Lombardy," in ibid., pp. 60–82.

30. Delille, *Le maire*. See also Gérard Delille, "Echanges matrimoniaux entre lignées alternées et système européen de l'alliance: un premier approche," in *En substances. Textes pour Françoise Héritier*, ed. Jean-Luc Jamard, Emmanuel Terray and Margarita Xanthakou (Paris, 2000), pp. 219–52; Gérard Delille, "Consanguinité proche en Italie du XVIe au XIX siècle," in *Epouser au plus proche. Inceste, prohibitions et stratégies matrimoniales autour de la Méditerranée*, ed. Pierre Bonte (Paris, 1994), pp. 323–40; Gérard Delille, *Famille et proprieté dans le royaume de Naples (xve-xixe siècle)* (Rome, 1985).

31. Heinz Reif, *Westfälischer Adel 1770-1860: vom Herrschaftsstand zur regionalen Elite* (Göttingen, 1979); Christophe Duhamelle, *L'héritage collectif. La noblesse d'Église rhénane, 17e-18e siècles* (Paris, 1998).

32. Cordula Nolte, "Gendering Princely Dynasties: Some Notes on Family Structure, Social Networks, and Communication at the Courts of the Margraves of Brandenburg-Ansbach around 1500," *Gender and History* 12 (2000): pp. 704–21; Teuscher, *Bekannte*, pp. 39–113; Roger Sablonier, "The Aragonese Royal Family around 1300," in *Interest and emotion. Essays on the Study of Family and Kinship*, ed. David Warren Sabean and Hans Medick (Cambridge, 1984), pp. 210–40; Heinz Reif, "Väterliche Gewalt und 'kindliche Narrheit.' Familienkonflikte im katholischen Adel Westfalens vor der französischen Revolution," in *Die Familie in der Geschichte*, ed. Heinz Reif (Göttingen, 1982), pp. 82–113.

33. Teuscher, *Bekannte*, pp. 135–79.

34. Wolfgang Reinhard, "Oligarchische Verflechtung und Konfession in oberdeutschen Städten," in *Klientelsysteme in Europa der frühen Neuzeit*, ed. Antoni Maczak (München, 1988), pp. 47–62, here pp. 55–57; Sabean, *Kinship*, pp. 141, 143–47, 158, 174; Delille, *Famille et parenté*, pp. 350–75; Volker Press, "Patronat und Klientel im Heiligen Römischen Reich," in Maczak, *Klientelsysteme*, pp. 19–46, here p. 20.

35. Sabean, *Kinship*, pp. 143–47.

36. Teuscher, *Bekannte*, pp. 84–113.

37. Chistian Maurel, "Stuctures familiales et solidarités lignagères à Marseille au XVe siècle: autour de l'ascension sociale des Forbin," *Annales ESC* 41 (1986): pp. 658–82.

38. Morsel, "Geschlecht," pp. 259–325, here pp. 297–317.

39. Simon Teuscher, "Parenté, politique et comptabilité. Chroniques familiales du Sud de l'Allemagne et de la Suisse autour de 1500," *Annales HSS* 58 (2003): pp. 847–58.

40. Sabean, *Kinship*, pp. 239, 256–60, 370–73, 559–71; David Warren Sabean, "Exchanging Names in Neckarhausen around 1700," in *Theory, Method, and Practice in Social and Cultural History*, ed. Peter Karsten and John Modell (New York, 1992), pp. 199–230.

41. On celebratory familial writing, see Tamara Michelle Zwick, "The Correspondence Between Public and Private: Women, Kinship, and Bürgertum in Early Nineteenth-Century Hamburg," (Ph.D. diss., UCLA, 2004); Dieter Barth, "Das Familienblatt— ein Phänomen der Unterhaltungspresse des 19. Jahrhunderts," *Archiv für Geschichte des Buchwesens* 15 (1975): pp. 121–316. See also Marion Kaplan, *The Making of the Jewish Middle Class: Women, Family, and Identity in Imperial Germany* (New York, 1991); Elisabeth Joris and Heidi Witzig, *Brave Frauen, aufmüpfige Weiber: Wie sich die Industrialisierung zur Alltag und Lebenszusammenhänge von Frauen auswirkte (1820-1940)* (Zürich, 1992); Gunilla-Friederike Budde, *Auf dem Weg ins Bürgerleben: Kindheit und Erziehung in deutschen und englischen Bürgerfamilien 1840-1914* (Göttingen, 1994); Jürgen Kocka, "Familie, Unternehmer und Kapitalismus: An Beispielen aus der frühen deutschen Industrialisierung," *Zeitschrift für Unternehmergeschichte* 24 (1979): pp. 99–135.

42. Sabean, *Kinship*, p. 452. These associations usually included in their membership the wives of the male descendants as well as their daughters (but not their daughters' children)—somebody had to do the work!

43. A good example for all of this is Uta v. Delius's genealogical work based on her keeping of the extensive family archives of the Delius family, with indications of the periodical family gatherings that continue till today, *Deutsches Geschlechterbuch. Genealogisches Handbuch bürgerlicher Familien*, vol. 193 (Limburg an der Lahn, 1987). For a noble family with an *eingetragener Verein*, see Rüdiger von Treskow, "Adel in Preussen: Anpassung und Kontinuität einer Familie 1800-1918," *Geschichte und Gesellschaft* 17 (1991): pp. 344–69.

44. Albert Goodwin, "Prussia," in idem, *Nobility*, pp. 83–101, here p. 97. Spring, *Law, Land and Family*, pp. 95–97, 113.

45. Raymond Carr, "Spain," in Goodwin, *Nobility*, pp. 43–59, here. p. 54. See the important work by Ulrike Vedder, "Majorat: Literature and Law of Succession in the 19th Century," in *A Cultural History of Heredity II: 18th and 19th Century*, ed. Hans Jörg Rheinberger and Staffan Müller-Wille (Berlin, 2003), pp. 175–86.

46. Among the many works to consult, Friedrich Zunkel, *Der Rheinisch-Westfälische Unternehmer 1834-1879: Ein Beitrag zur Geschichte des deutschen Bürgertums im 19. Jahrhundert* (Köln, 1962); Leonore Davidoff and Catherine Hall, *Family Fortunes: Men and Women of the English Middle Class 1780–1850* (Chicago, 1991); Philipp Sarasin, *Stadt der Bürger. Bürgerliche Macht und städtische Gesellschaft* (Göttingen 2. Aufl., 1997), pp. 91–136, 198–215; Jon Mathieu, "Verwandtschaft als historischer Faktor. Schweizer Fallstudien und Trends, 1500-1900," *Historische Anthropologie* 10 (2002): pp. 225–244.

47. Sabean, *Kinship*, p. 451.

48. D. C. Coleman, *Courtaulds: An Economic and Social History, Volume 1: The Nine-teenth Century: Silk and Crape* (Oxford, 1969). For a larger view on the issues adumbrated here, see Davidoff and Hall, *Family Fortunes*.

49. Coleman, *Courtaulds*, p. 106.

50. Coleman, *Courtaulds*, pp. 150, 182–210. See Zunkel, *Unternehmer*, pp. 9–23, 72–73, 94–95; Kocka, "Familie, Unternehmer und Kapitalismus"; Manfred Pohl, *Hamburger Bankengeschichte* (Mainz, 1986), p. 29; Brigitte Schröder, "Der Weg zur Eisenbahnschiene. Geschichte der Familie Remy und ihre wirtschaftliche und kul-turelle Bedeutung," in *Deutsches Familienarchiv. Ein genealogisches Sammelwerk*, 91 (Neustadt an der Aisch, 1986), pp. 3–158, here p. 53; E. Rosenbaum and A. J. Sher-man, *M.M. Warburg & Co. 1798–1938: Merchant Bankers of Hamburg* (New York, 1979), pp. 1–20; Hartmut Zwahr, "Zur Klassenkonstituierung der Bourgeoisie," *Jahrbuch für Geschichte* 18 (1978): pp. 21–83.

51. Coleman, *Courtaulds*, pp. 203–9.

52. One of the few studies to explore the issue is Jacqueline Bourgoin and Vu Tien Khang, "Quelques aspects de l'histoire génétique de quatre villages pyrénéens depuis 1740," in *Population* 33 (1978), pp. 633–59.

53. Sabean, *Property*, pp. 355–415; Delille, *Famille et propriété*, pp. 365–77.

54. Erwin Hölzle, *Das alte Recht und die Revolution. Eine politische Geschichte Württem-bergs in der Revolutionszeit 1789-1805* (Munich and Berlin, 1931), pp. 29, 104, 110–2; G.W.F. Hegel, "Ueber die neuesten innern Verhältnisse Württembergs besonders über die Gebrechen der Magistratsverfassung," in Georg Lasson, ed., *Hegels Schriften zur Politik und Rechtsphilosophie* (Sämtliche Werke 7) (Leipzig, 1913), pp. 150–4; Gustav Schmoller, "Der deutsche Beamtenstaat vom 16. bis 18. Jahrhundert," in *Untersuchungen zur Verfassungs-, Verwaltungs- und Wirtschafts-geschichte* (Leipzig, 1898), pp. 289–313; Alfred Dehlinger, *Württembergs Staatswe-sen in seiner geschichtlichen Entwicklung bis heute*, vol 2 (Stuttgart, 1951, 53), pp. 920–63.

55. Reif, *Westfälischer Adel*.

56. Carr, "Spain," p. 45.

57. Roberts, "Lombardy," pp. 78–80.

58. Christopher Johnson is studying the familial dynamics of a nineteenth-century French provincial family through a voluminous correspondence. For a glimpse into the richness of his results, see "Das 'Geschwister Archipel': Bruder-Schwester-Liebe und Klassenformation im Frankreich des 19. Jahrhunderts," in *L'Homme. Zeitschrift für feministische Geschichtswissenschaft* 13 (2002), pp. 50–67. He speaks of the "hor-izontalization" of kinship in the nineteenth century.

59. For a detailed discussion of marriage prohibitions, see Sabean, "The Politics of Incest and the Ecology of Alliance Formation," in *Kinship*, chap. 3.

60. Françoise Zonabend, "Le très proche et le pas trop loin: Refléxions sur l'organisa-tion du champ matrimonial des sociétés structures de parenté complexes," in *Eth-nologie française* 11 (1981), pp. 311–84; Delille, *Famille et propriété*, pp. 269–84.

61. See the discussion of the literature in Sabean, *Kinship*, pp. 398–427; Delille, *Famille et propriété*, pp. 271, 327.

62. Cf. David Warren Sabean, "Kinship and Prohibited Marriages in Baroque Germany: Divergent Strategies among Jewish and Christian Populations," in *Leo Baeck Insti-tute Yearbook* 47 (2002), pp. 91–103.

63. Sabean, Kinship, pp. 428–48; Mathieu, "Verwandtschaft," pp. 238–42; Raul Merzario, "Land, Kinship, and consanguineous Marriage in Italy from the Seven-teeth to Nineteenth Centuries," in *Journal of Family History* 15 (1990), pp. 529–46;

Jean-Marie Gouesse, "Mariages de proches parents (XVIe-XXe siècle)," in *Le modèle familial européen: normes, déviances, contròle du pouvoir* (Actes des séminaires organisées par l'école française de Rome 90) (Rome 1986), pp. 31–61; Sandro Guzzi, *Donne, uomini, famiglia, parentela. Una dinastia alpina nell'Europa pre-industriale 1650-1850* (Habilitation thesis Berne 2005, forthcoming).

64. A great deal of evidence is gathered in Sabean, *Kinship*, pp. 449–510.

65. Cf. Johnson, "Geschwister Archipel"; David Sabean, "Inzestdiskurse vom Barock bis zur Romantik," in *L'Homme. Zeitschrift für feministische Geschichtswissenschaft* 13 (2002), pp. 7–28.

66. Coleman, *Courtaulds*, p. 33.

67. Coleman, *Courtaulds*, p. 4–43, 203–5.

68. Martin Oppenheimer, "Lewis Henry Morgan and the Prohibition of Cousin Marriage in the United States,"in *Journal of Family* History 15 (1990), pp. 325–34; Guenther Roth, *Max Webers deutsch-englische Familiengeschichte 1800-1950* (Tübingen, 2001), pp. 539–44.

Chapter II

Bringing it All Back Home

Kinship Theory in Anthropology

Sylvia J. Yanagisako

This chapter focuses on theoretical and methodological developments in the anthropology of kinship that may be useful in reevaluating the old hypothesis of the decline of kinship in Europe from the middle ages onward. Rather than attempt to summarize these recent developments, my goal is to explore their implications for rethinking the history of European kinship. Once anthropologists recognized that what we had considered the universal basis of kinship in all human societies was, in actuality, a projection on other people of our own cultural beliefs about nature, culture, and biology, we were spurred to reformulate our theories and methods for studying kinship. Indeed, we were compelled to rethink what we mean by "kinship" and to blur the boundaries between what we had defined as the domain of kinship and other cultural domains. In the second half of this chapter, I suggest that an institutional approach to cultural domains, which has been integral to dominant sociological conceptions of modern society, has limited our vision of what kinship is all about. I make this argument by examining Weber's ideal type of modern capitalism and his concept of economic action, both of which relegate kinship to the margins of modern European society. The melding of Weberian and Durkheimian perspectives in the Parsonian theory of structural differentiation in modern society obscures the significance of kinship in shaping meaning and social action outside the restricted family. I suggest that historical research that reads across the boundaries of the cultural domains and social institutions charted by Parsonian theory will produce a richer under-standing of the diverse ideas and practices of kinship in the European past and of the processes that led to their homogenization in the con-cept of "modern European kinship."

After Schneider, After Nature

With some trepidation at the perils of periodization, I define the "recent" period of anthropological theorizing about kinship as marked by the publication of David Schneider's cultural analysis of American kinship in 1968. While there are several aspects of Schneider's methods and conclusions with which I do not agree,[1] his innovative analysis of American kinship instigated a radical rethinking of the core concepts and methods of the comparative study of kinship in anthropology. Schneider argued that for Americans, "the family is formed according to the laws of nature and it lives by rules which are regarded by Amer-icans as self-evidently natural."[2] Sexual reproduction is the core symbol that defines the family as a unit, distinct from all other cultural units. It entails the "facts of life" which define the members of the family and differentiate them from each other. Children are the products of the sexual union of husband and wife and, consequently, they are con-nected to their parents "by blood"—which is a symbol of "diffuse, enduring solidarity" (Schneider 1980). According to Schneider's U.S. informants, a blood relationship is an objective fact of nature and, as such, cannot be terminated. Marriage has contrasting, distinctive fea-tures. Persons related by marriage, including spouses, are not related "in nature," but rather by "law"—in other words, the enactment of a code for conduct. The distinction that Americans draw between relatives by blood (consanguinity) and relatives by marriage (affinity) reflects the dichotomy between substance and code for conduct which, in turn, is the manifestation of a higher level dichotomy in American culture: the dichotomy between the Order of Nature and the Order of Law. Whereas a blood tie is based on shared substance, marriage is not; whereas a blood tie endures, marriage is terminable.

By explicating the symbolic system through which Americans con-struct genealogical relations and a system for classifying different kinds of relatives, Schneider denaturalized kinship and laid bare its cultural foundations.[3] In *A Critique of the Study of Kinship*, moreover, Schnei-der argued convincingly that the anthropological study of kinship "derives directly and practically unaltered from the ethnoepistemology of European culture."[4] He demonstrated that, in spite of their claim to be studying kinship as a social phenomenon, anthropologists' definitions of kinship had consistently been rooted in biology because they had always been about relationships based in sexual procreation. The two key concepts that had guided the anthropological study of kinship since the nineteenth century were the "Doctrine of the Genealogical Unity of Mankind," which presumed that people everywhere reckon their kinship relations through genealogical links and the idea that blood is thicker than water, which attributes the strength of kinship ties to nature. [5]

Until Schneider demonstrated that anthropological kinship theory was rooted in the symbolic system to which most Americans ascribe, anthropologists had assumed that all people who know the "facts of life" reckon their kinship relationships using a genealogical grid which maps consanguinity and affinity. The genealogical relation between any and all kin could be determined by using combinations of the basic units of father, mother, husband, wife, son, and daughter.[6] Any particular kinship system was merely a cultural elaboration of the biological facts of human reproduction, even though anthropologists recognized that there were significant differences in how far these genealogical maps extended, how the relations in them were classified, and how specific kinds of relatives were supposed to behave with each other.

In contrast to other people's classificatory systems of kinship terminology, which lumped together categories of kin that we keep separate, our descriptive system of kinship terminology was viewed as an accurate reflection of natural categories. As Lewis Henry Morgan, who is often considered the father of kinship studies, wrote in 1870:

> As a system it is based upon a true and logical appreciation of the natural outflow of the streams of the blood, of the distinctiveness and perpetual divergence of these several streams, and of the difference in degree, numerically, and by lines of descent, of the relationship of each and every person to the central *Ego*. It is, therefore, a natural system, founded upon the nature of descents, and may be supposed to have been of spontaneous growth.[7]

We now recognize that the so-called natural system to which Morgan referred is a culturally specific system of symbols and meanings in which "streams of blood" symbolize social commitments and, moreover, chart the normative flow of property and status. In other words, blood constitutes kinship symbolically rather than naturally. The ties that bind are produced by culture, not nature.

As Franklin and Mckinnon note, Schneider's critique of kinship was part of a broader, reflexive shift in anthropology in the 1970s and 1980s, which rejected objectivist approaches to culture in favor of hermeneutical approaches.[8] His critique of the ethnocentrism of the "natural" and "biological" basis of kinship theory led the shift away from structural-functional approaches to kinship, exemplified by the works of Radcliffe-Brown, Evans-Pritchard, Fortes, and Goody, and the structuralist approach of Levi-Strauss, who treated the nature-culture dichotomy as a universal structure of the human mind. While some anthropologists bemoaned Schneider's critique as the death of kinship studies, others were moved to pursue research that did not take for granted that kinship everywhere is defined by, or limited to, genealogically based relations. The strategy of this new generation of kinship scholars was to ask, rather than presume to know, what kinship is all about in the societies we study.[9]

The impetus to break out of the boundaries of a genealogically defined domain of kinship continues in anthropology, as can be seen in the volume, *Cultures of Relatedness*, edited by Janet Carsten. The authors of the essays in this volume "describe relatedness in terms of indigenous statements and practices—some of which may seem to fall quite outside what anthropologists have conventionally understood as kinship."[10] For example, Sharon Hutchinson reveals that among the Nuer, who have become a paradigm of lineage-based society, relatedness has come to be understood not only in terms of blood and cattle, but also through the media of money, paper, and guns.[11] The transformability of Nuer idioms of relatedness documented by Hutchinson contrasts starkly with Evans-Pritchard's claim that the so-called agnatic principle is the basis of Nuer social structure.

Following his analysis of American kinship, Schneider suggested that, like the domain of kinship, the domains of religion and nationality in American culture are structured by the same symbolic opposition between the Order of Nature and the Order of Law. He pointed out that in the United States, people become members of a family, a nation, and a religion in remarkably similar ways: "In American culture, one is 'an American' either by birth or through a process which is called, appropriately enough, 'naturalization.' In precisely the same terms as kinship, there are the same two 'kinds of citizens,' those by birth and those by law."[12]

Schneider proposed that while kinship, nationality, and religion differ at the level of norms and the level of behavior, at the pure level of symbols and meanings, they "all ... seem to 'say' one thing."[13] They are all concerned with unity of some kind, which he defined as "diffuse, enduring solidarity."[14] He went on to suggest that the boundaries between kinship, nationality, and religion are not so well marked, at least in cultures influenced by Judaism and Christianity.

Schneider never fully developed the implications of this intriguing observation, nor did he attempt to resolve its conceptual weaknesses—not the least of which was its essentialist and ahistorical concept of European-American and European culture. This is a topic to which I will return later in this chapter. Yet, his observation of the common structure of meaning that organizes kinship, nationality, and religion in the United States incited a generation of anthropologists to analyze the intermingling of symbols and meanings among what had been previously treated as distinct cultural domains.

The Permeability of Domains

Feminist anthropologists, in particular, were inspired to investigate the permeable boundaries between kinship and a number of cultural domains, including gender, religion, ethnicity, race, class, and nation.[15] For example, Schneider's insight that sexual procreation is the core symbol of American kinship led my colleague, Jane Collier, and I to realize that both gender and kinship have been defined as cultural domains by the supposedly natural act of sexual procreation. This, in turn, led us to recognize that gender and kinship constitute a single field of study. Assumptions about gender have pervaded ideas about the so-called facts of sexual reproduction, which were commonplace in kinship theory. Much of what anthropologists had written about the atoms of kinship, the axiom of prescriptive altruism, the universality of the family, and the centrality of the mother-child bond was anchored in assumptions about the natural characteristics of women and men and their natural roles in sexual procreation.[16] The standard units of anthropological kinship charts were, after all, circles (female) and triangles (male), about which a number of things had been assumed. Above all, kinship theorists had taken for granted that they represent two naturally different types of people and that the fixed and enduring difference between them is the basis of human reproduction and, therefore, kinship.[17]

Arguing that such naturalized differences cannot be presumed to be the prediscursive, universal basis for kinship and gender, Jane Collier and I proposed a model of kinship and gender that does not begin by taking 'difference' for granted and treat it as a natural fact but, instead, tries to uncover the cultural meanings that pervade people's concepts and shape their relations. My later work with Carol Delaney extended the argument that naturalization is a power-saturated form of symbolic action to demonstrate how productive it is of social inequalities. Along with the other contributors to our volume, *Naturalizing Power*, we examined the power of naturalizing discourses to authenticate an "order of things"—for example, gender constructs—in which inequality and hierarchy come already embedded.[18]

In her discussion of the cultural implications of new reproductive technologies, Marilyn Strathern has argued along similar lines that naturalizations are culturally specific practices that confine knowledge to particular domains.[19] Because kin ties are said to be grounded in primordial, natural facts, kinship provides a useful example of naturalization as knowledge: "Nature, at once intrinsic characteristic and external environment, constituted both the given facts of the world and the world as the context for facts ... it also had the status of a prior fact, a condition for existence. Nature was thus a condition for knowledge."[20]

Developments in new reproductive technologies have radically altered both the given "facts" of the world and the conditions of knowledge. As Janet Carsten notes,

> relationships, which in the past would have been seen as having their basis in nature...may now be seen as either socially constructed or as natural relations which are assisted by technology....The more nature is assisted by technology ... the more difficult it becomes to think of nature as independent of social intervention. It follows from this that knowledge itself, which previously was seen as 'a direct reflection of nature,' as Schneider put it, no longer has such a grounding in nature. It is not just nature, then, but knowledge itself which has been destabilised.[21]

The work by Strathern and other anthropologists studying new reproductive technologies broadly expands what the term "kinship" can be used to understand; this now includes knowledge practices. Where kinship is defined as the meeting place between nature and culture, as it appears to be in England and the United States, it plays a crucial role in shifts in knowledge practices and vice versa.[22] Far from heralding the death of kinship in anthropology, the critique of kinship has revitalized it. Recent anthropological studies of kinship such as the essays in Franklin and Mckinnon's volume, *Relative Values: Reconfiguring Kinship Studies*, have broken out of their confinement to the domestic domain to investigate "new sites of kinship production, [including] the biogenetics lab, the transnational adoption agency, and cyberspace."[23]

Reading Across Domains

If it appears that the anthropological study of kinship has recently wandered far afield from its original focus, this is precisely my point. Much of what is innovative and productive in recent kinship studies in anthropology transgresses the boundaries between kinship and other domains that were formerly treated as distinct spheres of meaning and action. Asking how cultural domains have been formed and transformed in relation to each other and how actions are constituted by ideas and meanings from several domains challenges the mid-nineteenth-century view of social institutions and cultural domains as the basic building blocks of society. As Schneider pointed out in *A Critique of the Study of Kinship*, the "quartet of kinship, economics, politics and religion" was purported to fulfill functions considered indispensable to the orderly reproduction of society.[24] Despite the shifts in anthropological theory in the nineteenth and twentieth centuries, this quartet has proven resilient. Yet, it has never been clear where one cultural domain ends and where another begins.

Cultural domains are culturally specific, but they usually come with claims of universality. This is part and parcel of their seeming to be given-in-nature or god-given. The apparent logic and naturalness of these domains is a consequence of the way they are made real through the institutional arrangements and discourses people encounter in everyday life. People whose lives are organized along institutional fault lines that are the products of hegemonic cultural domains encounter the boundaries of these domains directly in their everyday lives. This is what makes religion seem to be about God rather than about gender and politics, and what makes the family seem to be about reproduction and childrearing rather than about the economy and gender.

Cultural domains, moreover, usually come with prohibitions against reading across them. The confinement of cultural interpretation to the space inside domains is especially rigid when it comes to the sacred. Sacred meaning may be read into other domains, but the reverse is not acceptable. Indeed, what defines the scared is that which is sealed off from readings emanating from other cultural domains. What constitutes the sacred, of course, differs from one instance to another. For some it is religion, for others it is science, and for yet others, it is the family.

Reading across domains is by no means new to anthropology. The standard analytic strategy of cultural anthropologists is to read across the domains of other cultures, especially those in so-called simple societies that lack formal social institutions resembling our own and so are deemed to be less differentiated. Among these other societies, the intermingling of religion and politics (e.g., African kingship), of ritual and economy (e.g., the potlatch of Northwest coast Indians), and of religion and kinship (e.g., ancestor worship) made it useful to read across cultural domains, however sacrilegious or foolish this might have seemed to the natives. In our own society, which social theory has characterized as more functionally and institutionally differentiated, cultural domains were not to be read across so cavalierly. In particular, our sacred domains of religion and science could not be read across. Yet, clearly people's ideas about the biological "facts" of kinship are rooted in beliefs about science and religion.

While social institutions and cultural domains have a profound impact on ideas and practices, people do not necessarily organize their everyday actions according to these divisions. Rather, people think and act at the intersections of domains and institutions. As a consequence, all social action is constituted by meanings from several domains. To assume that political discourse is what shapes politics and that kinship discourse is what shapes kinship is to accept the boundaries of cultural domains as given, rather than analyze them as the products of historical processes of domain making.

A productive question is to ask how culturally specific domains have been dialectically formed and transformed in relation with other cultural domains, how meanings migrate across domain boundaries, and how specific actions are constituted by ideas from multiple domains. In other words, we need to historicize cultural domains and trace both the historical process of their production and their effects. Questioning the boundaries that have defined the analytic domains of kinship, economy, gender, politics, and religion, is not the same as abandoning the study of the meanings and actions included in those domains. Calling into question the assignment of "motherhood" to the domain of "kinship" does not deny either the existence of physiological processes of human reproduction, nor the importance of studying ideas and practices of motherhood. Rather, questioning the assumption that motherhood is fundamentally structured by these physiological processes opens up paths of inquiry that will lead us to the productive analysis of other cultural meanings and social processes that are inscribed in motherhood. In other words, discarding the assumptions that have defined kinship as a domain of study need not entail discarding the study of the relations located in that domain.

Reading across domains in our own society has been made difficult by an intellectual division of labor, which is institutionalized in the academy in the form of disciplinary knowledge. This intellectual division of labor is itself a product of a prevailing model of modern society,

according to which each of the functions required for its orderly reproduction is fulfilled by a different social institution, which is, in turn,
governed by a distinct logic. The economy is governed by the market,
politics by the state, religion by the church, and kinship by the family.
Indeed, this institutionalization of domains is one of the distinguishing
features of so-called modern society.

In the next section of my chapter, I suggest that the institutionalization of domains is an integral feature of both our dominant model of
modern society and the thesis of kinship decline in Europe. I argue that
while institutions are useful analytical concepts and foci of study, an
institutional model of society can obscure our vision of both past and
present, constraining our understanding of what kinship is all about. I
make this argument by examining Weber's concept of modern capitalism and his allied concept of economic action—both of which have
been crucial to our model of modern European society.[25]

Weber and the Exclusion of Kinship from Economic Action

At the core of Weber's treatise, *Economy and Society*, is his concept of
"economic action" which rests on the distinction between action oriented
towards the satisfaction of a desire for utilities and action oriented toward
the satisfaction of other desires.[26] Utilities are defined as "the specific and
concrete, real or imagined, advantages (*Chancen*) of opportunities for
present or future use as they are estimated and made an object of specific
provision by one or more economically acting individuals."[27]

For Weber, it is the subjective meaning that processes and objects
have for human action which determines whether they are economic
actions. While he concedes that actions may be oriented towards multiple ends and shaped by multiple considerations, Weber assumes that
they can be classified on the basis of their "*conscious, primary* orientation."[28] Indeed, he is confident enough of our ability to discern the primary orientation of social actions to draw an even finer distinction
between economic action and economically oriented action. The latter
concept includes actions that take account of economic considerations
even though they are primarily oriented to other ends.[29] Only actions
whose conscious, primary orientation is to economic considerations
qualify as economic action.[30]

Modern capitalism with its calculative spirit and singular goal of
profit and accumulation is accordingly distinguished from the economically oriented actions undertaken by the large capitalist households in

the medieval cities of northern and central Italy.[31] Because these households were committed to a principle of solidarity in facing the outside
and to a "household communism"—that is, a communism of property
and consumption of everyday goods[32]—Weber considered them to be
based on "direct feelings of mutual solidarity rather than on a consideration of means for obtaining an optimum of provisions."[33] Hence, he
concluded, they have a "primarily non-economic character." According
to Weber, "Willingness to work and consumption without calculation
within these communities (the family, comrades in the army, and religious communities) are a result of the non-economic attitudes characteristic of them."[34]

Weber's early work on medieval Italian capitalism led him to conclude that the legal and accounting separation of the business enterprise from the household was crucial for the emergence of modern
Western capitalism. While this separation may have been a significant
innovation, Weber's error was to misconstrue the *legal and accounting
fiction* of separation—which was put in place for the purpose of limiting individual and familial financial liability—as a de facto separation of
family relations from business relations. In other words, Weber turned
a legal fiction of the separation of the family from the firm into a social
theory in which kinship and economy in modern capitalist society were
treated as distinct institutions shaped by distinct orientations. At the
core of Weber's distinction between modern capitalism and earlier
forms of capitalism and profit seeking, therefore, is a concept of economic action that assumes social actors whose desires, sentiments, and
orientations are already organized into distinct cultural domains and
who formulate social actions accordingly. As I argued earlier in this
chapter, however, all social action is constituted by a complex mix of
sentiments, desires, and meanings that cannot be neatly contained
within the boundaries of analytic domains (even when the social actors
themselves believe in the integrity of these domains).

Weber's model of economic action in modern capitalist society ban-
ishes kinship from the economic domain. Kinship is summarily denied
a place in the web of sentiments, orientations, and goals that shape economic action. Weber's concept of modern capitalism, along with
Durkheim's theory of the progressive evolution of the division of labor
in human society, [35] has been a crucial component of the vision of capitalist modernity that has dominated social theory since the nineteenth
century. According to this model, which was further developed by Talcott Parsons, the structural differentiation of functions is a central feature of modern society. The structures that organize and enable this
differentiation are social institutions. Kinship, which once organized a

wide range of functions, becomes restricted to the functionally reduced "conjugal family" that specializes in biological and social reproduction—childcare, socialization, and the emotional and psychological nurturance of workers.[36] Other functions are transferred to other modern institutions, including the state, the market, and the church. This thesis of the decline in the importance of kinship has an unmistakable gendered character, as it is the symbolically male functions that are lost. The contraction of kinship to the symbolically female domain of the private, domestic family governed by sentiment and communalism endows kinship with a traditional character in contrast to the progressive, male world of the modern economy.

It is little wonder, therefore, that beginning in the nineteenth century, kinship occupied a privileged place in anthropology. The other side of the coin of its marginality in modern European historiography and the sociology of modern society was its centrality in anthropological models of premodern, non-state societies. Nineteenth-century social evolutionary theorists assumed there was no family in early (non-European) societies and no kinship in late (European) societies. In the schemes of Morgan,[37] Maine,[38] and Spencer,[39] the decline in the political and economic functions of kinship, the contraction of kinship to the nuclear family, and the increasing importance of the conjugal bond distinguished the West from the rest of the world and from its own past. In short, the decline of kinship was part and parcel of what made Europe modern.

Modern European Kinship and the Production of Anthropological Knowledge

Anthropology has come a long way from its early-twentieth-century view of non-Western societies as ahistorical, static formations that can be reduced to structural principles—such as the agnatic principle among the Nuer of Sudan—or to core values—such as duty among the Japanese. In addition, the hermeneutic turn away from objectivist approaches to culture has encouraged us to critically assess the processes through which "culture areas"—such as Europe—have been constructed, rather than merely discovered, through historically situated discursive and material practices. Broad generalizations about regional and national cultures have come under increasing scrutiny, and today few anthropologists would defend a concept as broadly sweeping as "African kinship" or "modern Asian kinship." Yet, terms such as "European" or "Western" society and "European kinship" continue to be used freely and uncritically by anthropologists, along with historians and other social scientists. Theoretically nuanced and historically contextualized analyses of kinship in other societies are commonly juxtaposed against a European kinship which is presumed to be modern. A generalized and dehistoricized model of modern European culture and society serves as the foundation for the production of anthropological knowledge about other societies. Modern Europe, as a relatively homogeneous cultural order, has been, in short, crucial to the epistemology of anthropology.

European historians have a crucial role to play in helping cultural anthropologists to break through this essentialist, static view of modern European kinship. Investigations into the history of kinship in Europe—in all its diversity and transformations—hold great promise for challenging the evolutionary teleology of prevailing theories of modern society and for pushing anthropology beyond its naturalization of Europe toward a more rigorous understanding of both the transformation of kinship and the formation of kinship studies.

The tracing of the core constructs of both American kinship and kinship theory to a European ethnoepistemology of nature, culture, and biology raises the question of whether a cultural system of symbols and meanings of the sort described by Schneider is indeed pervasive throughout Europe and, if so, for how long has this been the case? If, as recent anthropological research has shown, people's understanding of the facts of life are affected by new reproductive technologies,[40] then it seems highly likely that in the past, people's understandings were also affected by significant transformations in science, philosophy, politics, and economy. Certainly, understandings of blood as substance have changed, as Franklin and McKinnon have suggested, "from the Bible's transubstantiation of divinity through Abraham's seed, to Morgan's transubstantiated kinship across rivers of water and blood, to modern biology's definition of human nature and kinship in terms of genetic codes."[41] To trace shifts in ideas about blood, substance, nature, conduct, sex, gender, and law—all of which appear to be deeply implicated in European-American kinship—historical research must investigate the cultural understandings through which people assess kinship relations and formulate kinship practices. This means that we need to reconstruct not only the marriage alliance strategies of historical subjects, but also the cultural meanings that informed these strategies.

There remains, of course, the crucial issue of regional and national variation in kinship practices, to which several chapters in this volume give voice. Related to this is the question of regional and cultural variation in what constitutes kinship among scholars. The French sociologist,

Martine Segalen, has described French kinship studies as distant, both from the English position toward pedigree, as well as the U.S. obsession with biology.[42] She claims that in France, the attention paid to biology has not been as great as in British or U.S. anthropology because there is a common assertion that kinship is first and foremost social. Her discussion raises the question of whether kinship and pedigree in Britain—which in the nineteenth century was the concern of aristocrats and the upper class—is the same as kinship and pedigree in France, which was the concern of small peasant landowners and newly landed bourgeoisie for whom genealogy was crucial to succession and inheritance of farmsteads and workshops. The contrast between Britain, where there are no restrictions on testations, and France, where restrictions were imposed by the Napoleonic code, is one obvious aspect of this diversity.

Questions of variation in Europe, in turn, compel us to ask when and where a particular view of the facts of life became hegemonic in Europe and through what discursive and material processes. Having concluded that what Lewis Henry Morgan viewed as a natural system "based on a true and logical appreciation of the natural outflow of streams of blood"[43] is neither natural nor logical, we may suppose that neither did these ideas arise and spread by spontaneous growth. How, where, and when did such ideas become hegemonic?

Finally, it would be productive to ask how the identification of a particular system of ideas and practices pertaining to family and kinship relations came to be identified as a distinctive feature of historical transformation and how this contributed to the process through which modern Europe was constituted. Here I suggest that we consider the possibility that modern European kinship is more accurately construed as a discursive process rather than a fixed ensemble of beliefs, norms, and practices that can be tracked across time and space. Indeed, both modern European kinship and the thesis of kinship decline might be more productively treated as discursive processes that entail the selective identification and decontextualization of elements that are, in actuality, embedded in complex configurations of ideas and practices which cannot be uniformly deemed to be signs of the decreasing or increasing social significance of kinship. Tradition —as we anthropologists have learned from historians—is always a selective process. So is modern European kinship.

Notes

1. See, for example, my disagreement with the static, structuralist aspects of Schneider's approach and the isolation of meaning from social action, Sylvia J. Yanagisako, "Variance in American Kinship: Implications for Cultural Analysis," *American Ethnologist* 5, no. 1 (1978), pp. 15–29; and Sylvia J. Yanagisako, *Transforming the Past: Tradition and Change in Japanese American Kinship* (Stanford, 1985).

2. David Schneider, *American Kinship: A Cultural Account* (Chicago, 1980), p. 34.

3. Schneider was not the first to notice the commonalities between Euro-American understandings of kinship and the conceptual categories of kinship study. Both Ernest Gellner and Rodney Needham had previously commented on this; Ernest Gellner, "Ideal Language and Kinship Structure," *Philosophy of Science* 24 (1957): pp. 235–42; and Rodney Needham, "Discussion: Descent Systems and Ideal Language [Response to Gellner]," *Philosophy of Science* 27 (1960): pp. 343–72.

4. David Schneider, *A Critique of the Study of Kinship* (Ann Arbor, 1984), p. 175.

5. Schneider, *Critique*, p. 174.

6. Schneider, *Critique*.

7. Lewis Henry Morgan, *Systems of Consanguinity and Affinity of the Human Family* (Lincoln, 1997), pp. 468–69.

8. Sarah Franklin and Susan McKinnon, "Introduction," in *Relative Values: Reconfiguring Kinship Studies*, ed. Sarah Franklin and Susan McKinnon (Durham, 2001), pp. 1–28, here p. 2.

9. See, for example, Marshall's 1977 study of interpersonal relations among the Trukese of Micronesia. Rather than limit his study to relations of consanguinity and affinity, Marshall examined a range of ways that Trukese define kinship in relation to the sharing of land, food, labor, residence, and support; Mac Marshall, "The Nature of Nurture," *American Ethnologist* 4 (1977): pp. 643–62.

10. Janet Carsten, "Introduction," in *Cultures of Relatedness: New Approaches to the Study of Kinship*, ed. Janet Carsten (Cambridge, 2000), pp. 1–36, here p. 3.

11. Sharon Elaine Hutchinson, "Identity and Substance: The Broadening Bases of Relatedness Among the Nuer of Southern Sudan," in ibid., *Cultures of Relatedness*, pp. 55–72.

12. David M. Schneider, "Kinship, Nationality and Religion in American Culture: Toward a Definition of Kinship," in *Symbolic Anthropology*, ed. Janet L. Dolgin, David S. Kemnitzer, and David M. Schneider (New York, 1977), pp. 63–71, here p. 67–68.

13. Schneider, "Kinship," p. 67.

14. Schneider, "Kinship," p. 67.

15. See Strathern on kinship and class: Marilyn Strathern, *Kinship at the Core: An Anthropology of Elmdon, A Village in North-West Essex in the Nineteen-Sixties* (New York, 1981); Yanagisako on kinship and ethnicity: Sylvia J. Yanagisako, "Variance in American Kinship," pp. 15–29; eadem, *Transforming the Past: Tradition and Change in Japanese American Kinship* (Stanford, 1985); and eadem and Carol Delaney, ed., *Naturalizing Power: Essays in Feminist Cultural Analysis* (New York, 1995)); Yanagisako and Collier on kinship and gender: Jane Fishburne Collier and Sylvia Junko Yanagisako, ed., *Gender and Kinship: Essays Toward a Unified Analysis* (Stanford, 1987)); Delaney on kinship, gender, and religion: Carol Delaney, *The Seed and the Soil: Gender and Cosmology in Turkish Village Society* (Berkeley, 1991);

Carol Delaney, "Father State, Motherland, and the Birth of Modern Turkey," in Yanagisako and Delaney, *Naturalizing Power*, pp. 177–99); and Williams on kinship, race, and nation: Brackette F. Williams, "Classification Systems Revisited: Kinship, Caste, Race and Nationality as the Flow of Blood and the Spread of Rights," in Yanagisako and Delaney, *Naturalizing Power*, pp. 201–38.

16. Claude Levi-Strauss, *The Elementary Structures of Kinship* (Boston, 1969); Meyer Fortes, "The Structure of Unilineal Descent Groups," *American Anthropologist* 55 (1953): pp. 17–41; idem, *Time and Social Structure and Other Essays* (London, 1970); Robin Fox, *Kinship and Marriage: An Anthropological Perspective* (Baltimore, 1967); Ward Goodenough, *Description and Comparison in Cultural Anthropology* (Chicago, 1970).

17. Jane Fishburne Collier and Sylvia J. Yanagisako, "Toward a Unified Analysis of Gender and Kinship," in Collier and Yanagisako, *Gender and Kinship*, pp. 14–50, here p. 32.

18. Yanagisako and Delaney, *Naturalizing Power*.

19. Marilyn Strathern, *After Nature* (Cambridge, 1992); Marilyn Strathern, *Reproducing the Future: Essays on Anthropology, Kinship and the New Reproductive Technologies* (Manchester, 1992).

20. Strathern, *After Nature*, p. 194.

21. Carsten, "Introduction," p. 10.

22. Marilyn Strathern, *After Nature*, p. 87.

23. Franklin and McKinnon, "Introduction," p. 8.

24. Franklin and McKinnon, "Introduction," p. 181.

25. My discussion of Weber will, of necessity, be limited and cannot do justice to the wide range of complexity of his scholarship on modern society. For a more extended discussion, see Sylvia J. Yanagisako, *Producing Culture and Capitalism: Family Firms in Italy* (Princeton, 2002).

26. Max Weber, *Economy and Society: An Outline of Interpretive Sociology*, ed. Guenther Roth and Claus Wittich (Berkeley, 1978), p. 68.

27. Weber, *Economy and Society*, p. 68. In addition to "goods" (nonhuman objects which are the sources of potential utilities) and "services" (utilities derived from a human source, so far as this source consists of active conduct), "social relationships which are valued as a potential source of present or future disposal over utilities are ... also objects of economic provision" (p. 69). This definition of utilities opens up his definition of "economic action" to a much broader range of actions that might be initially surmised. Indeed, it makes it difficult to distinguish economic action from other social actions, including those oriented toward establishing and maintaining kinship relations and friendships. Thus, what seems at first glance to be a rigorous and narrow definition of economic action turns out, on closer scrutiny, to rest on concepts that blur the boundaries of the definition. The problem is not that Weber's definitions are not sufficiently rigorous, but that his analytic strategy of differentiating economic action from other social actions is ill conceived.

28. Weber, *Economy and Society*, p. 64.

29. "As distinguished from 'economic action' as such, the term 'economically oriented action' will be applied to two types: (a) every action which, though primarily oriented to other ends, takes account, in the pursuit of them, of economic considerations; that is, of the consciously recognized necessity for economic prudence. Or (b) that which, though primarily oriented to economic ends, makes use of physical force as a means. It thus includes all primarily non-economic action and all non-peaceful action which is influenced by economic considerations.

'Economic action' thus is a conscious, primary orientation to economic considerations" Weber, *Economy and Society*, p. 64.

30. Weber, *Economy and Society*, p. 64.
31. Weber, *Economy and Society*, p. 359.
32. Weber, *Economy and Society*, p. 359.
33. Weber, *Economy and Society*, p. 156.
34. Weber, *Economy and Society*, p. 154.
35. Emile Durkheim, *The Division of Labor in Society* (New York, 1997).
36. Talcott Parsons, "The Kinship System of the Contemporary United States," *American Anthropologist* 45 (1943):, pp. 22–38; Talcott Parsons and Robert F. Bale, *Family, Socialization and Interaction Process* (Glencoe, IL, 1955); Neil Smelser, *Social Change in the Industrial Revolution: An Application of Theory to the British Cotton Industry* (Chicago, 1959).
37. Morgan, *Systems of Consanguinity and Affinity*, pp. 468–69; Lewis Henry Morgan, *Ancient Society, or Researches in the lines of human progress from savagery through barbarism to civilization*, ed. Eleanor Burke Leacock (Gloucester, 1974).
38. Sir Henry Sumner Maine, *Ancient Law: Its Connections with the Early History of Society, and Its Relation to Modern Ideas* (Tucson, 1986).
39. Herbert Spencer, *On Social Evolution: Selected Writings* (Chicago, 1972); Herbert Spencer, *The Evolution of Society: selections from Herbert Spencer's Principles of Sociology*, ed. Robert L. Carneiro (Chicago, 1967); *Herbert Spencer: Structure, Function and Evolution*, ed. Stanislav Andreski (New York, 1971).
40. Carsten, *Cultures of Relatedness*; Strathern, *After Nature*; Franklin and McKinnon, *Relative Values*.
41. Franklin and McKinnon, "Introduction," p. 11.
42. Martine Segalen, "The Shift in Kinship Studies in France: The Case of Grandparenting," in Franklin and McKinnon, *Relative Values*, 246-73.
43. Morgan, *Systems of Consanguinity*, pp. 468-69.

TRANSITION 1

FROM MEDIEVAL TO EARLY MODERN KINSHIP PATTERNS

Outline and Summaries

The chapters collected in this volume approach the development of European kinship, not as a linear process of decline and contraction, but in terms of two major transitions—the first one leading from the Middle Ages into the early modern period, the second from the latter to the nineteenth century. These transitions also serve as an organizing principle for the book. We have arranged the essays in two groups, one for each of the transitions. Each group of essays is preceded by a short note presenting some overarching questions and summarizing the arguments of the individual chapters. This is the introductory note to the chapters concerned with the passage from the Middle Ages to the early modern period.

Between the fourteenth and the seventeenth centuries, and in the most diverse European social and geographical environments, we can observe the emergence of new kinship practices and new forms of kinship organizations that stressed elaborate role divisions and enduring hierarchic structures within and between descent groups. In the earlier Middle Ages, property devolution had often been relatively egalitarian, but had also varied strongly according to situational contexts. In the course of the later Middle Ages, many groups began to develop more predictable patterns of inheritance and succession, such as the ones based on patriliniality, primogeniture, and other single-heir principles, many of which reinforced inequality among members of kingroups. This went along with a growing inclination to stabilize patron-client ties through marriage alliances and to the use of kinship to form networks based on vertical rather than on horizontal dynamics—descent rather than alliance. These shifts in kinship were connected to the development of stable and secular political institutions and state-building, to the rise of new modes of delineating property rights, and to the establishment of less permeable social hierarchies.

Throughout the later Middle Ages and the early modern period, political entities such as urban and rural communes or princely, noble, and ecclesiastic territories became by and large increasingly stable and thoroughly organized. Traditionally, historians assumed that the establishment of such state-like institutions had weakened the cohesion of kingroups. As opposed to this, the chapters that follow argue that the emergence of formalized political institutions and the development of more rigid forms of kin organization were interrelated processes. At the passage from the Middle Ages to the early modern period, access to lordly rights, to offices, and to electoral bodies was ever more frequently and systematically regulated in terms of familial descent, birth order, and marriage. In many social contexts, wealth and power came to depend strongly on the possession of specific, tangible or intangible goods that lost their status if they were divided: manors, estates, houses, offices, privileges, or rights to participate in monopolies. Such goods often came to be treated as some kind of collective patrimony of families, lineages, or clans, and the desire to preserve them led to reorganizations of such groups along principles of hierarchy and a permanent inclusion or exclusion of individuals. Status groups, such as nobles, patriciates, and citizens tended to become less permeable, while affiliation to them increasingly depended on familial descent. While conceptions of kinship expressed in terminology and in visual representations during the early Middle Ages frequently had stressed extended networks of living people who were linked through marriage and *cousinage*, the ones of the late Middle Ages gave more weight to generational depth and the continuous perpetuation of groups over many generations.

The chapters in this first section approach such developments from different angles. They examine the role of kinship within varied political institutions ranging from princely lordship (Spiess, Hohkamp) to ecclesiastic territories (Duhamelle) and communal government (Teuscher, Derouet). The chapters take up examples from regions as diverse as Hesse, the southern Rhenish territories, Provence, and Tuscany. Essays that narrow down on individual regions (Teuscher, Derouet, Calvi) are supplemented with approaches that ask about developments of a pan-European scope (Delille). While some chapters focus on shifts in marriage patterns (Duhammelle, Delille), others concentrate on how kinship was put to use in conflict and cooperation

(Derouet), or discuss what implications shifts in the organization of kingroups had for gender relations (Hohkamp, Calvi). The authors do not subscribe to a uniform vision of the major trends in the development of European kinship between the Middle Ages and the early modern period. They do, however, share the opinion that such developments need to be approached in terms of shifts in the ways in which kinship mattered rather than in terms of a traditional narrative about a constant decline of its importance.

*   *   *

Karl-Heinz Spiess examines long-term trends in the development of inheritance and succession patterns among German princes and counts between the high Middle Ages and the seventeenth century. Traditionally, historians have bemoaned that many of these magnates far into the early modern period continued to divide their territories among several of their children, which has often been ascribed to their failure to understand the importance of preserving stable states. As opposed to such interpretations, Spiess explains why most noblemen long preferred to provide as many children as possible with possessions that enabled them to perpetuate their dynasty's status. He draws a sketch of a slow spread of the exclusion of daughters and younger sons and the rise of primogeniture—a process for which he distinguishes several phases. In particular, Spiess discusses changes in the use of ecclesiastic offices to provide sons that were excluded from succession with alternative careers, and he points to the different effects the Reformation had for Catholic and Protestant families. Spiess argues that both the resilience of earlier patterns of frequent divisions and the eventual emergence of single heir systems were based less on considerations of state-policy than on dynastic strategies that had to be adapted to new political constellations.

Simon Teuscher discusses how the elite of the city of Bern at the end of the Middle Ages relied on kin in the politics of the city council and in other areas of cooperation. Historians have long assumed that urban government institutions intensified their control over society by breaking up traditional kin ties. In contrast, this chapter argues that the expansion of urban government in many ways went hand in hand with the emergence of more coherent forms of kin organization. Although citizens frequently, and in the most diverse circumstances, invoked norms demanding unconditional support for kin, such norms were nowhere more consistently enhanced than in the context of government institutions. Here, kin conceptions were increasingly used in formal regulations of who was responsible for whom. During the early fifteenth century, such regulations mostly referred to a wide, bilateral conception of kinship that included in-laws. In connection with the emergence of more stable divisions of rank around 1500, both government procedures and individual citizens increasingly highlighted a narrow, patrilineal definition of kinship. This allowed ascribing political privileges to clearly delineated lines of descent and supported new perceptions of families as tightly and hierarchically organized groups whose members were supposed to commit to common goals.

Michaela Hohkamp examines implications of the rise of primogeniture among princely and royal dynasties in Western Europe from the end of the Middle Ages onward. Her chapter first takes issue with the widely held opinion that it was necessarily beneficial to the preservation and expansion of princely power when dynasties began to adhere to single-heir rules. Hohkamp demonstrates how first attempts to impose such rules also limited political opportunities and destabilized territories. Single-heir solutions often triggered extended feuds of succession between brothers who frequently also engaged their wives' dynasties. Secondly, Hohkamp discusses how primogeniture, once it was firmly established, changed the manner in which the European dynasties interacted. While the marriage alliances of the sons of a prince lost their former strategic importance for succession conflicts, the marriages of his daughters and their role as aunts became a focal point in the negotiation of interdynastic relationships. Rigid regimes of passing on territories along the axis between fathers and firstborn sons enhanced the weight of a complementary axis, the one between aunts and their nieces. Aunts frequently raised their nieces at their courts, engineered their marriages, and exerted great influence on dynastic politics.

Bernard Derouet explores connections between political structures and forms of kinship in the south of France, notably in Gascony, Languedoc, the Rhone valley, and Provence. His chapter revisits positions of scholars belonging to the school of Frédéric Le Play who had one-sidedly relied on the study of legal norms and his presumption that systems privileging a single heir had been dominating the south of France since time immemorial. Derouet suggests that primogeniture and other single-heir systems developed progressively from the period around 1600 onward, and he relates this to the formation of a specific type of communal small town government characteristic of a society of ranks. Here, offices neither became venal nor were they otherwise passed on by direct inheritance. Instead, there emerged electoral and fiscal systems that related political rights and privileges to the possession of specific pieces of landed property. Avoiding divisions of such property became key for the preservation of a family's social status. In the course of several generations, unequal inheritance and the tendency of excluded sons to marry below the social rank of their fathers gave rise to kingroups whose members were spread widely over the social hierarchy. Thus, kinship began to matter less as a horizontal network and pressure group than as a basis for cliental practices and the formation of vertically organized clans and factions.

Christophe Duhamelle examines how new forms of organizing family relationships in the nobility contributed to stabilizing the south-Rhenish ecclesiastical states of the Empire, the territories of the archbishoprics of Mainz and Trier, and the bishoprics of Worms and Speyer. Much like the communal offices of southern France, the leading positions in these territories—the ones of bishops and chapter canons—never became hereditary in a strict sense. Nevertheless, from the sixteenth century onward, narrow groups of lineages belonging to the imperial knighthood succeeded in monopolizing these offices, turning the ecclesiastical states into a kind of collective inheritance. This was the outcome of increasingly rigid forms of family organization. Not only were there ever more rigid rules introduced that limited the eligibility of canon positions to descendants of the families of former canons, but also, the canon families consistently intermarried among themselves, established *fidei commmissa*, reduced the number of children that were allowed to inherit and marry, and, ideally, designated one son for an ecclesiastic career and another one for marriage and the devolution of property to succeeding generations. Thus, both offices and property were passed on—along separate routes—significantly, from uncles to nephews.

Giulia Calvi concentrates on conflicts related to the activities of a single government institution in the Grand Duchy of Tuscany between the sixteenth and eighteenth centuries: the Magistrato dei Pupilli that was in charge of appointing legal guardians for orphans whose fathers had died without making a will. According to Calvi, the Magistrato provided women with roles that tempered the period's strongly patrilineal family and inheritance system. Widows were frequently considered the most reliable and unbiased representatives of their children's best interests precisely because women were largely excluded from inheritance. Despite the opposition of members of their deceased husbands' families, widows were in the large majority of cases appointed as guardians, a position that could provide them with the considerable economic power of a head of household. Calvi demonstrates how interventions of the Magistrato into family conflicts contributed to separating and engendering two types of rhetoric. The one mainly used in favor of agnates highlighted the preservation of patrimony or wealth, while the other one was biased for mothers and stressed emotion, love, and care for children. The exclusion of women from inheritance thus went along with their increased ethical empowerment and the emergence of notions which put them in charge of the domestic sphere.

Gérard Delille uses examples from a wide range of regions to suggest the existence of a widespread "European" or "Christian" system of marriage during the Middle Ages and the early modern period. Delille points to the frequency of repeated alternating marital unions between several lineages or branches of lineages in premodern elites. Such marriages tended to be concluded just outside of the limits of canonical incest prohibitions—for example, a marriage between a man and a woman followed by a subsequent one between their respective nieces and nephews. While the system was characterized by a few basic rules, it left a wide scope for considerations of the moment and adaptations to specific political contexts. In many places the system structured relationships of political patronage. It could, for example, connect lineages belonging to different social orders or tie the ones holding offices in the center of territories to the ones dominating local governments. Toward the end of the early modern period, such systems tended gradually to disintegrate. As the sale of offices, a monetized economy, and primogeniture became widespread, power relationships were less structured by the ancient far-flung lineages than by individual patrilines. As a result of this, there emerged two new patterns: on the one hand, frequent marriages between increasingly close blood relatives (such as first cousins or uncles and nieces), on the other, the spread of completely kin-exogamous marriages that were to become typical of the twentieth century.

Chapter III

Lordship, Kinship, and Inheritance Among the German High Nobility in the Middle Ages and Early Modern Period

Karl-Heinz Spiess

The political map of Germany was characterized in the late Middle Ages and early modern period by a great number of independent territories. In the fifteenth century, there were roughly twenty-five principalities and around 110 counties and small territories.[1] Anyone who is interested in the history of these territories is confronted with a riddle. Why did rulers divide these principalities and counties among their sons again and again, even though doing so weakened their political and economic positions? Why did rulers behave so self-destructively and not do everything possible to leave a united territory to only one son? Why did the territorial partitions that resulted from this inheritance practice increase dramatically in the thirteenth century and first ebb again in the second half of the seventeenth century? Finding answers to these questions is impossible without examining the problem of "kinship in the long run." It is not just a question of relations between fathers and sons, but brothers, too, found that they had to confront each other—often immediately after the death of the father. As long as daughters were not excluded from inheritance, the brother-sister relationship also came into play.

In older historical literature, the territorial lords' inability to prevent territorial division and their practice of bestowing privilege on only one son (typically the oldest son, in the sense of primogeniture) was strongly criticized. Hermann J. F. Schulze, in his seminal work of 1851 (groundbreaking in its abundant use of source material), staked out this position.[2] He regarded monarchy as the best form of government[3] and expressed himself decidedly negatively about the consequences of partitioned bequests, which in his mind brought *unsägliches Unheil über unser Vaterland* (unspeakable disaster upon our fatherland): "Die Geschichte der deutschen Territorien ist in diesen Jahrhundert fast nichts als eine Leidengeschichte der gekreuzigten Staatseinheit" (The history of the German territories in this century is almost nothing but a tragedy of crucified state unity).[4] On the other hand, those princes who ended the *egoistischen* (egotistical) policy of division and introduced primogeniture were celebrated by Schulze as *Wohlthäter der Menschheit* (benefactors of mankind) and as *Neubegründer ihrer Staaten* (new founders of their states).[5] In any case, it took a long time, "ehe der Deutsche auch nur das ABC des Staatslebens erlernte" (before the Germans learned even the ABCs of political life).[6] Later authors not only insisted on the development of political thinking as the prerequisite for the introduction of primogeniture, but also followed Schulze in his judgment of territorial divisions.[7] Indeed, they were able to cite contemporary authors who animatedly warned of the dangers to result from such divisions.[8]

A reconsideration has begun only in the last few years. Historians have started to ask why it has been assumed that princes, who behaved quite pragmatically and who productively developed legal norms on other subjects, should have acted so irrationally in the crucial area of succession rights.[9] And further, they have challenged the idea that the behavior of princes might be viewed through modern ideas of the state and its inviolability.[10] Finally, they began to reconsider dynastic thinking and understand that princes found the best strategy for guaranteeing the future of a territory to lie in strengthening an expanding dynasty.[11]

Recent research has raised the question whether the religious differences between Protestants and Catholics during the Reformation period had an influence on the practice of partition. The American historian, Paula Sutter Fichtner, has presented strong arguments for a causal connection between Protestantism and the rejection of primogeniture,[12] but already before the Reformation, there were significant differences in the stance of princes regarding primogeniture.[13] In order to get a handle on the issue, it is time to examine some of the salient features of state development and practices of succession over the long run, across the artificial break of the Middle Ages and the early modern period.

In the course of a reign, every ruler of a territory, whether a duchy or a county, was confronted with the question of how to pass on his possessions to his heirs. To begin the examination of possible strategies, I will first look only at the inheritance rights of sons, since the rights of daughters were subsidiary and could only be claimed in the absence of sons.[14] If a single son was available, there was no succession problem at all, assuming that the father did not, for some reason, contest the ability of his son to rule. But the presence of multiple sons did not challenge the validity of heirship of any of them, since all were considered to have equal rights; a partition of the territory between all sons presented the easiest and, as far as they were concerned, the most just solution.[15] Underlying claims of equality were notions of blood (or, perhaps better, birth) that transmitted both physical and character traits and legal rights.[16]

The options for a father were in any case limited by the size of the territory. A still undivided duchy was easier to partition than a county already much reduced by previous partitions. And of course, the problem was different for each ruler depending on the number of sons, and without any question, two sons were easier to satisfy than five. Finally, it was abundantly clear to any head of state that a continuation over generations of the practice of partitioning would necessarily lead to a disadvantageous pulverization. Already in the ninth century, with their well-known regulations on the division of the empire (*Reichsteilungsordnungen*), Charlemagne and Louis the Pious divided the empire into three, but simultaneously tried to prevent any further fragmentation, with the rule that in the next generation in each of the three realms only one son might succeed.[17]

Mention of Charlemagne is a reminder that in the time of the Franks, even the king was confronted with the problem of succession. Almost all the solutions which were later implemented at the level of princes and counts were already attempted in the Frankish royal house, from equal partition among brothers to single succession of the firstborn.[18] Only the indivisibility of the empire imposed by Otto I in the tenth century, which introduced individual succession, ensured that the empire itself was not seen as a partible bequest.[19] Still the happy coincidence that almost always only one son was available in each generation for the Ottonian and Salian rulers mitigated problems of fraternal conflict.

The tension between rule and kinship before the backdrop of inheritance rights across several centuries presents four phases.[20] The first, in which there was a widespread lack of territorial partitions, extends into the thirteenth century. The second phase begins in the middle of the thirteenth century, when any barriers to dividing duchies and counties disappeared. This phase was marked by a dramatic rise in partitions and the formation of groups of agnates whose claims to equality were recognized as legitimate. Along with accession to a portion of a territory, went marriage and the attempt to establish a new line. As this progressed, agnates monitored the situation carefully to ensure that if any line of the larger lineage died out, all the possessions fell back to the house and were not alienated by distant cognatic relatives. Still, rulers were concerned to prevent excessive territorial fragmentation and were careful to dictate ecclesiastical careers for younger sons when the situation called for it.

The second phase ended with the Reformation: princes and counts who became Protestant could no longer appeal to the Church to provide for their younger sons; contrariwise, the few remaining Catholic dynasties no longer had to compete with them to provide their sons with bishoprics to strengthen their entire ruling houses. This third phase was characterized by the continuation of partition in some territories and at some points of succession, while for others, already in the late Middle Ages, other territories put through rules and practices of primogeniture. During the second half of the seventeenth century, a fourth and final phase brought the triumph of primogeniture in virtually all of the dynasties.

*   *   *

The most important barrier to the partition of duchies and counties in the first phase was their status as imperial offices. Emperor Frederick I stressed this point in his famous constitution from 1158: "Preterea ducatus, marchia, comitatus de cetero non dividatur" (Duchies, margraviates, and counties may not be divided).[21] This notion was widely accepted. The office and the associated fiefdom were not partible, because fiefs as a matter of principle were always transferred intact to a successor. But allodial property could be dealt with quite differently, and that could be subject to claims by all of the sons. This could explain why many rulers, especially counts, recorded their castles as fiefs from princes or kings; they aimed to keep them intact as nuclei of lordship of their smaller territories. Vassalage, in this case, prevented the originally allodial castles from being subject to equal rights of inheritance.[22] Gifts and endowments to the Church had the same effect, because they also removed allodial property from the grasp of heirs and promoted the interests of the dynasty through protectorates, patronage, or the delivery of prayers.[23]

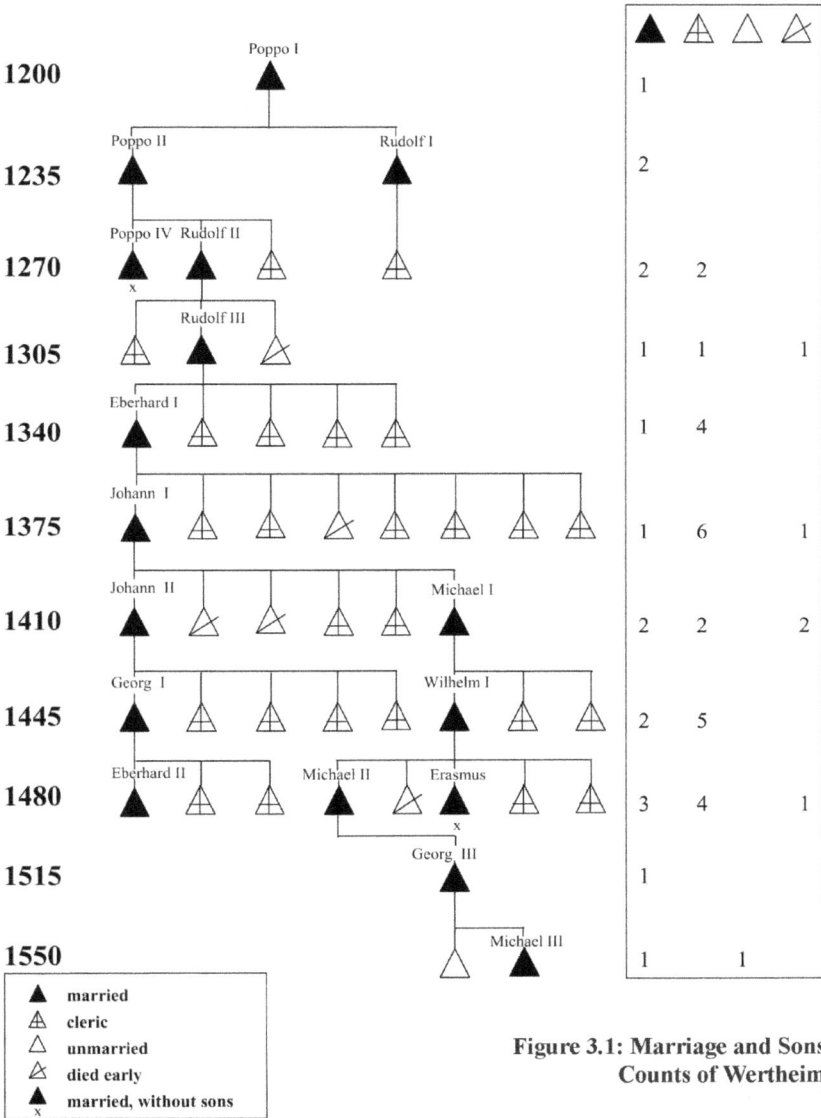

Figure 3.1: Marriage and Sons
Counts of Wertheim

In the thirteenth century—the beginning of the second phase—territories came to be regarded less as offices than as patrimonial properties that could be divided according to the number of sons. Apparently, a new understanding of dynasty, its reproduction, and expansion entered into the calculations that rulers had to make. A father with several sons now had to make a difficult decision. Allowing only one son to inherit may have prevented fragmentation, but it put the continuation of the dynasty at risk should that son fail to engender sons. In many cases, the solution was to allow two and sometimes more sons to marry and establish new lines of the dynasty.[24] Some fathers expected the second son provisionally to stay unmarried to see if the elder brother was able to reproduce. [25] And usually, the third, fourth, or fifth son was pressured into taking up an ecclesiastical career. The prebends of the cathedral collegiate churches allowed the sons of the higher nobility a standard of living adequate to their status. They could even look forward to election to a powerful German bishopric. For the son of a count, who might aspire to rule one of the three ecclesiastical electoral territories, this was a sufficiently promising perspective and explains why so many younger brothers accepted paternal demands to renounce their hereditary titles and enter the clergy. Such a move, in any case, might not be definitive, since many of them avoided ordination and could leave the Church to marry if their secular brothers failed to produce male offspring.[26] Figure 3.1 gives a quite typical example. Although the counts of Wertheim never issued a statute of primogeniture, they more or less practiced it. The division into two branches between Johann II and Michael I was occasioned by Michael's marriage, brought about by the pressure of the old count's second wife to see her son rule part of the territory instead of entering the Church.[27]

In the strategic thinking of rulers, there was a remarkable difference that developed between princes with large territories and counts with small ones. It was often a matter of prestige for princes to allow each son a portion of the territory, but counts and barons often could not indulge themselves in the same way. Their sons swamped the collegiate chapters and dominated them until princes began to send their sons into the Church in significant numbers in the fifteenth century.[28] Figure 3.2 shows the example of the Bavarian Wittelsbach dynasty, whose first ecclesiastical member was Ernst (1500–1560), bishop of Passau from 1517.[29]

How might a father deal with a concrete situation? Take a case where he allows three sons to stay secular, placing the rest in collegiate chapters. The sons of rulers were eager to claim their rights and powerful enough to insist on marriage and establishing new lines. Notions of equality supported each in the insistence on an equal partition of the territory. Some fathers in this situation would try to prevent fragmentation by prescribing a joint rule of the children, and even in the face of a great deal of evidence that this would not work for very long, some attempted such a constitutional solution. Ambitious sons sooner or later would have a falling out and divide up the land—often with

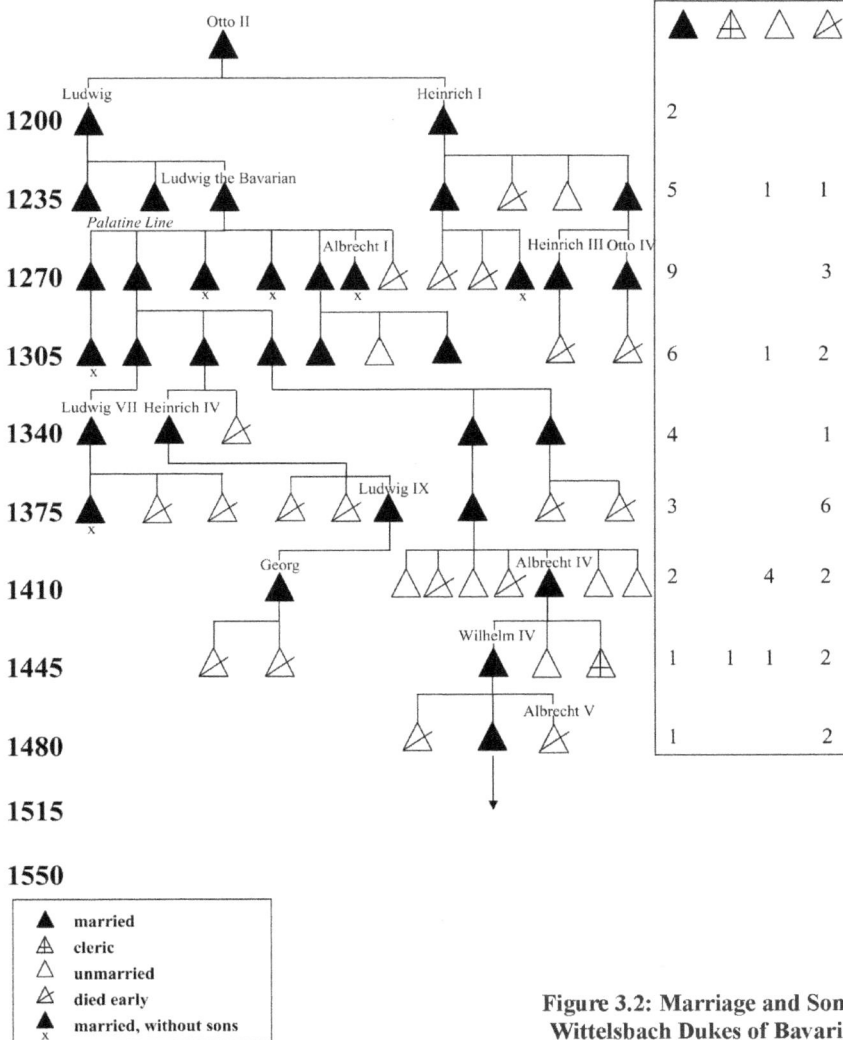

Figure 3.2: Marriage and Sons
Wittelsbach Dukes of Bavaria

considerable dissension. As a result, many a father preferred to establish a division in his lifetime, yet they almost always inserted clauses in
the house constitution to maintain common bonds between the future
rulers: a cloister, the archives, some revenues, or certain jewels were
declared to be joint property and owned by the dynasty as a whole. A
formal treaty was often the best instrument to avoid hostilities between
the new territories and their rulers. Another important means of con-
serving territorial unity was the prohibition on selling parts of a territory

to strangers without first offering it to the agnates. And one line was authorized to inherit the territory of the other in case its ruler died without any heir.[30] To give an example, the Wittelsbach dynasty divided its territories, the Duchy of Bavaria and the Duchy of the Palatinate, in 1329, but installed a clause that both territories should be reunited if one branch died out. This indeed happened more than four hundred years later, in 1777, and changed the political landscape thoroughly—not by war, but by kinship.[31]

Why did rulers not avoid all those problems by introducing primogeniture? In the history textbooks, it is commonplace to find reference to the famous Golden Bull from 1356 and the introduction of primogeniture into the secular electorates. Unfortunately, this is only half the truth, and the electors went on to divide their territories just as happily as ever. Respecting the Golden Bull meant that they just marked a certain undivided portion as the core of the electorate and continued to divide the other parts of the territory, like the Palatinate in 1410, which was partitioned four ways.[32]

Why did primogeniture as a strict rule not work? To begin with, as a rigid rule, it could be very risky if the eldest son proved to be unqualified to lead. For example, the barons of Hanau had introduced primogeniture in 1375, but altered it in 1414 after the firstborn son proved to be mentally disturbed. From then on, the first son was only allowed to rule if he proved to be suitable for government. In 1458, another alteration was made; now the son whom the father thought to be the best for the job was designated to rule.[33] But working out the mechanisms here was only part of the issue. In the political conditions of the late medieval period, brothers cut out of succession frequently could muster the resources to be troublemakers for their whole lives.

These considerations were perhaps even overshadowed by the fear of the extinction of a dynasty and the threat to the legacy of previous generations. Any ruler could observe how the failure of a line could disrupt the integrity of a territory. Even the nobility and towns of a land could be worried about this. The estates of the county of Hanau, for example, petitioned their lord to consent to the marriage of an agnate, the establishment of a new line, and the division of the territory.[34] Increasing the number of agnates was the best guarantee for a long-lived dynasty. Figure 3.3 shows the example of the Hohenlohes. Even though they continuously allowed partitions, nevertheless, in the sixteenth century, only two brothers were left to ensure the continuation of the dynasty.[35] Offering the contrary example, the counts of Wertheim, who practiced primogeniture systematically, died out in the sixteenth century. Even the Wittelsbachs, who allowed marriages and

avoided clerical careers, had, with Albrecht IV (1477–1508), only one
male to continue the dynasty.[36]

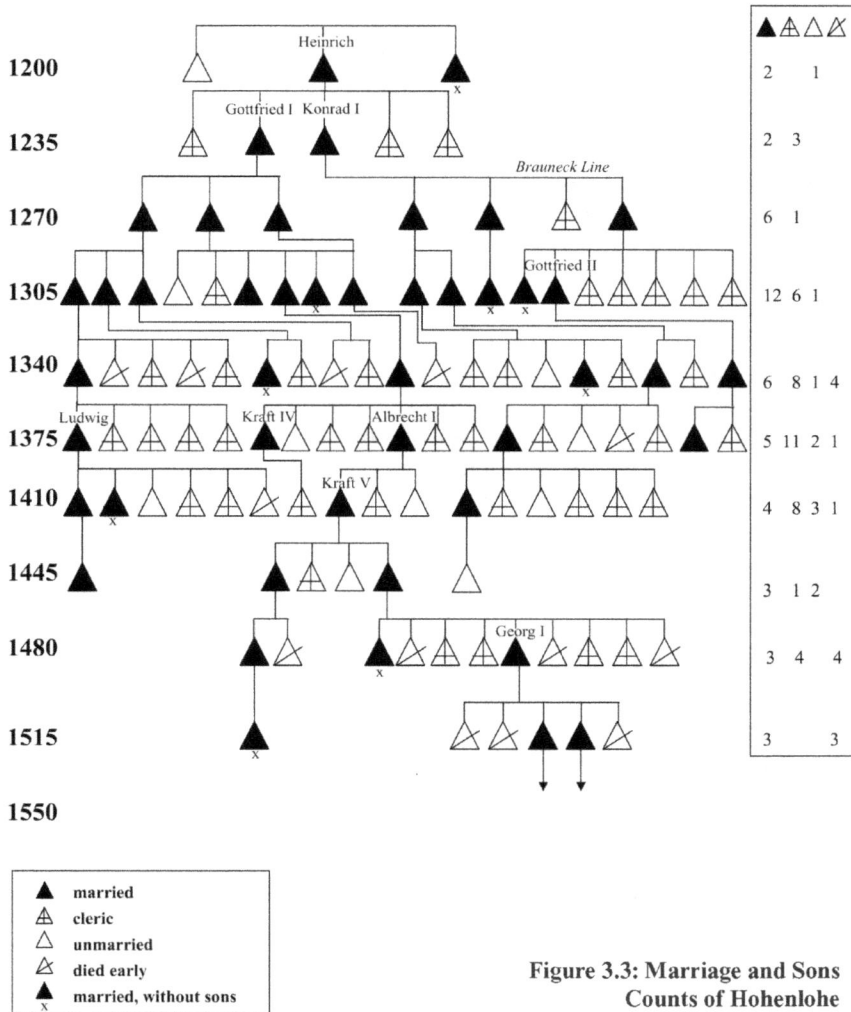

Figure 3.3: Marriage and Sons
Counts of Hohenlohe

Thus, in the later Middle Ages, the unimpeded practice of dividing a
territory and the dislike of primogeniture caused a dramatic increase in
the number of married princes, counts, and barons. All of them wanted
a share of their fathers' territories and split them up. Continuing to
produce sons and partitioning territories led to an enormous increase of
agnatic lines within a dynasty.[37]

How did the relationship between kinship and territory develop? First of all, the agnatic kin groups were always reminded of belonging to the same dynasty, because they kept the same name and title, even though they governed different territories. In addition, the right of pre-emption forced them to think of the agnates when selling a portion of the territory.[38] If the agnates of different lines were willing to cooperate, they could reunite the territory after some generations if one line was threatened with extinction. In 1392, Philipp VII and Philipp VIII of Falkenstein made a treaty, declaring each other brothers and heirs if one should die without a male heir. In this way, they managed a reunification of the territory their ancestors had divided more than a hundred years before.[39] The same aim could be achieved by arranging a marriage within the kin group. In Germany, enormous dowries, linked to status, were exchanged on the occasion of prestigious marriages: a princess was worth about 20,000 florins, a countess about 5,000 florins, to her husband.[40] Agnates, therefore, were anxious to profit from the exchange of dowries, and following canon law, agnatic lines of the same dynasty could arrange marriages four generations after a division of their territory had taken place.[41]

*   *   *

What about the daughters? Up to the fourteenth century, daughters, in principle, inherited an equal share of the paternal landed and movable property, with the exception of fiefs and offices. Their dowry was also regarded as part of their birthright. In the fourteenth century and later, more and more, daughters were forced to agree to renounce their hereditary title at the time of marriage, with the understanding that the dowry was the equivalent of the inheritance. Only if her father or her brothers died without leaving sons could a daughter's hereditary title become valid again.[42]

By marrying the future heiress, a reunification of a divided territory could be arranged. The counts of Katzenelnbogen, who had split up into two lines in the year 1260, arranged a marriage 125 years later between the heiress of the first line and the heir of the second.[43] The son of the couple was expected to reign the reunited county, and primogeniture was installed. For a few decades, the counts of Katzenelnbogen governed the richest and most powerful county in Germany until they died out, leaving the territory to be split up by collateral heirs.[44]

For the Katzenelnbogen, having only two lines, an arrangement was quite easy, but the Wittelsbach dynasty had split into six lines. When Prince Georg of Bavaria-Landshut had to accept the fact that he would die without a son, he knew that his territory would be inherited by

Albert, the next agnate of the Bavaria-Munich line. To prevent this, he bequeathed his territory in a 1496 will to his daughter, Elizabeth, and his son–in-law, Rupert, who was from the more distant agnatic kin of the Palatine Wittelsbachs, separated from the Bavarian branch of the dynasty as early as 1329. Of course he knew that this was contrary to imperial law and former dynastic treaties of the Bavarian Wittelsbach. Yet, his wish to favor his future grandson via his son-in-law and his daughter was stronger than dynastic reason, or, to put it in other words, family feelings were in this case stronger than the agnatic bond.[45] Such sentiment was contained in the common practice of calling a son-in-law "son," emphasizing potential affective bonds and close familial attachment.[46]

After Georg's death, prince Albert fought a fierce war against his agnate Rupert. He won it with the assistance of emperor Maximilian and gained the most important parts of the territory of Bavaria-Landshut. Small parts went to the emperor as a reward and to Georg's grandsons as compensation.[47] In this case, the heiress had been married to an agnate, a far distant one, but nevertheless, a member of the dynasty. Should an heiress become the wife of a prince not belonging to the dynasty, the territory threatened to be lost to strangers. The hereditary titles of daughters, in case their father lacked sons, proved to be dangerous for the stability of the territories. Towards the end of the fifteenth century, therefore, more and more, dynasties contracted treaties to deny daughters the right to inherit a territory so long as any males in any line of the dynasty were alive. This was a fundamental change! Whereas older treaties had allowed one line to inherit the territory of the other in case sons were lacking, they still gave hereditary title to surviving daughters—now only males could profit from the treaty. Of course, the practice by daughters of renouncing a hereditary title at marriage underwent a change, too. Now they could only inherit if no male of the dynasty at all were left. Still, the new practices were more often adopted by princes than by counts and barons.[48]

*   *   *

In the course of the Reformation, the religious landscape in Germany radically altered the political landscape. With the exceptions of the Bavarian Wittelsbachs and the Habsburgs, by the middle of the sixteenth century, all imperial princes and countless counts became Protestant. Even ten bishoprics converted to the Protestant confession and were swallowed by neighboring territories, in many cases, with the assistance of the bishop, a son from the dynasty. Thus, the Church lost its function for many princes and bishops as a means for providing for younger sons.[49]

In this third phase, the effects of the Reformation on the policies of Protestant princes deserve close examination. Surprisingly, primogeniture did not experience an upswing after the removal of the Church as a means for material support. Partitions seem to have increased, with religious issues playing a considerable role in calculations.[50] Princes also obviously did not attempt to reduce the number of their children through changes in their procreative behavior.[51] The frequent dying out of lines encouraged the opposite: securing the survival of the dynasty with as large a number of agnates as possible. And there was the added factor of high mortality rates for those unmarried sons who chose to support themselves through military careers.[52]

For Catholic princes, too, the Reformation, in theory, could have restricted material possibilities, in the first instance because ten lucrative bishoprics turned Protestant. With the reform of the Catholic Church culminating in the Council of Trent, new restrictions, to avoid the old scandals in selecting bishops, were put into place. Only a candidate who was at least thirty years old, ordained, and suited to the post was to ascend to a bishop's throne. And the reprehensible accumulation of bishoprics by one person was prohibited.[53] Had the reforms been strictly enforced, then putting princes' sons on bishops' thrones would have become more difficult. In any case, the reforms brought no improvement. In fact, the domination of the bishoprics by the two remaining Catholic ruling houses, the Wittelsbach and Habsburg, really began. And the popes, put into a difficult political situation and threatened with the loss of the powerful northwestern sees of Cologne, Münster, and Osnabrück, were quite ready to sacrifice reform measures to the power hungry princes.[54]

The Bavarian Duke Albrecht made the start, when in 1565, he gained the Bishopric of Freising (surrounded by Bavarian territory) for his eleven-year-old son, Ernst. The duke was forced to accept a compromise, which only allowed the little prince the secular right to rule the bishopric while a suffragan bishop and the cathedral college shared the religious duties until he reached his majority, but the duke had in fact brought the bishopric under his control. Despite an aversion to a clerical career, in 1573, at the age of eighteen, the reluctant adolescent Duke Ernst added the Bishopric of Hildesheim. After an attempt to secure the Archbishopric of Cologne failed, the Bishopric of Lüttich followed in 1581, and the three-time bishop finally did gain the Archbishop's throne in Cologne in 1583. The pope smoothed the way for him by issuing a letter of eligibility. Because the selection of a bishop as a bishop was impossible under Church law, only the cathedral college could nominate him, and only with two-thirds of the votes. Thanks to papal privilege, Ernst could be elected immediately, requiring only a simple majority. This privilege helped other princes' sons with election to cathedral colleges. In 1585, Duke Ernst went on to accrue his fifth bishopric. The ruling house of Bavaria invested vast sums (nearly a million Gulden) in the clerical career of Ernst and, in doing so, secured Bavaria a position in the European concert of powers.[55]

It is clear from the Wittelsbach example that the cumulation of bishoprics on one hand, was an important instrument for the expansion of power. Although such measures, already highly suspect under canon law, occasionally occurred in the fifteenth century, after the Reformation, they became frequently used church-political weapons.[56] To this was added the family-political aspect, because the few Catholic princes did not have enough sons to occupy each bishopric singly; ultimately, nine Bavarian Wittelsbachs held a total of thirty-three bishoprics. Another instrument that had already been occasionally used in the late Middle Ages, but was used systematically after the Reformation, was the office of the coadjutor with the right of succession. Originally created to support a bishop unable to rule due to illness or old age, the office of coadjutor now served to secure a quasi-succession. Using this device, the House of Bavaria managed to place their own family members on the bishops' thrones occupied by Duke Ernst.[57]

At the level of the Protestant counts, the unavailability of clerical benefices led to a significant rise of marriages with the consequential partition of territories among brothers. There seems to have been an effort by many counts to limit the number of possible births by delaying the first marriage of women, with the average age at marriage climbing from around seventeen years at the end of the fifteenth century to over twenty-three years in the sixteenth. Theoretically, this meant reducing fertility by almost four births, but still plenty of extraneous sons remained to keep the problem of succession severe.[58]

*   *   *

Given tenacious rejection of primogeniture well past the Reformation, it is surprising that primogeniture could so quickly triumph in the fourth phase, from the middle of the seventeenth century. This does not appear to have directly resulted from concerns with state-building.[59] Hardly anyone would link the introduction of the indivisibility of the empire under Heinrich I to progressive state-building. He clearly thought dynastically and strove above all to strengthen the royal dynasty he had founded by marrying his son to a king's daughter and naming him sole ruler of the empire. The princes in the late Middle Ages and the early modern period also thought of their dynasties and not of their states, and the introduction of primogeniture should, first of all, be understood as a strategic move to strengthen the standing of the dynasty, concentrating the political and economic power of the territory in one ruler.[60]

The necessity of such a step, which had so long been held off, can be traced to the consequences of the Thirty Years War. In light of the changed political and economic conditions, smaller territories no longer appeared competitive, particularly as the costs of a representative court life rose. Therefore, between 1650 and 1700, most dynasties were forced to introduce primogeniture.[61]

Looking back on kinship in the long run, the increase in the size of agnatic kin groups in the wake of partitions among brothers since the middle of the thirteenth century stands out. The marriages that accompanied partitions increased the number of agnates considerably. The end of clerical benefices with requirements for celibacy for princes and counts who had become Protestant resulted in a further rise in the members of dynasties after the Reformation.[62] Because, in principle, all sons were entitled to inherit, only the few voluntary renunciations of inheritance rights reduced the number of legitimate heirs. In the context of kinship and lordship, women played only a small role. Until the end of the fifteenth century, the subsidiary inheritance right of the daughter could, in absence of a son, lead to the fall of a territory to a daughter and thereby to a cognate. At the latest in the sixteenth century, agnates secured reciprocal inheritance rights through dynastic contracts and *fidei commissa*. This completed the exclusion of women from direct rule, because the marriage laws of the higher nobility excluded the wife from ruling and, at most, allowed widows to rule lands belonging to their dowers.[63] Only being a regent for underage sons offered a woman direct rule over a territory.[64]

*   *   *

In conclusion, let us return to the question asked at the beginning and attempt to outline answers. First, it needs to be stressed that the decision for or against a partition depended on the individual situation in each dynasty, and therefore, given the current state of research on the topic, it is too early to make generalized statements. What is missing is a comprehensive monograph on the long-term development of the law of primogeniture to replace Schulze's now obsolete book.[65] With great caution, one might say that princes and counts were conscious of the dangers of partition and that they attempted to minimize the detrimental consequences through appropriate stipulations. When they did partition anyway, in their view, they behaved entirely rationally. Because for them the good of the country was inseparably tied to the good of the dynasty, they perceived the extinction of the ruling house as the greater evil. Each ruler had, before his eyes, examples that demonstrated that, after the extinction of a dynasty, a country lost its independence and was divided among the collateral heirs.[66] The expansion of the agnatic family groups through the founding of new lines together with the consequent partitions appeared to be the best guarantee, in light of the high infant mortality rates, of the continuation of the dynasty.[67] Religious considerations may have played a contributing role,[68] but the biological argument remains decisive before and after the Reformation and, naturally, also after the introduction of primogeniture, as the following quote from the political testament of Prussian King Frederick the Great from 1768 illustrates:

> Wir haben Ansprüche an Mecklenburg, begründet auf einen alten Erbverbrüderungsvertrag, der erst beim Tode des letzten Herzogs gültig wird. Diese Herzöge haben dafür gesorgt, daß ihre Staaten nicht so bald an uns fallen; sie sind von einer Fruchtbarkeit, um ein Kaninchengehege zu bevölkern, während die Sterilität unserer Familie uns zu nahem Ende führt.[69]

> (We have claims to Mecklenburg, founded on an old reciprocal fraternal inheritance contract [*Erbverbrüderungsvertrag*], which are only valid after the death of the last duke. These dukes have provided that their states will not fall to us so soon; they are procreative enough to populate a rabbit colony, while the sterility of our family is about to bring us to our end.)

(Translation: Benjamin Marschke)

Notes

1. See the overview of the orders of the empire (*Reichsstände*) in the registry of 1521 in Herbert Grundmann, ed., *Gebhardt. Handbuch der deutschen Geschichte, vol. 2: Von der Reformation bis zum Ende des Absolutismus*, 9th ed. (Stuttgart, 1981), pp. 769ff.
2. Hermann Johann Friedrich Schulze, *Das Recht der Erstgeburt in den deutschen Fürstenhäusern und seine Bedeutung für die deutsche Staatsentwickelung* (Leipzig, 1851).
3. Schulze, *Recht der Erstgeburt*, p. 4: "Nur die monarchische Staatsform giebt die Möglichkeit zu Staatenbildungen höherer Ordnung, während Staaten, wo das ganze Volk unmittelbar herrscht, immer nur von geringem Umfang sein können" (only the monarchical form of government offers the possibility of developing

states of a higher order while states where the entire populace reigns unhindered can always be of a only lesser extent).

4. Schulze, *Recht der Erstgeburt*, pp. 11–12, 310–11.

5. Schulze, *Recht der Erstgeburt*, p. VI.

6. Schulze, *Recht der Erstgeburt*, p. V.

7. Hermann Wiesflecker, "Die politische Entwicklung der Grafschaft Görz und ihr Erbfall an Österreich", in: *Mitteilungen des Instituts für österreichische Geschichte* 56 (1948), pp. 329–384, here p. 346. Wiesflecker describes the counts after the partition as "völlige Nullen, die nur mehr hinter einem Habsburger oder Wittelsbacher oder Luxemburger gelegentlich zu zählen kommen" (complete zeroes, who only are only occasionally counted behind a Habsburg or Wittelsbach or Luxumburg). A similarly harsh judgement is passed on the lords of Eppstein by Karl E. Demandt, *Die Geschichte des Landes Hessen*, 2nd ed. (Kassel, 1980), p. 454.

8. Thus, Levold von Northof, in his chronicle of the counts of the mark, urgently warned that the county not be partitioned. Fritz Zschaeck, ed., *Die Chronik der Grafen von der Mark von Levold von Northof* (Berlin, 1929), p. 10: "quod satis patet in nonnullis dominiis ducatuum, comitatuum et aliorum dominiorum, que olim magni fuerunt nominis et potencie, que nunc per particiones diversas in heredes factas ad statum modicum sunt redacta."

9. Karl-Heinz Spiess, *Familie und Verwandtschaft im deutschen Hochadel des Spätmittelalters, 13. bis Anfang des 16. Jahrhunderts* (Stuttgart, 1993), pp. 199–200.

10. Ernst Schubert, *Fürstliche Herrschaft und Territorium im späten Mittelalter* (Munich, 1996), p. 22.

11. Wolfgang E. J. Weber, "Dynastiesicherung und Staatsbildung. Die Entfaltung des frühmodernen Fürstenstaates", in: *Der Fürst. Ideen und Wirklichkeiten in der europäischen Geschichte*, ed. Wolfgang Weber (Cologne, Weimar, Vienna, 1998), pp. 91–136, here pp. 94ff.; and Hans-Wolfgang Berghausen, "Eine 'der merckwürdigsten Urkunden in denen sächsischen Geschichten': Die Dispositio Albertina von 1499", in: *Zeitschrift für Historische Forschung* 27 (2000), pp. 161–177, here p. 165.

12. Paula Sutter Fichtner, *Protestantism and Primogeniture in Early Modern Germany* (New Haven, London, 1989).

13. Stefan Weinfurter, "Die Einheit Bayerns. Zur Primogeniturordnung des Herzogs Albrecht IV. von 1506", in: *Festgabe Heinz Hürten zum 60. Geburtstag*, ed. Harald Dickerhof (Frankfurt am Main, 1988), pp. 225–242; Hansmartin Schwarzmaier, "'Von der fürsten tailung.' Die Entstehung der Unteilbarkeit fürstlicher Territorien und die badischen Teilungen des 15. und 16. Jahrhunderts", in: *Blätter für deutsche Landesgeschichte* 126 (1990), pp. 161–183.

14. See below, p. 98.

15. Spiess, *Familie und Verwandtschaft*, pp. 272ff.; Hermann Schulze, *Das Erb- und Familienrecht der deutschen Dynastien des Mittelalters* (Halle, 1871), p. 57, gives an instructive example concerning the counts of Sayn in the year 1294: "proprietatem inter nos equaliter dividemus secundum quod nobis more patriae innatum est."

16. Weber, "Dynastiesicherung und Staatsbildung", p. 97.

17. Alfred Boretius, ed., *Capitularia regum Francorum* (Hannover, 1883), Nr. 45, pp. 126–130 and Nr. 136, pp. 270–273.

18. Rudolf Schieffer, "Väter und Söhne im Karolingerhause", in: *Beiträge zur Geschichte des Regnum Francorum. Referate beim Wissenschaftlichen Colloquium zum 75. Geburtstag von Eugen Ewig am 28. Mai 1988*, ed. idem (Sigmaringen, 1990), pp. 149–164; Brigitte Kasten, *Königssöhne und Königsherrschaft. Untersuchungen zur Teilhabe am Reich in der Merowinger- und Karolingerzeit* (Hannover, 1997).

19. Karl Schmid, "Das Problem der 'Unteilbarkeit des Reiches'", in: *Reich und Kirche vor dem Investiturstreit. Gerd Tellenbach zum 80. Geburtstag*, ed. idem (Sigmaringen, 1985), pp. 1–15.
20. Schulze, *Recht der Erstgeburt*, has only three periods because he does not see the Reformation as a new phase.
21. Heinrich Appelt, ed., *Die Urkunden Friedrichs I. 1158-1167* (Hannover, 1979), Nr. 242, pp. 34–36.
22. Spiess, *Familie und Verwandtschaft*, pp. 201ff.
23. Wolfgang Hartung, "Adel, Erbrecht, Schenkung. Die strukturellen Ursachen der frühmittelalterlichen Besitzübertragungen an die Kirche", in: *Gesellschaftsgeschichte. Festschrift für Karl Bosl zum 80. Geburtstag*, ed. Ferdinand Seibt, vol. 1 (Munich, 1988), pp. 417–438.
24. Spiess, *Familie und Verwandtschaft*, pp. 204ff.
25. Spiess, *Familie und Verwandtschaft*, pp. 288- 289.
26. Aloys Schulte, *Der Adel und die deutsche Kirche im Mittelalter. Studien zur Sozial-, Rechts- und Kirchengeschichte*, 2nd ed. (Stuttgart, 1922); Spiess, *Familie und Verwandtschaft*, pp. 301ff.
27. Spiess, *Familie und Verwandtschaft*, pp. 265ff. (graph from p. 266).
28. Weinfurter, "Die Einheit Bayerns", pp. 233–234; Karl-Heinz Spiess, "Erbteilung, dynastische Räson und transpersonale Herrschaftsvorstellungen. Die Pfalzgrafen bei Rhein und die 'Pfalz' im späten Mittelalter", in: *Die Pfalz. Probleme einer Begriffsgeschichte vom Kaiserpalast auf dem Palatin bis zum Regierungsbezirk*, ed. Franz Staab (Speyer, 1990), pp. 159–181, here pp. 175ff.
29. Spies, *Familie und Verwandtschaft*, p. 280.
30. A good overview of the territorial divisions is Reinhard Härtel, "Über Landesteilungen in deutschen Territorien des Spätmittelalters", in: *Festschrift Friedrich Hausmann*, ed. Herwig Ebner (Graz, 1977), pp. 179–205. See also Spiess, *Familie und Verwandtschaft*, pp. 276–277.
31. Karl-Friedrich Krieger, "Bayerisch-pfälzische Unionsbestrebungen vom Hausvertrag von Pavia (1329) bis zur wittelsbachischen Hausunion vom Jahre 1724", in: *Zeitschrift für Historische Forschung* 4 (1977), pp. 385–413.
32. See the Golden Bull in Lorenz Weinrich, ed., *Quellen zur Verfassungsgeschichte des Römisch-Deutschen Reiches im Spätmittelalter (1250-1500)* (Darmstadt, 1983), p. 382: "primogenitus filius succedat"; Spiess, "Erbteilung, dynastische Räson und transpersonale Herrschaftsvorstellungen", pp. 175–176, 179 (concerning the Saxony and Brandenburg electorates).
33. Spiess, *Familie und Verwandtschaft*, pp. 216ff.; Reinhard Dietrich, *Die Landesverfassung in dem Hanauischen. Die Stellung der Herren und Grafen in Hanau-Münzenberg auf Grund der archivalischen Quellen* (Hanau, 1996), pp. 43ff.
34. Spiess, *Familie und Verwandtschaft*, pp. 222–223; Dietrich, *Die Landesverfassung in dem Hanauischen*, pp. 119ff. (with many details). The estates of Bavaria-Munich opposed the statute of primogeniture of Duke Albrecht IV, too, but for other reasons. Weinfurter, "Die Einheit Bayerns", pp. 240–241.
35. Spiess, *Familie und Verwandtschaft*, p. 227.
36. See Figures 3.1 and 3.2.
37. See Figures 3.2 and 3.3.
38. See, for example, Fritz Ulshöfer, "Die Hohenlohischen Hausverträge und Erbteilungen. Grundlinien einer Verfassungsgeschichte der Grafschaft Hohenlohe seit dem Spätmittelalter" (Jur. diss., Tübingen, 1960); Werner Barfuß, "Hausverträge und Hausgesetze fränkischer reichsgräflicher Familien (Castell, Löwenstein-Wertheim)"

   (Jur. diss., Würzburg, 1972); Jörg Rogge, *Herrschaftsweitergabe, Konfliktregelung und
   Familienorganisation im fürstlichen Hochadel. Das Beispiel der Wettiner von der Mitte
   des 13. bis zum Beginn des 16. Jahrhunderts* (Stuttgart, 2002).
39. Spiess, *Familie und Verwandtschaft*, pp. 214–215.
40. Karl-Heinz Spiess, "Witwenversorgung im Hochadel. Rechtlicher Rahmen und
   praktische Gestaltung im Spätmittelalter und zu Beginn der Frühen Neuzeit", in:
   *Witwenschaft in der Frühen Neuzeit. Fürstliche und adlige Witwen zwischen Fremd-
   und Selbstbestimmung*, ed. Martina Schattkowsky (Leipzig, 2003), pp. 87–114, here
   pp. 98–99.
41. Spiess, *Familie und Verwandtschaft*, pp. 61ff.
42. Spiess, *Familie und Verwandtschaft*, pp. 243–244.
43. Spiess, *Familie und Verwandtschaft*, pp. 327ff.
44. Karl E. Demandt, "Die letzten Katzenelnbogener Grafen und der Kampf um ihr
   Erbe", in: *Nassauische Annalen* 66 (1955), pp. 91–132.
45. Reinhard Stauber, *Herzog Georg von Bayern-Landshut und seine Reichspolitik.
   Möglichkeiten und Grenzen reichsfürstlicher Politik im wittelsbachisch-habsburgischen
   Spannungsfeld zwischen 1470 und 1505* (Kallmünz, 1993), pp. 663ff.
46. Spiess, *Familie und Verwandtschaft*, p. 499; Cordula Nolte, *Familie, Hof und
   Herrschaft. Das verwandtschaftliche Beziehungs- und Kommunikationsnetz der Reichs-
   fürsten am Beispiel der Markgrafen von Brandenburg-Ansbach (1440-1530)* (Ostfildern, 2005), p. 65. The same custom existed in the cities. See Simon Teuscher,
   Bekannte—Klienten—Verwandte. Soziabilität und Politik in der Stadt Bern um 1500
   (Cologne, Weimar, Vienna, 1998), pp. 82–83.
47. Meinrad Schaab, *Geschichte der Kurpfalz, vol. 1: Mittelalter* (Stuttgart, 1988), pp.
   213ff.
48. Victor Meyer, "Zur Entwicklung der Hausverfassung der Hohenzollerischen Burg-
   grafen von Nürnberg und ersten Markgrafen von Brandenburg" (Jur. diss., Königs-
   berg, 1911), pp. 119ff.; Spiess, *Familie und Verwandtschaft*, pp. 331ff.
49. For an overview of the conversion of princes see Werner Paravicini, ed., *Höfe und
   Residenzen im spätmittelalterlichen Reich. Ein dynastisch-topographisches Handbuch,
   vol. 1* (Ostfildern, 2003), pp. 19ff. Regarding counts, see Ernst Böhme, *Das
   fränkische Reichsgrafenkollegium im 16. und 17. Jahrhundert. Untersuchungen zu den
   Möglichkeiten und Grenzen der korporativen Politik mindermächtiger Reichsstände*
   (Stuttgart, 1989), pp. 32ff.; Georg Schmidt, *Der Wetterauer Grafenverein. Organisa-
   tion und Politik einer Reichskorporation zwischen Reformation und Westfälischem
   Frieden* (Marburg, 1989), pp. 198ff.
50. Fichtner, *Protestantism and Primogeniture*, pp. 24ff.
51. Fichtner, *Protestantism and Primogeniture*, pp. 38–39.
52. Fichtner, *Protestantism and Primogeniture*, p. 17.
53. Hans Erich Feine, *Die Besetzung der Reichsbistümer vom Westfälischen Frieden bis zur
   Säkularisation 1648-1803* (Stuttgart, 1905), pp. 36ff.
54. Erwin Gatz, ed., *Die Bischöfe des Heiligen Römischen Reiches (1448 bis 1648). Ein
   biographisches Lexikon* (Berlin, 1996); Anton Schindling and Walter Ziegler, *Die Territorien des Reichs im Zeitalter der Reformation und Konfessionalisierung. Land und
   Konfession 1500-1650*, vol. 1–7 (Münster, 1989–1997).
55. Günther von Lojewski, *Bayerns Weg nach Köln. Geschichte der bayerischen Bistums-
   politik in der zweiten Hälfte des 16. Jahrhunderts* (Bonn, 1962), pp. 24ff.
56. Feine, *Besetzung der Reichsbistümer*, pp. 43–44.
57. Rudolf Reinhardt, "Kontinuität und Diskontinuität. Zum Problem der Koadjutorie
   mit dem Recht der Nachfolge in der neuzeitlichen Germania Sacra", in: *Der

dynastische Fürstenstaat. Zur Bedeutung von Sukzessionsordnungen für die Entstehung des frühmodernen Staates, ed. Johannes Kunisch (Berlin, 1982), pp. 115–155.

58. Schmidt, *Wetterauer Grafenverein*, p. 492.

59. This point is stressed by Thomas Klein, "Verpasste Staatsbildung? Die wettinischen Landesteilungen in Spätmittelalter und früher Neuzeit", in: *Der dynastische Fürstenstaat. Zur Bedeutung von Sukzessionsordnungen für die Entstehung des frühmodernen Staates*, ed. Johannes Kunisch (Berlin, 1982), pp. 89–114, here pp. 122–123.

60. Weinfurter, "Die Einheit Bayerns", pp. 228–229; Fichtner, *Protestantism and Primogeniture*, pp. 73ff. and Klein, "Verpasste Staatsbildung?", pp. 113–114 all stress the economic reasons for the introduction of primogeniture.

61. Fichtner, *Protestantism and Primogeniture*, p. 72.

62. Concrete numbers exist up until now only for regional studies. Spiess, *Familie und Verwandtschaft*, p. 279, shows that the number of sons of fifteen comital dynasties nearly doubles from the thirteenth to the fourteenth century. There is, however, a methodological problem, because the genealogical sources from the thirteenth century are rare and might not name all sons of a lord; Schmidt, *Der Wetterauer Grafenverein*, pp. 490ff. has statistics about the birth rate of Hessian counts from 1450 to 1648, with an increase in the sixteenth century and a noticeable reduction in the seventeenth century. Statistics for numbers of sons and daughters in the Habsburg dynasty within sixteen generations in: Andreas Hansert, *Welcher Prinz wird König? Die Habsburger und das universelle Problem des Generationswechsels. Eine Deutung aus historisch-soziologischer Sicht* (Petersberg, 1998), p. 264.

63. Spiess, "Witwenversorgung", p. 95.

64. Examples for the Middle Ages in: Edith Ennen, *Frauen im Mittelalter* (Munich, 1984); Spiess, *Familie und Verwandtschaft*, pp. 182–183; and for the early modern period, Heide Wunder, "Herrschaft und öffentliches Handeln in der Gesellschaft der Frühen Neuzeit", in: *Frauen in der Geschichte des Rechts. Von der Frühen Neuzeit bis zur Gegenwart*, ed. Ute Gerhard (Munich, 1997), pp. 27–54.

65. For England, see Eileen Spring, *Law, Land and Family. Aristocratic Inheritance in England, 1300 to 1800* (Chapel Hill, London, 1993).

66. Examples are the aforementioned territories of Katzenelnbogen and Bayern-Landshut.

67. Fichtner, *Protestantism and Primogeniture*, pp. 34–35.

68. Religious motives encouraged territorial divisions (Fichtner, *Protestantism and Primogeniture*, p. 69), but they did not cause them.

69. Richard Dietrich, ed., *Die politischen Testamente der Hohenzollern* (Cologne, Vienna, 1986), p. 657. The marriages of the king, of his brother, and his nephew were at that time all childless.

Chapter IV

Politics of Kinship in the City of Bern at the End of the Middle Ages

Simon Teuscher

While kinship has become an important topic among students of the late medieval nobility, it is only reluctantly discussed by historians dealing with the period's urban societies. This is, in part, a legacy of historiography. Historians of the European Middle Ages long tended to despise the nobility as a vestige of a waning age, while celebrating the period's urban citizenry as a pioneer of modernization. They also subscribed to the widely held assumption that kinship is important to traditional, but marginal to modern, social frameworks. The historiography of medieval cities has, much like the one on the nineteenth and twentieth centuries, brought about excellent studies of the organization of the nuclear family,[1] but demonstrated less interest in wider networks of relationships that were constituted by descent and alliance.[2] To the extent that historians of medieval cities mention kinship organization at all, they often refer to it as a structure in the process of disintegrating, which they mainly attribute to effects of urban government. As exceptional entities in the context of a "feudal" order, cities relied on innovative legislation and advanced administrative bodies, in which power was distributed by elections rather than by direct inheritance. Such forms of government, a frequent argument goes, needed to break

the strong ties to highly coherent kingroups that are seen as characteristic of medieval society.[3]

Rather than to assume a natural antagonism between urban government and kinship, this chapter examines how medium- to high-ranking
citizens relied on kinship in political as well as other arenas in the city
of Bern in today's Switzerland.[4] My approach is to investigate singular
interactions among kin that I trace in varied source material that
includes private letters, chronicles, administrative records, and mandates. I discuss examples from the decades between 1440 and 1520
that, with due reservations, can be used as indicators of major changes
in the organization and use of kinship between the Middle Ages and the
early modern period.

With an estimated number of five thousand inhabitants, no bishop
of its own, and a location off the major trade routes, late medieval Bern
was, by most standards, a small and unimportant town.[5] In political
terms, however, Bern gained considerable weight. As an imperial city, it
was largely self-governed, and between the late fourteenth and the
early sixteenth century, Bern conquered or purchased large areas of its
surroundings from the regional nobility and built what eventually
became the largest city-state north of the Alps, with a population of
roughly eighty thousand inhabitants. The expansion of the territory
went along with the establishment of an increasingly dense administrative organization headed by the city's council. This provided members
of the city's elite with growing opportunities to sustain themselves as
politicians, as the city's chatelains of rural districts, and as private owners of rural seigneuries under the city's overlordship. The particular situation of a small urban elite in charge of a large apparatus of territorial
lordship accelerated two developments that were under way in most
other European cities of the period. On the one hand, social mobility
that had been considerable until about 1400 slowed down, while citizens' social and economic positions increasingly depended on holding
office, political participation, and the use of "public" resources.[6] On the
other hand, administrative institutions were strengthened and claimed
to regulate ever more areas of life.[7] I will argue that both these developments were strongly interrelated with shifts in kinship-organization.

In what follows, I will first address contemporary normative conceptions of kinship and then lay out some general observations about the
reliance on kinship in day-to-day practices and politics. Subsequently I
will deepen a few observations by discussing two examples of how kinship was used. The first case concerns exchanges of political and other
favors among merchants in the 1440s, and the second deals with a
patrician's way of addressing kinship in a chronicle he wrote about his

life around 1520. Finally, I will address trends of the long-term development of kinship.

Two Conceptions of Kinship

Like many other European elites of the period, citizens of Bern used
two distinct manners of family-reckoning, a broad bilateral one that
included in-laws and a narrow one that was limited to lines of male
decent.[8] The broad concept was usually referred to by the term, *fründ*
(pl. *fründe*), that people used to address and describe almost anyone
beyond the nuclear family to whom they were related by paternal or
maternal descent or who belonged to a family into which they themselves, their siblings, or their children had married. The extensive use of
one single term indicates a limited interest in distinguishing between
consanguines and affines, generational orders, and degrees of kinship. A
few more specific terms did exist, but were rarely employed. Thus, with
regard to men, *fründ* was occasionally replaced by the barely more specific term *vetter* that designates a cousin in modern German, but around
1500, could refer to uncles, nephews, or in-laws as well. Contemporaries did, however, far more than modern German speakers emphasize
particularly close relationships to selected members of their extended
kin by addressing them in the terminology of the nuclear family, for
example, as "my brother" or "my sister."[9]

Such a kin-conception that was not only bilateral, but also included
in-laws, was in accordance with the city's inheritance patterns. All sons
and daughters had a right to an equal share of their deceased parents'
property, and spouses had a lot of leeway to delay the devolution of
property to the next generation by bequeathing it to each other.[10] Thus,
each marriage and each death entailed major divisions and mergers of
property. Passing estates from one generation to the next required
intensive cooperation—and frequently entailed fierce conflict—among
spouses, in-laws, and siblings who had to engage in temporary co-own-
ership, liquidate goods to compensate each other, or agree to receiving
shares in the form of acknowledgements of debt. From the perspective
of property, *fründe* appear as overlapping networks of people who, in
frequently shifting constellations, were likely to hold stakes in the same
property—if not in the present, then in the near past or future.

In the course of the fifteenth century and first among leading families, a different, more narrow conception of kinship referred to as
geschlecht or *stamm* was ever more frequently invoked. This conception
was patrilinear; affiliation in it was passed on from fathers to sons only,

while it stressed the perception that women were exchanged between kingroups through marriage. Such lineages did not overlap, but were strictly delineated groups that persisted over generations. Although the bilateral and the patrilineal conception of kinship seem incompatible, they rarely conflicted because they were invoked in different situations. Groups of actually interacting kin were consistently referred to as *fründe*, whereas the *geschlecht* was more of an abstract entity that its members invoked to make claims to status, honor, and political privilege. Contemporaries associated both concepts of kinship with strong obligations. In private letters and oral statements recorded in court protocols, citizens of Bern kept stressing that kin owed each other unconditional support in all kinds of situations and had to avoid disagreement.

Kinship in Day-to-day Cooperation and Government Procedure

Norms demanding solidarity among kin were largely uncontested in theory, but the fact that they were constantly invoked had everything to do with the inconsistency with which they were adhered to in practice.[11] The large majority of recorded normative statements about kin-solidarity were made by kin who admonished each other to live up to normative standards or complained about others' failure to do so. Although the ways in which kin really interacted were enormously varied, a few observations apply quite generally. As opposed to widely held notions about the importance of the household unit and the authority of house-fathers in premodern Europe,[12] the coherence within the nuclear core of the family seems to have been rather weak. The arrangement of marriages, for example, was controlled less by the parents than by a large number of more remote kin and nonrelated acquaintances. Fathers who claimed the right to make decisions about the education, careers, and activities of their sons and daughters in their twenties were frequently faced with disobedient children who pursued different plans without facing the impairing social sanctions this would have entailed in many elite groups of the early modern period.[13]

Both in trade, politics, and everyday routines, citizens of Bern tended to cooperate with individuals that they picked selectively and for rather short periods of time from a wide range of remote kin as well as from among other acquaintances. In situations of material need, people might first turn to one of their numerous *fründe*, but actual help was quite as likely to result from subsequent requests to wealthy neighbors, landlords, or friends of friends. In contrast to what came to apply in the

region in the early modern period, and especially in the nineteenth century, parents chose mostly outsiders to their kin as godparents for their
children.[14] To the extent that kin cooperated, they distributed roles,
such as the ones of leaders or followers, less according to the succession
of generations or the order of birth than in function of situational contexts and the participants' positions outside their kin group. Political
factions amalgamated around high-ranking officers and trade-networks
around particularly wealthy merchants. In many areas, actual cooperation among kin and among nonkin were very similar. Much like patrons
and clients without kinship ties,[15] kin of unequal status constantly negotiated the terms of their cooperation and uninhibitedly expressed their
expectation to receive a favor in return for every favor they granted.[16]
Such relationships were established or intensified when they promised
to be mutually beneficial, perpetuated over a few years, rather than several decades, and loosened again to give way to other constellations.

Although kingroups were permeable to outsiders and resembled
other groups as to their interior structures, the importance of kinship in
late medieval Bern should not be underestimated. Not only did property relationships compel kin to engage and dispute with each other
time and again, but the city's rapidly growing government system also
relied heavily on conceptions of kinship in order to define who
belonged to whom and who was responsible for whom. At the beginning of the fifteenth century, kinship was already used to regulate procedures of the city council. This council, simultaneously serving as the
legislative, executive, and jurisdictional power of the city, was practically the only institution that could make legally binding decisions.
Understandably, citizens frequently had a reason to show up in its
meetings, be it to complain about each other's misdeeds, to beg for
material support, to demand clemency, to ask to be appointed to an
office, or to complain about other officers.[17] For all these purposes, petitioners were supposed to present their cases in the company of a group
of bilateral kin who also served as mediators between the council and
individuals when it came to enforcing decisions. Even among the council members themselves, open partisanship was only considered legitimate as long as it followed lines of kinship.

Moreover, petitioners made their case by reminding the council of
their merits in the form of favors they themselves and past or present
members of their patrilineal kin had done to the city by serving in
offices, participating in wars, or lending money to the city. Accordingly,
the council frequently justified decisions concerning individuals by
referring to the degree to which the city owed gratitude to their lineages. Both contemporary conceptions thus played an important role in

the council politics—the bilateral one on a procedural level and the patrilinear one on an argumentative level. In a way, such regulations simply mirrored the high esteem for norms of kinship solidarity that contemporaries expressed in other contexts as well, if not in deeds, than in words. The specific dynamics of political, legal, and administrative procedure, however, strengthened the actual enforcement of such norms beyond what was usual in less formalized circumstances. And as government activity increased over time, the compelling character of such norms made itself felt in a growing number of situations.

Obtaining Support from Powerful Kin

The many ways in which reliance on kinship in government affairs reflected back on a wider array of interactions can best be captured through individual examples. The first case I would like to take up can be traced in a collection of accidentally preserved letters that were addressed to Peter Schopfer and written between 1438 and 1445.[18] During this period, Schopfer, a senior council member, served a term as the city's representative in one of the territory's districts that was located about thirty kilometers south of Bern in the Alps and included the small town of Thun. Like many of Bern's influential politicians of the first half of the fifteenth century, Peter Schopfer was also a wealthy merchant. He combined office-holding with participation in a promi-nent trade association with numerous agencies between southern Ger-many and Catalonia.[19] Many of two hundred extant letters Schopfer received were from his kin back in Bern who provided him with news about markets and politics, begged him for small and large favors, and asked him to help them bring personal problems to the attention of the city council. Some of Schopfer's kin addressed him in an intimate and informal tone and referred to regular mutual visits, while the letters of others abounded with marks of respect and polite phrases, or even indi-cate very infrequent interactions. Thus, one nephew made a rather fruitless attempt to get Schopfer to support his application for the post of the city's schoolmaster, but mixed up his uncle's first name, whom he addressed as "Hans"—rather than Peter—"Schopfer, my particularly dear good *fründ.*"[20]

An interesting relationship to zero in on is the one to Hans Kramer, an elderly grocer who is represented by fourteen letters, at least six of which he wrote within a few weeks. Kramer alternatively addressed Schopfer as *fründ*, brother, or *vetter*, but was his in-law, probably the husband of a sister of Schopfer's deceased first wife. The two men made straightforward arrangements for a plot of land that Kramer's wife and Schopfer's son had inherited together.[21] They also did business with each other; Schopfer sold oil to Kramer that he probably got from south of the Alps, while Kramer sold him iron from Bern to retail in Thun. They worked on separate accounts, but seem to have gotten along very well and constantly asked and granted each other small favors. Before buying an exceptionally inexpensive load of oil from a third party, Kramer made sure that Schopfer found buyers for his oil. In return, Kramer could expect Schopfer to keep oil in reserve for him to buy so he would not run out of supply should his Christmas sales go well.[22]

Against this background, Schopfer's reluctant response to another of Kramer's requests comes as a surprise at first. When one of Kramer's sons unexpectedly died, he found out that his daughter in-law was hurrying to collect money from the debtors of her deceased husband. Kramer feared that she intended to leave the city with the money in order to remarry, without giving her children their share.[23] When Kramer asked Schopfer to take his grandchildren's case up with Bern's city council, his letters took on an unprecedented deferential tone. He had to repeat this request in no less than five successive, increasingly desperate-sounding letters, and ultimately even offered to pay for Schopfer's travel.[24] Kramer wrote that he was too old and too inexperienced with politics to talk in a meeting of the council, that his wife had such a toothache that she could not leave their house, and that they had no other kin to turn to in this matter. He flattered his kinsman by saying that the council would be more moved by a single word spoken by Schopfer than by an entire Sunday sermon presented by an old man like himself. While Kramer and Schopfer, in dealing with a common inheritance and in trade, had found areas in which they easily cooperated to their mutual benefit, they were very unequal partners in the domain of politics. Kramer admitted that he was in no position to return a political favor, but reminded Schopfer that the grandchildren themselves would grow up and come to understand that they owed him for his help.

After several fruitless requests, Kramer brought up an additional argument that seems to have been the one that changed his kinsman's mind. Kramer reported that "everybody" in Bern, "rich and poor" gave him the advice to have Schopfer deal with the case, and that many people began to rumor that Schopfer was neglecting his kin.[25] Kramer thus referred to the period's equivalent of a public opinion that demanded that Schopfer live up to the norms of kin solidarity. From the last in the series of Kramer's letters we learn not only that

Schopfer brought the case of the semi-orphans to the city council after all, but also how this entailed a transition from equality to hierarchy in the relationship between the two men. Now Kramer complained that Schopfer had traveled to Bern to talk in the council without stopping by at his house to tell him how the case was developing, and whenever he asked other people, they refused to tell him without Schopfer himself being present.[26]

The letter exchanges between Peter Schopfer and his kin illustrate several points. The constantly invoked norms demanding unconditional kin-solidarity did by no means automatically translate into corresponding practices. The actual manners, in which kin interacted on a daily basis, rather were subject to constant negotiations about a quid pro quo in the exchange of favors. A greater pressure to act or to appear to be acting in accordance with norms of unconditional kin-solidarity was primarily felt in public domains and matters of government. There, agreements could not solely be based on juxtapositions of individual interests of the moment, but rather had to be legitimized by rules of a more general character, such as the obligation of kin-groups to assume a representative function in advocating each other's cases.[27] Habitual relationships among kin frequently had to be reconfigured in order to meet the specific requirements of government procedures, which quite frequently implied that people who had previously interacted on equal terms developed relationships that were nearly extensions of the hierarchical and authoritarian structures inherent to government institutions.

Keeping Account of Merits

The second case takes us to the 1520s, when Ludwig, a member of the prominent patrician lineage von Diesbach, wrote a memoir-like chronicle about his and his *geschlecht*'s past.[28] This manuscript of about forty-five pages was meant to be a continuation of a now lost volume about the lineage's history that Ludwig's uncle had written a few decades earlier. In his preface, Ludwig declared his intention to write about "those who have been good and those who have been bad to me, so that my children and their descendants, for better and for worse, will know how to act accordingly."[29] In what follows, Ludwig presents less a coherent account of his life than a list of unrelated experiences. Much like in contemporary bookkeeping, almost each of the chronicle's entries begins with the word "item," but also leads into an assessment of who had incurred a debt of gratitude toward Ludwig's *geschlecht* and to whom its members should remain grateful. Such reports added up to a hoard of merits of the kind citizens used when negotiating with the city council or with other individuals and wanted to justify their demands as claims to favors in return.

Ludwig's chronicle extensively elaborates on the financial and emotional sacrifices he took upon himself to serve his city. Lengthy descriptions of events during Ludwig's youth that he spent as a page at the court of the French king Louis XI demonstrate how the king developed an ever-higher esteem for Ludwig and his lineage. This reputation, Ludwig argues, permitted him to broker favorable treaties for the city, when he later returned to the king as an ambassador of Bern.[30] He makes the intention behind such arguments explicit when explaining why he agreed to serve a term as the city's chatelain in a remote part of the territory. Four of the highest-ranking officers of Bern, he writes, had come to his home and promised that if he accepted this office, the city would not be oblivious of its debt of gratitude both toward Ludwig himself and his offspring. At this point, Ludwig addressed his children directly: "Therefore, my children, do not forget to remind the authorities of their promise whenever you are presented with an occasion."[31]

In addition to drawing an account of merits, Ludwig made the case that he himself, rather than other members of his lineage, was the most reliable guardian of its best interests. In this particular respect, Ludwig's writing indicates tensions between the patrilinear conception of kinship that determined an individual's honor and political prerogatives and the bilateral one that corresponded to inheritance patterns and was supposed to regulate day-to-day cooperation. Ludwig was particularly prone to emphasize his patriline's best interests when writing about conflicts that had opposed him to other members of the Diesbach family in manners that were symptomatic of the period's inheritance system. For example, Ludwig relates how he overcame his older brother's stubborn resistance against dividing their deceased father's estate. This allowed him to compensate his wife's siblings for letting him succeed to the rural seigneury of his parents-in-law so that he could add a prestigious domain to his lineage's patrimony. Ludwig concluded by stating that the Diesbach lineage had incurred a debt of gratitude towards his wife and her family who supported him against his brother.[32] In another case, he admonished his descendants to remain grateful to his second wife. She had helped him win a legal battle against his sons from his first marriage who had claimed shares of their mother's inheritance and allegedly had done so with "indecent words and gestures."[33] Such narratives indicate how strongly Ludwig's social status, and in particular his position relative to his patrilinear kin, depended on arrangements he made with his wives and in-laws, many of whom he called "my brother" and "my sister."[34]

While Ludwig acknowledged the importance of his wives and in-laws, they had no permanent place in his lineage defined by a linear succession from fathers to sons. Ludwig's attempt to assess every turn of his life under the aspect of how it contributed to the status of his lineage was undoubtedly inspired by dynastic representations of the family in the period's nobility.[35] But his heavy investment in a patrilinear vision of kinship was just as clearly related to the workings of the city's communal political system, in which prerogatives were traded for merits. Ascribing merits to the *geschlecht* that remained unaffected by the constant fission and fusion caused by marriages allowed for accumulating them over decades and passing them on from one generation to the next. Merits could thus be treated as a kind of family-patrimony, an intangible capital convertible into legal and political privileges, which made patrilines an important basis of a stable system of ranks.

Dynamics of Change

In a development that began no later than the fifteenth century and continued far into the early modern period, family conceptions and norms demanding family coherence were integrated into a rapidly growing number of legal and administrative regulations. The use of kinship as an organizing principle had characterized procedures of the city council early on and was successively adopted in additional areas as diverse as taxation, relief for the poor,[36] or, to use a particularly telling example, sumptuary laws. The latter were primarily issued and revised in order to prevent citizens from overspending on representative clothing, jewelry, and celebrations. One thing such laws frequently limited was the circle of people that could be invited to baptisms, weddings, and other celebrations. Rather than indicating plain maximal numbers, such legislation delineated the types of relationship that made participation in such celebrations legitimate. Thus the council regulated the commemorative walks to the graves of recently deceased citizens that had used to be attended by large numbers of women. The first ordinance concerning this matter, issued as early as 1370, stated that participation in these walks should henceforth be limited to kin (*fründe*), and at most, two female neighbors.[37] Subsequent laws further narrowed the scope of legitimate participants, until a version of the early sixteenth century admitted "close kin" only.[38] Another series of laws regulated the carnival custom to visit each other's houses in order to be served cake.

A first, still quite tolerant mandate issued in the mid fifteenth century only forbade citizens to ask for cake from people who had not invited them.[39] A more strict mandate from 1522 stipulated penalties for offering cake to anyone but kin.[40] Quite consistently, this legislation aimed ever more at converting festivities that had used to bring together a broad range of acquaintances into family celebrations.

An increased reliance on kinship was not only increasingly mandated, but also further enhanced by political and social transformations. As government institutions got involved in the organization of broader and broader fields of urban life, citizens more often came under pressure to mobilize their bilateral kin as their representative supporters. At the same time, social hierarchies became less permeable,[41] which is likely to have given greater weight to family inheritance and family cooperation. The patriciate closed off and was increasingly successful at monopolizing the city's highest and most rewarding offices. Around 1500, members of leading families such as Ludwig von Diesbach still took great pains to justify claims to political privileges by recollecting their own and their ancestors' merits. By the early seventeenth century, the city council passed legislation that listed a few patrilines to which eligibility to higher offices should once and for all be reserved.[42] This development went along with an increasing emphasis on patrilinearity that began toward the end of the fifteenth century, when ever more *geschlechter* adopted coats of arms, established common burial sites, built their own chapels, and endowed their own pious foundations.[43] The emphasis on patrilineal, rather than bilateral, conceptions of kinship implied a greater stress on the pursuit of coherent family strategies over the long term, on the preservation of a patrimony of tangible and intangible goods, on mechanisms of permanent inclusion and exclusion, and on internal hierarchies. Kinship acquired qualities that allowed its use—attested in many social setting of the early modern period[44]—as an important substrate for new, more long-lasting kinds of patron-client relationships.

*   *   *

To sum up, the examples from Bern do not indicate that the expansion of urban government weakened rigidly organized kin groups. At the beginning of the fifteenth century, cooperation among kin was not structured by tightly organized, stable formations, but rather, selective formations, determined by individual interests of the moment, and subject to calculating negotiations about how favors were to be returned— in spite of constant invocations of norms about unconditional support for kin. More than anywhere else, pressure to abide by such norms was enhanced in the context of government institutions. Here, conceptions and norms of kinship increasingly assumed the function of rules that in a generally applicable, apparently objective, manner determined who was responsible for whom. Prescriptions to cooperate among kin according to the bilateral conception attempted to bring more predictability into contemporary practices of exchanging favors with frequently changing members of extended networks. And the emergence of stable divisions of rank went along with a growing emphasis on patrilinearity, which permitted an individual's political prerogatives to be determined through his affiliation with a clearly delineated stable group that could accumulate status over generations. The emergence of more coherent kinship practices and the expansion of government went hand in hand. This was due only in part to authorities' intentional attempts at disciplining the population. More importantly, individuals engaged in countless strategies of realigning and reinterpreting kinship relationships in manners that helped them assert themselves vis-à-vis the new institutional organization of urban society.

Notes

1. Studies that examine the nuclear family with some consideration for wider kinship networks include Martha C. Howell, *The Marriage Exchange: Property, Social Place, and Gender in Cities of the Low Countries 1300–1550* (Chicago, 1998); Christiane Klapisch-Zuber, *La maison et le nom. Stratégies et rituels dans l'Italie de la Renaissance* (Paris, 1990); Alfred Haverkamp, ed., *Haus und Familie in der spätmittelalterlichen Stadt* (Köln, 1984).
2. Important exceptions are: Christian Maurel, "Stuctures familiales et solidarités lignagères à Marseille au XVe siècle: autour de l'ascension sociale des Forbin," *Annales ESC* 41 (1986): pp. 658–82; Francis William Kent, *Household and Lineage in Renaissance Florence: The Family Life of the Capponi, Ginori, and Rucellati* (Princeton, 1977); Jacques Heers, *Le clan familial* (Paris, 1974).
3. Ultimately, this argument can be at least traced back to Jakob Burckhardt, *Die Kultur der Renaissance in Italien. Ein Versuch*. Neudruck der Uraugabe, ed. Konrad Hoffmann (Stuttgart, 1985), in particular, p 93. It has been further developed by: Heers, *Clan familial*, pp. 129–35, 265; Philippe Braunstein, "L'émergence de l'individu: Approche de l'intimité, XIVè-XVè siècle," in *Histoire de la vie privée. Vol. 2: De l'Europe féodale à la Renaissance*, ed. Georges Duby (Paris, 1985), pp. 526–619; Gerhard Dilcher, "The City Community as an Instance in the European Process of Individualization," in *The Individual in Political Theory and Practice*, ed. Janet Coleman (Oxford, 1996), pp. 281–302.

4. This article is an attempt to relate results of research that I have presented in greater detail in previous publications, including Simon Teuscher, *Bekannte—Klienten—Verwandte. Soziabilität und Politik in der Stadt Bern um 1500* (Köln, Weimar, Wien, 1998); idem, "Parenté, politique et comptabilité. Chroniques familiales du Sud de l'Allemagne et de la Suisse autour de 1500," *Annales HSS* 59 (2003): pp. 847–58; idem, "Chains of Favour. Approaching the City Council in Late Medieval Berne," in *Petizioni, gravamina e supplice nella prima età moderna in Europa (secoli XV-XVIII)*, ed. Cecilia Nubola and Andreas Würgler (Berlin, Bologna, 2004), pp. 311–28.

5. The most recent introduction to Bern in the late Middle Ages is Ellen J. Beer et al., eds., *Berns grosse Zeit. Das 15. Jahrhundert neu entdeckt* (Bern, 1999).

6. Hans Conrad Peyer, "Die Schweizer Wirtschaft im Umbruch in der zweiten Hälfte des 15. Jahrhunderts," in *500 Jahre Stanser Verkommnis. Beiträge zu einem Zeitbild*, ed. Ferdinand Elsener et al. (Stans, 1981), pp. 59–70; Hans Conrad Peyer, "Die Anfänge der schweizerischen Aristokratien," in *Luzerner Patriziat. Sozial- und wirtschaftsgeschichtliche Studien zur Entwicklung im 16. und 17. Jahrhundert*, ed. Kurt Messmer and Peter Hoppe (Luzern, 1976), pp. 1–28.

7. Christian Hesse, "Expansion und Ausbau. Das Territorium Berns und seine Verwaltung im 15. Jahrhundert," in *Berns grosse Zeit*, ed. Beer et al., pp. 330–47.

8. Teuscher, *Bekannte*, pp. 75–84. Cf. Anita Guerreau-Jalabert, Régine Le Jean, and Joseph Morsel, "Familles et parents. De l'histoire de la famille à l'anthropologie de la parenté," in *Les tendances actuelles de l'historie du Moyen Âge en France et en Allemagne*, ed. Jean-Claude Schmidt and Otto Gerhard Oexle (Paris, 2002), pp. 433–46; Joseph Morsel, "Geschlecht als Repräsentation. Beobachtungen zur Verwandtschaftskonstruktion im fränkischen Adel des späten Mittelalters," in *Die Repräsentation der Gruppen. Texte—Bilder—Objekte*, ed. Otto Gerhard Oexle and Andrea von Hülsen-Esch (Göttingen, 1998), pp. 259–325; Karl-Heinz Spiess, *Familie und Verwandtschaft im deutschen Hochadel des Spätmittelalters. 13. bis Anfang des 16. Jahrhunderts* (Stuttgart, 1993), pp. 494–531; Maurel, *Structures*.

9. Similar observations in Spiess, *Familie*, p. 499.

10. Friedrich E. Welti, ed., *Rechtsquellen des Kantons Bern. Stadtrechte*. Vol. I and II: *Das Stadtrecht von Bern*, 2nd ed. (Aarau, 1971), pp. 53–57. The most comprehensive analysis of the development of inheritance law in Bern is still spread out over several sections in Eugen Huber, *System und Geschichte des Schweizerischen Privatrechts* (Basel, 1886–1893). For a recent approach to a neighboring city with a very similar legal framework: Thomas Weibel, *Erbrecht und Familie: Fortbildung und Aufzeichnung des Erbrechts in der Stadt Zürich, vom Richtebrief zum Stadtrecht von 1716* (Zürich, 1986).

11. This section summarizes results concerning kinship in Teuscher, *Bekannte*.

12. Probably the most influential one of the studies to have made this point is Otto Brunner, "'Das Ganze Haus' und die alteuropäische 'Ökonomik,'" in *Neue Wege der Verfassungs- und Sozialgeschichte*, ed. Otto Brunner (Göttingen, 1980), pp. 103–27. For critical discussions of Brunner's notions and their reception: Claudia Opitz, "Neue Wege der Sozialgeschichte? Ein kritischer Blick auf Otto Brunners Konzept des 'ganzen Hauses'," *Geschichte und Gesellschaft* 20 (1994): pp. 88–98; David Warren Sabean, *Property, Production, and Family in Neckarhausen 1700–1870* (Cambridge, 1990), pp. 88–101.

13. Cf., for example, the contribution of Christophe Duhamelle in this volume and Heinz Reif, "Väterliche Gewalt und 'kindliche Narrheit.' Familienkonflikte im

katholischen Adel Westfalens vor der französischen Revolution," in *Die Familie in der Geschichte*, ed. Heinz Reif (Göttingen, 1982), pp. 82–113.

14. Erika Welti, *Taufbräuche im Kanton Zürich. Eine Studie über ihre Entwicklung bei Angehörigen der Landeskirche seit der Reformation* (Zürich, 1967); Abbé Berthet, "Un réactif social: le parrainage du XVIe à la révolution. Nobles, bourgeois et paysans dans un bourg perché du Jura," *Annales ESC* 1 (1946): pp. 43–50.
15. Teuscher, *Bekannte*, pp. 135–79.
16. For a broader perspective on notions of exchange in late medieval urban societies of the region, cf. Valentin Groebner, *Liquid Assets, Dangerous Gifts: Presents and Politics at the End of the Middle Ages* (Philadelphia, 2000).
17. For a more in-depth analysis of these procedures, cf. Teuscher, "Chains of Favor."
18. Regarding these letters, cf. Simon Teuscher, "Bernische Privatbriefe aus der Zeit um 1500. Überlegungen zu ihren zeitgenössischen Funktionen und zu Möglichkeiten ihrer historischen Auswertung," in *Mittelalterliche Literatur im Lebenszusammenhang*, ed. Conrad Eckart Lutz (Freiburg [Schweiz], 1997), pp. 359–85. On comparable letter collections from cities of the region: Mathias Beer, *Eltern und Kinder des späten Mittelalters in ihren Briefen. Familienleben in der Stadt des Spätmittelalters und der frühen Neuzeit mit besonderer Berücksichtigung Nürnbergs (1400–1550)* (Nürnberg, 1990).
19. Hektor Ammann, *Die Diesbach-Watt-Gesellschaft* (St. Gallen, 1928).
20. Burgerarchiv Thun, Thuner Missiven II 261, for Schopfer's lukewarm reaction, cf. ibid. II 680.
21. In several of the letters, Kramer shifts back and forth between these terms: Thuner Missiven 666, 676, 682.
22. Thuner Missiven 671, 676.
23. The type of conflict Kramer feared was indeed frequent. As in many places during the period, Bern had a system that presented a widow with children with two alternatives. She could either refrain from remarrying, stay with the children on her husband's estate, and retain the right to its usufruct, or she could remarry, in which case she had to divide her husband's estate with the children and had to renounce her right to bring them up. The dilemmas this legal situation entailed are addressed in the chapter by Giulia Calvi in this volume and vividly described in Christiane Klapisch-Zuber, "The Griselda Complex," in *Women, Family and Ritual in Renaissance Italy*, ed. Christiane Klapisch-Zuber (Chicago, 1985), pp. 213–46.
24. Thuner Missiven 660, 664, 666, 668, 682.
25. Thuner Missiven 668.
26. Thuner Missiven 665.
27. The distinction between a representative kin that one had to recur to for official purposes and the habitual kin that exchanged favors on a daily basis has been developed by Pierre Bourdieu, *Esquisse d'une théorie de la pratique, précédé de trois études d'ethnologie kabyle* (Geneva, 1972), pp. 71–-80.
28. For this genre, cf. the series of articles on "écriture et mémoire familiale" *Annales HSS* 59 (2004): pp 785–858; Raul Mordenti, *I libri di famiglia in Italia: Geografia e storia* (Rome, 2001), vol. 2; Pierre Monnet, *Les Rohrbach de Francfort. Pouvoirs, affaires et parenté à l'aube de la Renaissance allemande* (Geneva, 1997), pp. 115–215.
29. The text is edited in Urs Martin Zahnd, *Die autobiographischen Aufzeichnungen Ludwig von Diesbachs. Studien zur spätmittelalterlichen Selbstdarstellung im oberdeutschen Raume* (Bern, 1986), pp. 26–115, here p. 26.
30. Zahnd, *Aufzeichnungen*, pp. 82–84.

31. Zahnd, *Aufzeichnungen*, p. 86.
32. Zahnd, *Aufzeichnungen*, pp. 72–76.
33. Zahnd, *Aufzeichnungen*, p. 112–14.
34. For example, Zahnd, *Aufzeichnungen*, pp. 88ff.
35. Cf. Christiane Klapisch-Zuber, *L'ombre des ancêtres: essai sur l'imaginaire médiéval de la parenté* (Paris, 2000).
36. Teuscher, *Bekannte*, pp. 84–94.
37. Welti, ed. *Rechtsquellen Bern*, vol. I and II, pp. 162 (no. 205), 327 (no. 232).
38. Rudolf Steck and Gustav Tobler, ed., *Aktensammlung zur Geschichte der Berner Reformation 1521–1532* (Bern, 1918–1923), vol. 1, p. 89 (no. 344).
39. Friedrich E. Welti, ed., *Rechtsquellen Bern*, vol. I and II, p. 432 (no. 400) (Bern 1971).
40. Steck and Tobler, ed., *Aktensammlung*, vol. 1, p. 14 (no. 68) (Bern 1918–1923).
41. Peyer, "Anfänge," pp. 16–18.
42. Hermann Rennefahrt, ed., *Rechtsquellen des Kantons Bern. Stadtrechte.* Vol. V: *Verfasung und Verwaltung des Staates Bern* (Aarau, 1959), p 367f..
43. Citizens adopted almost all of the representative devices used by lineages of the lower nobility as discussed by Morsel, "Geschlecht als Repräsentation." A comparable investigation for the city of Bern remains to be conducted, but important elements are gathered in Luc Mojon, *Die Kunstdenkmäler des Kantons Bern. Vol. 4: Das Berner Münster* (Kunstdenkmäler der Schweiz) (Basel, 1960).
44. Cf. Wolfgang Reinhard, "Oligarchische Verflechtung und Konfession in oberdeutschen Städten," in *Klientelsysteme im Europa der frühen Neuzeit*, ed. Antoni Maczak (München, 1988), pp. 47–62; Ulrich Pfister, "Politischer Klientelismus in der frühneuzeitlichen Schweiz," *Schweizerische Zeitschrift für Geschichte* 42 (1992): pp. 28–60; Gérard Delille, "Echanges matrimoniaux entre lignées alternées et système européen de l'alliance: un premier approche," in *En substances. Textes pour Françoise Héritier*, ed. Jean-Luc Jamard, Emmanuel Terray, and Margarita Xanthakou (Paris, 2000), pp. 219–52.

Chapter V

Sisters, Aunts, and Cousins

Familial Architectures and the Political Field in Early Modern Europe

Michaela Hohkamp

In his brief statement about the Franco-Austrian relationship, the European Enlightenment intellectual, Johann Daniel Schöpflin (or Jean Daniel Schoepflin), "Professeur D´Histoire et D´Eloqu. Membre de L´Académie Royale des belles Lettres en France, et de la Société Royale en Angleterre" wrote: "Four queens issued from the house of Austria brought to the throne of France all the graces and virtues of their sex. These illustrious marriages seemed to allow friendship and a durable peace, but by a fatality that one could scarcely imagine, these remedies were converted into a disastrous poison which rendered the illness more incurable than ever."[1] In this way, Schoepflin reflected on the consequences of the War of the Spanish Succession at the turn of the eighteenth century and drew attention to the advantages of kinship and the disappointed political hopes connected to them. He thereby touched on one of the most central problems of writing the history of the early modern period, namely the meaning of kinship networks among ruling houses for political relations in Europe.

Historical research into the political role of ruling houses of the Holy Roman Empire during the early modern period is concerned with diverse, overlapping phenomena. On one hand, early modern princely courts expanded the structures of authority step by step and constructed the institutions that led to the modern state. On the other hand, the ruling families were always tied up with their complex, extensive kin relations.[2] Studies which have focused on the development of the territorial state have described ruling houses as "oligarchies with not that many powers" that "formed relatively unrelated regional clusters."[3] Seen this way, complex family ties appear as "a dynastic political arrogance"[4] that was not necessarily beneficial for early modern state-building processes, because their centrifugal forces obstructed territorial consolidation—from a historiographical viewpoint, a principal foundation of dynastic or state authority. Because territories literally lost ground in the countless partitions in the late Middle Ages and the early modern period, they have been characterized as irrational by the relevant scholarship, while primogeniture has been generally viewed as the realistic means to maintain and expand territorial authority. In their detailed studies of families and kinship in the late Middle Ages, Karl-Heinz Spiess and Jörg Rogge have argued against automatically judging territorial partitions negatively, but rather to view them as "practices of late medieval magnates," who, "after due consideration, developed particular solutions specially tailored to the nature of their territories."[5] These solutions took into account the "membership in the particular stratum of nobility," the exigencies of "social prestige," the extent and availability of divisible territories, and alternative "careers," such as clerical offices for cadets.[6]

Territorial partitions have to be understood not simply as an expression of territorial irrationality, but more generally as highly complex social and cultural political negotiations that affected the entire competence and household dynamics of princely families. It should be understood that these families were themselves part of extended networks of kin. Cultural historians are therefore presented with an opportunity to reevaluate the transmission of lordship from the perspective of these kinship-networks. In what follows, I will examine selected examples from the end of the fifteenth until the beginning of the eighteenth century of conflicts over succession in imperial ruling houses with European-wide family ties. I will argue that while primogeniture brought advantages for rulers, it brought certain disadvantages by limiting the capacity for political negotiation or, alternatively, by drastically reducing opportunities for securing a position of power through familial networking. Furthermore, I will show that as a consequence of the normalization of succession by firstborn males, the entire construction of early modern kin-networks was reconfigured. In particular, the traditional father-son axis in family ties was supplemented by an aunt-niece axis, which allowed inheritance claims to be reconceptualized.

*   *   *

From the late fourteenth century, and increasingly from the fifteenth and sixteenth centuries, it is possible to recognize a tendency among the territories of the Holy Roman Empire towards limiting the number of male successors to two or three or even to a single heir. In this inheritance system, the one who bequeathed his possessions or rule could choose his own successor. Because this meant that other offspring, who also had succession rights, were excluded from succession, such a decision had to be confirmed by anyone with succession rights. They had to agree publicly to the testament or, at least acquiesce, which was then ratified by the king or emperor.[7] Unigeniture usually meant celibacy for younger brothers (*Nachgeborene*), or, even with adequate material support, a substantial loss of status. This might only partially be made good if a brother of the successor could make a career as a cleric.[8] Hence, bequests were not always accepted by younger brothers without protest.

The proceedings in the house of the Margraves of Baden at the turn of the sixteenth century offer a clear example of a purposeful use of unigeniture. Christoph I of Baden had many sons and daughters, because his marriage with Ottilie of Katzenelnbogen was well blessed with progeny. The reign of Margrave Christoph was characterized by his attempt to connect together the widely strewn Baden territories and to round off his territory. The opportunity to do so was offered by the marriage of one of his younger sons with the single daughter and heiress of his neighbor, Count Rötteln, who in return for agreeing to his daughter's marriage demanded, that his future son-in-law be declared the single successor to the margraviate of Baden. Because at this point there was already an agreement in place that Christoph would take over Rötteln's territory after the count's death, the demands of the father of the bride were not taken seriously, whereby the entire marriage project was abandoned. Shortly thereafter Christoph found a politically attractive alternative for himself and his son. The choice fell on a daughter of the powerful neighbor the prince-elector of the Palatinate. This plan came to fruition, and in 1503, Margrave Philipp of Baden married Elisabeth of the Palatinate. The price for this marriage, though, was also Philipp's unigeniture.[9] But this time, the deal seemed fitting: the Prince-Electors of the Palatinate were counted among the most powerful ruling houses in the Empire on the eve of the War of the Wittelsbach succession.[10]

While the father was ready to reach a decision to skip over his remaining sons in favor of the lucrative marriage of one son, the brothers of the chosen successor were by no means ready to acquiescence. Margrave Christoph of Baden's testament of 1505 was therefore vehemently contested by his other sons. In this conflict the ruling margrave could still assert himself. After Bernhard, the second of his sons, refused to accept his testament, Christoph forced him to leave court and forcibly sent him into service with the Spanish.[11] Unimpressed, Bernhard maintained his refusal and gained support from his younger brothers, Ernst and Christoph.[12] While Ernst was spared, this resistance cost his brother Christoph his freedom. Their father had him arrested and forced him to acknowledge the testament.[13] Forewarned, Ernst tried other means. He began to work towards a marriage with Margravess Elisabeth of Brandenburg-Ansbach, and they married in 1511. With help from the granddaughter of the powerful Margrave of Ansbach, Albrecht Achilles, Ernst was successful in placing pressure on his father and his fraternal opponents. The dramatic end of the story is well known. Following further clashes, which did not leave the relationships between the brothers untouched, Baden was partitioned in 1535; the old Margrave was declared insane and arrested due to his *corporis debilis*.[14] The remaining potential successors were excluded after Bernhard and Ernst were declared his successors.

*   *   *

The legal historical literature of the nineteenth century showed little understanding for the late medieval and early modern practices of succession, which were, clearly, strongly influenced by the social context and political considerations. Unigeniture, or single son succession, was often regarded as a kind of "state lottery," necessary if one wanted to profit from the succession of a single son without automatically selecting the firstborn.[15] Since the nineteenth century, legal historical and state-centered historical scholarship has regarded uni- and primogeniture and the *Bevorzugung der Erstgeburt* (privileging of the firstborn) generally as suitable measures for securing power and rulership.[16] Prior to the apotheosis of the national imaginary, however, in the academic world, primogeniture was not necessarily seen as unquestionable. During the eighteenth century, discussions about the nature of the state raised the issue of whether the maxim, *primogenitus filius succedat*[17] (from the Golden Bull of Emperor Charles IV for the electoral territories of Bohemia, Brandenburg, the Palatinate, and Saxony), was relevant for the other territories of the Empire.[18] In the context of these debates, so-called *deductiones* appeared, juridical broadsheets, which argued for the succession rights of latter-born sons, indirect male heirs, or female heirs against the rights of a primogenitus. With their help, succession in a direct father-son line was cast into doubt and new claims were formulated. For example, primogeniture was seen as legally suspect because of the lack of imperial or royal ratification, or because it was against legal principles.[19]

By now it should be clear that primogeniture in early modern Europe was neither discursively nor practically the *conditio sine qua non* of the development of princely power as has been portrayed by historical scholarship focused on state building. From contemporaries' perspective, rule was not exclusively rooted in a territory, but based just as much on familial ties, which, in turn, could be created through politically strategic marriages. Because politically promising marriage alliances could only be made when the candidates were suitably outfitted, territorial partitions could make perfect sense to contemporaries. Landgrave Philipp of Hesse, for example, followed this kin-oriented principle and partitioned his territories among his successors. This is especially noteworthy because Philipp himself had ruled over all Hessian territories, since he had inherited as the only living male heir at the beginning of the sixteenth century. The vociferous conflicts both over his predecessor's right to rule[20] and over the right of his mother to rule[21] had been enough to push the Hessian landgraves to the periphery of the group of powerful princes in the Empire. Philipp's morganatic marriage and the resulting Empire-wide conflicts extenuated this process. In this crisis situation, rule over the whole territory of Hesse was not passed on undivided, but partitioned among four male heirs, creating the fragmentary territories of Hesse-Darmstadt, Hesse-Marburg, Hesse-Rheinfels, and Hesse-Kassel.

At the beginning of the seventeenth century, the second landgrave of Hesse-Kassel, 55-year-old Landgrave Moritz, came under pressure from his son, Wilhelm V, to abdicate in his favor. To regulate the succession, therefore, an agreement was reached by father and son, according to which Juliane, the second wife of the old landgrave, and their children were to be provided for, while Wilhelm V, the son from the first marriage, would actually succeed his father's rule. In the end, the agreement came to nothing, because the old duke had reserved the right to make changes to his testament. By 1632 when Duke Moritz died, the younger brothers had not confirmed the primogeniture agreement, nor had the emperor ratified it. Instead, after the death of Landgrave Moritz, it came to *schweren Irrungen* (grave quarrels)[22] over the succession between the heirs from Hesse-Kassel and their distant relatives in Hesse-Darmstadt. In the context of this conflict, the head of the house of Hesse-Darmstadt, Georg II, the grandnephew of the late Landgrave Moritz, issued a mandate prescribing primogeniture for Hesse-Darmstadt and "obtained special imperial privileges and letters concerning sole undivided rule and succession according to the right of primogeniture."[23] With this knowledge in the back of his mind, Wilhelm V of Hesse-Kassel, too, travelled to Vienna with a petition for imperial ratification of the primogeniture agreement he and his father had concluded.

In the partitioned Hessian territories, the desire to mandate primogeniture to make the succession of distant relatives difficult was based on the
experience of conflicts over succession among their own predecessors,
neighboring houses, and more distant princely relatives. The brothers'
feud[24] in the Hessian house in the second third of the fifteenth century
should be mentioned here, as well as the conflict resolved militarily several years before between the two uncles of the Hessian princes,[25] the
Wettiner brothers Friedrich the Gentle and Wilhelm the Brave.[26] The
Wettiner brothers were respectively married to a sister and a daughter of
the Habsburg Kings and Emperors Friedrich III and Albrecht II, and had
already, by the middle of the century, entered into serious conflict over
succession to both their fathers. The Habsburgs themselves also offer
prominent examples of conflicts and political problems involving brothers, cousins, and uncles.[27] Because the Hessian landgraves were related to
the Habsburgs as in-laws through manifold marriages,[28] it can be assumed
that information was regularly available about past and current proceedings at the respective courts. Both competing Hessian second cousins at
the beginning of the seventeenth century, Wilhelm V of Hesse-Kassel and
Georg II of Hesse-Darmstadt, would have known about the mechanics of
succession conflicts well beyond the circle of their own relatives. And the
conflicts of their direct predecessors, which they had personally experienced, would have offered very current instructional material. This last
conflict, which in the early phase of the Thirty Years War became particularly explosive, demonstrated the confused and confusing consequences
of claims to succession when a primogenitor and his descendants in the
direct male line (*Leibslehenerben*) were not explicitly privileged over
other male heirs. To shield his rule against the graspings of the second
cousin from Darmstadt and to secure his *ius territorialis*, a declaration of
primogeniture was the right means for Wilhelm V. But then such a form
of succession, based as it was on natural qualities would, in the future,
make it impossible both to adjust succession procedures according to the
situation and to integrate countless male heirs into the kind of family
architecture that previously had been geared towards securing and
expanding the dynasty and its power.

*   *   *

At this point, it should be clear that succession procedures in the early
modern period were highly complex social and political negotiations
which affected distant relatives as well as close family and which were
also conditioned by the experiences of the participants. Duo- or unigeniture did not change this, but rather reinforced the importance of
politically promising marriages in the devolution of rule, because it was

marriage that could provide the social, political, and cultural capital that was needed to compete for power in the first place. The ties of kinship created by countless politically attractive marriages were constantly reproduced by both male and female heirs with their spouses and in-laws. In contrast, where primogeniture as the firm legal right of the firstborn son to succession was practiced, the devolution of rulership became a quasi-natural process, making marriage strategies aimed at positioning in fraternal competition superfluous. When younger brothers were excluded from succession, their entire cultural, social, and political position also changed, and marriages lost their function in the competition among brothers. In houses that had chosen a primogenitor as the natural and exclusive legitimate successor, inappropriate marriages, celibacy, and alternative careers in the clergy or military were not just a means to get rid of burdensome competitors,[29] but arrangements for the material support for superfluous heirs whose social-political roles diminished, but whose function as biological reserve increased.[30] Male agnates were not well suited for the maintenance, stabilization, and renewal of politically important familial ties through marriage, and such functions were transferred to sisters.

Sisters, in the context of this inheritance pattern, were not only sisters, as the *Zedler'sche Lexikon* from the middle of the eighteenth century defined them, but also wives. Because "Schwester ist eigentlich eine Weibsperson, welche nebst anderen von einem Vater oder von einer Mutter gezeuget worden, und wird so wohl in denen Römischen Rechten, als auch bey den lateinischen Schrift=Stellern daher Soror gennenet, weil sie nicht allein ganz besonders (seorsum) gebohren, sondern auch bey ihrer Verehelichung von dem hause, darinnen sie gebohren, abgesondert, und in eine andere Familie versezet wird..." (Sister is basically a female person who is begotten, besides others, by a father or a mother, and is called *Soror* in Roman law, as well as by Latin authors, because she is not only born completely separately [*seorsum*=apart from the rest], but is also separated from the house in which she was born through marriage and placed in another family...").[31] That definition of "sister," totally different from "brother," is closely tied to her *Absonderung* (separation) into another family. This implicitly points to another familial position of a sister as wife and member of another house, namely the aunt. [32]

Early modern aunts fulfilled the widest range of functions in the familial network. They took in their nieces and nephews at their own courts and frequently raised and educated their nieces. For example, Margarete, daughter of King Maximilian I and governor in the Netherlands, who had her nieces and nephews brought to her own court after her brother Philipp died and his wife Juana displayed signs of madness. One of these children raised at the court of Margarete, Maria, succeeded her aunt in the office of governor. This closeness to the aunt continued in the next generation. Maria took in her nieces and nephews, the children of her sister Isabella, at her court after Isabella's husband, the Danish King Christian II, was deposed and imprisoned by his cousin.

Aunts did not just help at times of crisis, but also directed marriage politics, among other things. At the beginning of the sixteenth century, Elisabeth von Ansbach, a daughter of the Margrave Albrecht Achilles and sister of the margrave Friedrich the Elder of Ansbach, used her kin relationships and her political knowledge to marry off her niece with the same name, the daughter of her brother Friedrich, to Baden, and not to Württemberg as expected. Elisabeth was herself married to Eberhard VI of Württemberg, the successor of the first Duke of Württemberg Eberhard the Bearded (1495), and was the duchess of Württemberg until the deposition of her husband in 1498. After it became clear that the couple would remain childless, she took in her niece. When the opportunity appeared for this niece to marry Ulrich of Württemberg, the son of her imprisoned brother-in-law Heinrich von Württemberg, she intervened actively in the planning and instead negotiated a marriage for her niece with one of her own second cousins, Margrave Ernst of Baden.[33] (See Figure 5.1: Elisabeth of Ansbach as Aunt and Niece.) Because this marriage offered a chance for Ernst (one of the younger sons of the house of Baden, as mentioned above) to politically support his claim to a part of his father's succession, leading to the 1535 partition of Baden, the familial activities of the aunt had wide-ranging political implications. This is even more significant because a repetition of the Ansbach-Württemberg alliance in the marriage of Elisabeth with her cousin Ulrich would have fit the prevailing marriage pattern.[34]

The most famous example of such an aunt-niece axis is the alliance of the French royal house with the Habsburgs through their Spanish relatives, which ultimately brought on the War of Spanish Succession. When Charles II, King of Spain since 1665, died in 1700, a long European war over his succession broke out, which quickly grew into a concern for all of Europe. Both of Charles's marriages, first with Maria Louisa of Orléans and then with Maria Anna of Palatinate-Neuberg, were without children. Therefore, the need to regulate the succession was seen early. The first agreement of the parties with familial claims to the Spanish succession goes back to the year 1688. Both the Hapsburg Emperor of Austria, Leopold I, and the French King Louis XIV had married sisters of the Spanish King Charles II, and both made claims. These

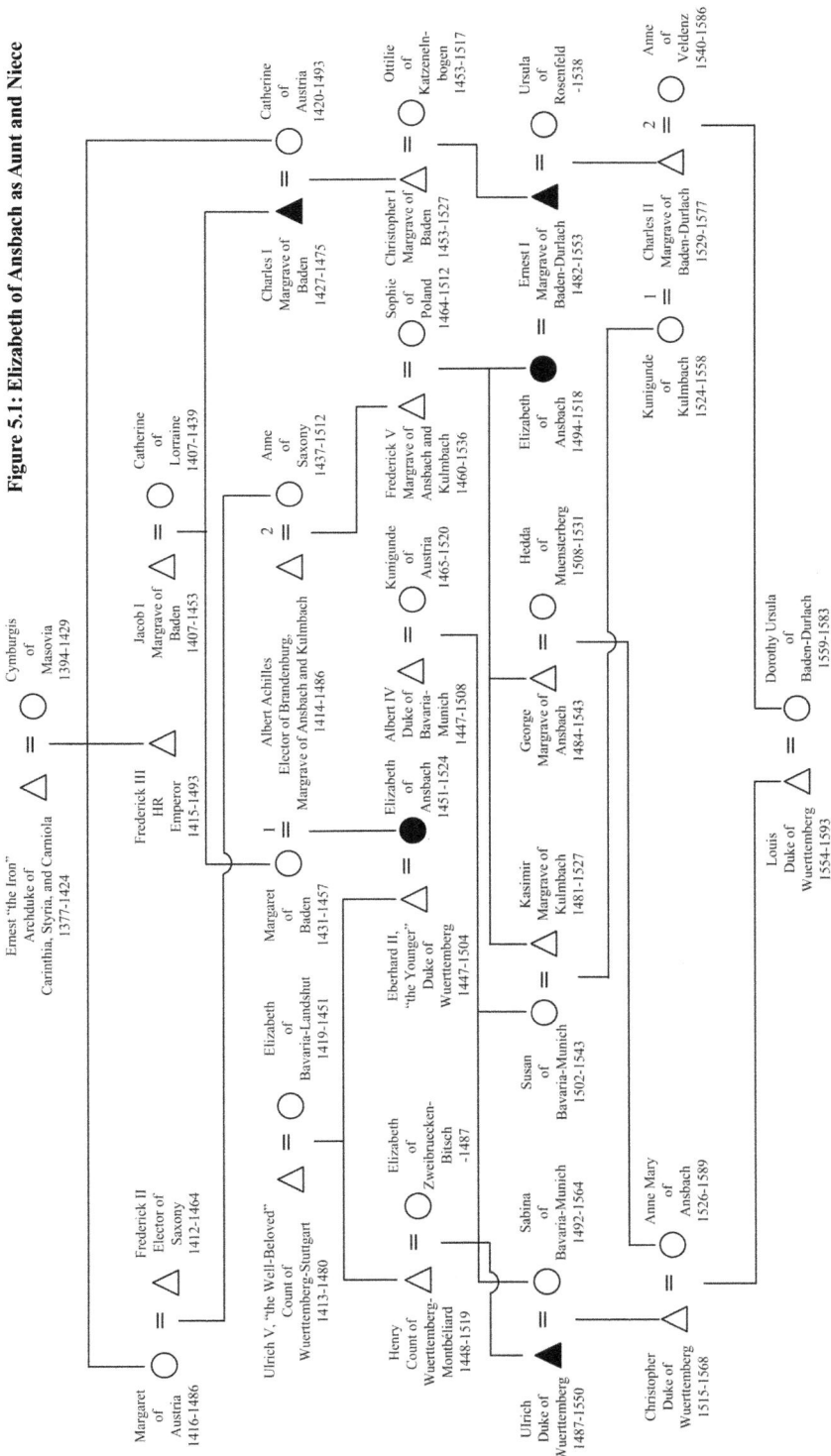

Figure 5.1: Elizabeth of Ansbach as Aunt and Niece

Figure 5.2: Aunts and Nieces

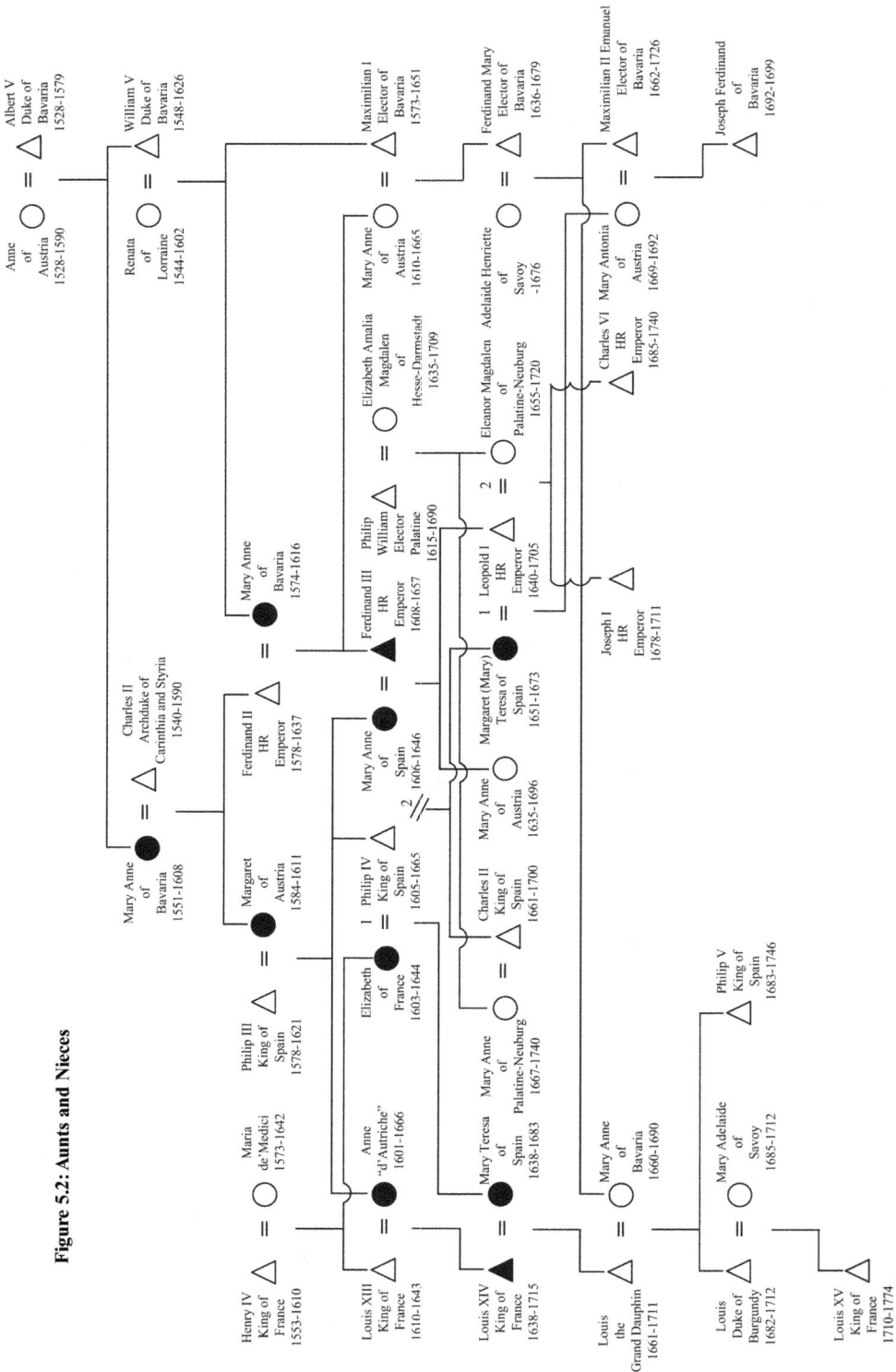

two agreed to partition the Spanish territories in a secret accord in January 1688,[35] but by the early 1690s, Charles II failed to cooperate. Several years after the birth of Joseph Ferdinand, great-nephew of Charles II, to the Wittelsbach ruling house in 1692, Charles selected him as his heir (1698). As the successor to Charles II of Spain, he was also in line for succession to the Spanish Netherlands and the colonies; Charles II's two brothers-in-law, Louis XIV and Leopold I, were to be compensated with Naples and Sicily (for France) and Milan (for Austria).[36]

With Joseph Ferdinand, Charles II had selected the son of his niece, Maria Antonia, and her husband, Elector Maximilian II Maria Emanuel of Bavaria. Maria Antonia was the daughter of Charles II's sister Margareta Theresia and the Emperor Leopold I (See Figure 5.2: Aunts and Nieces). All of these negotiations fell apart when the designated Spanish successor, Joseph Ferdinand, died in February 1699. Again, the French King and the Habsburg Emperor stood opposite each other as equally legitimate successors. Both were not only married to sisters of Charles II, but they were also cousins of Charles II, the nephews of Charles's predecessor, Philipp IV, and the sons of two aunts of Charles II. Louis XIV was the son of Charles's aunt Anne, who had been married to Louis XIII, and Leopold I was the son of Charles's aunt Maria Anna, who had been married to Emperor Ferdinand III. These manifold familial connections were a result of aunts and nieces marrying members of the same houses over two generations. The Spanish aunt-niece pair Anna and Maria Theresia married the French Kings Louis XIII and Louis XIV. The other Spanish aunt-niece pair Maria Anna and Margarete Theresia married the Emperors Ferdinand and Leopold. Put differently: the sons of the sisters of a pair of siblings each married the daughters of the brothers. From the perspective of classical ethnological theory, such marriages were patrilateral cross cousins, which, in European culture, perhaps mitigated the canon law prohibition against cousin marriages.

In terms of potential succession rights, these parallel marriages of two aunt-niece pairs to the male French and Austrian relatives led to an absolute stalemate. Charles's brother-in-law, Louis XIV, sought out political alliances and, even before the death of Charles, agreed with Holland and England to a partition agreement which was not acceptable to Austria. On the other hand, Charles II, in the last months of his life, had let himself stray further from familial principles, and after the death of his great-nephew, Joseph Ferdinand, he named as his successor another great-nephew, Philipp of Anjou. In contrast with Joseph Ferdinand who was a son of a niece, Philipp of Anjou was the son of a nephew of Charles II. If, for a moment, we look away from the political implications, which indicate Philipp's selection as a success of French diplomacy, then it remains that from the familial perspective, the Spanish King Charles II had first privileged the son of a niece (the grandson of his younger sister) over the son of a nephew (the grandson of his older sister) in the succession. The significance of the fact that both of the great-nephews that Charles selected as his successor were sons of the Wittelsbach siblings Maria Anna and Max Emanuel must be investigated at another time. It remains that Philipp of Anjou, the son of a nephew of Charles II—who from the perspective which favors the male line of succession, was actually the most legitimate successor as the closest male relative of Charles II—ultimately succeeded to the throne of Spain. It should be recognized, too, that this resolution was not uncontested. Philip could assume rule over Spain only after a tremendous European war was fought, in the course of which (as Schoepflin remarked in his brief work), the Rhine, as the new border between France and the Habsburg lands, was filled with countless corpses.[37]

Conclusions

The tendency to privilege a primogenitus in succession over other male agnates has been observable in the larger territorial states of the Empire since the sixteenth century. This tendency turned the political, social, and cultural processes of succession into a naturalized mechanism in which brothers, as well as uncles, nephews, and cousins were excluded from succession, forced to abdicate their right to rule, and compelled to adopt celibacy and/or a clerical career. Their opportunities to maintain, confirm, or build new kinship ties were thereby significantly reduced. In societies in which kinship figured importantly in the political field in that it positioned protagonists socially and culturally, this meant a loss of political power for most male family members. The indivisible transfer of territorial possessions is a maxim that, in most scholarship of the late Middle Ages or early modern period, stands undisputed as a politically rational course of action. But from a perspective that regards kinship as the nucleus of politics in the early modern period, the same maxim can appear disadvantageous for the political positioning of princely rule. Once many male children were excluded from the succession process, the beneficial maintenance of dense familial ties was only possible by developing an aunt-niece axis parallel to a father-son axis. Schoepflin thought that the extremely close kin networks between ruling houses represented a kind of "arrogance," but from a gender perspective, they can be interpreted as a reconstructed field within which the politics of the early modern states were played out as succession became "naturalized" through male primogeniture.

(Translation: Benjamin Marschke)

Notes

1. Jean Daniel Schoepflin, *Discours sur L'Alliance de la France et de la L'Autriche, prononcé à Strasbourg, le 26, Fevrier, 1739* (no publication information), p. 7.
2. Cf. Paul-Joachim Heinig, "Maximilian und die Frauen. In den Fängen der dynastischen Politik," in *Kaiser Maximilian I. Bewahrer und Reformer. Katalog zur gleichnamigen Ausstellung vom 2.8.2002-31.10.2002 im Reichskammergerichtsmuseum,* ed. Georg Schmidt-von Rhein (Wetzlar, Ramstein, 2002), pp. 69–81, here p. 70.
3. Peter Moraw, "Kaiser Maximilian I. (1493-1519). Bewahrer und Erneuerer," in ibid., pp. 17–29, here p. 22.
4. Alfred Kohler, *Karl V. 1500-1558. Eine Biographie* (Munich, 1999), p. 99.

5. Karl-Heinz Spiess, *Familie und Verwandtschaft im deutschen Hochadel des Spätmittelalters. 13. bis Anfang des 16. Jahrhunderts* (Stuttgart, 1993), pp. 99f.; Jörg Rogge, *Herrschaftsweitergabe, Konfliktregelung und Familienorganisation im fürstlichen Hochadel. Das Beispiel der Wettiner von der Mitte des 13. bis zum Beginn des 16. Jahrhunderts* (Stuttgart, 2002).

6. Spiess, *Familie und Verwandtschaft*, pp. 200–1.

7. See Hermann Johann Friedrich Schulze (Gaevernitz), *Das Recht der Erstgeburt in deutschen Fürstenhäusern und seine Bedeutung für die deutsche Staatsentwicklung* (Leipzig, 1851), pp. 120ff.

8. See [Anonymous], *Kurzer Begriff derer Gründe, welche das gleiche Erbfolge=Recht in denen Fürstlich Solms=Braunfelsischen Landen gegen ein neuerlich anmaslich aufgestelltes Erstgeburts=recht vertheidigen und behaupten. Zur geschwinden Einsicht zusammen getragen aus denen bey höchstpreißlich Kayserlichem Reichs=Hof=Rath verhandelten Acten In Sachen derer regierenden vier jüngern Herren Fürsten Gebrüdern zu Solms, entgegen Dero ältesten Herrn Bruder auch regierenden Fürsten zu Solms* (no publication information, 1775), p. 23.

9. See Konrad Krimm, "Markgraf Christoph I. und die badische Teilung. Zur Deutung der Karlsruher Votivtafel von Hans Baldung Grien," *Zeitschrift für die Geschichte des Oberrheins* 138 (1989): pp. 199–215, here p. 210.

10. See Krimm, "Markgraf Christoph I.," p. 212. Krimm argues here that the Baden policy fell under the shadow of that of the Palatinate after the battle of Seckenheim in 1462.

11. See Krimm, "Margraf Christoph I.," p. 213.

12. See Berthold Sütterlin, *Geschichte Badens* (Karlsruhe, 1965), p. 312.

13. See Krimm, "Markgraf Christoph I.," p. 213.

14. See Generallandesarchiv Karlsruhe (in what follows: GLAK), D 1165, Urkunde Maximilians I. vom 15.1.1516.

15. See Schulze (Gaevernitz), *Recht der Erstgeburt*, p. 125.

16. See Schulze (Gaevernitz), *Recht der Erstgeburt*, pp. 120, 125.

17. See Wilhelm Klank, *Die Entwicklung des Grundsatzes der Unteilbarkeit und Primogenitur im Kurfürstentum Brandenburg* (Leipzig, 1908), p. 6.

18. See Johann Jacob Moser, *Teutsches Staatsrecht*, Teil 12, 3. Buch (Leipzig, 1743); Johann Stephan Pütter, *Beyträge zum Teutschen Staats– und Fürstenrechte*. Teil 2 (Göttingen, 1779).

19. See *Kurzer Begriff derer Gründe*, passim. This deduction is about the legitimacy of the privileging of the firstborn in the princely Solms-Braunfels lands. It is argued that primogeniture is not a legal process. In previous times in the aforementioned territory, there was occasionally only a single successor who ruled. However, in these cases, it was coincidence or had to do with governments in which the brothers had consented. This could not serve as legal precedence.

20. See Volker Press, "Eberhard im Bart von Wurttemberg als Graf und Fürst des Reiches," in *Adel im alten Reich. Gesammelte Vorträge und Aufsätze*, ed. Franz Brendle et al. (Tübingen, 1998), pp. 41– 69, here p. 57. See also Cordula Nolte, "Der kranke Fürst. Vergleichende Beobachtungen zu Dynastie- und Herrschaftskrisen um 1500, ausgehend von den Landgrafen von Hessen," *Zeitschrift für historische Forschung* 37 (2000): pp. 1–36.

21. Cf. Pauline Puppel, *Die Regentin. Vormundschaftliche Herrschaft in Hessen 1500-1700* (Frankfurt, Main, 2004). About the history of Hesse, see Karl E. Demandt, *Geschichte des Landes Hessen*, rev. Nachdruck der 2. neubearb. und erw. Aufl. von 1972 (Kassel, 1980).

22. [Anonymous], *Unparteyische, in facto et jure vest=gegründete, Vertheidigung des Hochfürstlichen Hauses Hessen-Rheinfels so wohl in Betrachtung des neulich bey demselben eingeführten Erstgeburts=Rechts, Als der Fähigkeit seiner jezigen Prinzen, in Hessischen Landen zu succediren. Mit Beylagen sub Litteris A, B, C.* (1751), p. 6. The rivalries between the two principalities led finally to the so-called Hessian War (Hessenkrieg) of 1648.

23. *Unparteyische, in facto et jure*, p. 4.
24. See Reimer Stobbe, "Sophie von Brabant und Anna von Mecklenburg – zwei Frauen in Schlüsselstellungen für die Geschichte der Landgrafschaft Hessen und des hessischen Adels im Mittelalter," in *Hundert Jahre Historische Kommission für Hessen 1897-1997, Teil 1*, ed. Walter Heinemeyer (Marburg, 1997), pp. 59–87, here pp. 78ff.
25. Anna, the sister of both Wettiners Friedrich and Wilhelm, was married to Count Ludwig I (Landgraf) of Hessen. The two sons of this couple were the opposing princes Ludwig II and Heinrich III in the Brother's Feud (Bruderfehde).
26. See Herbert Koch, *Der sächsische Bruderkrieg (1445-1451)* (Erfurt, 1910); Rogge, *Herrschaftsweitergabe*, pp. 154ff.
27. I mean here the conflicts among the Habsburgs in the time of King Matthias (who died in 1619). In the fifteenth century, there was a war between Albrecht VI and his brother, Emperor Friedrich III. See Wilhelm Baum, *Die Habsburger in den Vorlanden 1386-1486. Krise und Höhepunkt der habsburgischen Machtstellung in Schwaben am Ausgang des Mittelalters* (Wien, 1993).
28. Their kinship ties to the Habsburgs were through the Wettiners: Friedrich the Gentle (1412–1464) was the brother of the Wettiner Anna (1420–1462), married to the Hessian landgrave, and Friedrich was married to Margarete (1416–1486), a sister of the Habsburg Emperor Friedrich III (1415–1493). In any case, the Hessian counts were related through the House of Baden and the Counts of Katzenelnbogen to the Habsburgs, because Ottilie von Nassau Dillenburg, married to count Philipp Junior of Katzenelnbogen, was the mother of the Countess of Baden, Ottilie (1453–1517), who through marriage with Count Christoph I was the daughter-in-law of the Habsburg Katharina, a sister of Emperor Friedrich III, because the emperor's sister Katharina was married to Karl I, the Count of Baden. A son of this couple, Christoph I, was married to Ottilie von Katzenelnbogen. Her mother had married (her second marriage) Oswald von Thierstein, the Habsburg governor in Alsace.
29. As in the case of the Wettiner brothers, Friedrich and Wilhelm, who in the middle of the fifteenth century pushed aside their brother Sigismund to the Würzburg bishop's throne and thereby satisfied his succession claims; see Rogge, *Herrschaftsweitergaben*, pp. 148–49.
30. Therefore, younger siblings in the seventeenth century often addressed their older brothers as father; see Sophie Ruppel, "Geschwisterbeziehungen im Adel und Norbert Elias' Figurationssoziologie," in *Höfische Gesellschaft und Zivilisationsprozeß. Norbert Elias' Werk in kulturwissenschaftlicher Perspektive*, ed. Claudia Opitz (Köln, 2005), pp. 207–24, here pp. 215, 219. See also Sophie Ruppel, *Zwischen Konflikt und Kooperation. Geschwisterbeziehungen im deutschen Hochadel des 17. Jahrhunderts* (Frankfurt, Main, 2007).
31. "Schwester," in *Grosses Universal-Lexicon aller Wissenschaften und Künste, welche bißhero durch menschlichen Verstand erfunden und verbessert worden* ... verlegt von Johann Heinrich Zedler in Halle und Leipzig [...], Bd. 36 (Halle, Leipzig, 1743), (Ndr. Graz, 1962), Spalte 480–483, here 480.
32. See Ebba Severidt, *Familie, Verwandtschaft und Karriere bei den Gonzaga. Struktur und Funktion von Familie und Verwandtschaft bei den Gonzaga und ihren deutschen Verwandten (1444-1519)* (Leinfelden-Echterdingen, 2002), p. 9.
33. See Krimm, "Markgraf Christoph I.," p. 213.
34. The incidence of aunts and their nieces marrying members of the same house increased considerably in the high nobility starting in the sixteenth century.
35. Spain, America, Milan, Sardinia, the Balearic Islands, and the Canary Islands were to go to Austria; the Spanish Netherlands, the Franche Comté, Navarre, and the African possessions, as well as the Philippines and the Kingdom of the Two Sicilies were to fall to France. See Klaus-Ludwig Feckl, *Preussen im Spanischen Erbfolgekrieg* (Frankfurt, Main, 1979), p. 209.
36. See Feckl, *Preussen*, p. 27.

Chapter VI

Political Power, Inheritance, and Kinship Relations

The Unique Features of Southern France (Sixteenth-Eighteenth Centuries)

Bernard Derouet

The close connection between political structure and forms of kinship is obvious in early modern European societies. Yet, this relationship is more complex than one would tend to think at first, and it is not merely a matter of dynasticism or mutual support among kin to monopolize important official positions. The particular context of southern France between the sixteenth and eighteenth centuries offers an interesting illustration of this complexity, and we cannot understand the relationships between kinship and the political system if we do not take practices of property devolution into consideration. The issue of succession is central: the inheritance not just of public offices, but of private patrimony within families, is at stake. This chapter seeks to show how the progressive development of a system of primogeniture among local elites in southern France closely accompanied specific forms of access to power appropriate to a society of hierarchy and status. How kinship and politics were related was less determined by "horizontal" networks and interest groups than by client-structured distributions of power.

The populations examined for this study are those of southern France—Aquitaine, Gascony, Languedoc, the Rhône valley, and Provence, with the exception of the mountainous zones.[1] Within these regions, our attention will focus upon the rural world and local political practices, on elites of the village or the *bourg* (a small town having strong ties to the surrounding countryside.) Our interest in these regions lies in their profound originality compared with the rest of the kingdom—especially the northern half of France—regarding both local political systems and inheritance practices. On these two points especially, the southern regions underwent significant developments between the sixteenth and eighteenth centuries. We will show how the two issues are connected and articulated with each other and how they affected kinship relations.

A Turning Point in Practices of Succession

More than any other region, the south of France poses problems in terms of inheritance and succession. Certainly such practices varied widely there until the eighteenth century, but they seem to have undergone important developments particularly over the course of the three or four centuries preceding the Revolution. These assertions rely upon the most recent research, though the question is still not definitively clarified and enough uncertainty remains to require further research. On this subject, we will be confined to a few comments and a rapid sketch.

There is a longstanding and still widely held notion that the southern half of the country was everywhere the stage for a familial system privileging a single heir from time immemorial. This consensus originated in nineteenth-century debates about the *Code civil*, and more recently it has fed upon a somewhat questionable interpretation of works on the history of law.[2] Paradoxically, it has also been reinforced by regional monographs from historians and anthropologists who, beginning in the 1980s, analyzed various southern societies and their practices of succession in considerable depth. Although these scholars readily chose regions of primogeniture and stem-family, they did not claim that their descriptive analyses could be transposable to the entirety of southern France.[3]

In reality, it is mostly the mountainous regions of southern France that practiced primogeniture early and very widely, beginning, in some cases, before the sixteenth century.[4] But they represent only a portion of southern France in terms of geographical area and especially of population. From the point of view of succession, the situation was much less drastic and less consistent in the regions of Aquitaine, Gascony, Languedoc, the Rhône valley, and Provence, a rather significant area, which is the subject of the present study. In these regions, substantial sections have been identified where egalitarian inheritance was practiced in the early modern period. This involved either complete equality among all the children or, more often, equality among all the male children (since daughters had dowries and were excluded from actual inheritance).[5]

Of course, we do not find a rigid equality here comparable to that imposed by customary law in some provinces north of the Loire River (especially in the west). Generally, the southern regions followed Roman law and used wills, which would grant sufficient liberty to the head of the family to plan his succession. Where inheritances were not settled by a will, equality was applied to all the children, daughters as well as sons. Moreover, even in cases where a will had been drawn up, its intent was not always to give an advantage to one child at the expense of the others. The will could have designated multiple children or even all of the brothers and sisters as collective heirs (*héritier universel*). And if one of the children was occasionally given preferential treatment over the others, notably in the allocation of the family home, this served often as compensation for the fact that the child had remained with the parents until their deaths, caring for them in their old age. In other words, it is impossible to reduce the diversity of such situations to one single formula. But the overall picture certainly emphasizes frequent moderation in the allocation of benefits, with considerable flexibility to achieve some final equity in the estate, without a systematic attempt to conserve the patrimony intact in the hands of one single descendent.

Above all, we must distance ourselves from the stereotype of these behaviors as frozen over time, for there is increasing evidence that such practices evolved between the sixteenth and eighteenth centuries. This change was gradual and varied according to the different rhythms of each province, but its direction is clear: it consisted of an expansion of the benefits granted to one child at the expense of the others, generally a son, most often the eldest, to make him the true heir-successor of his family.[6]

Another aspect of this transformation deserves our attention: its intensity seems to have varied according to social category. For one thing, the shift was clearest among landowners, both large and small. But overall and at least at first, conversion to the new familial system was the most complete and the most systematic among the upper or middle social strata of villages and small towns. These groups included medium- or large-scale *ménagers* (landowning farmers who lived entirely off of their property), rentiers, bourgeois, people of independent means, minor officials, merchants, members of the liberal professions, and so forth. It must be said, of course, that we do not yet have enough local monographs addressing the issue available to present this assertion as entirely proven, but most of the evidence currently points in this direction.[7] It is precisely these social categories which are the most directly involved in the exercise of local power and the most dramatically subject to the functioning of political institutions.

Significance and Stakes of Local Power

At the same time as the southern regions underwent this gradual change in forms of social reproduction, they also experienced a marked development in political organization at the local level.[8] To be sure, in these regions, the strength of the commune was long-standing, often supported by charters and, sometimes already in the twelfth or thirteenth centuries, the communes developed as "free cities" (*villes de franchise*). In any event, communes were recognized as legal entities and had representative political institutions such as consulships.[9]

Yet, not everything depended upon the Middle Ages.[10] During the early modern period, we witness a strengthening of the powers and privileges of the commune of inhabitants who, faced with the seigneur—and often, upon the occasion of conflicts with him, resolved through settlements that were to their advantage—acquired real written statutes, won a more complete freedom of assembly, and increased their autonomy over the management of their affairs and their internal organization. Many rights traditionally falling under the seigneur's jurisdiction, and tied to his *pouvoir de ban* or to his *dominium* over noncultivated lands, were bought out or taken over by the commune in return for an annual financial indemnity. However, it is important to be clear that this gradual weakening of the power of the *seigneurie* did not result in the promotion of an individualist society, free of all constraint, but consisted more in the commune's recovery of the powers of collective management, whose exercise it assumed in its own name.

As a result, the southern commune of inhabitants, enjoying true autonomy, represented an essential structure of social organization, one of those corporations characteristic of society under the Old Regime. This stands in marked contrast with what happened in northern France, where only true cities commanded such status—not villages or small rural towns. In southern France, the commune managed both itself and, through its own institutions, a number of tasks which were at once both public services and monopolies (such as the mill, the butcher, and many other services which, elsewhere, would come under the jurisdiction of either the seigneur or private initiative).[11] Furthermore, in southern France, where the communal estates could be relatively substantial (moors, scrublands, woods, fallows, and pastures), the commune held a landed patrimony that gave it an additional foundation and an important role in the management of local economic life.[12]

Public life was therefore characterized here by the broad range of local political responsibilities and by self-government. In this respect, we must underscore the important role held by the assembly of inhabitants, which was convened regularly and often elected its representatives, called, depending upon the province, jurats or consuls. Even if these officials were subject to control and supervision, their power was real and they played a prominent political role—a situation very different from that of the *syndics* who represented the villages of northern France. There, faced with the seigneur and the monarchical state, the territorial commune often remained rather weak, and public responsibilities (restricted largely to the collection of royal taxes and the administration of religious buildings) were rarely sought after if not entirely avoided.[13]

By contrast, the south of France experienced an intense political life at the local level. Minor offices connected with collective life were numerous, and the positions of communal management were especially prestigious and vigorously sought. Although they conferred real power, they were perhaps most coveted for their prestige, celebrity, and social recognition. These were expressed through a complex symbolic system, the most famous aspect of which was the wearing of the *chaperon* (hood), an honorary clothing sign reserved for the holders of these offices and linked to their power of justice.[14]

The Link between Politics and Patrimony

The increasingly powerful stakes tied to local political life, for which the sixteenth to eighteenth centuries constitute an essential turning point, offer an interesting framework through which to understand the simultaneous developments in family and succession practices. However, we must first be careful to avoid heading down the wrong track. One could assume, a priori, that this shift toward a single inheritor-successor system followed from the necessities inherent in the very nature of these political offices, along the lines of what happened regarding venal "offices" created by the Old Regime monarchy (offices of justice and finance). Although they served a public function, such offices were patrimonial, with succession indivisible among the heirs of a family. Sometimes they prompted a transfer from father to son (often the eldest, but not always), thus serving as pretext and framework for the formation of "patrimonial lines" focused on the retention of an office transferred to a single successor from generation to generation, a little like the phenomenon of noble titles.[15]

Such an interpretation is not relevant for the villages and small towns of the South. It is true that from the end of the seventeenth through the eighteenth centuries, the monarchy tried to create and sell mayors' offices in charge of community management. But this innovation had only limited success, and even when it was practiced, many communities succeeded in circumventing this compulsory system by purchasing the office of mayor themselves and combining its function with that of jurat or consul.

As for these latter positions, they were not venal and therefore did not give rise to a sort of "patrimonialization." The consuls were elected by the assembly of inhabitants, and their terms of office were short, generally lasting one year.[16] At each new assembly, the political personnel had to be changed, at least in part. The principle preventing immediate reelection of departing consuls remained generally well respected,[17] even though it was possible for some to have these offices reconferred upon them later in life. In short, an official did not himself designate his successor—whether it be his son, a relative, or another person—and the system prevented any appropriation and therefore any transfer of a particular political position within a familial line, even informally.

Therefore, we must proceed in another direction in order to understand the link between these political practices and the increasing shift in familial strategies toward a system of primogeniture. In fact, two particular features of this southern rural society must be introduced here: its very strongly hierarchical character (in both deed and image) and the function which patrimony serves—specifically landed patrimony—as a source of prestige and power at the local level and as a means of access to political administration.

Firstly, the place of the hierarchical principle. In spite of the very self-managed character of the local community in the south, and in spite of the existence of a representative political system (involving the election of leaders, at least in some regions), we must not rely upon appearances, which would lead us to believe we were in the presence of a true village democracy. Important decisions were rarely made in plenary assembly and, in fact, actual power belonged to the consuls and to the limited group which was appointed with them. This council met often and, along with the consuls, constituted a quasi-permanent authority over the management of affairs.

Moreover, even though the role of the plenary assembly remained important in choosing officials, the method of election or appointment was actually fundamentally *censitaire* (based on the poll tax). To that effect, the inhabitants were divided into different categories or classes. With the exception of very small villages composed almost entirely of peasants, the majority of communities in Languedoc and Provence utilized this system and differentiated among different groups of citizens by classifying them hierarchically in the electoral process. Although local variants were numerous, the classes into which local residents were organized generally depended upon occupation or visible social status (person of private means, landowner working his own property, merchant, artisan, *travailleur de terre*, i.e., day laborer, etc.). They also relied for the most part upon income and wealth, measured by the amount of taxes paid.

The membership of each person in a class simultaneously determined the electoral college within which he voted and the type of position for which he could seek election. For example, in the towns of Provence with three consuls, the first class citizens elected the first consul and they alone were eligible for this position; the same held true for the second class of citizens vis à vis the second consul, and so forth. In a way, such a system guaranteed each social stratum that it would be represented within the administration of the community. However, in practice, the consuls' influence depended upon their class, and the first consul remained the principal figure.

Naturally, this system was socially unequal—it privileged the rich at the expense of the poor. But beyond this obvious statement, it was not always perceived from within as an arbitrary seizure of power, for this system corresponded to a specific conception of political rights. The richest, because of their income or their capital, were those inhabitants who paid the highest taxes (both to the king and for the needs of the community), and therein lies the idea that they had more rights in the administration of collective interests, since they were more directly invested. These notables, referred to in many contemporary texts as "the most visible" (*les plus apparents*) of the community (a rough equivalent of the medieval concept of *sanior pars*), but also as "the most invested," had more legitimacy in handling public affairs. According to this line of reasoning, they better represented the community and felt justified in speaking and acting in the name of all.

We must add that it was not so much wealth in and of itself which legitimized power, nor the nature of one's profession, but above all, the social position conferred by the ownership of land (and its expanse, its value, or its estimated income). Here it is land which, fundamentally, was the basis of the social hierarchy and of all notability—it is land which indicated status and allowed people to be classified in comparison with one another.

In this respect, it is also highly significant that most of these southern provinces had a fiscal system different from the rest of the kingdom. This difference had to do with areas of so-called "real taxation" (and not "personal"); each individual paid a tax, not according to an assessment of all his forms of income, but in proportion to the amount of real estate which he owned. In the same manner, in cases where the community was able to tax its members in order to meet its own expenses, each was asked to contribute according to the size and value of his estate. To that end, at the end of the Middle Ages or the beginning of the early modern era, the southern communities had introduced detailed *compoix*, land registries, which were regularly kept up to date and according to which taxes were levied. This system must be seen as much more than a mere fiscal novelty lacking further significance, for in fact, it bears witness to a very specific conception of the social order. It was the land and not the man who paid the tax, and, as a logical consequence, it was the land which determined for each person his rights and also his duties.[18] In fine, it was also the land that determined access to political functions and the honors with which they were associated.

A Society of Ranks

The fiscal system does not explain everything, but it is a good indicator of the true values of a society. For the southern half of France, the close geographical alignment between regions of real taxation and regions of substantial and strongly structured territorial communities has been well demonstrated. A perfect counterexample is the Bordeaux region in the Midi, which fell under the category of personal taxation.[19]

We are now better prepared to understand the progressive change in succession practices of these village elites because the transformation seems intimately linked with the existence of a society of ranks. Its hierarchical character was still further exacerbated in the early modern era by strengthened local political institutions, and by an increase in the property tax-based aspect of political representation.[20]

The specificity of southern France lies in the fact that, even among the common classes of the population, there existed an extreme sensitivity to this notion of rank—to the desire to behave according to it, keep it, and to show it off. Naturally, this is an aspiration that concerned the middle and upper fringes of society especially. For these groups, above all, the preoccupation was with not losing social status, not falling back down the social ladder. The shift in succession practices toward a single heir seems to have been a response to such aspirations. The partition of an inheritance, even if practiced only among the male children, could in fact have had disastrous consequences from this point of view. This is particularly true in a world of landowning farmers and landlords, where it is not always possible to accrue enough property to set up several children simultaneously in a class equivalent to that of their father. The most important consideration was to leave intact the part of the patrimony composed of real estate. This was the very basis for notability, prestige, and social status, even for those with other sources of income, figures such as merchants, traders, members of the liberal professions like lawyers, or holders of small offices.[21]

Those who held positions of power were certainly not lacking in opportunities for involvement in the economic dealings of towns or villages. Consuls managed the collective patrimony and were in charge of the budget, they decided upon ways to use the communal lands, and they presided over the auctioning off of farms, by which income was produced from the property and monopolies of the community. With few exceptions, however, it seems that they rarely used their power directly with an eye toward personal gain. The benefit of their institutional position really lay more in the opportunity that it provided to create or maintain a network of clients. Indeed, favors bestowed to one group or another could in turn lead to benefits of an economic nature, but only eventually, deferred over time, and in an indirect manner. In fact, we must see things from the other way around: wealth seems to have been less the objective sought through political power than the necessary precondition to *attain* this power, whose stakes are situated on a much larger scale. At a certain moment, it appeared that only a change in behaviors of succession was likely to protect this possibility.

It is also revealing that the practices of primogeniture and the preservation of patrimonial integrity would be developed more among local elites and peasants of a certain affluence (at least at first)—that is to say, among the minority of the population for whom, after all, such conduct was least imposed by financial necessity. One can suppose, certainly, that this more restrictive attitude was linked to demographic growth and to the increasing scarcity of uncultivated or affordable lands to exploit. This made it more difficult to set up several descendants at the same level as their parents, unlike what had taken place in the fifteenth and even the sixteenth centuries, when such possibilities remained open. For all that, the very identity of families who first reacted to this closure of the lands suggests that the new behaviors were dictated less by reasons of survival than by motivations of a symbolic and political order, including the desire to protect and maintain a certain social status.[22]

In the same way, one could observe that in the eighteenth century, among the elites of villages and small towns, the matrimonial strategies accompanying the practice of a single successor did not always aim to preserve the patrimony in its current state, but rather to strengthen it and thus to achieve upward social mobility. This is demonstrated by the development in this era of marriages between two heirs, which resulted in the merging of two inheritances.[23] Even so, such forms of alliance were rare in peasant societies traditionally practicing primogeniture, as in the Pyrenees: one avoided them because they had the effect of making a "house" disappear, and instead, one systematically married an heir to a non-heir of another family (eldest-youngest marriage type). And when it was not possible to avoid such marriages between two heirs, the consequences were most often overturned in the next generation through the designation of two heirs in the family, each regaining one of the patrimonies that had been temporarily merged. While marriages of this type were rare in the peasant populations with pronounced primogeniture practices, they have relatively frequently been observed among the nobility, a social group whose familial practices over time have come to resemble those of *sociétés à maisons*. Without being entirely systematic, these unions between the heirs of two families were widely employed as tools in a deliberate strategy of extension of sovereignty and territorial conquest, whether among small seigneurs or at the level of monarchies themselves.[24] Thus, some forms of motivation which are at least similar in spirit—patrimonial augmentation and social mobility—seem to have also prevailed among the small rural notables of southern France.

Regarding this shift in succession and matrimonial behaviors, can we ultimately speak of a drift toward "noble" ideals and values? Actually, there are quite a number of facets to consider, and some elaboration is necessary to avoid any confusion. It would be inaccurate to see here the conscious, deliberate imitation of a model—in any event, certainly not an imitation of that part of aristocratic values which revolves around the idea of blood, of "race" (in the old sense), or of personal quality inherited from distant and illustrious ancestors. Besides, in these regions of southern France, where it was the land which made the man more than the reverse, it was not so much the noble who would be attractive as the seigneur, and above all the seigneury. It has often been observed that in these regions, a noble without land-based power was not much of a noble, even if he could invoke prestigious ancestors.

We are therefore led to suggest that even though there were some aspects of noble behavior among these rural bourgeois and notables of the Midi (sense of honor, hierarchy and rank, attraction to the exterior expression of social power), it was partly spontaneous or, in any event, it meant the sharing of certain values between the common elites and the landed aristocracy. Compared with northern France, the boundaries and distinctions between the noble and the common elites were certainly substantially reduced here—and in the nineteenth century, these two social groups would fuse in a more successful manner than elsewhere into what some have called a *société notabiliaire*, with a subtle mixture of the social values of both the nobility and the bourgeoisie. The southern ideal of *vivre bourgeoisement*, with all its implications of the valorization of a lifestyle of ease, concern for rank and status, and the deliberate display of social power that does not originate directly from economic power, is itself not so distant from *vivre noblement*. The two behaviors are rather comparable, though one cannot be presented simply as an imitation of the other.

Land played a fundamental role here as a source of notability and as a natural and privileged form of access to local power, but we must also understand that landed property was valorized not so much economically but as a marker of prestige, of social status, and also of rootedness, *enracinement*. This last notion is important and represents an entire facet of social recognition which led to political power.

At the foundation of this value system lay the idea that land was also territory and that it represented "more than just land", given its symbolic role and the rights that it entailed in the administration of public affairs. Far from a mental universe where land would be sought above all as a means of production, here there was a confusion, or a partial overlay, between the ideas of property and sovereignty. In this southern political system where, at its most extreme, the local community constituted less a community of inhabitants than an association of coproprietors, there was some sort of proportionality between the land one held and citizenship. Often a synonym for stability and seniority within the community, the landed estate was an essential criterion of this territorial membership or identity, granting the most important political rights and opening the door to the highest of political offices.

The Political Role of Kinship

Beyond the close ties existing between this original political system and the means of social reproduction of families, we now turn to consider what effects these connections could have had on kinship relations. In such a context, what were the social uses of kinship, and to what extent did they give rise to specific strategies regarding accession to power and its preservation? The answer is multifaceted, for although kinship did in fact play a role here, the manner in which it did was not necessarily what we would expect in other contexts.

On one hand, local political institutions themselves imposed restrictions upon the influence that relatives could have in supporting accession to office. Not only did nomination to positions of power often come from elections, but also, the terms of office were very short, without the possibility of immediate reelection. Further, many statutes in southern communities explicitly prevented the holding of a plurality of offices within a single set of relatives. For example, two brothers or even two cousins or second cousins could not sit simultaneously on the communal council, nor could one be consul while the second occupied another position of responsibility. These measures, which sought to maintain a certain balance among families, prevented the potential development of a monopoly of one extended family over the exercise of local power.[25]

To be sure, such stipulations merely impeded rather than completely eliminated the play of kinship relations. In some villages, which have been observed over time, certain extended families were more active than others in public service. After all, in order to be effectively exercised, these positions required a certain degree of education, contacts beyond the village itself, and considerable financial influence (especially to lend money to the commune).[26] So the number of people capable of satisfying these requirements was, by definition, relatively limited. Within that restricted group existed kin-ties, especially those resulting from marital unions formed within this local elite.

Nevertheless, compared with what was possible in other societies, it would be incorrect to suppose that kinship served as a medium here for the support of powerful networks with numerous branches, facilitating the multiplication of strong points of influence and the holding of strategic posts, or enveloping an entire regional area at the level of elites. Such a model, which privileges the quantitative aspect of kinship and where the multiplicity of relatives controlling important positions would allow collective monopolization of the exercise of political responsibilities and power, is not really pertinent here.

It is even less appropriate here, since collateral kinship is limited by the very consequences of the new system of succession. By more and more frequently concentrating most of an inheritance in the name of a single successor, these families condemned an increasing proportion of their younger offspring to a state of celibacy, a phenomenon which developed dramatically in the eighteenth century among these rural elites. Inevitably, this system had the ultimate result of reducing the density of coordinated networks of cousin and other family allies. The restrictive character of such a system, first indicated by marriages between heirs who thus merged their patrimonies, became ever more pronounced toward the end of the Old Regime and into the nineteenth century. Due to the early and widespread adoption of birth control, which sometimes resulted in a single child, a certain number of notable lines died out in this period for lack of descendents. Also, from the point of view of representation, those familial practices which favored the preservation and continuity of the patrimonial line were hardly compatible with an emphasis on the horizontal extension of the family.

Must one therefore conclude that kinship relations played only a minor role in the political practices of these small southern towns? To understand how kinship did indeed operate, we have to get at the effectiveness of familial relationships from a different angle. It is possible to show that a certain form of clientelism (very frequent in these small communities) relied upon the use of kinship relations by being entirely and closely tied to the familial mode of reproduction that we have described. On this point, we may return to some of the arguments proposed by Elie Pélaquier in his study of an early modern Languedoc community, Saint-Victor-de-la-Coste.[27] The development of the practices of primogeniture in the seventeenth and eighteenth centuries resulted in more and more frequent situations of either celibacy or social decline for the younger sons and daughters of a family. For here, as in many other societies practicing primogeniture, an heir married a spouse of his rank or higher; a non-heir, however, when able to marry, had to ally with a family ranked below his own (hypogamy). Some girls who received only a dowry were forced to accept marriage with an heir from a more modest family in order to establish themselves. Likewise a non-inheriting son, when he succeeded in avoiding celibacy, combined his dowry or his *légitime* with the dowry a non-inheriting daughter brought to him, which then afforded the establishment of a new familial entity whose financial means and status were certainly inferior to those of their origin.

Social decline or descent, caused by the differentiation among brothers and sisters through inheritance, could be repeated over many generations. After a certain period of time, then, multiple descendents from the same ancestor were to be found in widely varied positions in terms of economic and social status—the extended family thus being represented at every level of the social body of the community.

Elie Pélaquier demonstrates how this social dispersion of relatives at different levels could ultimately create cohesion in social relations, insofar as the ties born of marital alliances partially masked or softened the antagonisms which these very inegalitarian and hierarchical societies would otherwise entail. We can also venture the hypothesis that politically speaking, such forms of solidarity which transcend divisions of rank, occupation, and wealth constituted a milieu favorable to the phenomena of factions and "clans," which typically structured the political debate and often polarized local conflicts. In the small rural communities of the Midi, these factions, consolidated by a complex mixture of kinship ties and patronage-type subordination, were recruited from top to bottom of the social ladder, without associating people together by occupational or wealth strata.[28]

The relationship between kinship and political practices provided the basis for the uniqueness of southern villages and small towns in the early modern era. Unlike elsewhere, where kinship was instrumentalized to attain, preserve, or monopolize power within the elite, kinship in the Midi allowed the emergence of interdependencies that could be described more as "vertical" than "horizontal." These relationships served as the basis for the development of a very specific, largely clientele, form of political life.[29]

In terms of kinship, however, nothing is ever simple and unilateral. How best to describe the system which seems to have fallen into place in the middle of the early modern era, somewhere around 1600-1650? First of all by the practices it replaced: so long as several children, or in fact several brothers, could be coheirs, it was a good strategy to try and expand the number of kindred branches represented within the local elite. Several local examples show that the most influential extended families of a town or village were those who knew how to increase in number in this manner, succeeding best in establishing these different collateral branches *at the local level*. The very number of relatives, the mutual support that they facilitated, and the stability and the rootedness which they represent were all factors favorable to a certain continuity of power. At that time, it was not impossible to see two brothers serve as consuls one after the other.

The transition to primogeniture and to the "patrimonial line," as we have seen, radically altered the role of kinship in local political practice, favoring instead vertical types of interdependence. All the same, must we limit ourselves to this statement, in such an abrupt formulation? In fact, if the uppermost stratum of society with real access to power had become basically a collection of "elder branches" from different families, they were no less closely knit by relationships which fall under the heading of kinship, but where alliance played an essential role this time. The notables of the community had woven themselves together through ties of marriage in a very substantial way. This is no big surprise: even if, as we have seen, the practices of primogeniture were inevitably accompanied by phenomena of social decline and hypogamic marriages for the non-heirs, for their part, the heirs married at their own social level (homogamy), with endowed daughters belonging to the same social stratum. Therefore, family alliances also resulted from these unions between social equals, even if in the first generation the relationship was simply seen as one between in-laws. In the next generations, relationships were built around the female line.

On the basis of these statements, then, can we not formulate a more complex and nuanced hypothesis concerning the practices of kinship, the political system, and this society of ranks with which primogeniture is perfectly aligned? For the moment, it remains purely a hypothesis which requires eventual confirmation through appropriate research on the ground. But we may justifiably wonder whether we are not in the presence of a *double* orientation of the system of kinship. We know that, on one hand, what really counted in this southern society, as in others close to the Mediterranean world, was kinship along the *masculine* line—which had as its starting point the bond between brothers, and then subsequently among their respective descendnts (especially carriers of the same patronymic). This agnatic type of link, no longer involving families of the same status and social level, remained no less operative, but in the form of patronage interdependencies which we have drawn attention to here.

Yet at the same time, between the eldest branches constituting elite familial groups of the same social level and often united through marriage, it is possible that a certain cohesiveness was provided by the awareness of being bound by a kind of alliance focused more upon *affinity* and kinship along *female* lines. These were certainly less crucial than agnatic lines, yet they are never unimportant even in the most extreme patrilinear societies. Ultimately, there were two axes of kinship coupled with two different ways of perceiving their workings. The existence of this double system of interdependencies allows us to understand why the shift toward more vertical clientele relationships, in spite of its tenacity, did not entail permanent violent confrontations of familial clans within local society. Without question, this facilitated the maintenance of a certain equilibrium among the principal families of notables, guaranteed regular alternation of access to political offices, and in the long term, allowed a certain form of "power sharing" among different members of the local elite.

(Translation: Kelly J. Maynard)

Notes

1. Although they are located in the southern half of France, of course, mountainous regions such as the Pyrenees, the Massif Central, and the Alps constitute a rather unusual case from the point of view of succession practices and local communal forms; hence, they should be treated separately.
2. The polemics of the nineteenth century should be put in the context of the writings of Le Play and his followers concerning the effects of egalitarian legislation stemming from the Revolution and the *Code civil*, as well as debates surrounding testamentary rights. Regarding the history of law, see Jean Yver, *Essai de géographie coutumière* (Paris, 1966). This remarkable study, centered upon juridical norms, has been read too often as if it described social practices. The southern half of France, though certainly strongly influenced by "written" (Roman) law, was often characterized without nuance as being a center of maximum inequality of succession. Here I take the liberty of citing my own previous work on this issue: Bernard Derouet, "Les pratiques familiales, le droit et la construction des différences," *Annales HSS* 52 (1997): pp. 369–91.
3. Notably Alain Collomp, *La maison du père. Famille et village en Haute-Provence aux XVIIe et XVIIIe siècles* (Paris, 1983); Elisabeth Claverie and Pierre Lamaison, *L'impossible mariage. Violence et parenté en Gévaudan, XVIIe, XVIIIe et XIXe siècles* (Paris, 1982); Isaac Chiva and Joseph Goy, eds., *Les Baronnies des Pyrénées* (Paris, 1981, 1986).
4. The clearest case, from the point of view of both intensity and duration of primogeniture practices, is that of the Pyrenees. The Massif Central is somewhat similar, although with variations by region. For the Alps, the assertion is only partially borne out, for single child succession became established with great difficulty in the face of strong agnatic tendencies (favoring all the brothers).
5. One example, among many others, from the Narbonne region of lower Languedoc, is Paul Cayla, *Essai sur la vie des populations rurales à Ginestas et dans ses environs au début du XVIe siècle, 1519-1536* (Carcassonne, 1938). For Gascony, see Gregory Hanlon, *L'univers des gens de bien* (Talence, 1989), especially p. 97; and Gregory Hanlon and Elspeth Carruthers, "Wills, Inheritance and the Moral Order in the 17th-century Agenais," *Journal of Family History* 15 (1990): pp. 149–61, especially pp. 151–55.

6. In the area of Lectoure (Gascony), this progressive shift from equality to an increasingly pronounced practice of primogeniture beginning in the seventeenth century has been demonstrated by Pierre Féral, "Le droit successoral égalitaire et ses conséquences agraires dans le Lectourois," *Bulletin de la Société d'histoire et d'archéologie du Gers* (1949): pp. 37–47; for Languedoc, see Christian Chêne, "Testament, fortunes et religions. La pratique testamentaire à Ganges de la fin du XVIe siècle au début du XVIIIe siècle," in *Confluence des droits savants et des pratiques juridiques* (Milano, 1979), pp. 181–220, especially p. 198. Overall, see Elie Pélaquier, *De la maison du père à la maison commune. Saint-Victor-de-la-Coste, en Languedoc rhodanien, 1661-1799* (Montpellier, 1996).

   For the region of Provence, it seems that one may broaden the observations of Collomp (*La maison du père*): the existence of "lineage hamlets" (*hameaux lignagers*) suggests the presence of frequent divisions among brothers, before some stronger tendencies toward unity of succession subsequently appeared. I have always preferred this hypothesis, which is also supported by Dionigi Albera, notably in "Familles, destins, destinations. Entre mosaïque et portrait-robot," *Le monde alpin et rhodanien* (1994): pp. 7–26.

7. See Féral, *Droit successoral*, especially p. 43. At Saint-Victor-de-la-Coste, Elie Pélaquier argues that on the eve of the Revolution, the practice of choosing one privileged heir had become fairly widespread; however, some evidence suggests that it had first become apparent among local elites and the *ménagers*. For these groups, patrimony remained stable or even grew in the eighteenth century, even though small parcels of property turned out to be undergoing a process of fragmentation as a result of population growth. Moreover, it is among the bourgeois and *ménagers* that the tradition of the dowry paid partly in kind and especially in land disappeared the earliest. See also Jacques Frayssenge, Sylvie Groueff, and Elie Pélaquier, "Parenté, patrimoine et émigration dans les communautés rurales du Larzac héraultais," in *Pays et familles du Caylar (Hérault)* (Nîmes, 1996). For the social distribution of *fidei commissary* substitutions (which allowed for the transfer of patrimony without division), see Jean-Marie Augustin, *Les substitutions fidéicommissaires à Toulouse et en Haut-Languedoc au XVIIIe siècle* (Paris, 1980). In rural zones, this method of patrimonial preservation was widely practiced among two social groups in particular: relatively well-off landowning peasants and the bourgeois of small towns (the latter sometimes practicing the system even more than the bourgeois in cities). See p. 240.

8. Here, too, we will leave aside the rather particular case of the mountain zones, which differ due to specific constraints related to the management of space (a very powerful presence of communal property with a strongly structured territorial commune organization developed early within the framework of the village or valley).

9. To avoid any ambiguity, in this text, the word "commune" will be most often used, though in France, during the period between the thirteenth century and the Revolution, this entity was mainly referred to as *communauté* or *communauté d'habitants*.

10. Monique Bourin-Derrau, *Villages médiévaux en Bas-Languedoc: genèse d'une sociabilité méridionale, Xe-XIVe siècles* (Paris, 1987). The author clearly shows that in the region of Béziers, the village and the commune as we understand them in the modern era are a "medieval creation." This evaluation, though no doubt applicable to other southern regions as well, must not disguise the reality of subsequent changes to the system, whether regarding the weakening of the weight of the *seigneurie*, the rise of oligarchies and poll tax–based systems, or the increased role of local political authorities (which become more permanent and draw their authority less frequently from limited mandates for particular occasions).

11. It is in the southeast that this aspect was the most spectacular: see, for example, Raymond Collier, "Essai sur le 'socialisme' communal en Haute-Provence," in *Actes du 90e congrès national des sociétés savantes* (Paris, 1966), pp. 303–33.

12. Due to the necessity of presenting in a synthetic manner certain features which most of the southern communities shared, we are forced to leave aside here the infinite diversity of concrete local situations. On these, see, for example, Maurice Bordes, *L'administration provinciale et municipale en France au XVIIIe siècle* (Paris, 1972), pp. 184–91.

13. Obviously, this is a generalized assessment, which would need to be qualified according to certain local particularities. For example, in the east (Franche-Comté, Alsace, Lorraine, Burgundy, etc.), and overall in the regions most recently brought into the kingdom, provincial representation and local autonomy were somewhat better preserved than, for example, in the whole of the regions of the Paris Basin.

14. The bibliography on the communities of inhabitants of southern France is considerable. To gain a working familiarity, refer to the great provincial syntheses (which must be consulted in any case), such as Maurice Bordes, *Institutions et vie communales dans les campagnes méridionales aux XVIIe-XVIIIe siècles* (Auch, 1977); Michel Derlange, *Les Communautés d'habitants en Provence: au dernier siècle de l'Ancien Régime* (Toulouse, 1987); Georges Fournier, *Démocratie et vie municipale en Languedoc: du milieu du XVIIIe au début du XIXe siècle* (Toulouse, 1994); Anne Zink, *Clochers et troupeaux. Les communautés rurales des Landes et du Sud-Ouest avant la Révolution* (Talence, 1997); Jean-Pierre Gutton, *La sociabilité villageoise dans l'ancienne France* (Paris, 1979); and René Pillorget, *Les mouvements insurrectionnels de Provence entre 1596 et 1715* (Paris, 1975).

15. In fact, even in the world of venal offices, this assertion could prompt controversy, and the reality was apparently rather more complex. The outline sketched here seems to be confirmed among the elites of certain provincial cities, for example, at Montauban: see Margaret Darrow, *Revolution in the House: Family, Class, and Inheritance in Southern France* (Princeton, 1989). Conversely, a study of the circles of Parisian parliamentarians suggests the existence of more subtle strategies, allowing the transfer of the office along female lines, for example, while some sons purchased another position on the "market" of offices. On this function of the office in the social reproduction of the nobility of the robe, see the excellent analysis by Robert Descimon, "Conflits familiaux dans la robe parisienne aux XVIe et XVIIe siècles: les paradoxes de la transmission du statut," *Cahiers d'histoire* 45 (2000): pp. 677–97.

16. For reasons of space, we are deliberately simplifying here the method of appointing the consuls, which actually varied considerably from one village to the next and according to province. It could happen that the seigneur chose them, but from a list that was submitted to him beforehand. In Languedoc, the appointment of consuls and of the council members often took place through a complex system of co-optation in which the consuls about to leave office would intervene at first, then the seigneur, but even this was done in front of the communal assembly, whose role, though informal, was hardly negligible. It is in Provence that direct election took on the greatest role, though this is not to say that the representative principle and the role of the assembly of inhabitants was unimportant elsewhere.

17. There are exceptions, of course, especially in the communities that did not have sufficient elite inhabitants available for these regular changes in political leadership.

18. We note in passing that this system involved the nobles as well. Contrary to what took place in the northern half of France (regions of personal taxation), in the

south, nobles did not have the privilege of exemption from taxes according to their capacity as noble *person*. It is the *lands* themselves that were "noble" or "common" in character, and a seigneur could enjoy a fiscal exemption only if he held lands of noble character. Conversely, a bourgeois who managed to buy a seigneury could enjoy the exemption for the noble lands that were directly tied to it.

19. Zink, *Clochers et troupeaux*.

20. This strengthening of the oligarchic character of local power, visible in most of the southern regions in a sometimes informal manner, took a very institutional form in Provence through the communal statutes put into place in the sixteenth and seventeenth centuries. This meant a real historical evolution, as Michel Derlange shows in "En Provence au XVIIIe siècle: la représentation des habitants aux conseils généraux des communautés," *Annales du Midi* 86 (1974): pp. 45–67.

21. Many historians, like Michel Derlange for Provence (*Les communautés d'habitants*), have pointed out the ambiguous position of shopkeepers and even of large-scale merchants in southern communities. Except in the case of the cities which turned decisively toward industrial activity (like Marseille), these groups, despite their wealth, often had difficulty being accepted within the first class of citizens. Many only succeeded in entering the elite and performing important political functions by converting a significant portion of their wealth into land, which then conferred the notability necessary for the shouldering of responsibility or taking on leadership roles at the center of the territorial collective. The political system is truly based upon the poll tax, but it is not wealth as such which functions as the principle of social classification, but rather the place occupied in the property-owning hierarchy of the region. See also Michel Derlange, "De la répartition fiscale de la capitation à la définition d'un corps social: l'exemple provençal," *Annales du Midi* 92 (1980): pp. 281–300, especially pp. 298–99.

22. However, let us be clear that such an interpretation concerning the development of primogeniture practices in these regions can only be proposed for the period of the Old Regime. The nineteenth century would experience *another* important advance in these practices, but concerning the small- and medium-sized landowning peasantry above all, and this time for largely economic reasons. On this other phenomenon and its context, see Pierre Deffontaines, *Les hommes et leurs travaux dans les pays de la Moyenne Garonne (Agenais, Bas-Quercy)* (Lille, 1932); Bernard Derouet, "Marchés et transmission: les apports de l'Enquête de 1866," in *Terre et Marchés. Stratégies familiales et logiques économiques, 17e-20e siècles*, ed. Gérard Béaur, Christian Dessureault, and Goy Joseph (Rennes, 2004).

23. See Pélaquier, *De la maison du père*, who observes this behavior especially in the middle peasant class (the *ménagers*): he demonstrates an attempt to concentrate inheritances, to accumulate and not merely preserve them, which allowed some families of the upper levels of this social stratum access to the bourgeoisie.

24. Cf. Michel Nassiet, *Parenté, noblesse et Etats dynastiques: XVe-XVIe siècles* (Paris, 2000).

25. The increasing hold of a small group of notables over communal power was not at variance with the desire to maintain a certain kind of equilibrium at this level, "to avoid the collusion of patronage, the intrigues and conflicting loyalties, the dictatorship of a few. The rule is that power must be shared through collegiality, through supervision of the council members, through annual rotation and a reasonable period of time off. Each could then go about his business, become a successful contractor for the commune, supervise the communal administration as a counselor,

serve each role in turn, and enjoy the prestige of being consul at least once in his life" Derlange, "En Provence," p. 66 (translated quote).

26. It happened fairly frequently that the consuls, whether current or former, would be creditors for the commune. Whatever the underlying reasons for these loans, they bring to light the necessity for political leaders to have at their disposal significant financial resources. Of course, this could only work in favor of the succession of one single son within the families who sought access to local power. As for the communities themselves, the increasing possibility of having their own budget could only serve to reinforce the poll tax–based character of the designation of these leaders.

27. Pélaquier, *De la maison du père.*

28. René Pillorget, who inventoried the typology of conflicts in Provence during this period, notes that in spite of their diversity, they reveal more coalitions of this type more readily than direct confrontations opposing different "classes" identifiable by their membership in a particular level of the social hierarchy. See René Pillorget, *Les mouvements insurrectionnels de Provence entre 1596 et 1715* (Paris, 1975).

29. As this essay (first presented at the conference in the Hague in March 2002) was being finalized, it seemed necessary to situate it briefly in relation to the exceptional work just recently published by Gérard Delille, *Le maire et le prieur. Pouvoir central et pouvoir local en Méditerranée occidentale, XVe-XVIIIe siècle* (Paris, Rome, 2003). Several ideas developed here largely support the analyses of Delille, especially those regarding the relationships between the political system, marriage practices, and the cohesiveness of lineage. I fully support the historical model proposed in this book—which concerns primarily the areas of Italy and Iberia—while also believing that it must be qualified in the case of southern France, whose societies present some specific characteristics. If the role of wealth in the access to power (or even to nobility) is actually real there, then the role that the relationship to the land plays seems to me to require substantial emphasis for these regions as well. Moreover, the fundamental turning point represented by the transition to primogeniture, in both the Midi in France and among Italian and Spanish elites, seems to me to be open to slightly different interpretations. In southern France, it is more difficult to connect this shift with the relationship between local and centralized power, or to the fact that the latter was able, at a determined moment, to do without the mediation of local lineage groups in controlling regional populations, substituting instead a system of venal offices or specialized staff foreshadowing the modern civil service. Nevertheless, it is true that I consider local power in southern France at a more microregional level than is the case in Delille's analysis.

Chapter VII

The Making of Stability

Kinship, Church, and Power among the Rhenish Imperial Knighthood, Seventeenth and Eighteenth Centuries*

Christophe Duhamelle

The German Enlightenment harshly criticized the ecclesiastical territories of the Holy Roman Empire. According to Enlightened publicists, no sound and sustained set of policies was possible, because prince-bishops and archbishop-electors were elected, a custom, they thought, that could not create stability.[1] Indeed, many factors in the ecclesiastical states appear to have prevented continuity. To begin with, every bishop and archbishop after the Viennese Concordat between Pope and Emperor in 1448 was chosen by a cathedral chapter. It was difficult for a family to have two members elected consecutively as a prince in the same state. Each election, expressing the dissensions in the chapter, caused a policy change; and as the "prince-maker," the chapter reinforced its privileges each time, ensured a great amount of autonomy for its own estates, colonized an increasing number of state offices, and compelled an elected bishop to moderate his policies.[2] Secondly, in each chapter, the canons were chosen by the other canons, first by a general approval of the ability of the candidate, secondly by the choice of one canon according to a rotation called *Turnus*. There was no possibility to create a hereditary position in the strict sense of the word. The third reason was celibacy. The high clergy only loosely followed this rule at the end of the Middle Ages and at the beginning of the sixteenth century, but celibacy was more strictly observed afterwards because of the (slow) penetration of the new Catholic rigor into the chapters. Consequently, the construction of stability could not simply be based on the transmission of power through inheritance.

In spite of these reasons, the ecclesiastical territories of the south Rhenish part of the Empire (i.e., primarily, the archbishopric-electorates of Mainz and Trier, the bishoprics of Worms and Speyer) showed a high degree of stability, provided that one focuses on the ruling group in these states: the same family names are represented in the chapters throughout the last two centuries of the Holy Empire.[3] A relatively small number of noble lineages monopolized the greatest part of all positions in the chapters. Among the 601 canons elected in the chapters of Mainz and Trier between 1600 and 1803, for instance, 265 (44%) came from only sixteen lineages[4] (a little more than 10% of all lineages represented in these chapters). Furthermore, the overwhelming majority of princes were members of these families of canons. Although no visible continuity was ever created, during the whole period, some lineages produced many princes who, moreover, were closely kin-connected with other princes of other families.[5] Among thirty-three princes elected between 1599 and 1800 that I studied, twenty-three were nephews or grandnephews of another prince-bishop (and were often also brothers, brothers-in-law, or cousins of other princes), and six others were not nephews, but still close relatives of a prince (brother, brother-in-law, cousin). There were no "self-made men" among the Rhenish ecclesiastical princes.

The question dealt with in this chapter is, therefore, how did a leading noble group manage to create a collective stability—or a collective inheritance—in the ecclesiastical states of the south Rhenish Holy Roman Empire, even though these states were characterized by the disrupting rules of election and celibacy? I tried to address this question by studying the twenty most successful lineages of the Rhenish imperial knighthood, one of the institutionalized groups of the German nobility, directly subject only to the Emperor (although these nobles did not live in Austria), and not to a territorial prince.[6] The answer to the question is to be found in the institutionalization of a kin-protecting system of accession to the chapters, in a very precise managing of marriage, and in a peculiar evolution of family forms.

The Proofs of Nobility

To begin with, the thoroughly institutionalized framework of proofs of nobility both allowed families of the knighthood to turn chapters into their own gardens and, consequently, forced them to adapt their familial behavior continuously to this position of power. The proofs that every candidate had to show in order to be appointed a canon became stricter and stricter. Although, theoretically, this system was not permitted by canon law, it existed in fact and was even strengthened in the seventeenth century.[7] Following this policy, the Rhenish imperial knighthood achieved not only a monopoly on the chapters (and on their enormous incomes), but also an exclusion of every family that had not found its way to the chapters before 1600.

The form of proofs permitted this exclusion: a candidate had to show that every ancestor, man or woman, for four or five generations, had been a member not only of an old noble family, but also of a *stiftsfähig* family, i.e. one where a member had previously been elected as a canon. This system compelled families to record every familial event very precisely and to take care of their archives. The "collective inheritance" depended on a technical know-how that other families could not achieve and that came to be expressed and proudly exhibited in a specialized literature. The titles of these records (the genealogical compilations of Humbracht and Hattstein, for instance[8]) represent the group's self-esteem, and each chapter offers an institutionalized description of kinship, featuring ascending genealogies, looking exactly like nobility proofs.

These proofs "by quarterings" are different from the French system of proofs "by degrees," which considered only the male ancestors of one noble (or, in some cases, the male ancestors of his father and his mother, but not his grandmothers and so on). Under these circumstances, mésalliance implied social suicide for members of the imperial knighthood, destroying any hope of presenting irreproachable proofs for five generations. Thus, the possible matches for a marriage among this group were not numerous: an analysis of the 691 men and women married to a member of the group under study between 1600 and 1800 shows that the majority came from a very narrow circle of closely related families. They belonged to only 283 lineages, and more than half of the partners came from only 46 lineages. Since a "mésalliance" had such devastating consequences on the ability of a descendant to enter the chapters, it was unacceptable and very strongly punished by the family. Aside from two or three exceptions—the culprit then being disinherited—all married men and women avoided the new nobility;

more than 73 percent of the partners belonged to the relatively narrow group of the imperial knighthood, and more than 79 percent came from lineages producing one or more canons of the German cathedral chapters between 1600 and 1803. One could hardly imagine a more closed matrimonial field.

Of course, the restricted alliance policy of the Rhenish knighthood was not just the mechanical result of the system of proofs. Above all, it reflected the nature of power. This system was "centered" rather than "polarized," since, in the ecclesiastical states, there was no counterweight to the domination of the nobility. Within the oligarchy, pedigree offered the main ticket to the elite. Other oligarchies in Europe displayed similar dynamics, prompting their characterization as "centered" by historians to grasp a situation where the field of alliance was contained within the group.[9] In contrast, where there was a strong monarchical power, aristocracies were forced into processes of constant renewal and redefinition. Individuals could certainly marry among the rich and powerful, but they also sought out daughters from freshly noble and ascending families (the way one proved nobility being a symptom rather than a cause). In such situations, dowry became a flexible instrument for organizing a complex marriage market. Such a "polarized" field of alliance, magnetized by an external force, characterized both the high nobilities and lower levels of the aristocracies of France and England.[10] Sweden and Denmark offer good examples of a rapid shift from one type to the other, occasioned by an abrupt rise of royal power. In the case of Denmark, the growing professionalization of the army caused a shift in the criterion of choice for marriage partners from pedigree to function—an evolution also present in the Holy Roman Empire among the militarized nobilities of Hesse and Bavaria.[11]

The Management of Marriage

The narrow field of alliance within the Rhenish nobility did indeed create many problems. The first one arose from considerations of consanguinity, solved by contracting marriages at the very limit of forbidden degrees. Among the ninety-six couples belonging to the twenty lineages under study, exactly 50 percent were related by a fourth or fifth degree of consanguinity. But the relatively small number of narrow consanguinity cases (under the fourth degree) is striking, especially among "canon families," who would have had no difficulty obtaining dispensations. It appears that the chances of being elected a canon grew if the displayed proofs featured a full range of connections with other line-ages of the group, and choosing kin who were not too close as marriage partners had a certain logic to it. The apparent contradiction between the narrowness of the ruling group and the necessity for diversifying alliances—to sustain collective rule—was solved by complex mecha-nisms that tended to constantly reinforce kin-relationships without focusing too much on one lineage: the exchange of spouses between two, three, or more lineages, linking marriages in affinal chains and the like, composed a broad canvas with a remarkable virtuosity in a way shown in other studies of different groups of the European nobility.[12] In the Rhenish case, the density of these mechanisms was even greater because the system of proofs strictly forbade the intrusion of newcom-ers in the game.

The second problem with the narrow field of alliance was the ten-sion between the high rate of unmarried male canons and the neces-sity of assuring familial continuity. In practice, the brother who was designated to marry needed neither to be the firstborn nor the youngest, but was a chosen one, who may have been selected, among other reasons, for his ability to have children[13]: the proportion of child-less couples decreased from 25.78 percent for those married between 1600 and 1649 to 9.30 percent for those married between 1750 and 1800 (the lowest rate found among the European nobility of the early modern period[14]). In this situation, the restriction of marriage was not as devastating as for a declining oligarchy like the Venetian aristoc-racy,[15] for instance, and the vigorous fertility here contrasted with the biological decline that affected the dukes and peers of France. This fer-tility cannot be mechanically explained by the decline of marriage age among women or by the progress of wet nursing, but does indicate a coherent system of reproduction.[16] As a matter of fact, both declining nuptiality and high fertility made it possible for the lineages to survive and for a great majority of the male adults to become canons (more than 60% in the first half of the eighteenth century)[17]. Of course, solu-tions had to be found to cope with the fact that numerous women did not find husbands because the majority of men became canons. They abandoned the unprestigious local noble convents and tried to gain access to the few female chapters of the Holy Roman Empire. They also contributed to the creation of new institutions in the eighteenth century[18]. Moreover, the daughters were used to extend the field of alliance into useful but not *stiftsfähig* nobility groups (in Vienna, for instance). In some cases, as among the von Walderdorff, the unmarried women were settled on the same secondary family estate, generation after generation: the family contract in 1733 stated clearly that the five single sisters might marry only "against the expectations" of their brothers, and the contracts in 1786 and 1793 again organized the life of other singles in the old city estate in Limburg.[19] The testaments made by three of these women in 1757 and 1758 show how familial objects descended from one Limburger generation of unmarried women to the other, but the women transmitted the bulk of their little savings to "the one, who is chosen for continuing the Walderdorff lineage:"[20] even these "victims" of familial discipline contributed to reinforce its principles.

The third problem for the narrow field of alliance had to do with its social disadvantages. Marriage operated more as a consolidation of equals than an opening towards new horizons, and it could prevent families from benefiting from other opportunities, consigning them to a closed specialization. Dowries show particularly well that this sort of marriage lacked social dynamism. Throughout two centuries, they remained at a low level (between 2000 and 4000 Rhenish Gulden), even though families became considerably richer and other nobilities, like the English, had to cope with a tremendous dowry inflation.[21] For all of these reasons, opening new doors through marriage was tenuous and required caution and skill. One had to look for *stiftsfähig* matches offering a new opportunity, and to use, again, very precise mechanisms (rechained marriages and the like) to melt these matches in the old pot of the chapters' oligarchy. The Rhenish knighthood managed, thanks to these mechanisms, to overpower the weaker Franconian imperial knighthood in the Franconian chapters (Bamberg, Würzburg). This "weakness" was caused by the conversion of the vast majority of the Franconian knights to Protestantism, making them progressively unable to become canons. But a lineage did not have to be Catholic at all in order to be *stiftsfähig*, and marrying Franconian knights did not endanger the ability to present proofs of nobility. Marriage created connections to the few Franconian families that, remaining Catholics, did not have enough males to fill all the canon positions of the local chapters.[22]

The management of marriage therefore permitted both the exclusion of other groups and the great specialization of the imperial knighthood as an ecclesiastical elite. But this specialization was not just a matter of excluding others; it also came from an internal reconfiguration. The system of marriage reacted successfully against dramatic changes in the regional and confessional context and reshaped the familial logic itself.

The Adaptation of the Families

At the end of the sixteenth century, the ecclesiastical specialization of the Rhenish imperial knights was not as important as it later became. But increasing religious and institutional antagonisms were reducing their opportunities in other territories. The Palatine Electorate, for example, became Calvinist and an enemy of the Emperor, and was no longer a suitable place for a Catholic imperial knight to make the kind of career that had been possible at the end of the Middle Ages.[23] Such circumstances narrowed down the career possibilities of the Catholic knighthood in some areas, just as new ones were being opened up. Although the new Protestant aristocracy tried to secularize chapters in order to retain wealthy prebends, they failed in their attempts to do so in the southwest of the Empire. The War of Cologne (1582–1583) brought conflicts on this point to a climax, resulting in most chapters remaining Catholic, offering great possibilities to the lineages that continuously adhered to, or returned to, the old religion. In addition, the younger sons of ruling princes who, at the end of the Middle Ages, had almost always been elected prince-bishops, could no longer compete for these functions—with the important exceptions of the Bavarian Wittelsbachs in the northwest (especially as archbishop-electors of Cologne) and of the Austrian Hapsburgs in the southeast.[24] In the middle, along the Rhine and the Main, the field was open for the knights themselves, who rapidly monopolized not only the chapters, but also the bishoprics. When, from the end of the seventeenth century onwards, members of converted dynasties of princes tried to recover a position in the ecclesiastical territories, they faced a tough resistance from the chapters and gained only limited success.[25] The archbishop-electors of Mainz, for instance, were almost all sons of counts or princes in the century preceding the Reformation (von Isenburg, von Nassau, von Brandenburg), but were imperial knights from 1546 until the suppression of the Electorate in 1803 (except for one, a member of the converted dynasty Palatinate-Neuburg, in 1729–1732). In short: Catholic knights lost many career opportunities, but experienced a dramatic rise in the ecclesiastical field. As a result, the familial forms (like shared inheritance, multiplication of marriages, lineages with many branches, inheritance for women, and so on) that were once useful for extending the range of possibilities proved suddenly to be a threat for the new specialization, prompting a new "Malthusian" management of family size and emphasis on celibacy.

The maintenance of stability consequently depended on a profound change in family organization, begun for the most part in the seventeenth century, but completed in the eighteenth. First, the great number of branches inside one lineage (more than ten at the beginning of the seventeenth century for the von Metternich and the von Eltz, for example) was abruptly diminished through "suicide" (no marriage among—sometimes numerous—siblings) or through "recuperation" by marrying inside the lineage (there were, for example, five marriages between ten of the von Dalbergs over three generations[26]). The possibility for all knights, male and female, to take away a part of the family fortune was reduced by the progressive institution of *fidei commissa*, which practically excluded women from inheritance and defined male descent more strictly. The "legal" lineage came to be defined in terms of descent from the founder of the *fidei commissum*. It was perceived as important to bring together different branches who could not inherit from one another any more, through the mechanism of marriage between remote relatives bearing the same name and still considering themselves as parts of the same lineage. To avoid facing the same problem again, the number of children allowed to marry was dramatically reduced.

These developments reflected the specific strategical situation of "canon families:" primogeniture, for example, never became the rule, even when strict settlement spread, because the best career for a knight—to be elected a bishop—was often entered into by the firstborn son. Even among aristocracies that implemented primogeniture, like many Italian nobilities, the importance of ecclesiastical careers could convince some families to break the privilege of inheritance for the firstborn son.[27] The Rhenish knighthood carried this logic through, making "ecclesiastical primogeniture" the common rule, which, in addition, allowed the generation gap to widen, so that uncles were old enough to make way for their nephews in the cathedral chapters.[28] The knights managed all the better to bring family organization into harmony with social specialization, since they managed the whole process themselves: their contracts had the value of enforced law because they were not subjected to any external law. An example will perhaps help to see how the system worked: Franz Adolf Dietrich von Ingelheim married Maria Ursula von Dalberg, and they had twenty-two children between 1683 and 1706—a dramatic case of intensified fertility. Five sons attained adulthood, but the fifth, Johann Philipp von Ingelheim, born in 1698, was the only one who married (a Dalberg, like his mother). When Johann Philipp's firstborn son became a canon in Wurzburg in 1739, his father's two brothers with prebends in this chapter were old enough to have become full-right canons and able to help bring in their nephew.

The evolution of these families changed the position of each individual. The role of the canon and of the married woman in the family can be studied as good examples for this change. Numerous canons contributed a great deal to the fortune and glory of their lineages. They constantly passed on their own inherited family goods to their married brothers and transmitted by testament their (in many cases considerable) acquired money, collections, and estates to their lineages. But they were well aware of these contributions and were therefore able to reshape familial practice according to their own ideals of "canon families." They concentrated their legacies on one heir, defined as the (only) marrying nephew, even though the law required nonacquired family goods to be divided among all heirs. Acting in this way accelerated the restriction of nuptiality and encouraged the vocation of the majority of males to ecclesiastical careers. The way they dealt with the succession to property opened the way to strict settlement. Moreover, canons were eager to control the management of the family fortune they (and their predecessors) created. Many testaments or family contracts established "overviewing boards": the canons belonging to the family gathered once a year and asked the married head of the family to justify his accounts and take their advice.[29]

For women, the evolution was more radical. They were gradually excluded from participating in the circulation of wealth between the lineages as their shares in family goods were progressively diminished, culminating in a decision by all imperial knights in 1653 to abolish their inheritance claims. Even the possibility for a widow to bring goods from her first marriage into a second one was progressively reduced and finally suppressed in the eighteenth century. This process was crucial for the increasing emphasis on male descendance. As a quid pro quo, women acquired from the families into which they married increasingly more substantial dowers than the dowries they brought in. The dowries themselves progressively lost value from inflation and from the fact that they made up an ever smaller portion of the estates of the increasingly wealthy knighthood. Losing their power to transmit goods from one lineage to the other, but gaining a right for more financial and emotional regard from their husbands' families, women came to play a more passive part in the interfamilial game, but a more integrated role in their families of orientation. For one thing, marriage contracts increasingly specified them as the natural guardians for their minor children. In both cases (canons and wives), therefore, the place of every individual in the family evolved in a complex way, each case the result of bargaining, with losses balanced by compensations.[30] Some of the developments, such as guardianship, can only be followed from one contract to the other, and were not the result of legal changes, nor did they follow a linear trend. It is clear, however, that, firstly, the role of the widow's own family decreased. The last marriage contract[31] that foresaw the coguardianship of a widow and a member of *her* family was signed in 1629. Subsequently, tutors were either taken from *both* families or no condition was set. Secondly, the role of the widow herself increased. In 1644, a contract gave the widow the right to choose the guardians herself, after which this right appeared regularly. Moreover, the contracts reduced the guardians' control more and more, and explained, for example, that they were competent only for "great decisions" (like the sale of an estate), that they had to be authorized by the knights' corporation before diminishing a widow's rights, or that no guardians at all were needed as long as the widow stayed with the children. In spite of a great variability from one contract to another (a contract of 1686, for instance, established the widow as the sole guardian, but is the only contract to reduce her rights to the acquired goods), the evolution led, as in other noble groups, to a better position of the widow, but with less support from her own family.[32]

The family itself came to be based on a new self-representation that enhanced male descent in place of the extended kin on which so-called collective domination depended. This focusing on a narrow conception of male descendance rather than on a large kin network is perfectly illustrated by the family contract of the von Dalbergs in 1723.[33] Annual meetings of the lineage's men featured this new conception, where the chairman wore the "wolf's necklace" to which every male Dalberg, at his majority, added a gold sheet engraved with his name and the date. In a similar way, the organization of the "collective inheritance" in the ecclesiastical states reflected this new family pattern: the significance of maternal relatives in elections diminished, for example. Before 1675, the bishop uncles of newly elected bishops were always mothers' brothers, but after 1693, they were always fathers' brothers.

This shift in the practical kin-networks towards the father's family is also to be found with marriage choice. At the end of the period, the system that both avoided consanguinity and contained alliances within the broad kinship network began to fall apart. On one hand, the Rhenish knights (especially their daughters) began to marry into noble families far beyond the traditional Rhenish or Franconian reservoir. This evolution was in keeping with the extension of ecclesiastical success. Between 1750 and 1800, 38.97 percent of all canonries of the group were held outside of Trier, Mainz, Speyer, and Worms, a significant increase from earlier (23.39 percent between 1600 and 1649). Furthermore, the lineages studied here, although much narrower than before and encompassing fewer individuals, managed to find positions in an unprecedented number of sixteen cathedral chapters within the empire. The widening of the alliance field was loosening the matrimonial coherence of the Rhenish knighthood and also reflected the growing particularism of each family searching out a niche beyond the home region. While the opening to new families and regions was going on, a parallel and opposite trend led to closer consanguineous marriages, which was due in part to the increasing emphasis on male descent. A telling statistic underlines this point.[34] In the seventeenth century, 58 percent of all the marriages concluded between consanguines out to and including the fifth degree were concluded at the limit—at the fifth degree. But in the eighteenth century, this figure fell to 32 percent, as the marriage partners were chosen from ever closer blood relatives. Furthermore, wives were increasingly chosen from paternal rather than maternal kin. Matrilateral marriage choice (in consanguineous marriages) in the seventeenth century, the period when maternal kin were crucial for succession to high office, made up a full 34.5 percent of such marriages, a percentage that fell to 16 in the eighteenth century, when patrilateral criteria came to dominate.

Collateral Domination, but Patrilineal Transmission of Property

The developments that we have sketched here permitted the Rhenish aristocracy to establish a continuous domination of the southwest ecclesiastical states. There are many testimonies to the self-confident appropriation of the Rhenish Church by the aristocracy. The luxurious tomb plates in the cathedrals of Worms or Mainz are covered more by colorful representation of noble quarterings than by religious motifs, and the pulpits and altars are decorated with the arms of the Rhenish lineages. The lists of canons in Trier or Mainz clearly show the oligarchical monopoly: in the chapter of Trier, for example, composed of forty canons, there was at least one von Eltz throughout the two centuries, three or more of them in half this time, and even six or seven of them between 1675 and 1712! In funeral orations for archbishops, their ecclesiastical dynasties were openly celebrated, despite the idea that election incarnated divine choice.[35] All these facts, and more, may give the impression of an unchallenged rule, interrupted only by the French Revolution and the subsequent upheavals in Germany (suppression of the ecclesiastical states in 1803 and of the Empire in 1806). But familial discipline both made for stability and endangered it. The focus on

male descent helped to accumulate the fruits of ecclesiastical monopoly, while eating away at the roots of its success.

The two representations of kinship (the one founded on collateral
networks, the other on dynastic interests) were increasingly distinguished
from one another. All along, the aristocratic and oligarchical imperial
knights still held onto numerous conceptions of "kin," "lineage," "name,"
Freundschaft, and *Familie*, although the two partly opposed conceptions, reflecting strong institutional frames of mandatory proofs of
nobility and male descent of the *fidei commissum*) became dominant.
Still, this double evolution was not necessarily contradictory and could
be managed through a functional distinction between the collective
inheritance supported by the larger bilateral kin-group and the perpetuation and accumulation of fortune by the narrow, agnatic family.

The role women played strikingly illustrates this distinction. As we
have seen, women lost the ability to transfer wealth from one lineage
to the other, but this evolution paradoxically reinforced their function
as "alliance producers." Given the demographics and marriage policies,
they brought more in-laws and allies to their families than their brothers. To start with, the average number of men marrying per generation
decreased slowly from 1.35 between 1600 and 1649 to 1.09 between
1750 and 1803, whereas the average for women started higher and rose
slightly from 1.88 between 1600 and 1649 to 1.90 between 1750 and
1803.[36] To put the situation another way, between 1600 and 1649,
46.09 percent of all married men had at least one sister-in-law (brother's
wife), as opposed to 16.67 percent between 1750 and 1800. At the end
of the eighteenth century, a canon searching for allies in his chapter to
be elected bishop had twice as many chances to find sons of his father's
sisters than to find sons of his father's brothers. Even then, it is a question of allies and support, while the suitability of a candidacy derived
from agnatic descent and patronymic succession (following the schema
paternal uncle/nephew). Maternal kin, having lost the function of
succession (the earlier schema maternal uncle/nephew) could still be
mobilized for support. Although women figured less in the formal
transmission of property and power, they became increasingly important in weaving together the more informal ties that were crucial to
maintain the whole system of oligarchical domination in running order.

The increasing distinction between wide kinship and male line
sometimes led to situations of conflict. Indeed, the coherence of the
group was endangered during the eighteenth century by the diverging
strategies of families trying to broaden the investments of their
acquired capital, both social and financial (many of these families,
thanks to the accumulation of ecclesiastical prebends, had annual

incomes exceeding one hundred thousand florins, more than many princes of the Empire).

Struggle for power and better fortune was fierce among the knighthood, but was always tempered by the complex alliances that created dense lines of kinship within the group and by the principle of election, which gave each lineage its chance at a slot. The von Dalbergs, for example, gained the seat of archbishop-elector at the beginning of the seventeenth and end of the eighteenth century, but not much in between. However, they stayed part of the game because of their constantly reinforced alliances with almost every successful lineage during these two centuries. The struggle for power in the chapters would constantly be structured by family interests, but would also constantly be "relativized" by family ties.

Whatever conflicts existed in the group at the end of the eighteenth century—internal, ever changing, and astonishingly complex—a new danger of a different nature arose. The generalized kinship within the group was challenged by the emergence of a narrow core of especially successful families that gained the title of count from the Emperor. They no longer were interested in the old alliances with "mere" knights, although they were not particularly successful in breaking into the families of the old imperial counts.[37] This development added a small and airtight layer of "knights made counts" to the already complicated configuration of the German aristocracy. Moreover, each lineage tended to isolate itself and to seek a more exceptional destiny beyond the boundaries of the traditional Rhenish ecclesiastical field. Some of them acquired huge estates and a leading position in the Viennese aristocracy (Metternich, Greiffenclau, etc.), while others ascended into the narrow group of imperial princes (von der Leyen). In both cases, the new goals implied a radical shift in alliance policy.[38]

The von Schönborns, for example, experienced tremendous success in the German Church at the end of the seventeenth and beginning of the eighteenth century, and accumulated a great fortune.[39] Indeed, their name came to represent this period in the Empire's Church. With time, however, they had to face the growing distrust from other families who resented the growing gap between the von Schönborns and themselves, and they had to consider whether they could accept the opportunity for very powerful marriages that would have destroyed the perfection of their nobility proofs. The von Schönborns had been created imperial counts in 1701 and had immediately tightened their alliance field: before 1701, 10.53 percent of their marriage partners were counts or countesses, 94.44 percent afterward.[40] Like many of the most successful lineages within the imperial knighthood (von Metternich, von Stadion, von

Walderdorff), the von Schönborns partly solved the problem by creating two family lines in 1711, one staying at home, the other trying its luck at the Viennese court (with enduring success, as did also the Metternichs).

Beside this centrifugal move experienced by the most successful lineages of the Rhenish knighthood, discipline inside families became subject to internal criticism. Conflicts divided the families continuously: some contested successions ended up before the two imperial courts (the *Reichshofrat* and the *Reichskammergericht*), especially when the disinheritance of women spread among the knighthood. Despite the general agreement of 1653, which knights were eager enough to implement where their own daughters were concerned, they were far more reluctant to accept it if they could expect a succession through their wives. Beyond such issues of interest and familial strategy, the ideas of the Enlightenment opened novel areas for familial conflicts. Discipline itself was challenged by new ideas about an individual's pursuit of happiness and natural rights. The case of the canon Franz Karl von Waldbott-Bornheim is particularly well documented.[41] In 1790, Franz Karl decided to resign his prebends and to marry, breaking the iron rule of the ecclesiastical family (his younger brother had been chosen to be the only son marrying). The arguments Franz Karl referred to were typically inspired by Enlightened discourse—but, interestingly enough, so were the letters written by his parents, his brother, and his uncle, who expressed their strong disagreement in an emotional tone. Both sides of the argument about discipline depended on the *Zeitgeist*. Franz Karl wanted to marry the noble daughter of a military officer in order to begin a new career that was not so far away from classical noble horizons. It wasn't the noble style of life, but the specialization of the ecclesiastical knighthood that was questioned by Franz Karl and some members of his generation. Such internal criticism reinforced the centrifugal evolution.

The changes we have been following reveal that the system had considerable flexibility. It emerged from a series of choices and opportunities and from an overlapping of diverging interests. The stability of the group was ensured through concentration on male descent that, in turn, threatened the coherence of the knighthood as a global kinship group tied together by alliances and through the mediation of women.

Conclusion

The production of stability within the Rhenish imperial knighthood passed through the elaboration of a collective inheritance at two levels.

First, the monopoly of a power, not passed on by direct inheritance, but shared by the group (the canons electing the princes), led to an intricate system of global kinship, making each canon more or less the remote cousin of all the others and coheir in a system of domination. Second, ecclesiastical specialization succeeded only through the greater discipline of each individual family, resulting in a strict but balanced distribution of roles, with the celibate makers of fortune unable to transmit to their own children. These interconnected processes, partly in contradiction with one another, make the stability of the system appear paradoxical. The same lineages were present in the chapters for more than two centuries with surprising constancy, but only through continuous and complex adjustments between lineages and between each of their members. This dynamic stability suggests three conclusions.

First, the way a drastically reduced number of Catholic families managed to hold far more prebends after the Reformation than before demonstrates that confessionalization should not be studied as only a political and religious process of social constraint. Historians need to look into the creation of social niches created both through active social and familial strategies and within the context of the more encompassing political forces. Such so-called self-confessionalization should also be taken into account for studying social groups subject to disciplining authorities.

Secondly, the political, social, and confessional context appears, reciprocally, to have shaped family life and the representation of family, lineage, and kinship. Even if some developments observed for the Rhenish knighthood resembled broader processes (the rise of the *fidei commissum*, for instance[42]), its evolution was peculiar and, in some cases, diametrically opposed to what was going on in other nobilities. The repertoire of familial forms does not tell enough about social use, and a mere familial study of family history is doomed to neglect many of its own implications.

Thirdly, neither the context nor the familial repertoire "determined" the actual story of each family. Reading familial contracts or letters and studying the conflicts, successes, and failures of the players shows that context and repertoire were handled with inventiveness and were constantly recreated by—as well as creating—the frame of bargaining in every actual choice.[43] This story demonstrates how one can map the social and political context within which each family has to act and how the set of decisions tracks back into the encompassing social, political, and cultural processes.

Notes

*This article is based on a wider study: Christophe Duhamelle, *L'héritage collectif. La noblesse d'Église rhénane, 17e et 18e siècles* (Paris, 1998). This book contains a comprehensive bibliography, a list of sources, statistical material, and more developed analysis, which I cannot quote extensively in this paper.

1. Peter Wende, *Die geistliche Staaten und ihre Auflösung im Urteil der zeitgenössischen Publizistik* (Lübeck, Hamburg, 1966).
2. Günter Christ, "Selbstverständnis und Rolle der Domkapitel in den geistlichen Territorien des alten deutschen Reiches in der Frühneuzeit," *Zeitschrift für historische Forschung* 16 (1989): pp. 257–328; Günter Christ, "Subordinierte Landeshoheit der rheinischen und fränkischen Domkapitel," in *Landeshoheit. Beiträge zur Entstehung, Ausformung und Typologie eines Verfassungselements des Römisch-Deutschen Reiches,* ed. Erwin Riedenauer (Munich, 1994), pp. 113–34.
3. The lists of canons are edited by Peter Hersche, *Die deutschen Domkapitel im 17. und 18. Jahrhundert* (Bern, 1984).
4. "Lineage" here means all descendants from a remote common ancestor bearing the same name. Therefore, the von Metternich-Bourscheid, the von Metternich-Müllenarck, and the von Metternich-Winneburg-Beilstein, for instance, are regarded as different branches of the same lineage, although differentiated for many generations. The different families (defined as the actual living members of a narrow descendancy) of the imperial knighthood remained strongly aware (with varying interpretations) of being part of a lineage, as shown by the frequent marriages between remote cousins bearing the same names, when one branch died out. The heiress of the extinguished Metternich-Bourscheid, for example, married a Metternich-Müllenarck in 1691, considered explicitly by the marriage contract as kin, although the common male ancestor of both wife and husband was dead for more than 250 years. The memorial role of the name kept the lineage alive as a representation. The introduction of the *fidei commissum,* however, stressed a stricter comprehension of the *Stamm,* defined as all descending branches of the man (or men) having established the *fidei commissum,* but excluded every branch dating from a former partition. This restriction gained importance for inheritance, but did not overshadow the name-related definition of the broad lineage. The notion of *Freundschaft* (the loosely defined living group of parents, in-laws, relatives, allies, friends, etc.) also remained important. The concurring categories used in the actual networks challenge a strict definition.
5. Lists and short biographies of all bishop-princes and archbishop-electors of the Holy Roman Empire in Erwin Gatz, ed., *Die Bischöfe des Heiligen Römischen Reiches 1648 bis 1803. Ein biographisches Lexikon* (Berlin, 1990) and Erwin Gatz, ed., *Die Bischöfe des Heiligen Römischen Reiches 1448 bis 1648. Ein biographisches Lexikon* (Berlin, 1996).
6. A brief presentation of the imperial knighthood in English: Thomas J. Glas-Hochstettler, "The Imperial Knights in Post-Westphalian Mainz," *Central European History* 11 (1978): pp. 131–49.
7. Still fundamental on this topic: Andreas L. Veit, "Geschichte und Recht der Stiftsmäßigkeit auf die ehemals adeligen Domstifte von Mainz, Würzburg und Bamberg," *Historisches Jahrbuch* 33 (1912): pp. 323–58.
8. Johann Maximilian Humbracht, *Die höchste Zierde Teutsch-Landes und Vortrefflichkeit Teutschen Adels, vorgestellt in der Reichs-Freyen Rheinischen Ritterschaft [...]*

(Frankfurt, 1707). Damian Hartart von und zu Hattstein, Die Hoheit des deutschen Reichsadels, oder vollständige Probe der Ahnen unverfälschter adeliger Familien in alphabetischer Ordnung, nebst Ahnenprobe der Familien und mit den Stammwappen (Fulda, 1729–1740). Hattstein was an imperial knight himself. This pedigree culture of the ecclesiastical aristocracy, in particular, and of the German nobility as a whole explains why these genealogical records were so accurate and allow the current main German edition of genealogies—Wilhelm Karl Prinz von Isenburg, Frank Baron von Loringhofen, and Detlev Schwennicke, eds., *Europäische Stammtafeln: Stammtafeln zur Geschichte der europäischen Staaten, Neue Folge,* 21 vols. (Marburg/Frankfurt a. M., 1980–2002)—to be useful as a source for this research, as well as for others since.

9. For instance: Georg Schmidt, *Der Wetterauer Grafenverein. Organisation und Politik einer Reichskorporation zwischen Reformation und Westfälischem Frieden* (Marburg, 1989), p. 481.

10. Lawrence Stone, *The Crisis of the Aristocracy 1558–1641* (London, Oxford, New York, 1967), pp. 286–88; Jean-Pierre Labatut, *Les ducs et pairs de France au XVIIe siècle* (Paris, 1972), p. 184. See, for example, James B. Wood, "Endogamy and *Mésalliance,* the Marriage Patterns of the Nobility of the *Election* of Bayeux, 1430–1669," *French Historical Studies* 10 (1978): pp. 375–92.

11. The closed and stable oligarchy governing Sweden had to change its marrying behavior dramatically after the royal coup in 1680: Kurt Ågren, "Rise and Decline of an Aristocracy: The Swedish Social and Political Elite in the 17th Century," *Scandinavian Journal of History* 1 (1976): pp. 55–80. On Denmark: Svend A. Hansen, "Changes in the Wealth and the Demographic Characteristics of the Danish Aristocracy 1470–1720," in *Troisième conférence internationale d'histoire économique (Munich 1965)* (Paris, The Hague, 1972), vol. 4, pp. 91–122; Gunner Lind, "Military and Absolutism: The Army Officers of Denmark-Norway as a Social Group and Political Factor, 1660–1848," *Scandinavian Journal of History* 12 (1988): pp. 221–43. On Hesse: Gregory W. Pedlow, *The Survival of the Hessian Nobility 1770–1870* (Princeton, 1988), p. 45. On Bavaria: Walter Demel, "Adelsstruktur und Adelspolitik in der ersten Phase des Königreichs Bayern," in *Reformen im rheinbündischen Deutschland,* ed. Eberhard Weis (Munich, 1984), pp. 213–28, here p. 227.

12. For instance: Gérard Delille, *Famille et propriété dans le royaume de Naples (15e-19e siècles)* (Rome, Paris, 1985).

13. The sources, however, are silent on how the fertility of the chosen son was tested. Instead, they constantly insist on the fact that he was actually chosen (and not designated due to his birth rank), and the very fact that the infertility rate diminished to such a low level proves that the ability to continue the family was most certainly taken into account.

14. The rate of childless marriages is 13 percent in the nobility of Luxembourg in the eighteenth century (Calixte Hudemann-Simon, *La noblesse luxembourgeoise au XVIIIe siècle* [Paris, Luxembourg, 1985], p. 37), 12 percent in the Hessian knighthood between 1650 and 1899 (Pedlow, *Survival of the Hessian Nobility,* p. 54), 19 percent among the British dukes between 1730 and 1829 (Thomas Henry Hollingsworth, "A Demographic Study of the British Ducal Families," in *Population in History. Essays in Historical Demography,* ed. David Victor Glass and David Edward Eversley (London, 1965), pp. 354–378, p. 371), 24 percent among the Venetian aristocrats in the eighteenth century (James C. Davis, *The Decline of the Venetian Nobility as a Ruling Class* (Baltimore, 1962), p. 54), 35 percent among French dukes-peers between 1750 and 1799 (Louis Henry and Claude Levy, "Ducs

et pairs sous l'Ancien Régime; caractéristiques démographiques d'une caste," *Population* 5 (1960): pp. 807–830, p. 820).

15. In the eighteenth century, even among the only surviving sons, 64.7 percent did not marry at all, according to Davis, *Decline*. Recent studies show, however, that this demographical decline needs a revision: many marriages were not declared in the sources studied by Davis; Volker Hunecke, *Der venezianische Adel am Ende der Republik 1646-1797. Demographie, Familie, Haushalt* (Tübingen, 1995). In addition, the lack of interest in political power was not as strong as asserted: Oliver T. Domzalski, *Politische Karrieren und Machtverteilung im venezianischen Adel (1646-1797)* (Sigmaringen, 1996).

16. The average age at first marriage among women is very stable: twenty-two years, two months of age between 1600 and 1649; twenty years, five months of age between 1650 and 1699; twenty-two years, eight months of age between 1700 and 1749; and twenty-two years, seven months of age between 1750 and 1800. It is very difficult to know if wet nursing was increasingly practiced during the period. Wet nursing was far less present in Germany than in France, but was frequent among the aristocracy—not more frequent, however, than in regions with markedly lower birth rates in the nobility, such as France. Christophe Duhamelle, "La petite enfance en Allemagne, fin XVIIIe-début XIXe siècle. La vision des topographies médicales," *Revue d'Histoire Moderne et Contemporaine* 37 (1990): pp. 657–71.

17. In addition, the canons frequently cumulated prebends in several chapters.

18. For example, the female chapter Sta. Anna in Würzburg, founded in 1701/1714: Max Domarus, *Äbtissin Eva Theresia von Schönborn und das adelige Damenstift zur Heiligen Anna in Würzburg* (Würzburg, 1964).

19. Private archives of the count von Walderdorff, Schloß Molsberg, VI-60 and 65.

20. Private archives of the count von Walderdorff, Schloß Molsberg, VIII-AA, VIII-DD, VIII-CC.

21. The dowries among the English nobility has been multiplied by four (in constant value) from 1600 till 1725 and, at the time, represented more than the annual income of the wife's parents: Stone, *Crisis of the Aristocracy*, p. 290.

22. The evolution of the proportion of Franconian canonries among all canonries held by the group under study (16.13% in 1600–1649, 20.83% in 1650–1699, 20.33% in 1700–1749, and 23.53% in 1750–1803) and the evolution of the proportion of Franconian knights among the marriage partners (2.99% in 1600–1649, 8.29% in 1650–1699, 12.98% in 1700–1749, and 23.23% in 1750–1800) show that, in this case, the alliances followed the conquest of the chapters. Concerning the Westphalian chapters and nobility, the marriages preceded the ecclesiastical success, but the parallelism is also astonishing. The well-studied Westphalian ecclesiastical aristocracy was less specialized and more self-contained in its own region, and had to share the seats of bishops with families of counts or princes (Wittelsbach). See (also, as an exemplary study of the family forms of this aristocracy): Heinz Reif, *Westfälischer Adel 1770-1870* (Göttingen, 1979). In addition, cf. Johannes Freiherr von Boeselager, *Die Osnabrücker Domherren des 18. Jahrhunderts* (Osnabrück, 1990).

23. An overview in Volker Press, "Patronat und Klientel im Heiligen Römischen Reich," in *Klientelsysteme im Europa der frühen Neuzeit*, ed. Antoni Maczak (Munich, 1988), pp. 19–46, here pp. 24–26.

24. But even the Emperors did not manage to break the knights' monopoly upon the Rhenish ecclesiastical States. A recent overview in Matthias Schnettger, "Der Kaiser und die Bischofswahlen. Das Haus Österreich und die Reichskirche vom Augs-

burger Religionsfrieden bis zur Mitte des 17. Jahrhunderts," in *Reichsständische Libertät und Habsburgisches Kaisertum*, ed. Heinz Duchhardt and Matthias Schnettger (Mainz, 1999), pp. 213–55.

25. Rudolf Reinhardt, "Konvertiten und deren Nachkommen in der Reichskirche der frühen Neuzeit," *Rottenburger Jahrbuch für Kirchengeschichte* 8 (1989): pp. 9–37.

26. The percentage of the marriage partners belonging to the same lineage as their wives or husbands did show when this reduction of the size of the lineages occurred by means of the absorption of one branch by the other: 2.99 percent in 1600–1649, 4.15 percent in 1650–1699, 4.58 percent in 1700–1749, and 2.02 percent in 1750–1800.

27. Renata Ago, "Ecclesiastical Careers and the Destiny of Cadets," *Continuity and Change* 7 (1992): pp. 271–82.

28. Heinz Reif, "Zum Zusammenhang von Sozialstruktur, Familien- und Lebenszyklus im westfälischen Adel in der Mitte des 18. Jahrhunderts," in *Historische Familienforschung*, ed. Michael Mitterauer and Reinhard Sieder (Frankfurt a. M., 1982), pp. 123–55.

29. The *fidei commissum* contract of the von Metternich-Müllenarck in 1722 (*Landeshauptarchiv* Koblenz, SM 969), for instance, explained that the canons had the right to take their money back if the married brother wasted the family wealth "by drinking, giving exaggerated gratifications, gambling, especially with cards or dice, by seeking too much luxury or by suing in court in an unreflected or unuseful way."

30. This balanced result resembles the issues of the debates on the English strict settlement: Lawrence Stone and Jeanne Fawtier-Stone, *An Open Elite? England 1540–1880*, abridged ed. (Oxford, New York, 1986), pp. 48–55; Eileen Spring, *Law, Land and Family: Aristocratic Inheritance in England, 1300 to 1800* (Chapel Hill, London 1993), pp. 148–80; Lloyd Bonfield, "Affective Families, Open Elites and Strict Family Settlements in Early Modern England," *Economic History Review* 39 (1986): pp. 341–54.

31. These indications are based on a sample of fifty-nine marriage contracts from 1600 to 1781. The details are in my doctoral thesis, Christophe Duhamelle, "La noblesse d'Église. Famille et pouvoir dans la chevalerie immédiate rhénane, XVIIe-XVIIIe siècles" (Paris-I, 1994), vol. 2, pp. 593–98.

32. Johnnes Arndt, "Möglichkeiten und Grenzen weiblicher Selbstbehauptung gegenüber männlicher Dominanz im Reichsgrafenstand des 17. und 18. Jahrhundert, " *Vierteljahrsschrift für Sozial- und Wirtschaftsgeschichte* 77 (1990): pp. 153–74. More recently: Martina Schattkowsky, ed., *Witwenschaft in der Frühen Neuzeit: fürstliche und adlige Witwen zwischen Fremd- und Selbstbestimmung* (Leipzig, 2003).

33. "Erbvertrag der Hochfreyherrlich Dalbergischen Familie," in Johann Ulrich von Cramer, ed., *Observationes juris universi*, 6 vols. (Wetzlar/Ulm, 1758–1772), vol. 3, p. 90–119.

34. The following statistics are based on the ninety-six couples, where both partners belonged to the twenty lineages under study and for whom five levels of ascendant ancestors (male and female) can be traced.

35. In 1724, for example, the Jesuit Christoph Voss, in his funeral oration for Philipp Franz von Schönborn, prince-bishop of Würzburg, remarked that Philipp Franz was born three days after his granduncle's death (the former archbishop-elector of Mainz, prince-bishop of Würzburg and prince-bishop of Worms Johann Philipp of Schönborn, 1605–1673), and added: "As if godly wisdom would have indicated at this very moment, by a mysterious drama, that when a Schönborn sun was setting down, another one was already rising up in order to project his sunbeams onto the

Franconian Fatherland"; Christoph Voss, *Traur-voller und unvermutheter Niedergang der Fränkischen Sonne...* (Würzburg, [1724]), p. 4.

36. The calculation takes into account only siblings with at least one brother or one sister, marrying in order to avoid the statistical effect of the variable percentage of nonmarrying siblings throughout the period.

37. Schmidt, *Wetterauer Grafenverein.*

38. On this evolution, which the era of the French Revolution and Empire led to its climax: Christof Dipper, "Die Reichsritterschaft in napoleonischer Zeit," in *Reformen im rheinbündischen Deutschland,* ed. Eberhard Weis (Munich, 1984), pp. 53–74. See also, for example, the current research of William Godsey: "Noble Survival and Transformation at the Beginning of the Late Modern Era: The Counts Coudenhove from Rhenish Cathedral Canons to Austrian Priests, 1750–1850," *German History* 19 (2001): pp. 499–524.

39. The growth of the Schönborns' fortune between 1642 and 1729 has been estimated at almost 6,000 percent. Alfred Schröcker, "Besitz und Politik des Hauses Schönborn vom 14. bis zum 18. Jahrhundert," *Mitteilungen des österreichischen Staatsarchivs* 26 (1973): pp. 212–34.

40. In the German aristocracy (including the princes), every member of a family, male or female, bore the title. In contrast, however, an aristocrat's wife bore the title of her husband only if she had a sufficient rank in the aristocracy by birth.

41. About sixty letters and judicial documents: *Landeshauptarchiv Koblenz,* 54–32, 499 and 54–32, 500. See Christophe Duhamelle, "Der verliebte Domherr. Ein Familienkonflikt in der rheinischen Reichsritterschaft am Ende des 18. Jahrhunderts," *Historische Anthropologie* 5 (1997): pp. 404–16. Other cases in the same period and among similar nobilities: Heinz Reif, "Väterliche Gewalt und kindliche Narrheit, Familienkonflikte im katholischen Adel Westfalens vor der französischen Revolution," in *Die Familie in der Geschichte,* ed. Heinz Reif (Göttingen, 1982), pp. 82–113; Jörg Engelbrecht, "Adlige Familienkonflikte am Ende des 18. Jahrhunderts. Das 'Journal d'amour' der Luise von Hompesch aus den Jahren 1797/1798," *Rheinische Vierteljahrsblätter* 53 (1989): pp. 152–77.

42. J. P. Cooper, "Patterns of Inheritance and Settlement by Great Landowners from the Fifteenth to the Eighteenth Centuries," in *Family and Inheritance: Rural Society in Western Europe 1200–1800,* ed. Jack Goody, Joan Thirsk, and Edward Thompson (Cambridge, 1976), pp. 192–327.

43. Pierre Bourdieu, "Les stratégies matrimoniales dans le système de reproduction," in *Annales ESC* 27 (1972), pp. 1105-1125.

Chapter VIII

Rights and Ties that Bind

Mothers, Children, and the State in Tuscany during the Early Modern Period

Giulia Calvi

Paternal Branches, Maternal Branches

From the fourteenth through the nineteenth centuries, the death of a paterfamilias in Tuscany prompted the interest, attention, and intervention of the Court of Wards (Magistrato dei Pupilli). Dilemmas of an emotional nature ranging from economic concerns to choices in the area of education gradually shifted from the private sphere to the public domain of the court and to the language of petitions and judicial decisions.

Charged with protecting the weakest members of the community, the Magistrato dei Pupilli assumed the guardianship of orphans (lacking fathers), the physically handicapped, deaf-mutes, and the insane. This last group was further divided into several classifications, which ranged from the frenetic to the melancholic, and also included the profligate, namely those who were accused of squandering the family inheritance. The institution of the Magistrato dei Pupilli dates from the end of the fourteenth century, but it underwent radical reforms over the course of the next hundred years and again in 1565.[1] The office maintained its responsibilities until the beginning of the nineteenth century, charged mainly with managing the inheritance of orphans whose fathers had died without making a will or without naming a guardian. Several

situations might lead to the handing over of custody to the Magistrate:
(1) if neither the mother nor any member of the paternal side of the
family declared him/herself prepared to accept guardianship and, therefore, the management of the inheritance; (2) in the case of a dispute or
absence of testamental guardians; or (3) when a widow guardian
decided to remarry. Finally, a father could directly appoint the Magistrato dei Pupilli and defer testamental guardianship of minors to it.

Through the documents preserved in the archives of this magistrature, we can trace the history of hundreds of boys, girls, and widows
subjected to the control and protection of officials. Male children
remained under the Magistrate's guardianship until the age of eighteen
and girls until twenty-five, though, in actuality, the guardianship of girls
ended at the time of their marriage or entry into a convent.

Widows came into contact with the Magistrato dei Pupilli when they
were to accept or refuse the guardianship conferred upon them by the
wills of their deceased husbands or, in the case of death *ab intestato*,
when the widows took the initiative in requesting guardianship of their
children. In this manner, hundreds of women's lives found concrete
expression through a public institution. In fact, it is the state, which in
its phase of centralization and expansion, legitimized these women in
their position as interlocutors in familial conflict. It is the state that
began to grant them the right to speak, insofar as their voices were
modulated according to the code found in the statutes and the decrees
of the magistrature, which were also considered to be state law.

Even when surrounded by co-guardians, a widow guardian enjoyed
considerable prestige and authority in legal terms, since she was entitled
to the usufruct (life use) of the family patrimony without actually
inheriting it. Rather, she managed the inheritance in order to consign it
subsequently to the legitimate heir(s), all the while remaining in the
house that she entered upon marrying and keeping her children with
her.[2] Moreover, this position was sanctioned by the *donna et madonna*
formulation of Roman origin. An expression that remained unchanged
over the "long *durée*" of the law (from the classical age through the
eighteenth century), this formulation is recurrent in legal texts, in sentences, and in husbands' wills. A widow was *donna et madonna* and
could remain so with the sole condition that she agree not to remarry:
her second wedding would forever remove her as the guardian of her
children, as well as end her right of usufruct to her dead husband's
property and use of the family home. Legally speaking, a remarried
widow was the equivalent of a dead widow; a guardianship handed over
to the Magistrate was irrevocable and could under no circumstances
ever be reassigned. It is also important to point out that only a father

or paternal grandfather had the legal capacity to hand over a guardian-ship because the guardianship itself was founded upon *patria potestas*, that is, paternal authority. As a result, mothers had no legal right to name guardians in their wills. When they died, they were deprived of the comfort (as specified in the statutes) that one finds from entrusting one's children to the care of people with whom one feels connected through trust or emotional ties.[3]

Placing children under the guardianship of the Magistrate was the end result of a series of renunciations, abandonments, and vacancies. The refusal to assume sometimes extremely heavy responsibilities, extreme poverty, or an unstructured family situation led officials to take on orphans who had often already lost their father some years before and who had been placed in unknown hands, without any of the cir-cumstances ever being reported to the magistrature. In more robust eco-nomic situations, however, the change in guardianship caused serious conflicts between the widow and the paternal side of the family—espe-cially the brothers of the deceased. The act of accepting guardianship was, in fact, the first step which officially sanctioned the position of the widow as *donna et madonna*, with all its inherent privileges. However, if her brother-in-law were named guardian or, in rare instances, her father-in-law, this step could also decree the expulsion of the widow, driven from her husband's house and deprived of her children.[4] The language of the statutes expresses well this polarity in the list of rela-tives who could become guardians: "paternal grandfather, mother, paternal grandmother, uncle on the father's side or full brother, cousin." This paradigmatic, exemplary divide between paternal and maternal sides of the family regarding a question of such economic and emo-tional complexity as the guardianship of orphans is well suited to pre-liminary investigation. We may observe how the position and role of women helped to temper the formal structure of the patrilineal system, breaking down its rigid construction by means of horizontal practices and behaviors. Furthermore, we see here the emergence of an emo-tional and informal bilateralism, which at the same time is measured on the basis of privileges and roles whose juridical and social weight is explicit and officially recognized.

Managing an inheritance and functioning as head of the family con-stitute visible evidence of influence and power. Roman law gave to guardianship of minors the definition *munus musculorum*, and public obligation, which is why the sphere of activity of a guardian widow goes beyond the boundaries of the domestic space.[5]

This is a point upon which the ecclesiastical tradition agrees, a tradi-tion whose treatises concerning widows glorified their heroine-like virtue, their chaste solitude, and the difficult conquest of a "second freedom," finally removed from the sexual appetites of a husband. Virgin or chaste, the women who wanted to excel in areas normally reserved for men also had to escape the slavery of marriage. The extreme example of Judith, widow at the head of an army, offered to the social imagination the representation of a transgression which also marked the recovery of precisely that which a woman's calling to marriage sentenced her to lose: ownership of her body ("neither having possession of her body, nor being able to raise her head from this yoke, obliging her to serve more than once the debauchery and unbridled libido of the man"[6]).

The tradition of the church fathers, especially Ambrose, associated with the widow who renounced a second marriage the idea of freedom, control, and strength of body and soul which made her an asexual model, ipso facto virile. No doubt it is precisely the ambiguity of this sexual status which was the basis for the prestige of the *donna et madonna*; as the head of the family, she enjoyed custody of her children and commanded considerable power in the management of the inheritance and the household, always with the condition that she not remarry.[7] In juridical and social practice, her candidacy for guardianship stood as an alternative to that of her brother-in-law. Thus, if the death of a married man caused tensions, the most significant and the most intensely experienced conflict set the widow of the deceased against his brother. The resolution of such a confrontation was relatively simple (at least formally speaking) if there existed a will which named the guardian. However, in cases to the contrary, it was the Magistrato dei Pupilli's responsibility to entrust one or the other of the opponents with guardianship. Such a choice also meant taking a stand regarding the weight of the maternal family in comparison with the paternal. It was therefore simultaneously the representation of current social discourse as well as of the bilateral practices connecting kinship and transmission.

* * *

Between 1648 and 1766, if we add up all the data concerning Florence and its territory, there were 1,503 cases of legal guardianships (i.e., when fathers died intestate and therefore did not name guardians) (see Tables 8.1 and 8.2). In such instances the Magistrato dei Pupilli preferred to provide for the entrusting of minors to their mother or to their paternal uncle. Following is the data for Florence:

Table 8.1: Guardianships in Florence 1648–1766

Total guardianships:	614	
Guardianships granted to mothers:	463	(75.4%)
Guardianships granted to the paternal side:	139	(22.6%)
	117	to the paternal uncle
	16	to the older brother
	5	to the paternal grandfather
	1	to the paternal grandmother
Unidentified guardianships:	12	(1.9%)

Table 8.2: Guardianships in the Florentine Territory 1652–1733

Total guardianships:	889	
Guardianships granted to mothers:	620	(69.7%)
Guardianships granted to the paternal side:	254	(28.5%)
	234	to the paternal uncle
	20	to the brother or male cousin
Unidentified guardianships:	15	(1.6%)

Overall, then, of 1,503 legal guardianships, 1,083 (72%) were entrusted to mothers; 393 (26.1%) to members of the paternal side of the family; and 27 (1.7%) to unidentified guardians.

A second kind of data confirms this tendency for the magistrature to place increasing value upon the bilateral component of the familial group. In order to accept the guardianship, it was necessary to provide a guarantor whose responsibility lasted for one year and whose name had to be submitted for the approval of officers. In rare cases (which can nevertheless serve as indicators of a trend), the exact relationship between guardian and proposed guarantor is specified in the records. In Florence, the widow relied upon her brother in forty-six cases, while in twenty-six cases, she was assisted by her brother-in-law. This difference narrows in the area outside of Florence: 107 female guardians had their brothers by their sides, 94, their brothers-in-law, while 11 widows were aided by a son who had come of age.

The overall set of data collected highlights the fact that widows from the city had more power and prestige than those from the area situated outside of the walls of Florence. The slightly higher percentage of guardianships entrusted to widows living within the city walls, as well as the presence of their own brothers as guarantors, underscores the fact that the female, maternal side of the family had taken on more importance in urban contexts. By contrast, the paternal side predominated in rural areas, probably insofar as the inheritance was comprised above all of landed property. This seems to reinforce the findings of some anthropological investigations carried out in the area of the Mediterranean which establish a connection between the dispersion of settlements and the social atomization of women (on one hand) and the fact that these women have less power.[8]

Though this data is certainly fragmentary and discontinuous, nevertheless, there emerges an overall, long-term tendency that seems to me unequivocal. The action of the Magistrato dei Pupilli was based upon a precise conception of the central role of mothers, and this jurisprudential activity sanctioned—in the practice of relationships, feelings, and trust—a broadening of the structure of kinship beyond the rigid limits of patrilineal descent.

In my opinion, the widening of reference points which serve as the basis for the intervention of the Magistrato dei Pupilli and which include the maternal family corrects a pessimistic conception of the dowry as an irrevocable element of exclusion, which definitively relegates women to subordinate status. To the contrary, here the fundamental place of widows—and the presence, hardly insignificant, of their brothers—must be equally ascribed to the fact that they had contributed in a substantial manner to the well-being of their families. Indeed, the dowry gave the maternal side of the family a right to intervene and guarantee the well-being of the children born from sisters or daughters. A widow's position as *donna et madonna* rested upon a solid pupillary heritage whose composition was bilateral and whose maternal component was sometimes superior to the paternal. Actually, the second wedding of a mother involved the separation of her dowry from the inheritance, often causing serious economic damage to the orphans. In this specific case, the dowry functioned as a factor empowering women of the elites and their families of origin. But this was not just true in situations of economic strength. Mothers were named as guardians and given custody of their children even or especially in the cases which specify the humble origin or poverty of the orphans ("given the smallness of the inheritance ... in light of the destitute condition"). Given the trifling administrative responsibilities, the magistrature had no fear of sparking conflicts with the paternal side of the family. Therefore, apart from the content of the patrimony, officers chose based upon the status of the head of the family, which involved the status of the widow.

Let us now consider for a moment the main function of this great divide, which existed between the custody of children and the transmission of the patrimony. A long juridical tradition sanctioned one single, essential condition determining the custody of an orphan: no line of succession could connect the guardian and the minor. Mothers often turned to Magistrates to protest the poor treatment (or even death, in extreme cases) inflicted upon their children by paternal uncles, direct heirs of the minors over whom they had held guardianship and custody. *Not* granting custody to someone who would benefit from the death of his charge was therefore a question of vital importance to the Magistrate, so in his statutes, he specifically prohibited the awarding of custody of a minor to anyone who would be "suspected of inheriting from him." Patrilineal succession and testamental practice were both structured upon a vertical line; Men would leave their wealth and name to their sons, brothers, and nephews—those who were included in the group of agnates. In short, paternal inheritance had to remain within the lineage. On the other hand, mothers were kept out of a testamental practice which excluded them from the hereditary line, given that, in their capacity as women, they only had the right to a dowry and, as widows, to the usufruct of their husband's inheritance. In the case of Florence, the city statutes stressed the impossibility for women to inherit from their children in the presence of any male descendants, legal or biological (nephews and grandnephews; sons of the paternal grandfather, the uncle, the brother or the sister; the heirs of these last). But it was precisely this exclusion of women from the transfer of property that rendered them safe as guardians of their children in the sense that, not being the heirs of their offspring, mothers stood to gain nothing by their deaths. It is in this way and with this reasoning that the sentences issued by the Magistrate peremptorily described the mother/children relationship as "above all suspicion," since it was guided by what was considered by jurisprudence to be "pure" love, namely removed from any interest in inheritance. Relieved of the weight of economic determination, liberated from all monetary ties, maternal affection was therefore represented in terms of "gratuitous charity and affection." Since mothers were the juridical guarantors of pure love, they were worthy of absolute confidence, and therefore could be entrusted with guardianship and custody of their orphaned children, even in the case of second marriages.

Thus, the relationship of a widow with her children involved the highest possible status—guardianship—but had absolutely no value in patrimonial transmission, since the mother remained outside of the male hereditary axis. The prestige of her cultural and emotional role was the direct consequence of her precarious position within the line of succession. In the symbolic order, the relationship of a widow with her children is located under the sign of a double exclusion. Insofar as she was a guardian whose only condition was that she not remarry, the widow safeguarded the separation between sexuality and the maternal role. On the other hand, if she were put in charge of the custody of minors, it was because, in never being able to inherit from them, she thus ensured an absolutely selfless love for her children—pure love. The prestige of these mothers was therefore based upon the fact that they had fulfilled their reproductive function and thereafter relinquished the essentially physiological exercise of maternity in order to then assume their functions within a set of rules governed by (conflicting) principles of ethical value coupled with patrimonial *loss* of value.

Conflicts

In official acts, administrative language took shape gradually, consolidating into fixed formulas that would recur until the nineteenth century. Therefore, the contrasts and conflicts which swirled around the cases we encounter in the sixteenth century constitute a paradigmatic point of departure by which we may assess the strategies employed by officers as well as those later adopted by families. I will now recount a particular family conflict, preserving the dialogic and dramatic tone that the sources express as thoroughly as possible. In this sense, I wish to emphasize the capacity of the protagonists of these stories to act, choose, and fight. Their relationship with the institutions which protected guardianship was formulated in terms of positive rapport, request, and intervention granting what were perceived both as individual and collective rights. Indeed, appealing to the Florentine magistracy not only implied calling for protection against the violence of agnates or the arrogance of local governments, but it also prefigured a terrain upon which different points of view and differentiated ethics developed and confronted one another. Thus, it is not necessary to consider women and children only as weak subjects in need of guardianship; we must also see them as protagonists capable of establishing their own standards, at least in some cases.

In the small towns of the Grand Duchy, local administrators, vicars, officers, and notaries, through letters and dispatches, reconstructed the background facts of a situation. The presence of these observers immediately set family conflicts on the stage, as it were, of a public sphere of influence, pressure, and power, which provided multiple voices and interpretations of events. Next to the mother, the children, the brother-in-law, and the grandfather, local civil servants, the Florentine court, and the Grand Duke intervened, taking into account both local statutes and those of the Magistrate (which were also regional state laws and in the process of being centralized). In most cases, it was the father of the widow, namely the most important member of the maternal side of the family, who made an appeal to the Magistrato dei Pupilli (and therefore, ipso facto, to the law of the state and to Florence) in order to assert his rights (and by extension, those of his daughter). On the other side, the brother-in-law, representing the paternal branch, used to his advantage local statutes and the *podestat*. In this sense, the administrative center functioned as the guarantor for women and the maternal side of the family, providing a controlled, composed authority against the centrifugal thrust of the periphery.

The last will of a husband was certainly determinant in controlling the existential course of his widow's life. However, the cultural practices of paternal lineages limited de facto the rights of widows as well as the privileges and freedom granted to them by their deceased husband's will.[9] Conflicts with relatives of the husband would reveal what the authority and autonomy of these women in fact signified, namely a potential critique of the patrilineal order.[10] The clashes between widows and brothers-in-law unfold a practice of widowhood in constant tension with the legal prerogatives, the last wishes of husbands, and the familial strategies of paternal agnates. It was thus that a widow, despite the privileges that the law granted her, could find herself caught in a crossfire in which the guardianship and custody of her children were at stake.

The stories of young women alone with their children remind us closely of the situations experienced by the medieval widows whom Christiane Klapisch-Zuber has studied, women who, in the family books, never spoke in the first person. We would seek in vain to find in the documents a direct expression of their desires or their wishes. We lack even indirect accounts of their deeds, their movements, their activities. The traumatizing events which concerned them—the loss of their husbands, the violent intrusion of brothers-in-law, the custody of their children, a new marriage—did not appear to concern them in the first person, since they were performed by the paternal sides of two lineages. They were but pawns, mere tokens in the relationships among the men who represented their respective lineages. If the widows were no longer sufficiently young and therefore not likely susceptible to immediate remarriage, they would equally guarantee the upholding of rules of patrilineal succession and the vertical transfer of property. Be that as it may, the control exercised by the state over guardianship gradually altered the context of negotiations, promoting the development of a public sphere which gradually broadened, and within which family conflicts were able to be staged and debated. Compared with the late medieval structure of family books based upon the memory of male heads of households, this new discourse legitimized a form of plural narration within which women and children were able to express themselves. Yet, the silence found in the sources for most of the sixteenth century represents a boundary between the *void* of female voices marking the written evidence of the private family in the Renaissance, versus the *abundance* of women's words filling the public pages of the Magistrate. In fact, it was here, in the transition from agnatic writing to administrative writing, that a space was opened for women and minors to voice their own experience of family life. It sounded like a new language, no longer only echoing the dry logic of patrimony and succession, but revealing the complex tangle of emotions that bound the various protagonists together.

Lucrezia

In 1625, after the death of her husband, Lucrezia Brunacci found herself involved in a violent family conflict, which set her brother-in-law and eldest son against the other children who had not yet come of age. Here, the paternal and maternal sides became entangled in an intrigue in which everyone would have something to say, thereby demonstrating an exceptional capability for self-defense and initiative.

Let us step backward for a moment and return to San Miniato on 2 October 1624, when Vincenzo Rimbotti died *ab intestato*, leaving four children: Jacopo, age eighteen; Bernardo, age twelve; Rinaldo, age seven; and Margherita, age five. His widow, Lucrezia Brunacci, was in her thirties and formally renounced guardianship in favor of her brother-in-law, GiovanMaria Rimbotti, who, in turn, presented his request to the Magistrate. An administrator unknown to the family was assigned and the children separated, put in the care of various relatives on the paternal side. The eldest, Jacopo, went to his uncle's; Bernardo and Rinaldo to a second uncle; and Margherita was entrusted to the care of the paternal grandmother after whom she had been named.[11]

The story did not end there. A few months later, on 23 April 1625, through the intermediary of a procurator, Lucrezia presented a petition to the Magistrato dei Pupilli requesting guardianship and custody of her children. Though she had certainly signed the act formally renouncing her children, she claimed she had done so under threat and violence. The procurator Squadrini stated as much before the officers of justice, asserting that "the aforementioned woman Lucrezia by dread and fear and by force was compelled to renounce the guardianship of the children she had born with the aforementioned Vincenzo ... claiming that the guardianship assumed by GiovanMaria Rimbotti her brother-in-law had been accepted without validity ... and as a result that the guardianship taken by the aforementioned officials on the same 4 April was not within their competence, but rather reverted to the woman Lucrezia." As proof of the violence suffered by his client, the case file included a letter written by eighteen-year-old Jacopo to his mother on 13 October 1624, just a few days after the death of his father.

> I want to ask you to give up guardianship as we had agreed, because I assure you that if you don't do it with love, you will be obliged by the Magistrato dei Pupilli to do it by force, with little satisfaction for you and uncle Lesandro. I cannot act as your guarantor, and even if I could, I wouldn't want to, and I am determined to stay in San Miniato and am already enrolled with a Master to learn. If Uncle Alesandro comes to you, let me know immediately so I can properly arrange things.

He then ordered her to consign "all the barrels that we have at home" to "a worker for Uncle Giovanbattista, whom we ordered to put in barrels the wine that will be coming to us." He concluded by instructing that she "take account of all our affairs so that no confusion ensue. Your son, Jacopo Rimbotti."[12]

On 10 March 1625, Lucrezia took up the pen and intervened directly, writing herself to the Grand Duchess Maria Maddalena. In the midst of these forceful actions, she recalled all that her relatives had failed to respect, especially the promise that she made to her husband on his deathbed to take care of their children. Vincenzo "indicated that [he] wanted her to manage their children's upbringing and that she was disposed in this to do the will of her husband" but this agreement had been broken by the intrusion of "the brother of her dead husband [who] frightened her with a letter which he had had written by her eldest son, and she was forced to leave her children to take refuge in Pisa with her brother and to renounce guardianship against her will." Away from home, Lucrezia could not get back her dowry. That is why she is being "tormented" by her own brother "because she intended to remarry."[13]

A few days later, the Chancellery of the Magistrate saw another letter arrive, this one with childlike, unsteady writing. It was Bernardo, the twelve-year-old son, who, in his own name and the name of his little brother and sister, wrote: "To be happy, I want to go back with *Signora* Lucrezia Brunacci my mother ... and another of my younger brothers, and Margherita my sister are happy to go back with our mother aforesaid and I have written for myself and for them who don't know how to write, I beg you because I am of minor age. ..."[14]

Graziadio Squadrini was one of the best-known procurators in Florence during this period, sporting a clientele well-stocked with patricians, court artists, and intellectuals. Thus, his influence during the proceeding to which he signed his name, the well-documented case file, and the sentence, a *rescriptum* from the Grand Duke who ordered the immediate administration of *spedita giustizia*, all led to the repeal of the first proceeding. In fact, the Magistrates decree that "the renunciation of guardianship made by the woman Lucrezia did not take place as it was made in dread, fear, and force."[15] The testimony of brother-in-law Giovanbattista Rimbotti made no difference, though he directly accused Lucrezia of having "abandoned" her children and squandering the inheritance.[16]

The officials therefore returned custody to Lucrezia, nullifying both the guardianship taken on by her brother-in-law and the one assumed by the Magistrate. Management of the property therefore passed to the mother as well, and the administrator who had just been named returned the guardian books to her. On 2 December 1625, Lucrezia began proceedings for the restitution of her dowry, and on 12 December, she also won custody of her daughter Margherita.[17]

The story of Lucrezia and her children opened with a scenario whose violence has subsequently become familiar. And yet the vicious exclusion of the widow, the arrogance of her eldest son, and the torments which her brother inflicted upon her were all countered by the adherence of this affair to the formalities imposed by the law. This safeguarded a space where points of view, wishes, desires, personal ties, and emotions could be expressed which ran counter to the interests of lineage. Violence, threats, and torments found their forms of expression through the intervention of the procurator, the testimonies and the petitions, all of which were attentive to and respectful of the standards imposed by statutes and deadlines. A mutual pact of communicative exchange was established between this woman and the Magistrate to the extent that she accepted the norms of legal language. In exchange, the Magistrate's function as guarantor emerged clearly, on the one hand, bringing to the surface the trusting relationship with the institutions that the widow nourished and, on the other hand, prompting the protective response of the court which restored her rights. And the few short lines written by little twelve-year-old Bernardo brought into further relief the power of emotional bonds and the intensity of feelings involved in the conflict.

Though, in this instance, a widow lodged a complaint and won satisfaction, often the explicit or underlying conflicts dragged on for long periods without resolution. This demonstrates that the privileges of the law which protected the widow were, in reality, subject to familial practices, connections—in short, to a culture still conditioned by the vertical relations of paternal lineage.

The fact that a woman passed to the head of a family actually implied a symbolic and social reversal of the familial structure, a turnabout which was constantly challenged by the paternal side. Decisions concerning both the administration of patrimony and the education and future of the children would open up disputes which never entirely died down, with brothers-in-law who sometimes lived in the same residence as the widow and her children. The problem of the house is particularly interesting and offers unusual viewpoints of the forms and relationship dynamics of these groups. To live under the same roof generally raised the question of maintenance for the children (why pay for it when one lives within the same walls?), often subject to the humiliations and greed of paternal uncles and cousins. The threads of these contrasts sometimes allow us to detect the need for autonomy on the part of mothers and children in relation to paternal relatives, a need which expressed itself in specific terms: to have one's own space.

In these conflicts, where each person stepped in and acted as a member of a group of blood relatives or of cohabitants, a thin but durable line marked the boundary between roles and forms of membership in a family. This desire for an enclosed, separate space, which physically delineated a threshold of privacy in emotional relationships, emphasized the fact that the mother/children nucleus could be displaced beyond the rules of paternal lineage, could go against these rules. The Magistrato dei Pupilli listened to this request and intervened, which reinforced the idea that these events undermined the vertical structure of the patrilineal system.

Generally speaking, the desire to have one's own home went hand in hand with wanting to live with one's children. However, this implied dividing up the inheritance of the family by dividing up household fittings and furnishings, which usually remained in the paternal home where the awkward presence of the brothers of the deceased weighed heavily. The minor children who would go to live with their mother received an alimentary sum for "food and clothing" to be paid at pre-arranged, allotted times along with the income from the inheritance left by their father. This caused continual appraisals, appeals, and requests. The paternal side would generally offer to settle these disputes by accommodating the orphans in the family house. To live under the same roof and be seated at the same table technically nullified the alimentary expenditure to be paid to the children, which allowed the men of the paternal side to hold tightly to the reigns of family governance.

Conflicts between widows and their brothers-in-law would smolder for long periods of time, and sometimes explode violently. In certain cases, spectacular gestures and dramatic blows from one party or the other disrupted the order of administrative procedures, which the Magistrate required be respected in order to protect the institutional ritual of neutralization of immediate and direct conflicts.

The act of placing children in their mother's care was evaluated on the basis of a solid tradition and a series of criteria, often debated in the actual practices that informed the officers when interviewing relatives and children. The *infanti* of less than three years were almost automatically entrusted to the care of their mothers, unless the latter had explicitly renounced custody—which could happen—by abandoning them to one relative or another. Daughters, too, were more easily placed with their mothers until the age of seven years, after which time the Magistrate often decreed that they be placed "in education" (*in serbanza*) in a monastery chosen by the paternal or maternal side of the family. Boys of more than five years were frequently entrusted to the father's family, which had to provide for their education.

Consideration was also taken for the health of the minor, if special care were needed, and in some cases, for their mental equilibrium, something which the texts of the period diagnosed by resorting to various nuances and degrees of melancholy. But generally, officers tended to attach more importance to the emotional influence and educative role of mothers in the absence of their husbands. Indeed, one observes in the sentences the recurring remark that if the father were living, a child of either gender (in other words, even male) would remain in the care of its mother until the age of three years. Without this masculine figure, and almost as if to compensate for this void, it was necessary to entrust a child to the mother's care beyond the usual threshold of seven years, on a case by case basis. The role of the mother was therefore gradually reinforced when the father was missing. Membership in the group of agnates on the father's side was obviously extremely important in the construction of identity for young boys, whose character would risk finding itself weakened by the extended proximity of their mothers.

Around the middle of the seventeenth century, this concern also appeared in sermons and treatises on the family. The Jesuit Paolo Segneri believed that the influence of mothers upon the education of their children was decisive, since it formed not merely "half the children," as Aristotle had observed, but "almost all" of them. Mothers' love was "disorderly and excessive" and, particularly for the eldest son, so stifling and exclusive that it rendered her "unfair toward the other children." Out of love for this son, she forgot to think about God, to recite her rosary, to practice the sacraments. In sum, she finally loses her soul in slavery to this "object of idolatry."[18]

This bond of passionate dependence between mother and male child, wherein the latter "has no responsibility for the excessive affection which his mother holds for him," is important; it is a symptom of the transition at work in the texts of the Renaissance—especially of Alberti—from the physiological conception of maternal love to a vision of the familial microcosm dominated by the maternal figure and her emotions. Indeed, the discourse of the family from the beginning of the modern era described an opposition between the perfection of paternal love, which endured over time because it was made visible through name, patrimony, and lineage; and maternal love, which became deeply rooted and survived exclusively in the nurturing body, and which therefore contained all the dangers of inconstancy, imperfection, and abandonment. Once removed from the immediate perimeter of his birth, the child could end up at risk of experiencing the futility of an emotion whose boundaries were fragile like those of the body and temporary like the presence of women in lineages. In this sense, Klapisch-Zuber, when describing the model of the good mother, depicts her in terms of a woman who, as a widow, devotes herself to her children and to their home, refusing to enter into a new marriage and thereby loving them with a love that "took its full value from its masculine connotations."[19] The virtues of this mother are therefore the masculine virtues of fidelity to lineage. On the other hand, in the text of the Jesuit Segneri, the emotional intensity of the maternal tie was produced by a long, daily journey built of care and attention, namely the "weight, suffering, and pain which the child is for its mother." This is why "the conjugal yoke was called the matrimonial bond rather than patrimony, since it has more weight for the mother than the father."[20]

This explicit recognition of the importance which the maternal line assumed in a family discourse separating the domain of transmission, on one hand, from that of emotions, on the other, went hand in hand with the practice of the Magistrato dei Pupilli. The sentences of this office reinforced the expansion of the autonomous domain of maternal care compared with the interests of the patrimony. And if the affection of a father had less power, Segneri explained further, it is because he was dominated by concern for leaving a patrimony: "The love of fathers then is not really as sensitive as that of the [mothers], nor as passionate toward his children, but marked instead by avarice in order to leave them a patrimony."[21] While in Renaissance texts family affection was identified with the interests and substance of lineages, in the second half of the sixteenth century, a different interpretation made itself felt, separating and engendering, as it were, the by now opposite meanings of "love" and "patrimony." In other words, if agnates used the rhetoric of money, mothers voiced that of emotions.

The domain of caregiving, strengthened by institutions and defined by juridical language, conferred its identity upon the maternal relationship, which, in time, developed autonomously from the patrimonial interests of agnatic lineages. This imbalance between formal exclusion from succession and increasing ethical empowerment allowed the maternal subject to emerge more and more clearly, to speak, and—over the course of the eighteenth century—to take control of the domestic sphere.

(Translation: Kelly J. Maynard)

Notes

1. Firenze. Archivio di Stato (ASF), Magistrato dei Pupilli et Adulti avanti il Principato, Statuti et Ordini della Corte et Magistrato delli Officiali de Pupilli et Adulti della Città di Firenze riformati il XX Agosto 1565, F.248; the edition of the *Statuti* from the Middle Ages is by Francesca Morandini, "Statuti et Ordinamenti dei Pupilli et Adulti nel periodo della Repubblica fiorentina (1388-1534)," *Archivio Storico Italiano* 408 (1955): pp. 523–51, 409 (1956): pp. 92–117, and 410 (1957): pp. 87–103; Caroline M. Fisher, "The State as Surrogate Father: State Guardianship in Renaissance Florence 1368–1532," (Ph.D. diss., Brandeis University, 2003). Fisher writes, "During the first century and a half of its existence this government service contributed to the survival of over 3,300 families, and the Pupilli served as guardians for over 8,000 individual orphans" (p. 26).
2. Martha C. Howell, in *The Marriage Exchange: Property, Social Place, and Gender in Cities of the Low Countries 1300–1550* (Chicago, 1998), argues that the privileging of the children against the widow in the inheritance law of the northern cities first started under the pressure of the market and the state—a new policy of building capital instead of the old policy of building up a unit of production based on the household.
3. Yan Thomas, "La divisione dei sessi nel diritto romano," in *Storia delle donne in Occidente. L'Antichità*, ed. George Duby and Michelle Perrot (Roma-Bari, 1990), pp. 103–76; Thomas Kuehn, *Law, Family and Women: Toward a Legal Anthropology of Renaissance Italy* (Chicago, 1991); idem, "Person and Gender in the Law," in *Gender and Society in Renaissance Italy*, ed. Judith C. Brown (London, New York, 1998), pp. 87–106.

4. Cristiane Klapisch-Zuber, *Women, Family, and Ritual in Renaissance Italy* (Chicago, 1985), in particular "'The Cruel Mother': Widowhood and Dowry in Florence in the Fourteenth and Fifteenth Centuries," pp. 117–31; Isabelle Chabot, "'La sposa in nero'. La ritualizzazione del lutto delle vedove fiorentine (secoli XIV-XV)" *Quaderni Storici* 86 (1994): pp. 421–62.
5. The guardianship of orphans was not exclusively a prerogative of Roman Law. See Marilyn Dannel, "Orphanhood and Marriage in Fifteenth Century Ghent," in *Marriage and Social Mobility in the Late Middle Ages* [Mariage et mobilité sociale au bas moyen age], ed. Walter Prevenier, *Studia Historica Gandensia* 274 (1989): pp. 99–111; Martha Howell, "Marriage, Family, Patriarchy in Douai, 1350–1600," ibid., pp. 9–34; Barbara Hanawalt, *Growing Up in Medieval London: The Experience of Childhood in History* (New York, 1993); eadem, "The Widows's Mite: Provisions for Medieval London Widows," in *Upon My Husband's Death: Widows in the Literature and Histories of Medieval Europe*, ed. Louise Mirrer (Ann Arbor, MI, 1992), pp. 21–45; E. Clark, "City Orphans and Custody Laws in Medieval England" *The American Journal of Legal History* 34 (1990): pp. 168–87; David Nicholas, *The Domestic Life of a Medieval City: Women, Children, and the Family in XIV Century Ghent* (Nebraska, 1985); Julie Hardwick, *The Practice of Patriarchy: Gender and the Politics of Household Authority in Early Modern France* (Philadelphia, 1998).
6. "… non havendo potestà del proprio corpo, né potendo levare il capo fuor di questo giogo, facendole mestieri di servir molte volte all'intemperanza e sfrenata libdine dell'huomo." Giulio Cesare Cabei, *Ornamenti della Gentil Donna Vedova* (Venezia, 1574); Cesare Lanci, *Esempi de la virtù de le donne* (Firenze, 1590); Giorgio Trissino, *Epistola de la vita che dee tenere una donna vedova* (Roma, 1523); Lodovico Dolce, *Dialogo de la institution de le donne* (Venezia, 1545); Giovan Battista De Luca, *Il cavaliere e la dama* (Roma, 1675); Barbara J. Todd, "The Virtuous Widow in Protestant England," in *Widowhood in Medieval and Early Modern Europe*, ed. Sandra Cavallo and Lyndan Warner (Singapore, 1999), pp. 66–83; Lyndan Warner, "Widows, Widowers and the Problem of 'Second Marriages' in Sixteenth Century France," ibid., pp. 84–107.
7. Antoinette Fauve-Chamoux, "Matrimonio, vedovanza, e divorzio," in *Storia della famiglia in Europa*, ed. Marzio Barbagli and David I. Kertzer (Roma, Bari, 2001), pp. 307–51.
8. George Ravis Giordani, ed., *Femmes et patrimoine dans les sociétés rurales de l'Europe méditerranéenne* (Paris, 1987); Francesco Benigno, "The Southern Italian Family in the Early Modern Period: A Discussion of Co-residential Patterns," *Continuity and Change* 4 (1989): pp. 165–94; David I. Kertzer and Richard P. Saller, ed., *The Family in Italy from Antiquity to the Present* (New Haven and London, 1991).
9. Nino Tamassia, *Il testamento del marito* (Bologna, 1905); Enrico Pincherli, *La vedova. Patria potestà, diritti patrimoniali, seconde nozze* (Torino, 1901).
10. Julie Hardwick, "Widowhood and Patriarchy in Seventeenth-Century France," *Journal of Social History* 26, no. 4 (1992): pp. 133–48; Giulia Calvi, "Maddalena Nerli and Cosimo Tornabuoni: A Couple's Narrative of Family History in Early Modern Florence" *Renaissance Quarterly* 45 (1992): pp. 312–39.
11. ASF., MPAP, Campione di Partiti, F.42, c. 156, 4 April 1625.
12. ASF., MPAP, Suppliche con informazione, F. 2290, n.176.
13. ASF., MPAP, Suppliche con informazione, F. 2290, n.176.
14. ASF., MPAP, Suppliche con informazione, F. 2290, n.176, 28 March 1624.
15. ASF., MPAP, Suppliche con informazione, F. 2290, n.176, 23 April 1625.
16. ASF., MPAP, Suppliche con informazione, F. 2290, n.176, 16 July 1625.

17. According to Cristiane Klapisch-Zuber, "The Cruel Mother," pp. 121–22, Florentine women in the Renaissance could not take any children with them, if they took the dowry out of the household of their deceased husbands. In the seventeenth century, things had changed somewhat, since the state was now mediating between family members. Yet, in principle, the rule was still valid. In this case, the paternal kin used the repayment of the dowry to take guardianship away from the mother.

18. Paolo Segneri, *Il cristiano istruito nella sua legge* (Firenze, 1686), xi, pp. 138–39; xii, p. 141; Elisa Novi Chavarria, "Ideologia e comportamenti familiari nei predicatori italiani fra Cinque e Settecento. Tematiche e modelli," *Rivista Storica Italiana* 100 (1988): pp. 75–102. A narrative of fatherly love is in Margaret L. King, *The Death of the Child Valerio Marcello* (Chicago, 1994).

19. Cristiane Klapisch-Zuber, "The Cruel Mother," p. 129.

20. Paolo Segneri, *Il cristiano*, vii, p. 171.

21. Paolo Segneri, *Il cristiano*, xxi, p. 143.

Chapter IX

Kinship, Marriage, and Politics

Gérard Delille

Today, most historians agree that in every historical age, kinship and marriage have been of central importance for the creation of political associations (parties, factions, local councils, etc.) and for the nature of their relationships, whether harmonious or conflicting. But in most cases, historians provide no more than general assertions based upon the recognition of some kinship or marriage link between the different protagonists without any systematic study of these relationships, which, in any event, would be difficult to conduct given the current state of documentation for the medieval and early modern periods. Frequently, kinship and marriage are perceived as factors that contribute, among so many others (clients, friends, individuals linked by economic interests or religious convictions), to the construction of political networks of variable size. The dangers of this type of approach are obvious. Connections between individuals and the description of their networks may reflect the subjective impressions of the historian rather than objective reality. In a letter dated 10 August 1567, for example, certain protagonists of political struggles in the large town of Altamura, in the region of Apulia, give a precise description of the network of relationships between the municipal council members of 1566–1567 and Giovan Vincenzo De Notariis, who presided over the formation of the council but was not himself a member. All were related to him by blood or through marriage, often very closely. But we only know by accident from the contents of this letter that the entire network must have led back to this obscure figure. If we had restricted ourselves to the study of relationships between the individual members of the council, we would have described a totally different kind of collectivity.

In-depth research on this subject is still rare. Among the most interesting, I would cite that of David Warren Sabean on Neckarhausen[1] and that of Wolfgang Kaiser on Marseille.[2] By the study of very different cases with very different methodologies, both, it seems to me, attempt to go beyond impressionistic approaches to reconstruct and understand the deep mechanisms that link kinship, marriage, and sociopolitical structures. These studies also place emphasis, quite rightly, upon the importance of political rituals and symbols of power. More recently, the contributions of Christophe Duhamelle on the nobility of the Rhenish ecclesiastical territories and Michel Nassiet on the Breton and French nobility have reevaluated connections between kinship and politics.[3]

It is still too often explicitly or implicitly assumed that a relationship constituted through marriage or kinship is a straightforward instrument to further a political goal. In fact, certain cases simply answer the structural exigencies of situations of conflict (against an outsider, my brothers and my cousins will be my allies; against my cousin, only my brothers will support me), while others may be neutral or even negative—the marriages between the royal houses of France and Austria did not prevent repeated armed conflicts between the two countries in the first half of the seventeenth and in the second half of the eighteenth century. Marriage can be a sign of submission, the gift from the vanquished to the victor, or the forfeit required by the latter—the treaty of the Pyrenees (1659), which marked the definitive defeat of Spain, expressly provided for the marriage of Maria Theresa of Austria with the future Louis XIV. Conversely, if marriages were to be arranged for immediate political ends, their goals were not always in harmony. From the point of view of the long term, they might involve the play of reciprocities, the so-called rules which govern the "circulation" of wives, encourage marriages to consolidate already pledged political relationships, or block the development of other strategies. To borrow a famous maxim from Voltaire, political choices create marriages in their own image, but the latter make good the former.

The difficulty—and the interest—of studies of these complex issues derives from the fact that they are situated at the juncture of the "structural"—of marriage patterns constructed and transmitted over a long period—and the "conjunctural," that which furthers immediate and individual short-term strategies. The present chapter aims, by means of an analysis of a certain number of significant examples, to reflect theoretical problems and practical methodologies.

The first question is whether, for the medieval and early modern periods, a "European" or "Christian" system of marriage exists, or whether there are general mechanisms of exchange that are identical, recur everywhere, and function independently of the sociopolitical configurations of the immediate environment.

In Arles, the Antonelle family studied by Baron Du Roure[4] rose, from the beginning of the fifteenth to the middle of the sixteenth century, from the condition of modest fishermen at Saintes Maries de la Mer to that of local village nobility. Guillaume, the eldest, still registered as "worker of Arles" in 1536, moved up to the rank of hosiery merchant in 1544, then to bourgeois in 1552 (his younger brother was a *laboreur* (tenant farmer). His children, Gonin and Antoine, were ennobled in May 1578, and François, the son of Gonin, assumed the office of Noble Consul in 1602. Until then, the marriages this family entered into were with families from the Arles bourgeoisie, giving access to a world that was scarcely more well to do but a lot better known in terms of genealogy than the small local nobility. Even if their marriages, taken together, appear to be randomly scattered, the various Antonelles would, however, in just under a century, repeatedly form marriages with the Icard, de la Rivières, and Destrech families.

The relationship with the Icard family, also originating from Notre Dame de la Mer, occurred in the following way (Figure 9.1).[5] In each generation, a marriage connects the two families, or rather the two lineages, since there was constant alternation from one line to another. The marriage of Etienne Icard to Catherine d'Antonelle was followed by that of their respective niece and nephew, Antoinette Icard and Louis d'Antonelle. In 1702, Marie Icard, daughter of Nicolas, married Etienne d'Antonelle, issuing from another line of cousins descended from Guillaume d'Antonelle. Only one marriage fails to strictly comply with this alternation between lines, that of Nicolas Icard with Marie d'Antonelle. The latter was, in fact, the granddaughter of Louis, and the marriage was therefore consanguineous in the third degree, whereas the others avoid all the canonical prohibitions of this type.[6] This exception to the rule is explained by a very simple fact. Marie d'Antonelle was the one and only heiress and was therefore designated to marry according to another frequently applied rule, one which brings to mind that of the *épiclérat* in Ancient Greece, a close cousin.[7]

The exchange between alternate male lines is complemented by marriages with the female lines that complete and greatly strengthen the kinship networks. In this way, during the first generation, Antoine d'Antonelle, brother of Catherine, married Marie, daughter of Antoine de la Rivière and Jeanne Icard, issuing from a line of cousins of Etienne

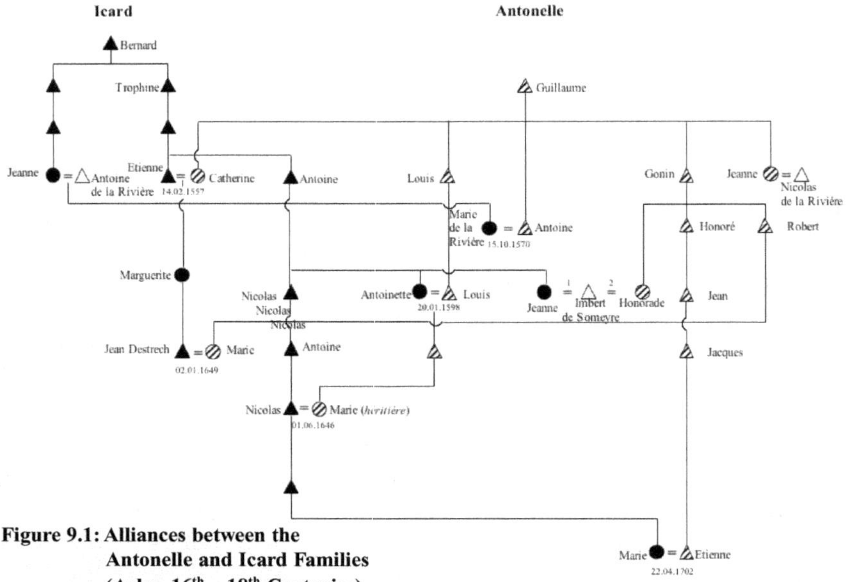

Figure 9.1: Alliances between the Antonelle and Icard Families (Arles, 16th – 18th Centuries)

Icard, Catherine's husband. Such crossings, through a daughter of one of the two families, are frequent. It is important to emphasize the matrilineal side of this system of relations.

Another feature concerning the relations between the different family groups should be emphasized. Among the sons of Guillaume d'Antonelle, it becomes clear, according to the expression used by the documents of the time, that Antoine—the one who married Marie de la Rivière—"created a branch," founding his own line, independent of those of his brothers and sisters. In fact, all his descendants would forge marriages with new families, the Reynauds, the Roux-Gonins, the Artauds, and the de Broglias, all of which had been strangers to the Antonelle family tree. This process of differentiation reappears in a continuous manner, as the family spreads itself. Among the sons of Gonin, François, the elder, sets in train a new circle of exchange from which the Icards, the de la Rivières, and the Desterchs are excluded.

We find the same practices among the other noble families of Arles. In the course of the development of a lineage, the exchange between alternate lines of two families does not extend to all of the new branches, but concentrates upon a certain number of them, while the others construct their own network of relations, which do not regularly cross the former. There is therefore progressive segmentation, but current research does not enable us to identify precisely how this process occurs, whether according to the order of birth of children, to the mechanism of hereditary transmission, to possible conflicts inside the family, to the political preferences and adhesion to different factions or parties. Is segmentation constant, or does it intervene at certain moments during the expansion of a lineage?

The study of these questions enables a better understanding of the connection between kinship and marriage, on the one hand, and political strategy as an institutionalized system and occasional conflict, on the other. I have endeavored, for the large rural town of Manduria in southern Italy, to show how, within the framework of great lineages, the older lines tended to maintain noble status, while the younger ones fell into the popular class (*populari*), which automatically led them to play divergent political roles—the offices apportioned to the two orders were strictly differentiated. Following the extinction of a principal line, the closest collateral line could, however, move up by reclaiming noble rank. Political conflicts could also modify this fine mechanism for maintaining internal hierarchy. In the 1580s, the "median" branches (third and fourth born) of the Pasanisa lineage seized municipal power and drove the only surviving senior member from the village, while keeping the lines descending from a fifth-youngest child in their status as commoners. They thus assured victory within their own lineage, their permanent anchorage within the local nobility, and their lasting political influence upon the community (still effective in the nineteenth century).[8]

While the mechanisms of segmentation and for maintaining hierarchies developed rapidly in the course of the sixteenth and seventeenth centuries, they were not the same everywhere. By the sixteenth century in Altamura, the younger members of noble families no longer descended to the ranks of commoners, because unlike Manduria, it enjoyed the title of Città (City) and the privilege of Nobilità separata (exclusive nobility). The competition between younger offspring was thus made more urgent and increased the hostility and tensions within lineages, but the "symbolic heritage" of families to which political privileges were linked remained anchored in the older lines. The principle of equal distribution that, still in the sixteenth century, governed the division of moveable goods and real estate between heirs did not apply to this so-called symbolic capital, which was often more important. It guaranteed access to certain kinds of power, to positions of responsibility, and to important sources of revenue and mechanisms of enrichment—thus demonstrating the importance of studying succession to different kinds of "goods."

Despite considerable institutional, political, and legal differences, marriages between alternate lines occurred just as frequently among the great families of Manduria as among those of Altamura and the noble families of Arles. Everywhere, this mechanism displays patrilineal lines around which long-term exchanges were organized, a secondary but substantial role for matrilineal lines, and segmentation inside the different family lines. In very extensive groups like the Meyrans, the Glandevès, the Forbins, or the Estang-Parades, these relations between alternate lines function in a very systematic way and structure an important proportion of marital unions. Within the great provincial nobility, women could circulate between certain families (the Castellanes, the Villeneuves, the Pontévès, the Vintimille-Lascaris, etc.) for centuries. I have shown elsewhere that this play between alternate lines, which enables the replication of marital unions while respecting legal restrictions applying to consanguines and close affinal kin, emerged in the Middle Ages and continued to the seventeenth century in numerous regions of Europe (southern and northern Italy, Estremadura, Burgundy, Belgium, and Saxony).[9] Except in very few cases (the butchers of Limoges, the great German noble lineages), they disappear completely in the course of the eighteenth and nineteenth centuries, leaving the way open for unions between simple family or sibling groups or individuals, each developing an independent game.

The exchange between alternate lines very much constitutes one of the fundamental elements of the so-called European system of marriage. Most often, it took the form of exchange between patrilineal lines, complemented by irregular and less frequent unions between matrilineal lines. Still, the combination of the two forms could sometimes be more balanced and systematic. This seems to have been the case for the west of France and for England. There, male lines were not clearly distinguished from female ones. The English royal family can boast Norman origins, but only by including several female cross connections that the Capetians—the French royal family—would never have taken into consideration in defining themselves as a dynasty. When a line developed through a female link, it could eventually lead to a change in the family name, which tends to mask the workings of the system and makes study of it very difficult. This situation should perhaps be related to customs of succession—in particular, the Norman custom that imposed a strictly equal division of inherited properties between all children, both sons and daughters.

The mechanism of exchange between alternate lines is in no way abstract and was not thought of in the long term as a kind of gigantic covering having to envelop all the successive generations and to bind together a fixed and defined collection of families. In fact, it resulted from the repeated application of short-term closed circuits, which were anchored in the actual lives of the families—in particular, in their demographic circumstances—while always responding to the same fundamental principle—the replication of marriage, not in the future generation, but through the collateral lines. The alliance between the uncle's nephew (or niece) with the aunt's niece (or nephew) was the simplest and the most common (Figure 9.2).

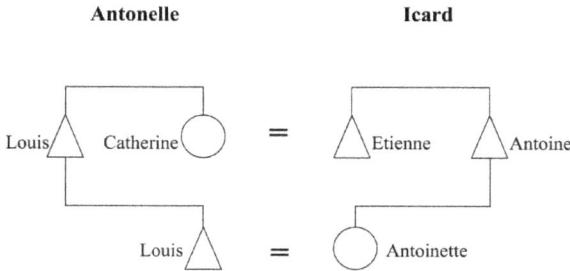

Figure 9.2: Marriages between Uncle/Niece and Aunt/Nephew (Antonelle and Icard Families, Arles, 16ᵗʰ Century)

This form recurs everywhere in Western Europe. It is enough that such a practice be repeated regularly in the course of generations to construct a system of exchange between alternate lines. This very supple mechanism could combine in every way possible the agnatic and uterine pathways as well as different generational levels. Again, the Antonelle family provides a very nice example of this (Figure 9.3).

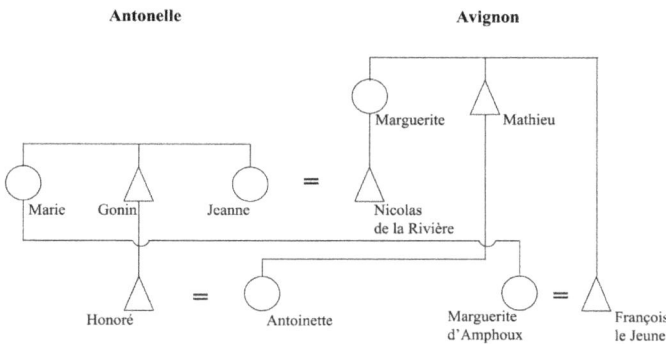

Figure 9.3: Integenerational Exchanges (Antonelle and Avignon Families, Arles, 16ᵗʰ Century)

Remarriages were also often used to complete the circles of exchange between collateral family lines, for example, the two marriages
of Imbert de Someyre made the respective nieces of Etienne Icard and
Catherine d'Antonelle sisters-in-law (Figure 9.4).

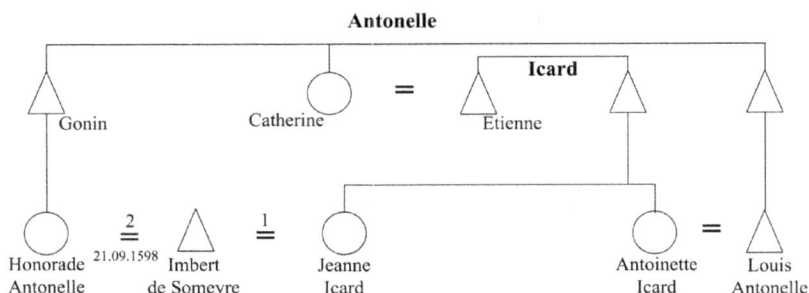

Figure 9.4: Remarriage and *bouclages*
(Arles, 16th Century)

I could add other examples, but this is not the place to give a minute
analysis of all these practices for forging links. It is enough simply to
stress the fact that they represent the most elementary forms, the atoms
of the wider, more fully constructed system of exchanges between
alternate lines, and that an attentive study of the genealogies—when
the data they provide are accurate and full—of noble and commoner
families, for the medieval and the early modern periods, shows that
they can be found everywhere recurrently. This does not mean that
there was complete uniformity. For example, in building connections
through remarriages, Burgundy seems to have had a high frequency of
marriages between a widower and a widow followed by those of the
children of the first marriages, while in the Germanic countries, it was
more usual for second marriages to be accompanied by the union of an
offspring from a previous marriage to a collateral relative of the new
partner (brother/sister or nephew/niece).[10] Furthermore, the chronology of the development of these mechanisms of alliance varied considerably, developing earlier in some countries (England) and later in
others (southern Italy).

What relationship does such a system of circulation through marriage have with political associations or allegiances and with political
struggles? This question emerges from our description of the maneu-
verings to form alliances and the construction of marital ties. These
developed in the context of very extensive restrictions (up to the fourth

degree of consanguinity or connection through marriage) imposed by the Church. In jumping from one line to another, families circumvented such restrictions while also regularly replicating unions and maintaining, at the heart of the system, a general principal of reciprocity.[11] However, there was no application of rigid rules or mechanisms of circulation. Two families could continue for four or five centuries with exchanges among alternate lines, but could also, at certain moments, break the trend and turn towards other partners. The nephews and nieces of earlier spouses might marry between themselves or might not, transferring the function of replicating the marriage link to other relatives or to other generations. Numerous factors, especially demographic vicissitudes, could intervene. There were not always brothers and sisters with their own progeny. Beyond this, considerations of an economic and political nature could intervene to disrupt a pattern of exchange.

Let us now return to the marriage form of uncle/niece with aunt/nephew, illustrated by the Antonelles and the Icards (Figure 9.2). The pathway through collateral relatives occurs in both cases in the masculine line (Antoine Icard and Louis d'Antonelle), and the second marriage—that of the nephew and niece—again unites an Antonelle with an Icard. The linkage, in this case, closes in on itself (the Antonelles have given a daughter to the Icards which has been returned to them in the succeeding generation) and cannot be repeated. But one of these collateral relatives could have been a woman—all types of exchange, combining male and female lines indifferently in fact seem possible—and the second marriage would have thus associated an Antonelle or an Icard with a representative of a third patriline. One would then be in the presence of an open network of generalized exchange (A marries B marries C) with very different implications from those of the first, patrilateral and closed. We see how much the rules, which govern the differentiation of elementary systems of kinship, underpin the complex system with which we are concerned here.[12] This is an important point, in theoretical as well as practical terms, but it cannot be developed in the context of this short chapter.

The choice between a crossed patrilateral or matrilateral connection and a parallel patrilateral or matrilateral connection culminates in the construction of different kinds of networks and, at any moment, the system can be opened or closed by the choice of one route or another. It is at this level that factors of a political nature can intervene.

This is particularly true as regards, for example, remarriages. In the fourteenth century, the multiple remarriages of Jean de Gruyère to women who were, themselves, widows, resulted in chains of generalized exchanges with the families of the spouses of these widows. In the

same way, the different marriages of Agnes of Württemberg and of
Kraft Hohenlohe-Weikersheim (thirteenth century), or those of Fer-
rante Pasanisa in Manduria in the seventeenth century, forged relationships with so-called families-in-law, formerly strangers to one another,
thereby recreating the network of marital unions. This mechanism of
opening up generally depends upon a second marriage with a widow.
But remarriages can also close up a cycle and express an endogamous
choice. It seems that this was the case in Arles with Imbert de Someyre
(Figure 9.4) who married two single girls successively, Jeanne Icard and
Honorade d'Antonelle. There would be no subsequent replication of
these unions.

Consequently, the challenge facing the historian is to attempt to
understand the exact combination of certain choices of kinship and of
marriage and their concomitant political implications, both in the
medium and the long term. In Verviers (Belgium) in the seventeenth
century, all the members of the Pirson sibling group married representatives—or their children—of the Le Pas de Sécheval sibling group. The
two families united—in a sense that was also political—to the highest
degree possible. They also strongly determined the political choices of
their descendants, who could not marry among themselves or put in
place a system of exchange between alternate lines for four generations
because all were close blood relatives. The linkage of uncle/niece with
aunt/nephew could not, for example, be activated because the nieces
and nephews were also first cousins. They were obliged to form unions
outside the two groups of origin and to initiate a program and a strategy of political action accordingly.

The system thus obeys general rules which are precise and, at certain
levels, constraining (replication of marriages through collateral family
links), but then leave a wide scope for opportunities for manipulation
based on political motives or objectives. The principle of reciprocity
remains powerful and, over time, changes the direction of strategies or
political choices, but, beyond this, it can be played in a variety of ways.

In concrete terms, how does such a coupling of kinship and marriage
with politics appear to the historian? In the case of Arles, abundant
documentation of communal institutions and local political life makes
it possible to identify precise configurations. In 1617, a document
establishes all the relationships of kinship and marriage existing
between all the members of the municipal council. As a result, the
presence of two distinct groups can be detected, one centered on the
families—or rather, on certain branches of the families—de la Rivière,
Procelet (a branch of the Fos family), Albe, Meyran, Romieu, and
another on the Quiqueran de Beaujeu, the Arlatan, the L'Estang-

Parade, the Boche, and another line of the Porcelets. Our Icards and our Antonelles appear in the first group, but in a marginal position. The latter is represented, in part, by new nobles who were able to assert themselves during the troubles arising from the wars of religion and, above all, at the time of the crisis of the League. The de la Rivières, who came to Arles towards the middle of the sixteenth century, were the leaders of the Catholic Party and did not hesitate at certain moments to rally the party of Philippe II and to unite with Spanish troops. Nicolas de La Rivière, husband of Laudune Porcelet and head of the Catholic party, was assassinated on 13 March 1652. One of his closest collaborators, Nicolas La Touche, married his widow and became leader of the Party of the League. He would end up being hanged, but not without first having married into the nobility of Arles under pressure from his soldiers, though without the so-called required quality and against all order and rule. The Icards and the Antonelles, united by marriage to the de la Rivières, were newcomers, but that was also the case for the Renauds, the Piquets, and the Brunets. On the other hand, the Porcelets, the Albes, the Meyrans, families of the old nobility, were represented only by particular lines. The second group seems more representative of the old nobility, and its Protestant sympathies leave hardly any doubt, even if many of the members moved to more moderate religious positions with the accession of Henry IV.

In this specific case, the violence of the political struggles ended the matrimonial exchanges between the two groups almost totally in the last decades of the sixteenth century. But it is interesting to observe that with the return of peace, the mechanisms of segmentation began once more to weave links between the antagonistic groups. From 1600, François Quiqueran, brother of Jean, one of the leaders of the Anti-League faction who would emerge as First Consul in 1617, married one Jeanne de La Rivière. Little by little, the marriages proliferated and the contours of the parties redefined themselves.

The problem of the endogamy or the exogamy of opposed factions is also important and complex. The cessation of marriage between two camps often indicated war, while the revival of such unions might follow from peace. In Mediterranean regions, these practices could still assume great solemnity. The peace might be signed by the parties in the presence of a public notary, and the marriage of members of the leading families of both factions might be celebrated with great pomp, with the entire community in attendance. There are abundant examples of this.

The exchange of women between adversaries had more than symbolic value. In Manduria, in the first half of the seventeenth century, the mayors of the village (from the faction of the town council) were always father-in-law or son-in-law, depending on the case, to the priors of the Mount of Piety, leaders of the opposed faction. As a consequence, peace was firmly guaranteed. This new circumstance indeed offers a remarkable perspective. The unions rapidly reestablished a classic mechanism of exchange between alternate lines, the significance of which was not a union of families, but simply the maintenance of a general political equilibrium between the groups. The representatives of families who played a subordinate role in each faction, or who were only *clients*, practiced these intermarriages between political rivals in a more limited way. However, there is also evidence of very different situations from those of Manduria in which strict endogamy within factions (with exchanges between alternate lines internal to each party) enabled the maintenance of strongly differentiated social, economic, and political identities and, in consequence, a relative tranquility between the groups. The circulation of women always responds to the same fundamental principles (reciprocity assured across collateral family lines) and to the same forms of linkage; however, its meaning varies considerably according to the specific political contexts in which it occurs. This, in turn, can be understood only by means of a precise study of the entirety of matrimonial relationships in relation to the political allegiances of the protagonists, but this is not always easy.

From all this, it may therefore be concluded that the political system of European Mediterranean societies can be described, a little like that of the Swat Pathans studied by F. Barth, in terms of a pragmatic dynamism based upon agreements made and unmade, choices and rejections, contracts, and transactions in which kinship and marriage constitute one element—a mode of action among others, which may be employed according to circumstances. [13]

This deconstructionist and narrowly synchronic vision of things is undoubtedly overstated, and the realities that confront the historian seem to me to be more complex. Firstly, observation of the political struggles in Arles, at Manduria, or in other Spanish communities (Caceres, Murcia[14]) shows that the pragmatic dynamism governing confrontations in reality consists of ordered, precise, and recurrent modes of behavior, in which the actors become involved and position themselves according to the nature of the conflict and the genealogical distance through blood or marriage with the protagonists. Cousins can be members of opposed factions, but if a conflict of a private nature opposes one of them to an outsider, the family unity is momentarily restored to confront it, and a whole series of peripheral alliances of friends, of *clients*, reposition themselves in response to this new reality. Once the conflict is resolved, each one returns to his previous position.

In the same way, a change in the social hierarchy is only conceivable through mechanisms that modify this genealogical distance (a marriage) or, in an indirect way, substitute it or prepare for it (sponsorship, loyalty, and protection). In Ravenna in the first half of the sixteenth century, when the Rasponis triumphed conclusively over the opposing faction, they were not content to simply kill the majority of male representatives of rival noble families, but obliged the latter to give their daughters in marriage to their allies from within the popular ranks who, through female heritage, succeeded those they had killed.[15] More commonly and less brutally, the social elevation of a family was often the result or the sanction of a long and shrewd political calculation of marital unions, which gradually brought about a reduction in the genealogical distance from members of a higher social class. In the fifteenth and even the sixteenth century, political strategy was not calculated, and in general was not constructed, outside of and independently of kinship. Such calculation in Mediterranean countries would not happen until the eighteenth and nineteenth centuries. I will return to this point.

Continuous fission and fusion drove both the system of kinship (through differentiation of senior and junior lines, which created social circulation, even inside lineages) and the political system (factions in conflict on matters of local concern could find themselves united against the intrusion of an external power). These forces acted in different time frames—long or very long-term for kinship, shorter or immediate for the political—and did not coordinate with each other—or only partially—even where there were constant efforts to try to reduce their opposition.

These local-level problems could also develop in a national, and even international, context. In Arles, the factions which took part in the wars of religion in the second half of the sixteenth century united with the great court factions (the Guises, the Coligny) which engaged in conflict at the highest level of the State, which often attempted to direct or to coordinate political and military operations across the entire country. In the case of France, this complex pyramid relationship is still poorly understood, and the religious character of the confrontation certainly contributed to greatly modifying the mechanisms of organization. But such constructions also occurred in Italy and Spain and have been the subject of extremely interesting recent studies. Thus, in the middle of the sixteenth century, the viceroy of Naples, don Pedro de Toledo, built a vast network which extended throughout the kingdom and beyond, to other Italian states, and brought within its web not just people from very different social strata, but equally, at the local level, those belonging to opposing factions.[16] Similar situations may be found in Spain. In

Logrono, rival factions led by don Pedro de Ariz y Yanguas and don Diego Ponce de Leon were both allied to the party of the Count-Duke of Olivares.[17] In general, relationships of a linear type (local faction a as client of central faction A, and b to B), which were probably predominant in France during the wars of religion, were in a minority here. Ties based on patronage clearly assumed a fundamental importance in the construction of these political pyramids. That does not exclude an important role for matrimonial unions—horizontally, at the level of different political groups, which compose the structure, as well as vertically, between distinct social levels, allegiances, and loyalties. The frontier between political patronage and matrimonial union is, moreover, often a lot more blurred and temporary than one might imagine. The client or protégé who succeeds can easily become a "relative" through marrying some representative of a junior line of the family or of another related family. Deciphering these complex interrelations of political patronage, marital unions, and power is, as we have said, proceeding apace, even if it is not easy. We must keep in mind, in the context of this chapter, that we find ourselves, in the sixteenth and at the beginning of the seventeenth century, still in the presence of hierarchical systems of intermediaries of power between the center and the periphery of the State. The internal economic, social, and political cohesion of these groups and their external positioning in relation to other groups still relies extensively—but not exclusively—upon mechanisms of kinship and of marriage.

In the case of the large town of Manduria in the region of Apulia, it is possible to trace from the fifteenth to the eighteenth century all the relationships of kinship and marriage of everyone who lived in the village. The relationships between all of the members of all of the municipal councils are thus known to us. For the second half of the sixteenth century and the beginning of the seventeenth century, there were, on average, 2.05 ties of blood and 9.57 links based upon marriage for all the councils (each comprised a mayor and four assessors—*nobile vivente*—and eight elected commoners). The ties deriving from marriage were thus much more numerous than those based on blood—almost all of which occurred through a female link—and these relationships constituted the essential means by which the councils were organized and structured right into the first decades of the seventeenth century. This conclusion can certainly be extended to a great number of political constructions in Western Europe during the same period, and the example of Arles alluded to previously is very similar to that of Manduria. The density of ties appears very similar inside the different sociolegal groups that compose the council, that is, the *nobili viventi* and the *popolari*. We find six relations of blood and thirty-eight of marriage between the nobles, against seven and fifty-four between the elected members. The ties that unite the two orders (*ceti*) are the most numerous: twenty-six of blood and ninety-three of marriage. This indicates that the two groups were not yet separated by rigid boundaries, that there was no sharply defined barrier (*chiusura*) between them. This, however, began to develop in the 1570s, and progressively imposed itself in the course of the seventeenth century. Up till then, both through heredity (the diversification and passing of lines of the same family from one order to another) and marriage (the exchange of women with all the political repositioning that it allows), the mixing between the two groups was constant.

The same study of these councils for the years 1695 to 1761 has provided evidence of the diminution by more than half of the average numbers of kinship and marriage connections (1.1 and 4 per council, respectively). The role of consanguinity and marriage fades, and already in the eighteenth century, the political structures appear to be very close to what they will be in the nineteenth and twentieth centuries: disjointed regroupings in which several closely or distinctly related individuals mix with one another. Economic, political, and ideological ties take precedence from then on over ties of blood. However, this does not mean that the latter have disappeared completely, for they reveal themselves in the long term at the level of political succession, which became, mostly, hereditary. From the middle of the seventeenth century, the dominant families, the Pasanisas, the Giustinianis, les Arnos, and so forth, regularly provided the mayors of the village, from father to son, in the same line, stabilized in their political role. Such situations were very unusual in the sixteenth century, when public offices passed from uncle to nephew, from grandfather to grandson, from cousin to cousin, utilizing the entire expanse of the lineage and not just a single line.

This claim regarding the diminution in importance of kinship and marriage in the eighteenth century should, however, be qualified, and the phenomenon defined precisely. The relationships inside and between the two *ceti* changed considerably. The ties between living nobles and commoners became rare. From this point on, the two orders were entirely separate. It is the relationships inside the stratum of the popular classes that now dominate massively: they represent 64.2 percent of kinship ties and 66 percent of ties of marriage. The weakening of ties in the group of *nobili vivanti* is, by contrast, apparent: a single relationship of blood and seven of marriage, and many of these derive after 1740 from families originating from the popular classes recently elevated into the nobility. The noble families that since the end of the sixteenth and the beginning of the seventeenth century, practiced rapid primogeniture with marriage, allowed only for the eldest son often reduced themselves to single lines. They turned towards totally exogamous marriages, forged most often outside the village or, more rarely, if the line was threatened with extinction, towards marriages with blood relations or very close relatives through marriage (uncle-niece, remarriage with a relative of the deceased first wife, then, towards the end of the eighteenth century, with the sister of the wife). For them, with either strategy, marital union was no longer an essential instrument in local political power. But the lower classes acted quite differently. They never opted for primogeniture and continued to organize themselves in expansive and interdependent lineages and to play the game of marriages between alternate lines that had characterized nobles in earlier periods.[18] Kinship and marriage remained important—though diminished—elements of their political practice and a lever for social elevation that certain legal or clandestine political groups knew how to exploit, sometimes even up to the present day.

The new system as a whole, as well as political opposition, came no longer, or only marginally, to be built upon kinship and marriage. The eighteenth and nineteenth centuries clearly signpost the victory of the line over lineage.

We should thus endeavor to understand why and how the old system of lineages disintegrated and how they progressively adjusted to the roles that kinship and marriage played in the development of political structures. An essential function of lineages and factions was to control territory and enable access to administrative and political posts to family representatives for the benefit of the whole group, all this in local settings where, in Italy as in Spain or southern France, the system for allocating official posts remained, in most cases based on election. There were several possibilities for putting an end to such a sociopolitical configuration. The one that effected the change worked through the mechanism of making public office hereditary, as in Spain and Italy. In France, the institution of election put severe limits on kinship and patronage for determining access to office.

In Castile and particularly in Old Castile, where the system of local government by the *linajes* remained very much alive right up to the end of the medieval period (Sora, Salamanca, Valladolid), the monarchy from the reign of Isabella the Catholic and the end of the *Reconquista* sought to bring an end to the often very violent struggles between *bandos* for the political domination of towns. To do this, it attempted to fix the public offices, notably those of the *regidores*, in certain families. It began by granting concessions for life (Isabella) and then, from the reign of Charles the Fifth, introduced the definitive sale of offices, which became a transferable inheritance from father to son. Here, as in many countries of Europe, the sale of offices emerged as one of the essential instruments in the transition to the inheritance of public offices. Systems of election became purely fictional, disappeared, or applied only to minor positions. From that time until the close of the reign of Philippe II, political struggles between factions seem to have been effectively quelled, at least in the important towns of the *realengo* (those under the dominion of the king). In smaller Castilian centers, where offices did not belong to the Crown, and in the towns of the Crown of Aragon—where a tradition of democratic election with strong representation from the popular stratum was solidly established—a move towards hereditary transference in the same family lines of the most important public offices took place (as in Manduria). These transformations in the countries of the Spanish Crown never led to a revision of the system that divided the society into orders (*hidalgos* and *pecheros*). Simply, the *mitad de oficios* (division of offices in half between nobles and commoners), which became general in the course of the sixteenth century, worked to the advantage of the small number of nobles within small communities.

In northern and central Italy, changes were not brought about by the privatizing policies of a few great families. On the contrary, the system of *ceti* was thoroughly overhauled. Everywhere, from the middle of the fourteenth to the end of the sixteenth century, we see the fusion of the nobles (*i nobili*) into a single group, comprising the old families of the nobility and the richest families from among the commoners. Such was the case, for example, in Genoa, with the reforms of Andrea Doria in 1528. This new ruling class, inside which all were equal, soon appeared closed.[19] A *Libro d'oro* (Book of Gold) provided a list of noble families who alone could attain to public office. Entrance proved to be difficult in the majority of cases. But also very quickly a heredity of fact and sometimes of right ensured that offices were assigned according to strict succession. In the case of the extinction of a line, the nearest line of relatives inherited. The electoral democracy disappeared; the electoral corps was reduced to a small number of those with entitlement, and the offices that remained elective were often of little importance. Everywhere, the extremely violent struggles between factions that characterized the end of the Italian medieval period came to an end. After the privatization of offices, there was no longer anything to dispute. The structure of shrewd and powerful political networks through marriage scarcely had any reason to continue to exist. Kinship and marriage became no more than residual supports of political strategy.

In Southern France (the situations described are also found in the north of France), the direct link between privatization of public office and adjustments in the political game seem less apparent at first. In France, the sale of public offices scarcely touched local positions before the end of the seventeenth century, and then only in a very limited way. Offices remained elective and could therefore, theoretically, continue to change hands according to the outcome of political struggles. In fact, in the violent conflicts that agitated the town of Marseille in the second half of the sixteenth century and the first decades of the seventeenth century, which W. Kaiser and R. Pillorget have clearly portrayed, the composition of factions still drew extensively upon consanguineal, godparentage networks, and marriage.[20] However, another mechanism emerged and progressively altered the rules of the game. While the system of orders remained formally in place, the membership of individuals was no longer determined by legal definition, but by wealth. At Aix, Draguignan, or Grasse, access to the consulate required membership in a certain social rank: nobles, knights, lords, bourgeois, merchants. But in the seventeenth century, rank in no way corresponded to a legal estate, but rather to a level of wealth. A person who enjoyed a certain level of income was noble. At Marseille, the regulations of Angoulême of 1585 made this clear: "No one can be First Consul who is not a gentleman, or well established or reputed as such, honestly possessing ten thousand escus…" We are in the presence of an elite electoral system involving a drift from rank to wealth. Neither the monarchy nor the city governments—as in Spain or in northern and central Italy—imposed a political solution to the problem of factions and power struggles, but they moved towards economic competition. To be noble, to attain official posts, one had to be rich, with the obvious consequence that the factions or political parties established themselves among the rich and no longer between relatives accorded different legal statuses. The system remained more fluid, more open than those that consolidated themselves in Spain or in Italy, since continuity in terms of the tenure of local offices was only assured by continuing wealth (the great offices of state were sold, but that is an entirely different issue). Moreover, political strategy retains a certain importance, since even the rich had to get elected. Kinship and marriage faded here as well, but in a way that is perhaps different from the preceding cases. However, a comparative study of their roll still has to be made.

By means of different mechanisms (sale of offices, jurisdictional privileges establishing an order of succession, strict hereditary transmission, the decisive role of wealth), the relationship between, on the one hand, the monarchies and central powers and, on the other, local powers, more and more became a relationship with persons, with individuals—or more precisely—with lines of individuals and no longer, as was generally the case in the medieval period, with groups of people strongly conditioned by the solidarity of "lineage." The spread of primogeniture that established itself progressively from the last decades of the sixteenth century and was adopted, little by little, by the entire ruling class, from the great nobility to the small well-to-do of the village, is only one of the most obvious expressions of this new relationship between the state and its subjects. Offices were acquired by heredity, and the younger relatives no longer had access to them. No longer useful for consolidating the power of the principle line, they were cast aside.

The fading of the role of consanguinity and marriage is also indicated in the course of the eighteenth and nineteenth centuries by a radical transformation of the old system of marriage circulation. Structures like the long-term exchange between alternate lines, or like the coordinated short-period uncle/niece and aunt/nephew marriages, were replaced by a system which encouraged two extremes: marriages between increasingly close blood relatives or affines (first cousins, uncle/niece, levirate or sororate); (endogamy) and marriages forged outside the limited circle of relatives or members of the community of origin (exogamy). The progressive diminution of consanguineous marriages in the last decades of the nineteenth century, then their virtual disappearance in the course of the twentieth century, would coincide with the rise of these individual, entirely exogamous marriage choices that have become the norm in modern societies. In the meantime, legal restrictions have also changed. In civil law today, they apply only to marital unions between specific individuals (I cannot marry my niece or the divorced wife of my brother, for example, without a dispensation) and no longer to entire groups of descendants (all my cousins up to those termed 'fourth cousins') or other relatives through marriage. Our system of kinship and marriage is intrinsically linked to the relations of power within a democratic regime. There is nothing to guarantee that this system will survive the disappearance or profound changes to contemporary power relations.

(Translation: Sheila Oakley)

Notes

1. David Warren Sabean, *Power in the Blood: Popular Culture and Village Discourse in Early Modern Germany* (Cambridge, 1984); idem, *Property, Production, and Family in Neckarhausen, 1700–1870* (Cambridge, 1990); idem, *Kinship in Neckarhausen, 1700–1870* (Cambridge, 1998).
2. Wolfgang Kaiser and Florence Chaix, *Marseille au temps des troubles, 1559-1596: morphologie sociale et luttes de factions* (Paris, 1992).
3. Christophe Duhamelle, *L'héritage collectif: la noblesse d'Église rhénane, 17ᵉ-18ᵉ siècles* (Paris, 1998); M. Nassiet, *Parenté, noblesse et états dynastiques: XVᵉ-XVIᵉ siècles* (Paris, 2000).
4. Auguste (Baron) Du Roure, *Les Meyran et leurs alliances. Généalogies provençales d'après les documents originaux publiés par le baron du Roure* (Paris, 1907). See also Abbé Bonnement, "Familles d'Arles," (Municipal Library of Arles).
5. I am excluding the 1562 marriage of Jean d'Antonelle, the natural son of Guillaume, the younger, to Marthe d'Icard, a merchant's daughter.
6. These were second cousins. Canon law forbade marriage as far as third cousins (fourth degree) without a dispensation.
7. Among the Antonelle family, Marie also had relatives who were so-called third cousins, descendants of Guillaume, brother of Louis. But it was from the uterine side that a cousin was chosen.
8. Gérard Delille, *Le maire et le prieur: pouvoir central et pouvoir local en Méditerranée occidentale (XVᵉ-XVIIIᵉ siècle)* (Rome, 2003).
9. Gérard Delille, "Echanges matrimoniaux entre lignées alternées et système européen de l'alliance: une première approche," in *En substances. Textes pour Françoise Héritier*, ed. Jean-Luc Jamard, Emmanuel Terray, and Margarita Xanthakou (Paris, 2000), pp. 219–52.
10. Gérard Delille, "Remariages, mobilité sociale et construction de réseaux d'alliance en Europe Occidentale (Xᵉ – XVIIIᵉ siècle)," in *Eheschliessungen im Europa des 18. und 19. Jahrhunderts: Muster und Strategien*, ed. Christophe Duhamelle, Jürgen Schlumbohm, and Pat Hudson (Göttingen, 2003), pp. 363–88.
11. Françoise Héritier, *L'exercice de la parenté* (Paris, 1981).
12. Claude Lévi-Strauss, *The Elementary Structures of Kinship (Les structures élémentaires de la parenté)* (London, 1969).
13. Fredrik Barth, *Political Leadership among Swat Pathans* (London, 1959).
14. For Murcia, see Maria Teresa Perez Picazo and Guy Lemeunier, "Formes de pouvoir local dans l'Espagne moderne et contemporaine. Des *bandos* au caciquisme au royaume de Murcie (XVᵉ-XIXᵉ siècles)," in *Klientelsysteme im Europa der Frühen Neuzeit*, ed. Antoni Maczak and Elisabeth Müller-Luckner (Munich, 1988). For Arles, Manduria, Cacerès, see Delille, *Le maire et le prieur.*
15. Cesarina Casanova, "Potere delle grandi famiglie e forme di governo," in *Storia di Ravenna. Dalla dominazione veneziana alla conquista francese*, ed. Lucio Gambir (Venice, 1992), pp. 39–129.
16. Carlos José Hernando Sánchez, *Castilla y Nápoles en el siglo XVI: el virrey Pedro de Toledo: linaje, estado y cultura (1532-1553)* (Valladolid, 1994).
17. Francisco Marcos Burgos Esteban, *Los lazos del poder: obligaciones y parentesco en una élite local castellana en los siglos XVI y XVII* (Valladolid, 1994).
18. Delille, "Echanges matrimoniaux."

19. For an exploration of all these issues relating to Northern and Central Italy in a book which is beautifully produced, the reader should consult Bandino Giacomo Zenobi, *Le "ben regolate città:" modelli politici nel governo delle periferie pontificie in età moderna* (Rome, 1994).
20. Kaiser and Chaix, *Marseille au temps des troubles;* René Pillorget, *Les mouvements insurrectionnels de Provence entre 1596 et 1715* (Paris, 1975).

TRANSITION 2

FROM EARLY MODERN TO NINETEENTH-CENTURY KINSHIP PATTERNS

Outline and Summaries

This book presents new ways of looking at the long-term development of European kinship from around 1300 to around 1900. We have suggested conceiving two major transitions. The first led from the late Middle Ages into the early modern period and was linked to processes of state formation and property consolidation. It can be associated with an increasing stress on vertical kin relationships. The second transition, starting in the eighteenth century, brought about a stronger stress on horizontal interactions. It was closely connected to aspects of class formation, political modernization, and new market dynamics. Each of these transitions led to important changes, and it can be argued that, contrary to widespread assumptions, kinship gained in significance in the course of modernization.

Beginning around the middle of the eighteenth century, alliance and affinity, rather more than descent and heritage, came to organize interactions among kin. During the early modern period, marriage alliances were usually exogamous, frequently cemented long-term clientage relations, and created complex patterns of circulation among different political and corporate groups and wealth strata. From the mid eighteenth century onwards, marriages became more and more endogamous, both in terms of class, milieu, and consanguinity. Cousin marriage, which had once been avoided or prohibited in most parts of the population, was at the heart of the new system—now marriage partners sought out the "familiar". These innovations were linked to the formation of social classes, to a new differentiation of gender roles within property-holding groups, and to reconfigurations in political institutions, state service, property rights, and the circulation of capital. If anything, the nineteenth century can be thought of as "kinship-hot," a period when people invested an enormous amount of energy in maintaining and developing extensive, reliable, and well-articulated structures of exchange among families over many generations.

The transition from early modern to nineteenth-century kinship patterns had many ramifications in social, economic, and cultural life. The bonds of reciprocity created by repeated marriages between close relatives were strengthened through other forms of cooperation such as godparentage, guardianship, tutelage, and legal representation. Over time, all these ties resulted in extensive kindreds and networks of kin. Along with the closeness based on familiarity came a stronger appreciation of romantic love, emotional accord, and similarity of personality as the basis of legitimate marriage. As the flows of sentiment and money operated in much the same channels, this was by no means contrary to material considerations. In fact, the new kin-constructed networks were the most important resource for capital accumulation and business enterprise, and contributed to the formation of classes and class cultures. Last but not least, they were the mechanism for political elites and officials to reproduce themselves. In the rapidly modernizing states, all over Europe, inherited family rights to office were replaced by a new order of talent, which in turn was mediated through connection and networking. In many instances, women acted as brokers: brokers of marriages, employment opportunities, apprenticeships, and business and political connections. Focusing on the historic contribution of women thus opens up a new understanding of what constitutes the political and leads to breaking up the clear line between the private and the public.

The chapters in the second part of the book show many aspects of the transition to, and the working of, nineteenth-century kinship in Europe. Some authors examine the framework for the activities of early modern traders and of the new industrial bourgeoisie (Fontaine, Joris, Gyáni, Sabean). Another issue treated is the effect of kinship use on political organization (Johnson, Joris). A third theme concerns problems of the development of mate selection and marriage (Mathieu, Sabean), and, finally, the chronology of kinship history and the interpretation of its basic trends are discussed (Fontaine, Mathieu, Sabean). Thus, the group of essays offers insights into mobility, gender, emotion and interest, property and capital, class, politics, and culture, some in a single locality, others in a single country or across large parts of the continent. There is, of course, room for different views and disagreement. A fruitful, productive hypothesis does not attempt to close a debate, but rather to open it by suggesting new ways of looking at both old and new facts. Our hypothesis of two major transitions in European kinship history has certainly started such a debate. It is important to note that the consequences at stake are far-reaching. The proposition challenges the artificial division between the so-called traditional and modern societies and a series of other time-honored opinions about the distinguishing characteristics of Western society.

*   *   *

Laurence Fontaine begins her chapter by looking at the historiography on mobility in Europe, which has failed to register the fundamental importance of kinship for migration patterns. Her own analysis highlights, by means of a few examples, the characteristics and functioning of the kin-structured migrant networks. She stresses their power as well as the unequal distribution of kinship ties within these societies. The new research on present-day diasporas is considered useful for reevaluating the nature of mobility in the past. Altogether, Fontaine argues that historic Europe produced extensive commercial networks founded upon the use and exploitation of kinship, which provided important resources of trust, information, and leadership. Paying attention to chronology reveals that there was significant variation by region and time. Many of the great networks of migrants developed between the fifteenth and the end of the eighteenth centuries. Rather than thinking of migration as a quantity that ebbed and flowed, Fontaine considers it a matter of constant adaptations, where different patterns of kin networks characterized different times and places. Even today, in many parts of the world, kinship groups, working on apparently archaic entrepreneurial models, are very common and remarkably successful.

According to Jon Mathieu, the multiplication of marriages between close relatives during the eighteenth and nineteenth centuries has been a central finding of kinship historians. There are, however, two interpretations to this trend that differ from each other both in their starting point and their focus. While the contraction thesis assumes a loosely defined endogamy in an early period up to the seventeenth century, the intensification thesis starts with predominant exogamy. Quite naturally, the differing assumptions about the trend influence its interpretation. The contraction thesis assumes that the significance of kinship was decreasing during economic and social modernization, while the intensification thesis, on the other hand, maintains that kinship mattered more, since it grew more important to develop new strategies to appropriate resources and status from the eighteenth century onward. Mathieu's chapter sketches the long-term history of kin marriages in Switzerland

and attempts to evaluate the plausibility of the two versions. For that purpose, it examines the meaning of social relations: How far did the consciousness of being related reach, and where did it normally cease? The results speak in favor of the intensification thesis.

Elisabeth Joris suggests that "gender" is not just a discursive category or a matter of legal definition—it "happens" in continually self-renewing practices, including kinship practices, in interpretations shaped by ambivalences, and in the construction of dynamic networks. On this general premise, her chapter analyzes various related kinship and gender issues. It explores the importance of marriage policy for the formation of the bourgeoisie, the implications of the politically constructed split between the public and the private spheres, familial sociability, the demand for flexible capital, and survival strategies of families. The focus of the essay is on the "long" nineteenth century, with most of the examples drawn from Switzerland. In this and in other countries, the failure of intellectuals to discuss kinship was the result of the split between the public and private spheres and the privileged status of "male" forms of representation in the public domain over forms of exchange defined as "private". Yet, despite the reduced legal capacity of the female sex, in practical terms, women's status was always flexible, contradictory, and multifaceted.

Christopher H. Johnson seeks to encourage debate about the place of kinship within associational and political life in nineteenth-century Europe through the careful examination of elite society in the Breton city of Vannes (France). How did kinship networks correlate with associational activities, and how did both connect with the local power structure and influence programs for civic betterment? Is kinship the missing factor in the analysis of bourgeois civil society, a factor always suspected but rarely articulated within the reigning discourse of individual achievement? The very idea of coupling civil society and kinship may seem incongruous to many historians of the modern age in as much as the first great advocates of the notion of civil society or the public sphere, such as Kant and Hegel, effectively defined it as antithetical to the family and kinship. According to this line of thought, it would seem that participation in civil society necessitated liberation from the family and that the truly problematic relationship was that between civil society and the state. The family would not disappear, but it defined a private sphere where women and children played an integral role on a field of sentiment, not reason, and were thus in need of shepherding as well as external representation by male heads of household. Yet the rich historical material presented in the article suggests that, in reality, family, kin, and the public sphere could not help but overlap, and while the latter seemed painted male, the place of women in this interaction was crucial.

Gábor Gyáni argues that the particular relevance of kinship to the development of Hungary's bourgeoisie was related to the fact that modernization was initiated by the former nobility. The modes of behavior and the value system of the landed nobility determined the formation of the middle class. Since a large part of that class was recruited from Jews, Germans, and other minority groups, family behavior was also characterized by ethnic and confessional diversity. In each of the different milieus, however, kinship ties served an essential function in fostering capital accumulation. The difficulty of financing industrial development was one of the most urgent problems in the late nineteenth century, and setting up and running a company by relying on family support was a very common practice. The play between material considerations and personal emotions underlying middle class marriage can be examined by looking at marriage contracts. They also provide insights into the roles males and females were expected to play in the family. The density of personal contacts and communication in urban environments is a good measure of how and to what extent kinship contributed to maintaining and enforcing the internal cohesion of class. Even in cases when there was a social distance between different families linked together by blood, the sense of internal solidarity manifested itself in the form of regular personal contacts. While consanguinity was essential for establishing and strengthening a kind of middle-class identity, the various forms of kin relations have always been used flexibly.

David Warren Sabean opens his chapter with two illuminating novels of society and manners published during the late nineteenth century. The first, Anthony Trollope's 1875 novel, *The Prime Minister*, is a tale of class milieu and family set in the context of English propertied provincial life, whereas the second, Theodor Fontane's *Frau Jenny Treibel* of 1892, is placed in the context of the social mobility and volatility of imperial Berlin. The novels give some clue as to what was on people's minds during the time, and they touch upon themes that together point to a special kinship strategy in nineteenth-century Europe: the reciprocal structuring of class and kin cultures; endogamy within class milieus (like with like); courtship within the context of family desires; repeated exchanges among allied families (cousin marriage); older women as gatekeepers and mediators of alliance (matrifocality); marriage as a connection point for the flow of capital and access to property; and erotic attraction between siblings and cousins. This pattern was the result of a fundamental reconfiguration of kinship developed gradually with the opening up of the economy and shifts in the nature of state government and administration. The first steps were taken around 1750, and the peak was reached between 1880 and 1920. An extensive, integrated, horizontally constructed set of kindred emerged, which provided structural support for the production and reproduction of class milieus.

Chapter X

Kinship and Mobility
Migrant Networks in Europe

Laurence Fontaine

Is the analysis of migration a useful way of approaching the question of whether or not there has been an intensification of kinship ties as part of the transition towards modernity? In addressing the subject, I am going to begin with the study of migrant networks. As migration is a subject that touches upon all aspects of life, there will often be echoes of some of the other themes explored in this book. I will begin by looking at how the historiography has related kinship to migration, and will then analyze the characteristics and functioning of migrant networks by means of a few examples. I will consider why historians have failed to reveal the extensive links between mobility and kinship, and will treat migrant networks in the context of the findings of economists on contemporary diasporas. Finally, I will underline the unequal distribution of kinship ties, even within societies that have produced extensive migrant networks.

Historiography

To understand how the historiography has linked migration with the family, we should first carefully consider how migration has been discussed, since the presuppositions underlying previous studies contain preconceived ideas regarding the connections between family and mobility, of which we need to be aware.

In general, within traditional models of migration, there is no reference to kinship because three major presuppositions contribute to making it invisible. Firstly, mobility has always been conceived of in opposition to sedentariness and as the option of last resort compared with other more highly esteemed manners of providing stability. Itinerancy has always been associated with break up; it is conceived of as a mechanism for regulating overpopulation, its "oxygen balloon," and signifies a slicing up of the community. The family plays a peripheral role in these movements—at best, it marks out the route. In fact, historians have written two juxtaposing histories of mountain villages: one, noble, of those who stay, and another, more ignominious, of those who leave. These histories are entirely separate, and the successes of those who depart are never conceived of as other than individual or familial (in the narrow sense) successes. Hence, it has been impossible to study socially and economically effective networks which link settled populations, migrants, and emigrants. It has also, hence, been impossible to consider occupations associated with migration as equal in status to so-called "rooted" occupations, whether as complementary or as alternative forms of employment.

This impossibility derives from models which valorize points of arrival to the detriment of points of departure, which atomize the social body, and which are founded upon a notion of the economy as unrelated to political contexts and the structures of social relations. Migrants are perceived as individuals and, at best, members of small family units. The departure is viewed as an individual choice, even if it rebounds upon the family and the group of origin. In this way, the migrants who appear in other social configurations, such as kinship or commercial networks, are thus either obscured or incomprehensible.

Two other presuppositions combine with that of the primacy of sedentariness to make the relationships between migration and kinship even more invisible. The first relates to the workings of the labor market, the complexity of which is never fully appreciated. The underlying image of it is that of a liberal economy, pure and simple, where supply and demand meet in perfect transparency. Even in the present age, this model is questionable; it seems a lot more ideological than real. In fact, there is a contradiction between the rational presuppositions that accompany these theories of poles of attraction and repulsion and the empirical analyses of employment in towns.[1] Indeed, in the early modern period, in the case of numerous professions, the market is segmented and partially controlled by specific social groups. All the studies of towns show the dominant role, in certain professions, of migrants of a precise geographical origin. The range of these occupations is broad and includes some requiring status qualifications, others linked to services, and still others offering only physical labor.[2]

The third supposition is a consequence of the notion of "limited goods," which has been, for a long time, at the center of analyses of regions characterized by migration and of peasant communities, and which rests upon the relationship between the distribution of agricultural wealth in villages and the number of their inhabitants. In explaining mobility, these studies emphasize the distribution and size of properties as well as systems of inheritance, which are regarded as central factors in the allocation of lands. Thus, within this analytical framework, two types of migration are identified: migrations arising from exclusion, when the balance between men and land resources is upset, and temporary migrations, which served as stopgaps for those awaiting the acquisition of village property—for example, upon the death of a father.[3] Starting from the principle that only the land created wealth for village peasants, these analyses overlook the fact that via the movement of men and money, peasants, who sold their knowledge and their physical labor or who lent money, were able to shift the frontiers of their local regions and demonstrate that village resources were more elastic than the single relationship between the ecosystem and the density of population would seem to suggest.

A historiography of the left has extended to the entirety of Western European peasant communities this model, which Chayanov put forward in relation to Russian peasantry. Each family unit is conceived of as an entity, which is simultaneously consumer and producer, and the relationship between the two functions changes with the progression of the family cycle. The goal of the peasant would be, in this context, to try to keep the relationship between consumption and production in balance, and migration becomes one of the means of achieving this equilibrium during periods of a pronounced rise in consumption.[4] In this essentially economic vision, albeit one with moral implications, the peasants are envisaged first and foremost as consumers who become producers only when their needs dictate. In this sense, migration is a passive phenomenon, resulting from an economy of shortage. It cannot be interpreted as deriving from a deliberate intention to accumulate wealth. The persona of the entrepreneur is denied to the peasant, reinforcing the image of migration as an option of last resort.

Against these models, the study of migrations from mountain communities—which are the best known, though lowland regions have produced similar migrations—provide other interpretations: work away from home takes migrants away from self-sufficiency and into an economy of risk. It signifies the pursuit of occupations that entail entrance into the world of contractors of peasant labor.

Among all the studies on migration, only those specifically concerned with diasporas have directly associated kinship with migration. Today, diasporas have become very fashionable, and the word tends to encompass all expatriate communities, irrespective of the original reasons for expatriation and the forms it takes. Traditionally, the notion is associated with the dispersion of the Jews after the fall of Jerusalem, as well as that of the Armenians, and even that of the Protestants forced to leave the kingdom of France after the revocation of the Edict of Nantes. Today, the word is used to evoke and to stress the ties between places of origin and of settlement in order to show the permanence of original cultural identities.[5] In fact, the word "diaspora" is hardly ever associated with migrations from mountain communities, quite the opposite. This modern usage has obliterated the Greek etymology and the original meaning of the term: "dissemination" or "dispersal of seed," which was used in reference to the colonies established by the Greek city-states beyond the peninsula, as well as to the economic and political relationships maintained with the mother country. Contemporary economists use the word in this way, and I am using it in the same sense to underscore the privileged economic and political relationships maintained between migrants and their country or place of origin.

Before entering into an analysis of diasporas from mountain regions, however, I would like to emphasize the diverse nature of migration and of the living conditions that pressured mountain dwellers to leave. The research I have conducted traced three forms of mobility. Firstly, there were individual and definitive migrations, which occurred among both the richest and the poorest inhabitants. Those from among the richest provide the key to understanding village society: they constructed networks that employed the physical labor of men from their villages of origin. It is of these that I am speaking here. Those from among the poorest were those who no longer had either land or physical labor to offer in exchange for their needs—the old, widows without resources, orphans from poor families. These people experienced a true migration of exclusion. Secondly, there were temporary migrations linked to the mobility of elites. The masons, the ironmongers, the grinders, peddlers, and haberdashers, who spread out into rural areas and small market towns, were tied to those who stayed by a double relationship of dependence—they were their debtors at "home" and obligated through commerce and recruitment. Finally, there were the large-scale migrations of the poorest who, at times of crises, abandoned their villages.

From the Middle Ages, in the Alps as in the Massif Central, one finds these mass exoduses, which sent out onto the roads isolated individuals as well as entire families.[6]

I lay stress upon this diversity to emphasize that migrants from the same village did not therefore all take part in an organized migration. However, the latter remain at the heart of rural community life.

Kinship in Migration

Can one see how these networks of migrants make use of kinship? An examination of mobility in premodern Europe reveals that diasporas from mountain communities played a very important role in the distribution markets between the fifteenth and eighteenth centuries. They were particularly extensive in mountainous regions such as the Alps, the Pyrenees, Scotland and the Massif Central, but also in lowland regions—the peninsula of Cotentin in Normandy, for example, has also accommodated structured networks of migrants.

Here are a few examples just as a reminder of the extent of these networks.[7] Post mortem inventories, record books, reports of trustees, and deeds of notaries reveal that Protestant residents of Dauphiné migrated between Switzerland, Northern Italy, Southern France, and Spain. Jean Giraud, one of my principal "informants," ran a shop in Lyon, like his father before him, and his father-in-law kept a shop in Geneva. The Giraud family made up only a segment of a much larger network, which connected other families linked to the same mountain range, like the Bérards, the Delors, the Horards, and the Vieux de Mizoen families. Since the sixteenth century, some of them had acquired bourgeois status, such as the Delors in Lyon and Geneva. The notaries' archives of villages show that others established themselves in Grenoble, in Burgundy, in Italy, in Germany, and along the road to Spain.[8]

*   *   *

The catholic Brentano family originated from the valleys of Lake Como. It depended upon four lines—the Brentano-Gnosso, the Brentano-Toccia, the Brentano-Cimaroli, and the Brentano-Tremezzo—to construct its network. The first arrived north of the Alps in the sixteenth century as simple *Höcker*, itinerant vendors of citrus fruits and spices, up until the turn of the eighteenth century when they succeeded in setting up town shops. A Brentano first appears in 1640 in Basel from where he was expelled. We then find his son, Carl, in Frankfurt in 1673. Within the Tremezzo line, the first Brentano to come to Frankfurt was Martino. In

1662 he obtained a license to sell his citrus fruits on a table, crouching like *Hockerer* traders, and sharing this license with the old and the infirm.[9] His son, Domenico, born in 1651 in Tremezzo, developed the business in association with his brothers-in-law, and opened a shop in Frankfurt in 1698. Nonetheless, he still continued to go back and forth between Frankfurt and his lands at Lake Como, where he had his family and where he died in 1723. The marriages between families from the same village enabled the Brentanos, through the associations they formed among themselves, to develop their branches in the Rhine axis. Not until the second half of the eighteenth century—or at least four generations after the first known Brentano—would Peter Anthony (Pietro Antonio), born in Tremezzo in 1735 and deceased in Frankfurt in 1797, attempt to integrate himself into Frankfurt society through marrying Maximiliane La Roche, his second wife, a product of the cultivated bourgeoisie and a friend of Goethe. At the beginning of the eighteenth century, the Brentanos took up residence in Amsterdam, Bingen, Brussels, Coblenz, Cologne, Krakow, Diez, Frankfort, Friberg, Heidelberg, Mannheim, Mainz, Nuremberg, Rothenberg, Rotterdam, and Vienna. If one adds to these towns those where their relatives opened shop, their establishments are to be found throughout the whole of northern Europe.[10]

In the eighteenth century, families from Briançon specialized in the printing business. Various lists make it possible to trace fifty or so Briançonnais surnames in the eighteenth century among those who ran bookshops in France, Italy, Spain, and Portugal. They controlled between a quarter and virtually the entire printing market in various countries within Mediterranean Europe: Spain, Portugal, and the south of France. If the newly affluent peddlers extended the network of shopkeepers, the mountain village continued to be a reserve of men who were clerks or itinerant tradesmen, as necessity required. Though this network of bookshops and itinerant booksellers originating from the region of Briançon seems to be the most important, it is by no means the only example. The editors Remondini of Venice, originating from Bassano, made their mark during the second half of the eighteenth century by means of a similar network, at a time when the entire Venetian publishing trade was in crisis.[11] Many other examples could be given, as much from the world of commerce as from that of craft production.

Before exploring the organization of these networks, I would like to underline why, apart from the presuppositions of studies on migration, they have evaded researchers. The reasons are, it seems to me, twofold. They relate to the purpose of the state in producing archives and to the practices of tradesmen. We know, after Michel Foucault's work, how much is difficult to fathom and to grasp, above all because the sources (registers of names, census returns, income tax forms) marry the points of view of the state and of the Church which have imposed the simple family unit as the basis for public records of bodies, souls, and properties. By relying solely on these sources, one risks taking the aim of these institutions (to control the reproduction of families[12]) to reflect the reality of family practices. The works of David Sabean and of Giovanni Levi have stressed the inadequacy of this family framework, even if, in their efforts to impose it, the state and Church have found determined allies in the heads of families.[13]

The invisibility of migrant networks to those who produce archives has been compounded by the determination of heads of families, in a general way, to prevent the State from interfering in their affairs. The reconstruction of these families is almost impossible, since the researcher cannot trace many of the children born during migration and in towns, in which migrants did not settle. Further, the migrating traders are registered in the archives as originating from the towns where they set up shop; their post mortem inventories present them as inhabitants of the place where they worked and, in most cases, the documents are silent about their origin and make no reference to the temporary nature of their urban residence. Their own account books help to reinforce this impression; when they note those with whom they do business, they do not mention that some of the merchants came from the same village, a fact that was self-evident to them, but only the place where they had settled, this being the only detail of importance for transactions. For example, the bookseller, Nicolas, indicates in his account book that he did business with Pic and Rome of Paris, with Giraud, Chicot, and Grengent of Lyon, and not that all these book traders originated from the Alps. Jean Giraud, himself, mentions in his record book Salomon, Arthaud, and Pic of Turin, Nicolas of Grenoble, of Arles, or of Puy, but not that all these are from La Grave in Dauphiné. We understand these practices—one does not record what is self-evident and of no use, only that which might vary or lead to confusion if omitted. The traders moved around and, moreover, each family could establish itself in several places, like the Pic family, which we find in Paris and at Turin, or like the Nicolas family itself. Thus, the trading networks only become evident if they are located at every point where they extend, beginning with the mountain communities.

Let us now briefly consider the organization of these networks. They were based upon a double structure, on the one hand, the kinship ties between those who open the shops and the depots in the main centers of European commerce and, on the other hand, a system of distribution founded upon the men from the villages of origin who pass through towns and rural villages distributing the merchandise. In this way, the organization of these networks rests on two main elements: on the strength of kinship ties and on the power of elites who act as labor-force contractors.

The strength of kinship ties is at the heart of the system. It provided initial capital needed for business and the capacity to form commercial companies that were very flexible, linked or unlinked, according to the needs of commerce, a death in the ranks, or the increasing affluence or impoverishment of the various members. Generally, the association lasted between one and six years. Each member provided capital and the profits were divided pro rata in accordance with initial investment. Within this family banking system, each associate put the main part of his inheritance and legacies into the company, as well as the dowry of his wife.[14]

Let us stop a moment on the subject of women. They are scarcely visible in the foreground, even if widowhood could lead some of them to manage the businesses of their deceased husbands, and even if, of course, we encounter them as wives and daughters of merchants, and as peddlers who knew how to use their status as the "weaker sex" and the indulgence of the legal system towards them to their advantage, in order to circulate forbidden books in the towns.[15] But their financial contribution, via the dowry, was fundamental to the constitution of companies, and provisions were made to prevent the withdrawal of capital by the widow or heirs of a deceased associate. The extant contracts show that capital was secured up until the end of the contract of association, and that, in particular, the widow of the deceased merchant received, at fixed terms, money arising from interest on the sums invested, but could not touch the capital. Commercial companies were thus endowed with structures that enabled them to deal with biological hazards.

Furthermore, participation in a common family structure developed a communality of interests that provided the main guarantee that business relations would be conducted to the advantage of everyone. Inbreeding was an essential mechanism to protect the banking system and allegiance to the commercial network. The exceptions to this rule may be put down to the adjustments that the migrants had to consent to in order to penetrate the market in the areas where they settled and to twist the state legislation that aimed to exclude or control them. The interdiction against marrying in the low lands was also part of the mechanism of commercial companies in that it left the possibility for men to move about easily in response to the needs of the company and the opportunity to oversee them via the family remaining in the village.

But, in doing so, these mechanisms reinforced the family structure of these societies.

Finally, women were the last ramparts against total failure. We know that between the sixteenth and eighteenth century, women experienced an extension of their judicial incapacity and, on the other hand, an increasingly greater protection of their financial interests.[16] Of course, there were numerous variations, depending on the region and its customs.[17] During the seventeenth century in France, legislation relating to the legal mortgage of estates was generalized from the written law of specific regions to the entire country, to the advantage of women, and was made applicable to the property of the husband and to common property, even if the woman could validly renounce the mortgage.[18] On the other hand, if during the union, the woman feared the ruin of her husband, she could ask for the separation of estates.[19] Families knew how to take advantage of these legal provisions to avoid total failure. They arranged to transfer the estates of the husbands to the wives and used the fact that they were privileged creditors to withdraw the properties of their husbands from the claims of creditors. In this respect, the institutions worked to the advantage of family companies.

The second fundamental characteristic of these migrant societies unites elites with village inhabitants. The relationship is of such importance that it is impossible to pass over it in silence under the pretext that it is no longer a matter of family relationships but of clientelistic relationships, because the basis of the wealth and the power of elites derived precisely from the work of the migrants that they controlled.

These trading organizations thus coordinated the working together of the entire social range within village communities with, at the top of the network, the merchants, some of whom were among the richest inhabitants of the towns in which they settled, and, at the other end of the commercial chain, men who had hardly any capital to offer in guarantee of merchandise which was entrusted to them. Taking into account the weak institutional framework of work relations in early modern Europe, the double structure of kin and village compatriotism proved to be very effective in enforcing trust, which was crucial for commerce at that time.

In fact, between established tradesmen and peddlers, the ties of trust were built upon their belonging to the same village and on the social hierarchies into which men there were locked. All the peddlers were indebted with regard to the merchants who employed them, and in the village they left family and property at the disposal of the merchants in case of a breach of trust. Peddlers were thus prisoners of multiple financial dependencies and hemmed into a system of social relations that both assisted and kept surveillance over them.

For the provider of funds from outside the valleys or for those who called upon the services of companies of workers, the highly hierarchical organization of village migration, its anchorage within the "elites" who simultaneously played the role of contractors of labor and that of privileged relay between town trading and itinerant sales, gave the maximum of guarantees. For example, the practice of having guarantors—which was very widespread—if it imposed mutual dependence and aid, also facilitated denunciation.

This ethic impressed upon the group was underpinned by the strategies of village elites who supervised each modification of an estate and closely followed every reversal of fortune. To do this, the elites relied simultaneously on their own families, village notaries, and other peddlers who gave them information on the state of properties and upon all the changes in the composition of families liable to affect the solvency of the peddlers. A chain of information and surveillance thus ran through village society. In this sense, it was very difficult for members of business networks to hide malpractice or to even imagine it, since community control was so strong. In addition, this organization enabled the control of the plurality of ties that bound individuals who worked for the network.

The great importance of kinship is evident in this construction of trust since, because of it, the partners had access to all the information necessary to control the behavior and capacities of the various members of the network. In fact, this structuring of labor was perfectly adapted to the institutional weaknesses of the markets of early modern Europe. Numerous labor markets at this time were founded upon the employment of teams, and workers were not recruited individually but through team managers—consider, for example, masons, porters, or soldiers. The control and direction of the village labor force by a few families was, thus, a form that offered a maximum guarantee to future employers.

These kinship networks were also perfectly adapted to the transmission of information and to the following of developments within markets. In fact, the settlement of families in the main places of European commerce enabled them to gain access to information regarding the supply and demand of different commodities and the prices of goods, and also to become aware of the restrictions and favorable terms which states and towns reserved for foreign trade. Furthermore, the refusal to put down roots gave networks the capacity to redeploy themselves in accordance with the needs of commerce and political transformations of states; all made information circulate and all moved about from place to place in response to needs and opportunities. A main feature of these networks was, moreover, their capacity to sell the newest and most sought after products (which indicates that their information system worked very well) and to mobilize great armies of workers for their purposes.

Finally, the way in which these Alpine networks knew how to exploit the diversity of regulations and rivalries between towns and states was a consequence of this organization based on family connections established over vast territories. The settling of Alpine printers in Avignon is a perfect example. Besides the guarantees that this type of organization of work offered to employers, these networks were perfectly adapted to "underground" activities and illegal trafficking. Mule drivers, mercers related to the printers, and peddlers hid and transported this merchandise, as highly prized as the book that is forbidden everywhere that it is in demand.[20] The part played by contraband in these business transactions is, of course, very difficult to establish, but one repeatedly comes across hidden activities in the archival records and one acquires a sense of the profits derived from an ability to manipulate or play about with the regulations.

What conclusions can be drawn? To reply to the question posed by this book, I would say that the development of commerce and its prerequisites, that is, the factors of trust, information, and leadership, confirm the intuition of the organizers: early modern Europe developed commercial networks founded upon the exploitation of extensive kinship networks. As proof, one can also point to a series of indirect indices that endorse these conclusions, since it is impossible to reconstruct the families of small merchants on a pan-European scale. However, the question of chronology calls for a more measured response. In fact, the situation varies from region to region, and the time when the great networks of migrants were at their peak in Europe differs according to their origin, but all sprung up within the broad timescale of the fifteenth to the end of the eighteenth century. By the nineteenth century, some had succeeded in maintaining this activity by virtue of an increased specialization in terms of new and luxury products and by redeploying themselves in new markets outside of Europe and in South America.[21] The lifespan of these migrant networks was extremely variable as they were caught between several dynamics—the desire of families to maintain them, the wish of the state to bring about their disintegration, and the institutionalization of the economy which made them, in many cases, increasingly less necessary. The Briançonnais network, for example, existed through the entire early modern age; in the eighteenth century, it was evidently at its most extensive, but it appeared in the sources from the sixteenth century. However, the wealth of the Alps in the fifteenth century and some allusions by travelers to the extent of itinerant trading in the valleys leads one to think that already quite early, merchant networks were very active. Moreover, account records and deeds of notaries show that the main families that composed this network conducted business together throughout these three centuries and continued to associate with one another, despite the geographic dispersal resulting from the Revocation of the Edict of Nantes. Rather than a cycle, it was a matter of constant adaptations until the French Revolution and the Napoleonic Wars closed the frontiers and crushed the networks throughout Europe. On the other hand, the Scottish networks that were active in Scandinavia developed earlier and declined sooner. The supreme position of the Dutch in the commerce of the Baltic from the sixteenth century, and the opening of the English market after the Act of Union, marked the decline in the migration of Scottish merchants and peddlers. Emigration no longer recurred, assimilation occurred progressively and, towards the end of the eighteenth century, the process was completed in Poland and Denmark.[22] The same thing occurred, but a century earlier, in Sweden, where the seventeenth century politics led to establishing roots and forming alliances with indigenous families.[23] As for the Italian networks of the Great Lakes, they began to break up in the nineteenth century. Rather than there being an apogee or peak with regard to European networks, it was a matter of constant adaptations of the products sold, the markets prospected, and the customers targeted. On account of their great susceptibility to political and economic vicissitudes, these adaptations and changes cannot be given a precise chronology.

Contemporary Diasporas

To understand the success of these kinship networks even today, I am going to investigate them in the light of works by contemporary economists. In fact, this type of network, which is still very prevalent and still remarkably successful, fascinates economists who also endeavor to explain the mechanisms at work in the economic success of these apparently archaic entrepreneurial models. Mark Granovetter, who has worked specifically on networks of Chinese businessmen, places two elements at the core of their success: the role of trust between members and the strength of the community. If trust is not lacking, explains Granovetter, it is because the community is so homogeneous that it is very difficult for its members to hide malpractices or to even imagine them. Furthermore, it is sufficiently strong to preclude conflict regarding the delegation of authority.

Chinese businesses are organized around kinship, credit, the pooling of capital, and the delegation of authority without fear of breach of agreements. In addition to the strength of communities, researchers point out that the position of individuals within groups and within kinship relationships is clearly defined, which limits the claims that individuals can have with regard to the business by comparison with other, more fluid, kinship structures where people belong to numerous interest groups overlapping with one another. One of the dangers in such joint undertakings is that of a requirement to distribute financial returns and favors beyond the financial capacity of the group.[24] The danger is real, since when one group is at the center of a business transaction, members of other linked groups can legitimately claim a portion of the profits. This multiplicity of possible demands creates a strong element of weakness as the studies of Clifford Geertz on Indonesian businessmen have underlined.[25]

Finally, researchers emphasize that the development of these businesses rests upon their capacity to create "business groups" through family alliances. Today, this phenomenon even has a specific name in each country: the *zaibatsu* in Japan, the *chœbol* in Korea, and the *grupos economicos* in Latin America. These groups are variable in size, structure, and legal forms of organization. Some of them derive from a single family group which extends its domination, by acquisition or alliance, as in Japan or in Korea, while in Latin America it seems that different groups arise independently and join together at a favorable moment.[26]

As economists have noted, trust is at the very center of the success of migrant networks, but it is not an element produced naturally through belonging to a community. It is the fruit of continuous work at social control based upon information, surveillance, behavioral constraints, limitation of choice, and financial dependence with, for the richest, the obligation to invest inheritance in the common business and, for the poorest, debt dependence. Thus, social organization conduces to the strengthening of family and community solidarity to the detriment of individual choice. And so it becomes apparent how the strength of groups is established and why so few conflicts of authority mark the history of these business networks. Moreover, whatever conflicts there are, are settled among themselves, outside of court, and the cases are rare in which migrant tradesmen openly declare war against one another, calling upon legal authorities. They prefer to settle their differences before an informal tribunal, made up of local merchants.[27] These practices also explain why these networks are underrepresented in the archives. However, beside the trust imposed inside groups, it should also be stressed that they are perfectly adapted to the lack of institutionalized trust from which the labor market suffers in general.

Secondly, one should stress, more than economists have done so far, the importance of the mobility of members as the basis of the success of business networks. It enables the best use of information in deploying and redirecting men in response to the needs of the market, and in moving them from place to place, without suffering the human and economic burdens caused by rootedness. Mobility has given a suppleness and adaptability to business transactions.

Kinship Distribution

If kinship appears as the context that enables us to understand the reproduction of families better, in particular those of the elites of high Alpine villages, it is not yet known whether all the families of the high valleys are thus positioned within wider kinship relationships. To evaluate the role of kinship, I looked at how kin took over from fathers and mothers in the case of orphaned children; that is, at a time when the solidarity of relatives is vital. This study, which was conducted on the basis of reports of "assemblies of relatives, neighbors, and friends," convened to decide the fate of orphans, provides evidence of a clear difference between the families of the elite and those of more modest inhabitants. The first find guardians and trustees without too much trouble, and numerous relatives attend the meetings, which can bring together twenty or so people. But above all, the concern within the village is reinforced by that of relatives who have left the village and who offer orphans apprenticeship contracts and employment in the low lands.

But outside these families, mobilization around orphans is very limited. Each time that succession poses a problem, the gathering of "relatives, neighbors, and friends" has trouble in finding guardians and trustees, and few relatives attend meetings. In the most favorable cases, only uncles, brothers, and brothers-in-law of the deceased parents concern themselves with the orphans. It is, moreover, from them that support is expected, and their absence is explicitly noted during the assemblies of relatives. If necessary, cousins participate in the meetings, but rarely on a regular basis, and their disinterest is not condemned. When "the relatives have not deigned to appear," the notary writes in the report that those absent will be pursued by law, but subsequent gatherings do not prove to be better attended. In fact, the number of those present at the meetings proves to be in inverse proportion to the need that the child has for family solidarity.[28]

Kinship thus proves to be a benefit unequally distributed. For the elites, "family space" (in the broadest sense) is indicated in the kinship relations present in the village and among those who have migrated. Nuclear families appear as links in a much larger social structure. They were interdependent and relied upon one another to affirm or develop their social or commercial position. The study of peddler networks shows that families relocated their members in diverse commercial towns in Europe in response to the necessities of commerce or when death left a strategic place unoccupied. Moreover, the analysis of the social records of these lineages reveals the shared determination to occupy as many fields as possible to enable the preservation of local power over people and markets. For that, families endeavored to exert their presence in a diverse range of geographic and social environments. The importance of occupying certain positions that favor the activities of the large family group thus directly influenced the careers that parents chose for their sons. Indeed, the exercise of certain occupations was all the more profitable if relatives were positioned in other geographic or institutional places. Thus, merchants aimed to have children in the justice system (as judges or lawyers), in the body of notaries, in the clergy of the village and in other towns to extend the commercial network.[29] All the Alpine elite practiced this diversification.

*   *   *

This professional diversification was, it seems to me, an essential feature of the society of the Old Regime, in that it enabled adaptation to the logics—and the hazards—of the economy, where private and public affairs were indissolubly linked. It offered an effective response to structures within the economy and the weakness of institutions. Wider kinship networks protecting individuals were both aggressive and demanding, countering the ideal of the narrow family that the state and the Church endeavored to impose. Those who were too poor to be able to make use of family connections attempted to enter into the clientele of those extended families that controlled the economic circuits beyond the village and the local region in order to guarantee work and subsistence for themselves.

Thus, the history of individual elite family unfolds within the broad context of kinship relations. Some relations were close and some were distanced, but they connected the elite and more modest families within a dynamic of patronage and connection. David Siddle has used the concept of the *gens* to designate the "nesting" of particular families within a network of kin.[30] Personal ties, founded in variable proportions according to place, credit, tenancy, or access to crucial local resources such as grazing rights, gave elites control over the physical labor of the villagers, which they used according to the changing needs of their economic situations.

Including these social, familial, and extrafamilial ties, as well as the geographic environment in which they operated in research, gives us a different insight into the meaning of mobility in societies characterized by considerable labor migration. Mobility can be understood, in the same way as sedentariness, as an intrinsic part of their functioning and not just a sign of destabilization, even if, in common with every other constituent of society, mobility brings about the gradual evolution of societies as much as their fragmentation.

(Translation: Sheila Oakley)

Notes

1. Jan Lucassen, *Migrant Labor in Europe 1600–1900: The Drift to the North Sea* (Beckenham, 1987), gives numerous analyses of these segmented and controlled labor markets.

2. Leslie P. Moch and Louise A. Tilley, "Joining the Urban World: Occupation, Family, and Migration in Three French Cities," *Comparative Studies in Society and History* 27 (1985): pp. 33–56; Ian W. Archer, "Responses to Alien Immigrants in London, c. 1400–1650," in *Le Migrazioni in Europe secc. XIII-XVIII*, ed. Simonetta Cavaciocchi (Florence 1994), pp. 755–74; Raffaello Ceschi, "Bleniesi milanesi. Note sull'emigrazione di mestieri dalla swizzeria italiana," in *Col bastone e la bisaccia per le strade d'Europa. Migrazione stagionali di mestiere dall'arco alpino nei secoli XVI-XVIII* (Bellinzona, 1991), pp. 49–72.

3. Giovanni Levi describes the majority of migrations by masons in this way: they are temporary in every sense of the term, they are migrations of expectation. "For them, to be a mason, amounts to settling oneself in a waiting room," "Carrières d'artisans et marché du travail à Turin (XVIIIᵉ–XIXᵉ siècles)," *Annales ESC* 45 (1990): pp. 1351–64, here p. 1358.

4. Alexander V. Chayanov, *The Theory of Peasant Economy* (Homewood, IL, 1966) (first edition in Russian, 1925); Lucassen, *Migrant Labor*, p. 99; Giovanni Levi, *Centro e periferia di uno stato assoluto. Tre saggi su Piemonte e Liguria in età moderna* (Turin, 1985), pp. 77–140; Franco Ramella, *Terra e telai. Sistema di parentela e*

manifattura nel Biellese dell'ottocento (Turin, 1983), pp. 78, 225–27. For a critical discussion of the concept of "the familial economy" and a review of the historiography, see Ad Knotter, "Problems of the Family Economy: Peasant Economy, Domestic Production and Labor Markets in Pre-industrial Europe," *Economic and Social History in the Netherlands. Family Strategies and Changing Labor Relations*, NEHA 6 (1994): pp. 19–59.

5. Steven Vertovec and Robin Cohen, ed., *Migration, Diaspora and Transnationalism* (Cheltenham, 1999), p. XVII.

6. For an analysis of the discussion on migrations from mountain communities, see Abel Poitrineau, *Remues d'hommes. Essai sur les migrations montagnardes en France aux XVII et XVIII siècles* (Paris, 1983); Lucassen, *Migrant Labor*; *Col bastone e la bisaccia*; Cavaciocchi, *Migrazioni in Europa*; Antonio Eiras Roel and Ofelia Rey Castelao, ed., *Migraciones internas y medium-distance en la Peninsula Iberica, 1500-1900* (Santiago de Compostela, 1994). The conclusions which I offer here are developed more fully in Laurence Fontaine, *Pouvoir, identités et migrations dans les hautes vallées des Alpes occidentales (XVIIe–XVIIIe siècles)* (Grenoble, 2003), pp. 218–25.

7. For more details, see Laurence Fontaine, *History of Pedlars in Europe* (Cambridge, 1996).

8. Unfortunately, I cannot retrace the forms of family ties in these commercial organizations. It is difficult to discern how precisely they used blood ties and marriage. The sources are fragmentary and greatly dependent upon chance, since many of the legal documents relating to transactions were not drawn up in the villages of origin but in those of migration.

9. Johannes Augel, *Italienische Einwanderung und Wirtschaftstätigkeit in rheinischen Städten des 17. und 18. Jahrhunderts* (Bonn, 1971), pp. 62–105, 193.

10. The index of Augel (*Italienische Einwanderung*) mentions seventy-seven Brentanos settled in the Rhine area between the end of the seventeenth century and the end of the eighteenth century. J. Rumpf-Fleck, *Italienische Kultur in Frankfurt am Main im 18. Jahrhundert* (Cologne, 1936), pp. 25–28, studies the different branches established in Frankfurt, and gives on pages 133 to 135 a list of the Brentanos, deriving from the four family branches, established in Frankfurt during the seventeenth and eighteenth centuries.

11. Mario Infelise, *L'editoria veneziana nel '700* (Milan, 1989), p. 237; and I Remondini di Bassano, *Stampa e industria nel Veneto del Settecento* (Bassano, 1980).

12. Michel Foucault, *Histoire de la sexualité*, tome 1: *La volonté de savoir* (Paris, 1976).

13. David W. Sabean, *Property, Production and Family in Neckarhausen, 1700–1870* (Cambridge, 1990), pp. 1–37. See also the discussion in Giovanni Lévi, *L'Eredità Immateriale, Carriera di un Esorcista nel Piemonte del Seicento* (Turin, 1985), chap. 2. Two studies clearly show the inadequacy of this framework: Huges Neveux, "Individu, famille et communauté à Villiers-Le-Bel (1573-1587) (d'après des Testaments)," in *114e Congrès national des Sociétés savantes* (Paris, 1989); *Histoire moderne et contemporaine* (Paris, 1990), pp. 405–19; David J. Siddle, "Articulating the Grid of Inheritance: The Accumulation and Transmission of Wealth in Peasant Savoy 1561–1792," *Itinera* 5/6 (1986): pp. 123–80.

14. Examples in Fontaine, *Pedlars*, chap. 1.

15. Sabine Juratic, "Les femmes dans la librairie parisienne au XVIIIe siècle," in *L'Europe et le livre. Réseaux et pratiques du négoce de librairie XVIe-XIXe siècles*, ed. Frédéric Barbier, Sabine Juratic, and Dominique Varry (Paris, 1996), pp. 247–76; G.

Sheridan, "Women in the Book Trade in Eighteenth Century France," *British Journal for Eighteenth-Century Studies* 15 (1992): pp. 51–69.

16. *La Femme. Recueils de la société Jean Bodin pour l'histoire comparative des institutions* (Brussels, 1962), vol. XII; Laurence Fontaine, "Women and Credit. Practices and Cultures in Early Modern Europe," in *Women and Credit: Researching the Past, Refiguring the Future*, ed. Beverly Lemire, Ruth Pearson, and Gail Campbell (Oxford, 2002), pp. 15–32.

17. Consider, for example, Normandy, where lineage was very important up until the end of the eighteenth century and remains very constraining for women who do not attain their full wealth until the death of their husbands.

18. Pierre Petot, "Le statut de la femme dans les pays coutumiers français du XIIIe au XVIIe siècle," in *La Femme*, pp. 243–54, here p. 251.

19. *La Femme*, pp. 247, 462.

20. Lodovica Braida, *Il commercio delle idee. Editoria e circulazione del libro nello Torino del Settecento* (Florence, 1995); and idem "Le commerce du livre en Genève et l'Italie au XVIII siècle: agents, obstacles, pratiques," in Barbier et al., *L'Europe et le livre*, pp. 279–307.

21. On these issues, see Fontaine, *Pedlars*, chaps. 2 and 7.

22. Thomas Riis, "Scottish-Danish relations in the sixteenth century," in *Scotland and Europe, 1200–1850*, ed. Thomas C. Smout (Edinburgh, 1986), pp. 82–96, here pp. 88–91; Jonathan J. Israel, *Dutch Trade Hegemony* (Oxford, 1989); A. Bieganska, "A Note on the Scots in Poland, 1550–1800," in Smout, *Scotland and Europe*, pp. 157–65, here p. 159.

23. Thomas A. Fischer, *The Scots in Sweden* (Edinburgh, 1907), p. 37.

24. Mark Granovetter, "Les institutions économiques comme constructions sociales: un cadre d'analyse," in *Analyse économique des conventions*, ed. André Orléan (Paris, 1994), pp. 79–94.

25. Clifford Geertz, *Pedlars and Princes* (Chicago, 1963), p. 123.

26. Granovetter, "Les institutions économiques," p. 88.

27. Augel, *Italienische Einwanderung*, p.199.

28. Examples in Laurence Fontaine, "Solidarités familiales et logiques migratoires en pays de montagne à l'époque moderne," *Annales ESC* 45 (1990): pp. 1433–50.

29. Examples for the Ticino in Sandro Guzzi, "Local Autonomies and Alpine Political Systems: The Italian Swiss from the Seventeenth to the Eighteenth Century," *Itinera* 12 (1992): pp. 229–55; and for the Dauphiné, in Fontaine, *Pouvoir*, p. 235. In addition, the payments in cereal that are often made in the country mean that related occupations also impact upon the family clan. Bakery is one of these privileged occupations. Ulrich Pfister has shown that, in the region of Zurich, peddlers and bakers came from the same Alpine villages: Ulrich Pfister, *Die Zürcher Fabriques. Protoindustrielles Wachstum vom 16. zum 18. Jahrhundert* (Zürich, 1992). Rose Duroux made the same observation about the Auvergne and Castille in the eighteenth and nineteenth centuries: Rose Duroux, "Les boutiquiers cantaliens de Nouvelle-Castille au XIXe siècle," *Mélanges de la Casa de Velasquez* XXI (1985): pp. 281–307.

30. David Siddle defines the *gens* in this way: "the widest set of kinsmen linked by family name and marriage who can, in certain circumstances, recognize a level of involvement in the affairs of any individual family ménage or lineage. So that individual family ménage under a head is 'nested' within a lineage which itself is nested within a gens," "Grid of Inheritance," p. 168.

Chapter XI

Kin Marriages

Trends and Interpretations from the Swiss Example

Jon Mathieu

For factual and methodological reasons, marriage is one of the best indicators of the historical development of kinship in Europe. In factual terms, marriage established long-term connections between categories of people for all sorts of exchange processes and thereby represented the center of the reproduction of kinship networks. Methodologically, the use or nonuse of relatives for marriage alliances can be more easily and systematically ascertained from the sources than their use for other purposes. An important result of research is the observation that marriages between close relatives multiplied in the eighteenth and nineteenth centuries. This multiplication is to be observed in quite varied regional and chronological contexts. Jean-Marie Gouesse, for example, examined the marriages of very close relatives for many countries over a long period and registered a real boom since circa 1750.[1]

We are still far away, however, from being able to comprehensively survey the European marriage trends of the last five hundred years. Additionally, their historical interpretation throws open quite a few questions. The problems already begin at the factual level. If one assumes that marriages in an earlier period were systematically made between distant relatives, then the multiplication of marriages between closer relatives from the mid eighteenth century onwards could be understood as a contraction trend. Furthermore, the fact that this narrowing down was coupled with marriages between completely unrelated people points towards a disruption of the older structures of endogamy. This is the position that Gérard Delille has presented in various works over the last two decades. The thesis of David Sabean is different. He argues that in the early eighteenth century, a shift from exogamous to endogamous marriage practices occurred, which peaked around the year 1880. This shift was an expression of an intensification of kinship relations—in the course of modernization, a "kinship hot society" developed in Europe.[2] These two accounts differ from each other both in their starting point and their main focus. While the first one assumes a loosely defined endogamy in an early phase and points to an increase in exogamous marriages in the eighteenth and nineteenth centuries, the second one starts with predominant exogamy and points to a later increase in endogamy. Naturally, the differing assumptions about the direction of the trend influence the historical interpretation. General to the debate is that this change in kinship (and both theses emphasize change) opens a wide field of interesting problems.

The following chapter pursues two goals. It first sketches the history of the marriage of relatives in Switzerland from the sixteenth to the nineteenth century, and then attempts to answer the question of which direction one can interpret the historical trend. Was there a contraction or an intensification of kinship, and which arguments can be put forward regarding the kinship change?[3]

In the early modern period, the area that is now Switzerland consisted of an association of urban and rural territories, later called cantons. Some of them joined the Reformation in the sixteenth century, while the others stayed with the old Church. Under the pressure of the French Revolution, this loose association, or *Corpus Helveticum*, developed around 1800, for a few years into the Helvetic Republic; the founding of a durable federal state with a general rule of law and administration came only in 1848. The use or nonuse of kin as marriage partners and the related question of the historical place of familial exogamy or endogamy is to be observed in this area in two interconnected sources: in the marriage laws (primarily in the Protestant territories) and in the marriage dispensations (mostly in the Catholic territories).

Before we turn to these two indicators of marriage trends, it seems necessary to counter the idea that in small communities, generally all the residents stood in close relation to each other, and that they therefore could not avoid marrying relatives. The creation of models and calculations do not confirm this common sense assumption. Theoretically, most people, even under relatively restricted conditions, had the choice of marriage partners among many unrelated people as well as a few relatives.[4] Measured by lawmaking and the issuing of dispensations, these alternatives played a varying role in different historical periods.

Marriage Law

In canon law, the prohibitions on marriage between relatives remained, in essence, unchanged from the thirteenth until the early twentieth century. In the collateral dimension of blood relatives, to which I will limit myself here, they generally included relatives of the fourth degree. Great-grandchildren of siblings (that is, third cousins)[5] were not allowed to marry, but more distant relatives were allowed. However, with special permission of the Church, one could marry inside this circle. The difficulty of getting a dispensation correlated to the closeness of the relation. In Catholic areas of Switzerland, the civil authorities and clergy occasionally debated the modalities of the dispensations and their theoretical justification, but the legitimacy of prohibitions itself was not questioned.[6]

Lawmaking developed differently in the areas that went over to the new confession. The reformers, prompted by questions regarding the allowance of marriages, fell back on Biblical texts and criticized the hierarchical and financially motivated issuance of dispensation: "What was formerly attained with dispensations and fees, should all be finished," dictated the Zurich marriage ordinance of 1525. Yet, the enactment of a binding law no longer perforated with special permissions proved quite difficult, because the Holy Scripture listed in Leviticus 18 and 20 only a limited number of forbidden relationships; even first cousins had to be allowed to marry, according to the Bible. In fact, liberalism ruled in Huldrich Zwingli's Zurich and in other allied areas during the early phase of the Reformation. But after only a short time, the prohibitions were again expanded; the negative reaction and the corresponding pressure from the populace may have been decisive. Marriages between siblings' children led to "many rumors, aggravation, indignation, shame, and repugnance among us and our neighbors." Even a marriage of relatives of the third/fourth degree could bring on a "clamor of some kinship."[7]

Important steps towards consolidation were two conferences in Zurich in 1533 at which delegates from Bern, Basel, Schaffhausen, and St. Gallen were present. Not the least of the reasons for the conference was the disputed question of kin marriage. The assembly, in its majority,

decided to extend the prohibition out to relatives of the third degree—
a limit which, with a certain flexibility and an omnipresent uncertainty,
became the norm for many Protestant areas, at least temporarily.[8] After
an especially conservative phase in the late sixteenth century, the
rolling back of the prohibitions emerged as the dominant trend, similar
to that in the German lands. In keeping with the political structure of
the *Corpus Helveticum*, the change manifested itself in individual territories, and especially in localized areas, even on the scale of individual
courts and communes. In 1591, Zurich renounced a briefly enacted
prohibition on relatives of third/fourth degree. A little later, dispensations for relatives of the third degree were introduced; they were initially disputed, but were normalized by the eighteenth century. In
1667, the struggle over dispensations for relatives of the second/third
degree began, and a century later, they were regularly issued. The development in the early modern period was similar in Schaffhausen. In
1737, Basel allowed marriages of relatives of the second/third degree,
but then returned briefly to the customary dispensation practice, only
to quickly organize that process more rationally. Things were taken a
step further in Graubünden, where the disputes were sometimes decided
by individual courts or communes. In 1766, the Protestant session
made marriages of the second degree (first cousins) eligible for dispensations, which, according to the minutes, pained the clergy more than a
little.[9] Geneva seems to have been ahead of them all. John Calvin had
attacked the canon marriage prohibitions in his early writings, but here
again, the lawmaking of the sixteenth century acted conservatively.
"Pour éviter scandale en ce qui de longtemps n'a point esté accoustumé,"
marriages between first cousins were forbidden and, in practice, the
prohibition was extended further. In contrast, the authorities were later
liberal and granted dispensations for marriages of first cousins, despite
protests from the consistory. In 1713, the prohibition was lifted entirely,
"puisque le mariage, dans ce degré de parentage, n'est point défendu
par la Loi Divine." Such cousin marriages were obviously no longer so
scandalous that they had to be prosecuted by the authorities.[10]

Thereby, Geneva anticipated the developments of the Helvetic Revolution, which in turn anticipated the developments in Swiss lawmaking in the nineteenth century. Shortly after its proclamation in the
spring of 1798, the Helvetic Republic was swamped with appeals for
dispensations from first cousins who wished to marry. These were
approved by the authorities without exception and without demanding
a fee. In light of their liberal role models in revolutionary France, any
different stance would have been surprising. When the question of a
general rule arose, the various opinions were expressed. Whether such

marriages were really "repugnant," whether they simply served the "piling up of riches," what natural law and Leviticus said about the matter, to what degree genetic disorders would be passed along—old and new arguments now flowed together in a multifaceted debate. The final draft, which was accepted by a considerable majority, determined the "freedom of the individual citizens" to be the first priority, with the result: "The civil law in the Helvetic Republic does not forbid marriages between first cousins or further degrees."[11]

The Helvetic Republic did not last long, so after a few years, the question again fell to the cantons. However, the change of opinion now accelerated on a broader scale. In Zurich, where, until the revolution, marriages of first cousins had not even been issued dispensations, the prohibition was dropped when fifty years later the civil law code was issued, the same code which was in part or in whole assumed by other cantons. With the enactment of the federal law regarding civil status and marriage of 1874, this liberal law was applied throughout Switzerland; the national civil law code assumed the same rule in 1907. In the preliminary commissions and in the parliamentary debates at both points, the marriage of first cousins was no real issue. There were "sanitary considerations" presented in opposition during the preparation of the civil law code, and an initiative was made to extend the prohibition anew, to which a third of the commission members agreed. Still, in comparison to the other problems facing the commission members and in comparison to the horror with which these relationships has been regarded at the beginning of the modern period, the reaction was limited.[12]

Thus, except for the canon rules, which for Catholics remained valid in their religious existence, the familial marriage prohibitions were rolled back three degrees over the course of 350 years. This is not the place to explore the multifaceted discourse that accompanied this change. Generally, we can assume that at no point did it represent a coherent whole.[13] One of the emotional roots of the opposition surely lay in the ideas of sexuality and pollution. It was said in the early seventeenth century that, if the circle of possible marriages were pulled in too closely, "then soon great and serious, yes, damnable incest would be considered acceptable." Similarly, in 1798, some argued that there should be a distance "fence" around incest: "It is better to be too strict with it than too mild."[14] In that period, the political argument was also popular: that the marriage of close relatives was merely an accumulation mechanism whereby money and property were concentrated in certain families. In the course of the nineteenth century, the new medical-biological view took the upper hand; that such marriages (which were particularly common among doctors' families) were responsible for every sort of bodily ailment.[15] That the lawmakers repealed the restrictions despite every counterargument is thanks not just to the new relationship between state, church, and citizen, which had developed since the revolution. Earlier juristic practice had already had to take into consideration the values of the populace to some extent, and here it appears that large groups surmounted their aversion to kin marriages, because they were increasingly interested in marrying their kin.

Marriage Dispensations

We can best demonstrate this last point with a contrast to marriage law: the number of individual dispensations. In the Protestant territories, quantitative figures are difficult to produce because of the changing standards and record keeping practices. Yet, the widely renewed dispensation policies already give a hint, and the literature also offers some quantifiable figures. In Zurich, the number of approvals of marriages in the third degree slowly climbed after the middle of the seventeenth century and reached an average in the eighteenth century of twenty-five cases per year, whereby the expensive concessions became a fiscal consideration. In Neuchâtel, after an early phase that is difficult to interpret, there was a dramatic increase in petitions and dispensations at the end of the Ancien Regime. Until the middle of the eighteenth century, the authorities never had to decide on more than one petition for a marriage of relatives per year, but in the last quarter of the century, this accelerated to an average of seven per year.[16]

Long-term developments in the Catholic areas are easier to follow on a broader scale, because the constant canon rules offer a more valid comparison between various periods. Additionally, since the Council of Trent, care was usually taken to record approved dispensations in the parish records, so that their numbers can at least be approximately reconstructed for many areas. Table 11.1 represents a sample of fourteen localities from seven cantons, compiled in conjunction with available demographic studies. The marriage of relatives was mostly only cursorily and partially dealt with in these studies (marriage of relatives was not one of the standard themes of such studies in the 1970s and 1980s), but the recourse to available materials is a good starting point for the expansion of data and has the additional benefit that the figures are easily put into the context of the contemporary local demography. The tables (11.1 and 11.2) show an increase and a narrowing of the marriage of relatives from the seventeenth to the nineteenth century. In a first phase, the proportion of marriages between distant relatives especially climbed, and in a second

Table 11.1: Permitted Kin Marriages in Catholic Localities of
Present-day Switzerland, Seventeenth to Nineteenth Centuries

Territory		1600	1700			1800			1900
GR	Camuns etc.	–	28/0	38/0	38/2	31/2	29/9		
GR	Tarasp	24/0	31/2	46/0	48/2	25/1	19/8		
LU	Entlebuch	–	–	4/–	11/–	–	–		
LU	Marbach	–	–	29/0	22/1	14/3	19/3		
SO	Lostorf	2/0	2/1	6/0	12/1	16/0	11/6		
SO	Oensingen	2/1	3/0	10/2	12/1	–	–		
SO	Starrkirch	0/0	2/0	1/1	8/1	11/1	–		
SZ	Freienbach	–	3/0	5/0	5/0	7/2	–		
SZ	Muotathal	–	0/0	29/1	42/2	29/2	26/6		
TI	Miglieglia	–	–	40/0	58/11	49/14	–		
UR	Urseren	–	–	37/3	38/6	43/9	–		
VS	Conthey	–	14/0	23/1	43/4	46/6	35/7		
VS	Leuk	–	2/0	17/1	13/1	13/5	10/5		
VS	Simplon Dorf	0/0	7/1	19/1	36/4	29/6	45/14		

NOTES:

a/b

a = permitted kin marriages up to and including the fourth degree of kinship as
    a percentage of all marriages.

b = permitted kin marriages up to and including the second/third degree of
    kinship as a percentage of all marriages.

– no information: not registered or not investigated.

GR = Grisons, LU = Lucerne, SO = Solothurn, SZ = Schwyz, TI = Ticino,
    UR = Uri, VS = Valais.

The figures are sometimes based only on shorter periods within the
    fifty-year-period.

For sources and specific periods investigated, see Appendix 1.

phase, the alliances between closer relatives increased.[17] In most areas,
the indicated totality of kin marriages reached its peak between 1750 and
1850; afterwards, it declined, perhaps because of declining registration,
too. On the other hand, in the nineteenth century there was an increase
in the marriage of close relatives almost everywhere—on average three-
or fourfold more than in the late eighteenth century. The marriage of first
cousins, especially, became an increasingly common practice.

Concerning the large differences between localities, we can only say that considerable local and regional variations in Europe must be regarded as normal.[18] A comment must be made, however, regarding the reliability of the sources. Without a doubt, the parish records used did not record all of the dispensations that were issued in reality, much less all of the marriages of relatives without dispensations. There was also considerable variation in record keeping; for example, in certain cases, local differences prove in the first instance to be differences in the quality of the available sources. However, it would be incorrect to assume that the records became generally more exact from the seventeenth to the nineteenth century. Already in the decades after 1600, the parish records in some places make a surprisingly disciplined impression; the clergy proved again and again that they were following the Tridentine rules regarding the issuing of marriage bans and the researching of possible disqualifications. The material for family reconstitution improved due to this conscientiousness, but the necessary motivation could also be withdrawn. This applies above all to the nineteenth century, when the state increasingly made dispensations a private matter, and especially after 1874, when dispensations were removed entirely from official records, so that we have only a few entries from the last decades of the nineteenth century.[19]

Table 11.2: Applications for Marriages of Close Kin in the Bishoprics of the Nunziatura di Lucerna, Sixteenth to Nineteenth Centuries

Time Years	Months	Territory	Applications –2nd/3rd Degree	Per year For CH	Proportion 2nd Degree	Proportion Consanguineal
1572–1584	156	BC	*1	* 0	–	–
1647	3	NL	6	** 16	33%	33%
1669	6	NL	23	** 33	13%	50%
1733–1734	14	BC	42	** 72	–	–
1809	12	NL	140	** 112	77%	90%
1817	12	CH	122	122	61%	81%
1869–1871	36	CH	839	280	69%	90%

NOTES: BC = bishopric of Constance. NL = Nunziatura di Lucerna before 1815, without the associated part of the Bishopric of Como. CH = Nunziatura di Lucerna after 1815, roughly corresponding to present-day Switzerland.
* The source mentions only dispensations up to and including the second degree (for all bishoprics).
** Estimate for CH based on the proportional figures from 1809 and 1817, subtracting only the large non-Swiss part of the bishopric of Constance.
SOURCES: 1572–1584: Archivio Segreto Vaticano, Fondo Benedetto XIV, bolle e costituzioni 4, fol. 108–20. 1647–1871: Archivio Segreto Vaticano, Archivio della Nunziatura in Lucerna 282, fol. 253–95; 278, fol. 485; 322, fol. 328–60, 304–15; 283, fol. 203–43, 416–22, 429–37, 474–75, 478.

Most dispensations were issued by the seven bishops whose dioceses include our areas of study, by the nuncio responsible for this area in Lucerne, and from the Pope in Rome. Generally, the greater the impediment to the marriage, that is, the closer the familial relationship of the couple, the higher up the hierarchy the dispensation was issued. In particular cases, however, the issuance of dispensations was again and again the object of controversy between the various officials, not least of all because of the substantial financial stakes which could be involved. The eighteenth century stands out as especially full of conflict; the nuncio's office disputed individual permissions with three of the bishoprics and with the Catholic confederation.[20] One explanation for the increase in disputes is the increase in the number of dispensations issued, which made the dispensations more lucrative. In Table 11.2 the available numbers of the applications for marriages between close relatives are listed (approved almost without exception), which were sent directly to Rome before the creation of the Lucerne nuncio in 1586, and were thereafter collected by the Nuncio and sent on to the Holy See. Because the dispensation procedure for these serious impediments to marriage was quite strictly regulated, one can assume that the figures represent a reliable indicator. As fragmentary as this source material may be, its message is just as unmistakable: the petitions for marriages between close relatives increased massively from the late sixteenth to the nineteenth century. This is valid, still, when one takes into account a certain centralization of the dispensation administration and the general increase in the population.[21]

Especially dramatic according to the available data, was the increase in the later phase, the period in which parish records are also dominated by marriages among close relatives. In the years before the suspension of the nuncio in Lucerne (1873) the negotiation of dispensations became a regular industry, dependent on preprinted forms and the telegraph.[22] Furthermore, Table 11.2 shows that the marriage circles of the nineteenth century, even within close kin, had tightened relative to those of the seventeenth century (there is a higher proportion of marriages with relatives of the second degree or closer), and in-law relationships no longer played such an important role in marriages between relatives as they did in the earlier period (there is a higher proportion of consanguineous marriages). Above all, the first conclusion is easily confirmed at the local level in many parish records.[23]

Generally, the developments in the area under study follow the international trend, which had its peak in the decades around 1900, and afterwards declined, sometimes abruptly. When the drop off in marriages between close relatives occurred exactly, I cannot say. When in the 1930s the first studies on "incest" in remote areas first appeared, the process had probably been underway for some time. The researchers, motivated by racial-hygienic doctrines, assumed then that the populations under study had carried on the same narrow marriage practices forever and ever, despite indicators to the contrary. Many historical demography studies of the 1970s and 1980s followed them in this point. The evidence could have shown a clear increase in kin marriages over time, yet their interpretation only pointed to the high incidence in a later period and explained that the local endogamy had not allowed anything else.[24] Thereby they fell back, mostly without being conscious of it, on an old explanation: the formula *ob angustiam loci*—because of the constrictions of the locality—belonged to the standard justifications for dispensations (just as, in turn, opponents of the marriage of relatives pointed again and again to the broad selection of marriage partners).[25] Yet, over the long term, it is shown that marriages between relatives increased when the population was experiencing strong growth and many localities were becoming bigger. According to the assumption that there was constant local endogamy (not realistic, but supported by stereotype), people would then have increasingly married relatives exactly when they could have married an especially large number of unrelated people.

Contraction or Intensification of Kin Relations?

Here the question arises, who of the marriage partners really were regarded as kin and who were not? As is mentioned above, Delille is of the opinion that Europe, until the seventeenth century, was dominated by an alliance system that was characterized by marriages among relatives at degrees outside the canonical prohibitions. The reciprocity between family branches and individual families via the "exchange of women" played an important role. He therefore regards the multiplication of marriages between relatives of the forbidden degrees during the eighteenth and nineteenth centuries as a contraction, and the many marriages between unrelated people in this period as a divergence, from the earlier comprehensive endogamy. Generally this manifests the decrease in significance that kinship suffered during economic and social modernization. Empirically, Delille relies heavily on the analyses of genealogies. Theoretically, his thesis falls in with the tradition of structural anthropology founded by Claude Lévi-Strauss.[26] Of the problems that this approach presents, we want to address one central one—were marriages outside of the fourth degree regarded as marriages between relatives at all? Or, said differently, how far did the consciousness of kinship reach, and where did it normally cease? These questions cannot be answered by genealogical research. They require an investigation of the meaning of such social relationships from the perspective of the historical actors to whom Delille gives little attention.[27]

One such historical actor, whose understanding and practice within our area of study we can reconstruct, is Martin Peider Schmid. Schmid belonged to the village elite of the Grisons. In the years following 1770, he wrote a voluminous chronicle, which contains countless hints at this issue. As Schmid retold his sometimes bitter life experiences, for example, he put kinship in terms of friend and foe. The greater the number of relatives, the better one could defend oneself, "by one person standing up for the other, be it with good advice, with good help, or even with violence, which should only be used in extreme cases; of such great importance are relatives." In another instance, he thought about the words of the preacher who, in his Sunday sermon, argued against rolling back the marriage prohibitions and thereby said, "How praiseworthy it is, to keep on observing a good and exact family order." Schmid shared this point of view, above all, because through exogamous marriages, "more relatives are bound up together into one party."[28] He gauged the size of any given kinship network based on the number of first cousins. To him, they were "close" relatives. Second cousins he held for only "good relatives," and third cousins he regarded on occasion as "still a little related." At this distance, though, the relationships were uncertain, and in some instances, Schmid was only able to reconstruct them with the help of the inheritance history. From his remarks, it is clear, moreover, that the living or recognized kinship relations inside these circles also varied subjectively; naturally, not every person in the same category would be handled and remembered the same.[29]

And how was it in the general population? The chronicler lamented at one point that the distant progenitors were no longer known in many peasant families, because to them work was important, but not their "name."[30] In fact, his personal horizon, which extended to the bounds of the canon rules, does not seem to be especially limited. A sign of this is the customary usage of kin denominators. The official documents of his home region teem with first cousins of the public clerks; they obviously found it difficult to distinguish and name closely related people in a neutral way. Second cousins of the clerks also appear in such sources regularly, but nowhere near as often as they should given their fourfold larger number. Further out, the use of family titles decreases dramatically. Third cousins were distinguished from other neighbors only sporadically or not at all.[31] It seems, then, that the kinship in this area was recognized out to the third or fourth degree, but surely not further.

Given the current state of the research, it is not easy to judge the situation in other parts of Switzerland. One indicator that can be used are the laws on legal disqualification or recusation. They were enacted to regulate and reduce the conflicts between public decision making and personal involvement due to kinship in court cases and in politics. So it was proclaimed in 1609 in the city of Bern that for some time, "with the exclusion of kinfolk much inequality has been wrought, and thereby disorder unleashed." In order to prevent such "abuses," the rule was issued that in elections, court cases, or other decisions, all blood relatives up to and including first cousins had to abstain.[32] In the volumes of Swiss juridical sources published thus far, one finds disqualification laws citing specific degrees of kinship for eight cantons. Some of them were already issued in the fifteenth and sixteenth centuries; most were from the decades after 1600. The issue seems to have been an especially relevant one at that time, but it remained important in the eighteenth century, and in the nineteenth century, part of the regulations were incorporated into the modern law code. This process of systematization and clarification of kinship relations by the state is of interest in many ways, but here we want to limit ourselves to the range of kinship.[33] Most edicts set the disqualification limit on relatives of the second or third degree; in some cases the fourth degree was included. Only in one canton and for a short period do we find a law that extends to kinship à l'infini for certain cases.[34]

As in the Swiss case, the majority of research from other parts of Europe shows that the range of the consciousness of kinship should not be overestimated. Raul Merzario demonstrates with many vivid examples in his investigation of the Como diocese how difficult it was for villagers of the early modern period to keep their genealogic memory straight or to refresh it for the clarification of possible impediments to marriage. According to him, the fourth degree of kinship was the distinct limit. Studies from France and from the German-speaking lands generally reach the same conclusions.[35] This is not to say that marriages between further distant kinship grades could not be the expression of purposeful politics—especially among the elites, for example, in the struggle for a dynastic right to rule passed on to a daughter. However, it is difficult to see how such marriages between distant relatives, in the case of normal society, could be the result of conscious strategies and, up to 1700, the basis for a comprehensive endogamous system of alliances.[36]

With this, Sabean's thesis—that the multiplication of marriages between relatives in the eighteenth and nineteenth centuries should be

regarded as a shift from exogamous to endogamous marriage practices—gains plausibility. An entirely different interpretation is bound
up in this thesis. Seen this way, the modernization process did not lead
to a decrease in the significance of kinship, but rather, to intensification
and increased importance.[37] Investigating how people perceived kinship can also improve the view of this particular period. As we have
seen, first and second cousins were regarded in our area of study as
"close" and "good" relatives, respectively, while third cousins were
regarded as "only a little related"; the aforementioned tightening of permitted marriages of relatives in the nineteenth century appears, in this
light, as a crescendo, even if the total marriages within the canon
degrees decreased after 1850. The intensification thesis is also supported by studies from gender history and research on modern bourgeois society. They show from various perspectives and on the basis of
entirely different sources how strongly Swiss society in the industrial
century was characterized by kinship.[38]

Furthermore, the intensification thesis is more plausible than the
contraction thesis for the assessment of the long-term developments in
lawmaking and administration. The intensification thesis assumes a
dialectical relationship or a negotiation process between the values
and interests of the population, on one side, and the public decisions
of the church and the state, on the other. The formulation and administration of marriage laws could in some areas anticipate the development, but on the whole, they were dependent on general changes in
public opinion. Against this, the contraction thesis ultimately relies on
a natural tendency of premodern societies toward familial endogamy.
That the "exchange of women" occurred in the degrees outside the
canon rules is supposedly thanks only to the constant repression of
Church and state authorities.[39] Historically, it is then difficult to com-
prehend why, in the Reformation period, the populace argued for
exogamy and why the authorities gradually dismantled their comprehensive marriage prohibitions.

Conclusions

Since the nineteenth century, many intellectuals have assumed that
kinship was an archaic organizational principle and that it could be dis-
regarded in analyzing the modern West. For example, the author of the
Swiss civil law code, Eugen Huber, wrote in 1901 that the restriction of
the individual and the marginal role of the state in earlier times had
given a tremendous role to familial associations, but that the traces of

kinship in the modern world were rapidly disappearing.[40] In any case, this assumption of a general decrease of significance may be applied more to the public representation of kinship than to its real use. Since the Enlightenment, the criticisms of dynastic principles, the conceptual separation of private and public spheres, and other causes have led to a diminishing of kinship in intellectual and political discourse. However, this does not mean that the development ran in the same direction at all levels. The difficulty of escaping from such *idées reçues* is demonstrated by the phenomenon of the marriage of relatives. It only represents *one* indicator relevant to the theme (one should consider other indicators), but for factual and methodological reasons, one should recognize it as critically important.

The area of present-day Switzerland, our area of study, has had a biconfessional character since the Reformation, and therefore allows a view at different variants of the process. The use or nonuse of relatives for marriage alliances is to be observed in two interrelated sources: in the marriage laws (primarily in the Protestant territories) and in the marriage dispensations (mostly in the Catholic territories). At the level of lawmaking, the marriage prohibitions were rolled back three degrees from the sixteenth to the nineteenth century. Around 1500, one could only marry his fourth cousin; by 1900, first cousins were acceptable as marriage partners. The dispensations for forbidden kin marriages, documented in local and central records, show a parallel development. They increased practically everywhere, and especially in the eighteenth and nineteenth centuries, became a common occurrence. In general, then, Switzerland followed a European trend which hit its high point around 1900. This shift hardly lets itself be reconciled with a general decrease in the significance of kinship. Research into the consciousness of kinship indicates that people did not systematically marry relatives of distant degrees in an earlier phase, and that there was no subsequent contraction trend, but rather that we are witness to a shift from exogamous to endogamous marriage practices. The use of kinship intensified and relatives became potential marriage partners during a certain phase of modernization.

Why? In the research, one finds a series of arguments based on demographics, economics, politics, and culture. Regarding the relevance of some factors, there is widespread consensus, while other explanations are still debated. Above all, arguments that link this shift in any way with demographic processes are disputed.[41] Generally, socioeconomic explanations are greeted with more agreement. The intensification of kinship occurred before the background of an opening and expansion of the economy and state. In this situation it was important to develop new strategies to appropriate resources and status. Since the inheritance of certain claims lost their value as society became more dynamic, many families shifted to more actively using kinship relations. For the process of class building, this was, as Sabean states, of almost infrastructural significance, because kinship endogamy formed the nucleus of class endogamy.[42]

(Translation: Benjamin Marschke)

Appendix

1. Permitted kin marriages, according to local sources (for Table 11.1)

The unpublished studies can be found at the university institutes. The parish registers that I consulted to gather more data are cited in an abbreviated manner ("and PR"); their location can be found in the studies. Where the period under study does not correspond to a fifty-year period, this is specified in parentheses. The abbreviations "GR," "LU," and so forth, indicate the cantons (see Table 11.1).

GR: Giusep Bass, *Quantitative Untersuchung zur Bevölkerungsgeschichte der Lugnezer Pfarreien Camuns, Cumbel, Lumbrein, Pleif, Vigens und Vrin von 1650–1850* (unpublished Lizentiatsarbeit, University of Basel, 1977), p. 80, and PR (Camuns etc. 1651–1700, not for all parishes, 1851–1874); Jon Mathieu, *Eine Region am Rande: das Unterengadin 1650–1800. Studien zur Gesellschaft* (Ph.D. diss., University of Berne, 1983), p. 169, and PR (Tarasp 1629–1635 and 1646–1649, 1850–1875).
LU: Silvio Bucher, *Bevölkerung und Wirtschaft des Amtes Entlebuch im 18. Jahrhundert,* (Luzern, 1974), p. 51, and PR (Entlebuch 1710–1729, 1765–1781, Marbach 1710–1749, 1850–1855).
SO: André Schluchter, *Das Gösgeramt im Ancien Régime. Bevölkerung, Wirtschaft und Gesellschaft einer solothurnischen Landvogtei im 17. und 18. Jahrhundert* (Basel, 1990), pp. 383–95, and PR (Lostorf 1750–1774 and 1787–1799, 1800–1819, 1850–1869, Starrkirch 1620–1649, 1800–1829); Theo Ehrsam, *Quantitative Untersuchungen zur Bevölkerungsgeschichte im solothurnischen Mittelland im 18. und frühen 19. Jahrhundert* (unpublished Lizentiatsarbeit, University Basel, 1975), pp. 86–91, and PR (Oensingen 1750–1789).

SZ: Urspeter Schelbert, *Quantitative Untersuchungen zur Bevölkerungs-geschichte der beiden Schwyzer Pfarreien Muotathal und Freienbach im 18. und frühen 19. Jahrhundert* (unpublished Lizentiatsarbeit, University Basel, 1976), pp. 45, 132, and PR (Freienbach 1801–1839, Muotathal 1681–1700, 1851–1874).

TI: Stephan Robert Epstein, *Miglieglia. Storia demografica e sociale di un paese, 1700–1849* (n.d. [after 1978, Historisches Seminar Basel SC 2901/27]), p 29.

UR: Anselm Zurfluh, *Une population alpine dans la Confédération. Uri aux XVIIe et XVIIIe siècles. Démographie et mentalités* (unpublished Thèse de doctorat, Université de Nice, 1983), p. 349 (Urseren 1801–1830).

VS: Jean-Henri Papilloud, *Histoire démographique de Conthey (Valais) 1680–1830,* (Fribourg, 1973), pp. 95, 206–7, and PR (Conthey 1683–1700, 1801–1825, 1851–1875); parish registers Leuk, communication by Lydia Brunner (Leuk 1657–1699, 1850–1869, and 1880–1899); database of the Forschungsinstitut für die Geschichte des Alpenraums Brig, and PR (Simplon Dorf 1641–1649).

2. Legal disqualification due to kinship in Swiss juridical sources (for note 34)

All cited volumes from: *Sammlung Schweizerischer Rechtsquellen, namens des Schweizerischen Juristenvereins herausgegeben von dessen Rechtsquellenstiftung* (Aarau, later Basel, since 1898). Cited are exemption articles detailing the degree of kinship; given the current state of publication, they come from eight cantons. Articles issued before 1600 are cited in italics.

BE: Die Rechtsquellen des Kantons Bern, Erster Teil: Stadtrechte, vol. 5, pp. 180–81, 527; vol. 7, p. *567*; Zweiter Teil: Rechte der Landschaft, vol. 1/1, pp. 186–87, vol. 2, p. 316, vol. 5, p. 312.

GL: Die Rechtsquellen des Kantons Glarus, vol. 2, pp. 706, 751, 752, *773*; vol. 3, pp. 1020, 1032, 1039, 1089, 1481; vol. 4, pp. 1551, 1593, 1633, 1698, 1772, 1881, 1955, 1980, 1982.

ZG: Die Rechtsquellen des Kantons Zug, vol. 1, pp. 163, 439; vol. 2, p. 982.

SG: Die Rechtsquellen des Kantons St. Gallen, Zweiter Teil: Stadtrechte, vol. 1/2, pp. 29, 30, 171; Dritter Teil: Landschaften und Landstädte, vol. 1, p. 172.

GR: Die Rechtsquellen des Kantons Graubünden, B: Gerichtsgemein-
den, Erster Teil: Gotteshausbund, vol. 1, pp. 306, 474, 522, 528; vol. 2,
pp. 310, 353–54, 416, 544; vol. 3, pp. *91*, 146, 242, 350; Zweiter Teil:
Zehngerichtenbund, vol. 1, p. 358.

AG: Die Rechtsquellen des Kantons Aargau, Erster Teil: Stadtrechte,
vol. 1, pp. *124*, 372, 418; vol. 3, p. 213; vol. 4, pp. 154, 185; vol. 5, pp.
303, 334–35, 430; vol. 6, pp. 390–91; Zweiter Teil: Rechte der Landschaft, vol. 3, pp. *64*, 271.

NE: Les sources du droit du Canton de Neuchâtel, vol. 1, pp. *156, 294*.

GE: Les sources du droit du Canton de Genève, vol. 2, pp. *403, 423*;
vol. 3. pp. *183, 250*, 570; vol. 4, pp. 115, 369, 576, 577.

Notes

1. Jean-Marie Gouesse, "Mariages de proches parents (XVIe-XXe siècle)," in *Le modèle familial européen. Actes des séminaires organisés par l'école française de Rome* 90
   (Rome, 1986), pp. 31–61 (for Spain, France, and Italy).
2. Gérard Delille, *Famille et propriété dans le Royaume de Naples (XVe-XIXe siècle)*
   (Rome, Paris, 1985); idem, "Echanges matrimoniaux entre lignées alternées et système européen de l'alliance: une première approche," in *En substances. Textes pour
   Françoise Héritier*, ed. Jean-Luc Jamard, Emmanuel Terray, and Margarita Xanthakou (Paris, 2000), pp. 219–52; idem, "Réflexions sur le 'système' européen de la
   parenté et de l'alliance," *Annales HSS* 56 (2001): pp. 369–80; idem, *Le maire et le
   prieur. Pouvoir central et pouvoir local en Méditerranée occidentale (XVe-XVIIIe siècle)*
   (Paris, 2003); David Warren Sabean, *Kinship in Neckarhausen, 1700–1870* (Cambridge, 1998); for the first volume of the Neckarhausen study and a preview
   article: idem, *Property, Production, and Family in Neckarhausen, 1700–1870* (Cambridge, 1990); idem, "Social Background to Vetterleswirtschaft: Kinship in
   Neckarhausen," in *Frühe Neuzeit—Frühe Moderne? Forschungen zur Vielschichtigkeit
   von Übergangsprozessen*, ed. Rudolf Vierhaus et al. (Göttingen, 1992), pp. 113–32.
3. I have presented part of the following text in another context in "Verwandtschaft
   als historischer Faktor. Schweizer Fallstudien und Trends, 1500-1900," *Historische
   Anthropologie* 10 (2002): pp. 225–44. For discussions, support with the archival
   work, and translation I thank Lydia Brunner, Urban Fink, Peter Hersche, Gabriel
   Imboden, Benjamin Marschke, Liliane Mottu-Weber, and Simon Teuscher.
4. Under the assumption, for example, that in a village of five hundred people, every
   parent and grandparent had two siblings and kinship marriages out to and including the third degree were forbidden, then 84 percent of households would have
   been eligible for marriage (Sabean, *Kinship*, p. 101).
5. The most common (Germanic and canon) counting method counted from the siblings as the first degree of kinship outwards. Siblings' children (first cousins) were

kin of the second degree, and so forth. Regarding uneven generational relationships, one spoke, for instance, of kinship in the second/third or third/fourth degree.

6. In the Swiss overviews, the question was handled cursorily; see Friedrich v. Wyss, *Die Eheschliessung in ihrer geschichtlichen Entwicklung nach den Rechten der Schweiz* (Basel, 1878), pp. 47, 80; Eugen Huber, *System und Geschichte des Schweizerischen Privatrechts*, 4 vols., (Basel, 1886–1893), vol. 4, p. 336; Anne-Lise Head-König, "Forced Marriages and Forbidden Marriages in Switzerland: State Control of the Formation of Marriage in Catholic and Protestant Cantons in the Eighteenth and Nineteenth Centuries," *Continuity and Change* 8 (1993): pp. 441–65, here pp. 443, 455–56.

7. Citations: "was bißhar mit dispensieren und umb gelt erlangt worden ist, sol alles uß sin; vil Nachred, Eergerniß, Unwill, Schand und Abschühens bi uns und unsern Nachpurn; gschrey von etwas früntschaft." See "Rechtsquellen von Zürich," in *Zeitschrift für Schweizerisches Recht* 4 (1855), pp. 103–98, here p. 117; Walther Köhler, *Zürcher Ehegericht und Genfer Konsistorium*, 2 vols. (Leipzig, 1932/42), vol. 1, pp. 74, 78–84, 239, 244, 264–5, 316, 325, 332–3, 342, 361, 375, 379, 384–6, 402, 410; Thomas Max Safley, "Canon Law and Swiss Reform: Legal Theory and Practice in the Marital Courts of Zurich, Bern, Basel, and St. Gall," in *Canon Law in Protestant Lands*, ed. Richard H. Helmholz (Berlin, 1992), pp. 187–201; the usual interpretation of the renewal of the prohibition emphasized the foreign policy importance (consideration of the Catholic territories) at the expense of the domestic policy.

8. Köhler, *Ehegericht*, vol. 1, pp. 419, 426–28, 435, 439.

9. Paul Wehrli, *Verlobung und Trauung in ihrer geschichtlichen Entwicklung von der Reformation bis zum Untergang der alten Eidgenossenschaft. Ein Beitrag zur zürcherischen Rechtsgeschichte* (Turbenthal, 1933), pp. 10–11, 16, 78–88; Roland E. Hofer, *"Üppiges, unzüchtiges Lebwesen." Schaffhauser Ehegerichtsbarkeit von der Reformation bis zum Ende des Ancien Régime (1529-1798)* (Bern, 1993), pp. 203–10; Willy Münch, *Ehehindernisse und Ehenichtigkeitsgründe im Basler Stadtrecht*, typoscript (Basel, 1943), pp. 46–54; Christian Simon, *Untertanenverhalten und Moralpolitik. Studien zum Verhältnis zwischen Stadt und Land im ausgehenden 18. Jahrhundert am Beispiel Basels* (Basel, 1981), pp. 115–17; Hans De Giacomi, *Das Eheschliessungsrecht nach den bündnerischen Statuten* (Chur, 1927), 97–104; Jon Mathieu, *Eine Region am Rande: das Unterengadin 1650-1800. Studien zur Gesellschaft* (Ph.D. diss., University of Berne, 1983), pp. 167–68.

10. Alfred Martin, *Exposé de l'ancienne législation genevoise sur le mariage* (Genève, 1891), pp. 24–26; Köhler, *Ehegericht*, vol. 2, 505, 635, 667; in addition, personal communication by Liliane Mottu-Weber.

11. "Das bürgerliche Gesetz verbietet in Helvetien die Ehen unter Geschwisterkindern oder in weiteren Graden nicht." See Hans Staehelin, *Die Civilgesetzgebung der Helvetik* (Bern, 1931), pp. 236–44.

12. Jürg-Christian Hürlimann, *Die Eheschliessungsverbote zwischen Verwandten und Verschwägerten* (Bern, 1987), pp. 66–79; and Schweizerisches Bundesarchiv Bern E 22/1985 and 1986 (materials relevant to the Federal Law Code of 24. 12. 1874).

13. Sabean, *Kinship*, p. 64; he also hints at modern anthropological arguments and their preformulation in historical texts.

14. "...da wirt bald große und schwäre, ja hochsträffliche blutschand für zulässig gerechnet; es ist besser, man seye hierüber zu strenge als zu gelinde." See Wehrli, *Verlobung*, p. 85; Staehelin, *Civilgesetzgebung*, pp. 245, 247.

15. Sabean, *Kinship*, pp. 444–48; regarding medical consultations in view of bourgeois cousin marriages, see Albert Tanner, *Arbeitsame Patrioten—wohlanständige Damen. Bürgertum und Bürgerlichkeit in der Schweiz 1830-1914* (Zürich, 1995), p. 193.
16. Hans Bänninger, *Untersuchungen über den Einfluss des Polizeistaates im 17. und 18. Jahrhundert auf das Recht der Eheschliessung in Stadt und Landschaft Zürich* (Zürich, 1948), p. 34; Jeffrey R. Watt, *The Making of Modern Marriage. Matrimonial Control and the Rise of Sentiment in Neuchâtel, 1550-1800* (Ithaca, 1992), pp. 116–20, 175–78.
17. The limit for the marriage of close relatives was set here at the uneven second/third degree: as a rule the authors of the local studies subsumed these marriages under the second degree (as in Freienbach, Muotathal; implicit in Urseren), the Lucerne Nuncio followed a similar practice.
18. Sabean, *Kinship*, for instance p. 407.
19. Examples of disciplined recording practices at an early point are Oensingen and Starrkirch; also the dramatic increase in Simplon Village does not reflect the quality of the sources; for the break of 1874, see note 12.
20. Archivio Segreto Vaticano, Archivio della Nunziatura in Lucerna 278, fol., 468, 477–80, 484, 485–91, 493–96, 498–553; Urban Fink, *Die Luzerner Nuntiatur 1586-1873. Zur Behördengeschichte und Quellenkunde der päpstlichen Diplomatie in der Schweiz* (Luzern, 1997), pp. 104, 117, 134; Alois Henggeler, *Das bischöfliche Kommissariat Luzern von 1605-1800* (Stans, 1906), pp. 152–55.
21. The population in 1650 of the area of present Switzerland has been estimated at 1.0 million. It climbed to 1.7 million by 1800, and to 2.7 million by 1870.
22. Archivio Segreto Vaticano, Archivio della Nunziatura in Lucerna 449, fol. 180–83, 360–434.
23. The increase of consanguineous marriages among kin marriages shows up less dramatically in our sample (Table 11.1); the nadirs do mostly fall in the period before 1750, but the differences are not very significant.
24. For the early studies, see Arnold Egenter, *Über den Grad der Inzucht in einer Schwyzer Berggemeinde und die damit zusammenhängende Häufung rezessiver Erbschäden (Albinismus, Schwachsinn, Schizophrenie u. a.)* (Zürich, 1934); an example from the younger generation is the study of Conthey, cited in Appendix 1.
25. See *Rechtsquellen 1855*, p. 117; Köhler, *Ehegericht*, vol. 1, p. 402; Staehelin, *Civilgesetzgebung*, pp. 240–41.
26. Françoise Héritier, *L'exercice de la parenté* (Paris, 1981), pp.137–67, considers marriages between distant relatives as a fundamental mechanism of the "complex" alliance systems, which operate with prohibitions and recognize no clear selection rules like the "elementary" systems; she tries to thereby integrate the European case in the anthropological exchange theory of Lévy-Strauss, which has difficulty with such systems. Delille's position follows along here, but is in some aspects more complex; for his studies, see note 2.
27. In a brief, early passage, Delille treated the "mémoire généalogique" and concluded that the limit normally lay between the third and fifth degrees *(Famille,* pp. 286–8); however, at one point in his work, on the basis of genealogical sources, he discusses kinship marriages out to the eighth degree; the later, necessarily selective quanitifications reach to the sixth degree *(Maire,* pp. 222–24).
28. Citations in Rhaeto-Romance, see Mathieu, *Region,* pp. 154, 170; briefly published in idem, *Bauern und Bären. Eine Geschichte des Unterengadins von 1650 bis 1800* (Chur, 1987), pp. 178, 184.

29. Citations in Rhaeto-Romance; Mathieu, *Region*, pp. 163–67; and idem, *Bauern*, pp. 182–83.

30. Mathieu, *Region*, p. 377; and idem, *Bauern*, p. 257.

31. I have never seen "third cousins" (*basdrins*) in primary sources, but see the remark in Jon Mathieu, "Die ländliche Gesellschaft," in *Handbuch der Bündner Geschichte: Frühe Neuzeit*, ed. Verein für Bündner Kulturforschung (Chur, 2000), vol. 2, pp. 11–54, here p. 41.

32. "…im abtretten der fründtschafften vil unglycheit gebrucht worden, damit ouch unordnungen ingerisen." See Hermann Rennefahrt, ed., *Die Rechtsquellen des Kantons Bern, Erster Teil: Stadtrechte* (Aarau, 1959), vol. 5, pp. 180–81, see also Simon Teuscher, *Bekannte—Klienten—Verwandte. Soziabilität und Politik in der Stadt Bern um 1500* (Köln, 1998), p. 77–78.

33. It supports the thesis developed by Teuscher, whereby the process of state building in the modern era led to the solidification of kinship; see Teuscher, *Bekannte*, pp. 75–113, 243–63.

34. For the nineteenth and twentieth centuries, see Rolf Geiser, *Über den Ausstand des Richters im schweizerischen Zivilprozessrecht* (Winterthur, 1957), pp. 3–4, 8, 42–43; for the older sources, see Appendix 2. The special case mentioned is Geneva, where at least from 1670 to 1692 there was no expressly mentioned exemption limit for criminal cases and votes; as mentioned above, Geneva shortly thereafter also became an exception regarding marriage prohibitions (see note 10).

35. Raul Merzario, *Il paese stretto. Strategie matrimoniali nella diocesi di Como, secoli XVI-XVIII* (Torino 1981), pp. 35–38, 141; Jean-Louis Flandrin, *Familles. Parenté, maison, sexualité dans l'ancienne société* (Paris, 1976), pp. 32–38; André Burguière, "La mémoire familiale du bourgeois gentilhomme: généalogies domestiques en France aux XVIIᵉ et XVIIIᵉ siècles," *Annales ESC* 46 (1991): pp. 771–88; Christian Maurel, "Construction généalogique et développement de l'état moderne: la généalogie des Bailleul," *Annales ESC* 46 (1991): pp. 807–25; Karl-Heinz Spiess, *Familie und Verwandtschaft im deutschen Hochadel des Spätmittelalters. 13. bis Anfang des 16. Jahrhunderts* (Stuttgart, 1993), pp. 42–43, 490–91; Margareth Lanzinger, *Das gesicherte Erbe. Heirat in lokalen und familialen Kontexten. Innichen 1700-1900* (Wien, 2003), p. 314; from an anthropological perspective: Jeanette Edwards and Marilyn Strathern, "Including Our Own," in *Cultures of Relatedness: New Approaches to the Study of Kinship*, ed. Janet Carsten (Cambridge, 2000), pp. 149–66, here 157–61.

36. For a well-researched case, see Christophe Duhamelle, *L'héritage collectif. La noblesse d'Église rhénane, XVIIᵉ-XVIIIᵉ siècles* (Paris, 1998), here pp. 102, 129–31, 142.

37. For Sabean's studies, see note 2.

38. Above all, see the studies of Elisabeth Joris, Heidi Witzig, Albert Tanner, and Philipp Sarasin, as summed up in Mathieu, *Verwandtschaft*, pp. 228–30.

39. Delille, *Famille*, pp. 368, 380–81.

40. Eugen Huber, *Schweizerisches Civilgesetzbuch. Erläuterungen zum Vorentwurf des Eidgenössischen Justiz- und Poliziedepartements, Erstes Heft* (Bern, 1901), p. 96.

41. Jean Sutter pointed out the effects of the demographic transition; Delille stressed the consequences of the expansion of primogeniture; Sabean concerned himself with the partition of land parcels and the related labor practices; regarding the last, see Jon Mathieu, "Ein Cousin an jeder Zaunlücke. Überlegungen zum Wandel von Verwandtschaft und ländlicher Gemeinde, 1700-1900," in *Politiken der Verwandtschaft*, ed. Margareth Lanzinger and Edith Saurer (Göttingen 2007).

Chapter XII

Kinship and Gender

*Property, Enterprise, and Politics**

Elisabeth Joris

Marriage, the socially sanctioned union of man and woman, is central to the reproduction of kinship, and determines the exchange processes between the categories of persons involved. In this process, patriarchal social structures have shaped the different spheres of action of male and female kin to a crucial extent, albeit varying according to historical context. In line with David Sabean's processual view on family—similar to E. P. Thompson's position that "class happens" —gender is also not a firmly fixed category; gender happens, as well.[1] In other words, according to the context, gender is not only revealed in discursive and legal standards, but it also "happens," in continually self-renewing practices, including kinship practices, in interpretations shaped by ambivalences, and as communicative action and the construction of dynamic networks. However, women and men rarely act solely as kin, and by the same token, they rarely act solely as "gender."

This chapter is an attempt to elaborate on David Sabean's hypothesis of the nineteenth century as "kinship-hot" by exploring the links between various levels and spheres in gender-specific terms.[2] I will also attempt to place the gender aspects of kinship into a broader context.[3] The overall legal, economic, and geopolitical conditions set the parameters and define the margins in which the paradoxes of gender-specific practices and their different forms become visible. I shall therefore focus primarily on Switzerland in the "long" nineteenth century, a key theme of my previous research work, but without neglecting the wider European context.[4] Most of the examples cited are drawn from Switzerland.

In an essay about kinship as a historical factor, Jon Mathieu points out that at the end of the nineteenth century, intellectuals, also in Switzerland—including the eminent legal historian Eugen Huber—assumed that kinship had lost its significance in the modern era.[5] They thus followed in the footsteps of the foremost representatives of an academically trained elite who, in many cases, had studied at universities abroad. In their quest to achieve the rational and systematic renewal of the state, these academics were convinced that estate and class-based connections were no longer central for the maintenance of power and control; henceforth, the key factors would be merit and professionalization. Until very recently, this conviction was reproduced, generally unchallenged, in Swiss historiography. By contrast, alongside Albert Tanner for Bern and Zurich and Philipp Sarasin for Basel, Heidi Witzig and I underline the importance of the marriage market and kinship relations for the consolidation of the bourgeoisie's position.[6] Based on our examination of numerous private bequests, especially letters, we noted in our regional study that in the nineteenth century, the development of kinship relations was becoming increasingly important in determining social position as well as in safeguarding livelihood, and that women—despite their subordinate status in law—participated to a significant extent in this process.[7] Thus, the negation of kinship as an analytical category is shown to be the outcome of the constructed separation between the public and the private spheres and the associated privileged status of "male" forms of representation in the public domain over forms of exchange which were defined as "private." This is reflected in the privileged evaluation of publicly archived sources compared with the laborious process of sifting through private archives.

Starting with women's transmission functions in relation to rights of control and property, I will explore, firstly, the importance of marriage policy for the development and consolidation of the bourgeoisie in the transition from the Ancien Regime to the modern era. In this context, I will examine the extent to which David Sabean's theory of hypergamy also applies to marriage practices in Switzerland. Secondly, in the context of the development of the capitalist economy, I shall discuss the kinship implications of the constructed separation between the public and the private spheres and the codification of private law. Thirdly, I shall examine the link between the feminization of responsibility for familial sociability and legally cemented social change. Fourthly, based on examples from the Swiss bourgeoisie, I shall explore the connection between the increasing demand for flexible capital and the development of kinship relations. And finally, I shall highlight the ways in which women contributed to the survival of families from different social classes during the nineteenth century.

Marriage, Control, and Property—or the Transmission Functions of Women

Since the late Middle Ages, marriage policy had formed part of the practice of power and control. It was an integral part of a strategy which aimed to expand and consolidate power and achieve social advancement. Harnessed into a multidimensional exchange process, women did not merely perform a passive mediating role. The union established by marriage was a means of enforcing claims in the political and social sphere. In this context, women acted as the representatives of their family of origin, as well as the family into which they married. The status of the women who married into a family varied according to different inheritance laws and the social prestige of their own kin.[8] This is clearly illustrated by Sandro Guzzi-Heeb, who cites the example of the widow, Marie-Julienne de Rivaz (1725–1791). Thanks to her extensive network of relationships, she was able to assert her position over the nephew of her deceased spouse and secured the post of presiding judge (*Burgrichter*) in the border region between France and present-day Switzerland for her son, whom she married to a niece of her own family. She thus opened the way for him to assume the highest offices in the canton of Wallis during the Helvetic and Restoration periods.[9] This shows that despite the prevailing patrilinearity and the reduced legal capacity of the female sex, in practical terms, women's status in various periods was always far more flexible, contradictory, and multifaceted than the legal provisions suggest, as well as being far more complex than the companionships of woman and man, based on complementarity envisaged by the Reformed Church from Luther onwards. As Claudia Ulbrich underlines, marital relationships were not partnerships; "integrated into a force field in which power was asserted," they were one element in a comprehensive structure of dominance and control as social practice.[10] This continued to apply beyond the end of the Ancien Regime and into the bourgeois nineteenth century, which is the focus of my interest.

As a class, the bourgeoisie developed out of the educated middle class during the transition from the eighteenth to the nineteenth century.[11] Unlike the situation during the Ancien Regime, ownership of land was no longer the determinant factor in the political and economic system of the modern era. Besides a family's social prestige, it was ability, individual achievements, and a profession legitimated by education which crucially determined social status in Switzerland, too, and influenced access to official careers. As class barriers fell and the competition for economic and public positions intensified, relationship networks played an important role and women's mediating function gained in significance.[12] As the path to political office involved elections, new alliances had to be forged. Not only did the geographical constituencies expand, the number of persons entitled to vote also increased. Furthermore, the opening of markets, freedom of establishment, and freedom of trade offered a wider range of social classes the opportunity for social and economic advancement. In this system of free competition and freely elected alliances, informal connections were important—especially since the bourgeoisie, which set the economic, social, and political tone, had little formal organization until well into the second half of the nineteenth century.[13] Kinship was of key importance as a prescribed network of relationships, which also had emotional overtones, but it was also important as a network which could be developed and expanded through new marriage-based alliances, that is, with in-laws. In the bourgeoisie, mediation between spouses' kinship groups was a crucial factor determining a family's social status.

Through marriage, a lasting connection was established between groups of persons, opening up the opportunity for many other highly diverse exchange processes. In these processes, women acted as brokers: of marriages, employment opportunities, apprenticeships, and business and political connections. Supposedly "freely chosen" economic partnerships and kinship connections overlapped. Depending on the stage reached in the development or consolidation of the bourgeoisie, marriage policy served either to open up the family or to exclude and isolate it.[14] In Switzerland, connections were formed between new and old elites, newly rich industrialists and the old aristocracy, and up-and-coming individuals from rural backgrounds with the urban elite.[15] Marriages between close relatives enabled existing social and political connections to be intensified, strengthening the family's social and economic position in a society based on competition. As Davidoff and Hall have shown in their study of the English middle class, not only sons, but nephews and sons-in-law became preferred business partners.[16] Networks which also pooled economic capacities became even more important once there were no longer any class-based privileges to prevent social demotion. Marriage strategies were thus integral to economic calculation. The marriage market, declared to be part of the private sphere, retained its preeminent importance alongside the labor and financial markets. However, in Switzerland, too—following the general trend in Europe, noted by David Sabean—the number of marriages between close relatives in a range of social classes increased over the course of the nineteenth century, both in the rural and the urban milieu. Thus, when searching for a bride, the gaze of Gottlieb Baumann, a small-scale milk merchant from eastern Switzerland, fell on Marie Gertrud Hafner, a poor orphan who lived and worked at the home of Johann Ulrich Hafner, Baumann's wealthy guardian and landlord of the Krone. The farmer, Conrad Hürlimann, who lived near Zurich, married Barbara Nägeli, his grandmother's grand-niece. Marie (Heim-) Vögtlin, a pastor's daughter who became Switzerland's first female doctor, was engaged to her kinsman Fritz Erismann, who, like Marie herself, came from a Pietist pastor's family. Only after he moved into the milieu of the Russian female medical students at the University of Zurich, was the engagement was broken off. The rural entrepreneurs who owned the textile factories were also interrelated by marriage, as were the old established factory owners' and merchants' families in Winterthur and Basel or the class-conscious Bernese aristocracy.[17]

Whereas David Sabean noted a predominance of hypergamy in Europe, that is, a family's advancement and the consolidation of its social position through the marriage of the women into a higher caste, the historical analyses published to date do not confirm this general trend for Switzerland.[18] On the contrary, in his wide-ranging study of marriage practices in the Bernese bourgeoisie, Albert Tanner notes that the sons of the aristocracy tended to marry "if possible, to someone of equal status or even into more refined social circles," whereas daughters had to "be content with a husband who, at least in terms of his family background, had a lower social status."[19] But what do "higher" and "lower" mean? "Lower"meant the marriage of an aristocratic woman to a wealthy member of the bourgeoisie. According to Tanner, in reality, "social demotion as a result of marriage [seems] to have been a rare occurrence."[20] So, despite his rustic origins, the "rural economist," Gustav Hürlimann, was able—thanks to his extensive lands—to marry the "poor, but refined Fräulein Luise Wehrli"[21] from an old established Zurich family. His sons, who became the husbands of wealthy urbanites, soon entered the most refined social circles in Zurich, into which two of their sisters also married.[22] These unions represented advancement for the Hürlimann family, but in social, not economic terms.

As regards to economic status, horizontal unions were the rule. The history of the De Bary family, who were silk manufacturers in Basel, is a good example of these horizontal unions. In 1823, Johann De Bary, a shareholder in his father's business, married Susette Sarasin, the daughter of another silk manufacturer.[23] Other members of this family were also connected by marriage to most of the leading families in Basel, both through kinship and, at the same time, through commercial links.[24] According to Philipp Sarasin, in this city, women's role was to connect the various upper middle class groups with each other. Sarasin does not discuss issues of hypergamy; on the contrary, he describes the case of Johann Jakob Schuster-Burckhardt, originally from Strasbourg, who later became a "full-blooded capitalist"[25] and whose meteoric rise was due to his marriage to a woman from the Basel upper class. Schuster married first into the banking and then into the silk manufacturing milieu, and soon became a driving force in the newly established Swiss Bank Corporation (*Schweizerischer Bankverein*), whose worldwide presence he drove forward.[26] Less meteoric but equally symbolic is the career of Heinrich Grunholzer from the Zurich Oberland. His father-in-law, Hans Heinrich Zangger from Uster, one of the largest textile producers in continental Europe, had no male heirs; however, he did have four daughters, three of whom married, thus opening up their husbands' paths into the economic elite. With the advent of general education between 1830 and 1848, Grunholzer progressed from being a simple primary school teacher. After studying at German universities, he became the director of various new educational institutions and was elected to Zurich's Education Council. He married Rosette, Zangger's youngest daughter. Grunholzer succeeded his father-in-law, not only as the head of the company, he also followed him into the federal parliament where, as a Member of the National Council, he became one of the most faithful followers of Alfred Escher, the industrialist, banker, and founder of the railways, who was the most influential politician of his day.[27] Although it was Grunholzer's wife Rosette who was coheir to the Zangger factories, Grunholzer now assumed a public role as an industrialist. Rosette, meanwhile, became a patron of music, thus establishing and deepening her relations with the urban educated bourgeoisie and consolidating her family's position as members of the Swiss elite.[28]

Nonetheless, there are clear indications of hypergamy in Switzerland, too. Various matrimonial unions in the family of the doctor, Johann Jakob Blumer, who was threatened with impoverishment in the rural canton of Glarus, are good examples. He married his eldest daughter to the son of the Paravicini family, who were textile manufacturers from Glarus. One of her sisters then married a brother-in-law, Jacques Paravicini. A third sister married a wealthy widowed merchant, and a fourth married a professor of Romance languages at the University of Basel. Finally, Emilie Paravicini-Blumer actively brokered the marriage of her youngest sister Katharina to Paul Usteri, a banker from the renowned Zurich family, Usteri-Usteri.[29] According to Tanner, in Zurich, unlike Bern, hypergamy seems to have become the increasingly dominant model of kinship relations through marriage. Around 1864, the offspring of former municipal officials' families—whose declining fortunes meant that they no longer belonged to the best circles—married women from bourgeois or middle class/petty bourgeois families in more than 70 percent of cases, and at least 10 percent of these women came from rural entrepreneurs' families. During the second half of the nineteenth century, this class increasingly included the wives of members of Zurich's old commercial aristocracy, who generally preferred to marry the daughters of doctors, merchants, and entrepreneurs from the city. Thus, the liberal member of the cantonal government, Heinrich Escher from Zurich, took the sister-in-law of the successful textile and machine manufacturer Caspar Honegger, from the Zurich Oberland, as his second wife, but did not wish Honegger to address him as "brother-in-law"— signifying equal rank—in public.[30] One of the most notable examples of hypergamy in Zurich—although it is atypical, as it did little to consolidate the position of the families involved—was the marriage of Eugen Huber, the author of the Swiss Civil Code, cited above. He fell in love with the young servant, Lina Weissert, while still a student. As a young professor and journalist at the *Neue Zürcher Zeitung*, he sent her to Geneva for two years in order to "develop her intellectual capacities" before marriage.[31]

Women could broker assets and advancement through marriage, but were rarely permitted to advance themselves or increase their own fortunes. Men presented themselves in public as personalities with individual talents and achievements, whereas women were viewed as the representatives of their families—both their families of origin and the family into which they married. As women were not granted any individual position, parents tended to consider the social ramifications for the family to a greater extent when marrying off a daughter; when marrying off sons, by contrast, they generally considered the impact of marriages on their individual social status.

The Public and the Private, Law and Gender

The separation between the public and the private domains was, and is, primarily political and is defined in legal terms, but it was also a gender-hierarchical system which legitimized discriminatory practices. Women, as well as kinship relations, were assigned to the private sphere. However, a more detailed analysis reveals the male-connoted constructional character of this separation—for women, too, operated outside the family circle, and within the circle of acquaintance and kinship that they developed, they influenced decisions of economic and political significance. Prominent public figures had family connections and female support to thank for their social and economic status, first and foremost. The relationships cultivated within the family were central to socialization. This was where domestic and economic interests, and private and political activities, overlapped. Leonore Davidoff and Catherine Hall sum this up aptly: "Public was not really public and private not really private despite the potent imagery of 'separate spheres'."[32] Nonetheless, underpinned by the legislation of the nineteenth century, the gender-connoted separation between the public and the private domains proved extremely effective. Not only were women denied access to the public sphere, but they also had no access to the professions, which was one of the fundamental categories of the bourgeoisie.[33] But they were also denied recognition of the Enlightenment's key demand in relation to the codification of private law, namely full legal capacity as the prerequisite for autonomous action, as well as the rights implicit in the concept of property—which Eugen Huber described as one of the "main foundations of today's society"[34]—that is, to dispose of the fruits of one's labor, to use one's own property, and to enter into contracts. With the explicit or implicit recourse to Rousseau's antirationalist and anti-individualist concept of "nature" and the associated notion of the difference and complementarity of the male and the female dispositions, the inequalities in the legal treatment of women and men needed no further legitimation. In restricting women's freedom of contract, however, the aim was also to preserve the husband's public position as head of the family.[35] Yet, the wife's position as the representative of her line of descent was weakened as a result.

The Ancien Regime had not recognized any separation between the private and the public spheres: family, household, and the economy were all elements of the social order and were thus subject to the control of the authorities. With the dawn of the modern era, class-based forms of tutelage disappeared.[36] However, women's capacity to act continued to be restricted in the nineteenth century, but now, the barriers were no longer class-based. They were gender-specific and enshrined in law, and women's reduced individual capacity to act was no longer regulated as part of the social order but through civil or private law, that is, through marriage, property, and inheritance law. The debates about legal reform which had taken place across continental Europe since the French Revolution all reflected similar attitudes to gender relations despite their different legal traditions. Admittedly, the principle of unmarried women's full legal capacity gained ground during the course of the nineteenth century—Switzerland's federal law of 1881 is a notable example—but like similar laws elsewhere in Europe, it had only limited application to married women.[37] Demands for freedom of contract, which is based on the equality of the contracting parties, were rejected on the grounds that married men's privileges had to be maintained—an argument which was presented with varying degrees of vehemence.[38] The husband was not only the head of the family; the most prevalent form of property rights in private law guaranteed husbands almost everywhere the right to dispose of their wives' property, even when they remained the formal owners. It was the legislator's will that it should be freely available to her husband as an economic resource. The situation was clearly described by the representative of women's interest at the time of the codification of Swiss law: "The merchant is not only a merchant per se; he is also the father of a family, and his property relations depend partly on the development of the law governing matrimonial property and inheritance."[39]

At the same time, the private or civil law which was developed on the basis of the French *Code Napoléon* in continental Europe greatly weakened, or virtually removed, the family of origin's inheritance claims in respect to the dowry, as well as its opportunities to exert influence over this asset.[40] Dowries continued to be negotiated between families and were of key importance when marriages were arranged among the propertied classes. In formal terms, the dowry was akin to an early inheritance, which, after marriage, generally remained the wife's property as a "woman's portion" or "special asset" and could not be disposed of without her consent. In the event of her death, the dowry did not revert to her family of origin unless—as was the widespread custom among the Bernese aristocracy—the family's claims had been regulated in a prenuptial contact.[41] In this context, the prenuptial agreement made in 1795 between the family of Dorothea Respinger and the silk manufacturer Johann De Bary from Basel is interesting: it was cosigned by a total of seventeen relatives. If Dorothea died without issue, the property she brought to the marriage would revert to her family of origin, whereas, if her offspring were living, her entire wealth would pass to the widower and their children. When Dorothea—by now a widow of almost eighty—died in 1851, her son and daughter and the grandchildren from the marriage of her deceased daughter inherited her property, as was usually the case in the nineteenth century.[42]

The property brought to the marriage was, directly or indirectly, part of the assets of the husband's firm and was thus removed from the wife's control. This loss of control over the dowry by the wife and her relatives was counteracted by the commercial relations between in-laws. Furthermore, the husband's control over the wife's assets remained limited in that the often much younger wives took over the reins of the company as their husband's heirs. There are many examples of independent action by widows, also in Switzerland, in the early nineteenth century. The marriage of Magdalena Wegmann (1764–1829) from Zurich to the artist Ludwig Hess was arranged by their fathers. Even as a wife, she—like her husband and her own kin—was actively committed to the principles of equality propounded by the French Revolution. Widowed young, she managed her husband's works— which were exhibited, inter alia, to the Emperor of Austria in 1815— with great expertise: "He did not speak to me, nor I to him, but if Linth-Escher, who showed him the paintings, was unsure of a particular point, I provided the necessary information."[43] She also ran a textile factory, took an active role in her only son's education, and arranged his marriage to a woman from an eminent Zurich family. Thanks to her close friendship with leading figures in the liberal movement, he was elected to the highest government office in Zurich canton. Marie-Catherine de Preux (1789–1871), whose first marriage was to a cousin from an old and influential family, was widowed young and was left with two children. She asserted her position vis-à-vis her kinsfolk and married the administrator of her extensive estates.[44] In the wake of industrialisation, widows often managed the family companies they had inherited, in which often substantial portions of their own wealth was invested. Thus in 1884, after the death of her husband Wilhelm Adolf Sutter, the widow Katharina Elisabeth Maria Sutter-Krauss took over, as a matter of course, the management of the family's vinegar- and polish-making company, in which her relatives had invested substantial funds on its establishment in 1857. After the death of her husband in 1877, Agatha Zweifel-Schmid, the mother of eight children, asserted her position against the procurists and took over the family's weaving firm, acting as advisor to her sons on matters of business until her death.[45] The publisher Verena Conzett was actively involved in the family printing works, which specialized in labor movement publications, even before her husband's suicide. Under her management, the company became one of the largest media corporations in German-speaking Switzerland.[46] As a widow, Franziska Dosenbach-Buchmann from Lucerne managed the company which she and her husband had built up, which specialized in factory-made shoes, drawing on the support of her thirteen children in this context. She held the reins of her highly diversified company even after her remarriage. Her second husband kept the accounts of her shoe empire and also opened up her route into Zurich's bourgeoisie, into which several of her children married, thus cementing their social advancement.[47]

Similarly, daughters who inherited companies often only appeared to confine their activities to transmission functions—instead, their husbands who had married into the family had to adapt to its ways. Heinrich Grunholzer-Zangger, for example, aligned his political positions to those of his father-in-law, which, over the long term, led to bitter conflicts with his former colleagues from his teaching days, such as the radical democratic journalist and politician, Johann Caspar Sieber.[48] In a marriage between relatives, such adaptation was by implication unnecessary, as it was replaced by kinship practices.

The long-dominant academic opinion that kinship is outdated as an analytical category is thus revealed as a misinterpretation which is based on the legally defined position of husbands instead of on social practice. Indeed, according to Margareth Lanzinger and Ellinor Forster, during periods of social transformation, kinship—as a "relationship network of direct relevance to daily life—and thus as a research-relevant category"—increased in importance.[49] Through informal kinship networks, women took an active role in the public discourses from which they were in principle excluded. Barbara Hess-Wegmann, for example, mentioned above, chronicled the impacts of the French Revolution on Zurich on behalf of her kin.[50] Some hundred years later, Gertrud Villiger-Keller, the daughter of one of the leading educationists and theorists driving forward Switzerland's transformation in 1848, was successful in her efforts to involve women in associations to implement the bourgeoisie's temperance policies. When a major fire broke out in Glarus, Emilie Paravicini-Blumer, together with Susanne Blumer-Heer—the sister of the highest government representative of the canton and wife of a Member of the *Ständerat*—performed outstanding organizational work within the Women's Committee.[51] Marie De Bary, an unmarried woman from a rich silk manufacturing family in Basel, was an active member of a committee which ran a home for deaconesses as well as being a founding member of the Young Women's Friendship Association, and for her work on behalf of soldiers wounded in the Franco-Prussian War of 1870 to 1871, received a foundation medal of the Geneva Convention and the International Committee of the Red Cross.[52] Three of the four unmarried Werdmüller daughters from the textile-making town of Uster, whose father was a pastor in the Reformed Church, excelled themselves not only as collectors of donations to the Basler Mission, but actively intervened in the political battles between liberals and conservatives by founding a free church based on the Pietist "awakening" movement. They also opened a Sunday school and a school for small children. They provoked a hostile reaction from factory owner and Education Council member Heinrich Grunholzer-Zangger, urged on forcefully by his wife.[53]

In sum, it is apparent that family ties were stronger or more important than gender boundaries.[54] Identification with the family into which a man or woman married was therefore as central to the family's prosperous development as it was to its business interests. As this identification was determined to a large extent by family background, the integration process into the new family was much easier if the spouses originated from the same milieu and shared common experiences. As guarantees of a good marriage, horizontal social links were preferred by parents when selecting a spouse for their children, making marriage within the kinship circle a favorable option. Women also created a matrilinear system of relationships through their development of familial sociability.[55] Consequently, a key feature of the nineteenth century was the coexistence of different concepts which reflected not only the provisions of inheritance law, but also the kinship practices of daily life.

The Feminization of Private Sociability

The new forms of sociability evolved primarily through the informal network of relationships and developed as early as the eighteenth century in the educated elite, which was not an "estate" in the proper sense.[56] This network of relationships offered important opportunities for the assertion of group interests and was an excellent tool to further individual careers. Women were granted an important role in this network of relationships due to the social competence assigned to them, with the result that this familial sociability, according to Rebekka Habermas, created a new public arena which "to some extent rendered gender-specific inequalities inactive."[57] In contrast to the widespread preference for the construction of patrilinear genealogical pedigrees in the nineteenth century, the emotional reference system was bilinear or even matrilinear in nature.[58] Through correspondence, gifts, visits, discussion groups, ladies' circles, and other gatherings, women created a semipublic arena in which the supposedly private linked into and overlapped with the public.[59] It was the women who drew all the information together and were thus able to shape the relationship networks to their own and their families' benefit. This is most apparent in their extensive correspondence, which increasingly became one of women's responsibilities in the nineteenth century.⁶⁰ Thus, the industrialist ,Walter Boveri, described his mother's writing desk as "a kind of command bridge for the whole household."⁶¹ From here, she kept relatives abreast of what was happening in the family. It was the women's responsibility for the domestic sphere—the family and the household—which created an implicit responsibility for the family's external relations as well. Control of this area was essential to create physical and psychological well-being and to anticipate and balance out potential emotional conflicts and economic damage. The control of the family's external relations became more important as the private wealth and the capital invested in the company increased, or as the political and professional career opportunities of male members of the family and kin grew in perceived significance. Thus, the responsibility for shaping the private sphere legitimized the mother's position as "captain"—to return to Boveri's analogy once more—thereby relativizing the provisions on the family's external representation prescribed by matrimonial law.

As well as promoting the flow of information, the extensive correspondence facilitated the communication process in general and ensured that family members were kept abreast of events. Letters were written regularly, perhaps weekly, whether or not the writer had any news to report. Letters were not primarily intended to be a form of exchange between two persons, but were circulated widely, thereby assuring even those who were only addressed indirectly of their position within the family.⁶² The correspondence maintained the unbroken connection between kin, especially the connection to the family of origin, despite geographical separation. As they were responsible for this communication, women created the conditions which defined the family as an emotional space and, in doing so, established the basis for its cohesion. Thus, even in the class-conscious Bernese aristocracy, women's key task was to ensure that family solidarity and social capital were preserved through the cultivation of kinship relations.⁶³ This same role was also performed by women in the rural bourgeoisie. In the mid nineteenth century, the siblings of a bankrupt textile manufacturer in the Zurich Oberland kept in contact after the father's death via the mother and sisters who lived very close to each other. In the words of one of the younger sisters who had moved away, this place was "a true center for all members of the family" who had "dispersed in all directions" ⁶⁴ The brothers, who were directors of textile companies, lived in England and France, while a sister lived in Alsace. Childless, Emilie Paravicini-Blumer also acted as a link between the relatives in her immediate neighborhood and those in Zurich and

Basel.[65] Not only did she correspond regularly with her sisters and nieces, but they also came to her house to meet their kinswoman who lived nearby. Luise Wehrli-Hürlimann, received her grandchildren and orphaned great-nieces and nephews every Wednesday at her home in Zurich, assisted by her unmarried daughter, Frieda.[66] Mothers, grandmothers and aunts also played a key role in arranging reciprocal visits to relatives on family days at New Year.[67] This focus on the mother and sisters can also be observed in less wealthy families. For example, the household of a municipality clerk from a large textile workers' village included two unmarried sisters of his wife, who originated in the factory workers' milieu.[68]

Kinship practices created a shared biographical background and deepened family bonds. In this process, women showed themselves to be skillful representatives of their own family's interests. In the bourgeoisie, the priority was to guide the marriage process by averting any conflict between emotional and material interests. Invitations, regular visits, and celebrations created the milieu in which emotional kinship and love could flourish between young women and men.[69] Outwardly, the mothers and other female relatives involved would underline the uniqueness of the bridal couple's emotional attachment while strictly controlling the selection of possible marriage candidates. This meant that the bride was supposed to talk about love but not about material interests, whereas the latter was naturally of far greater concern to her family, for marriage continued to be central to economic and social power, both of the family and the individual marriage partners.[70]

This environment, which was shaped by family-specific rituals and an apparent lack of compulsion in the private sphere, encouraged the emotional intensity of encounters between female and male relatives and between brothers and sisters. Whereas emotional connections between male and female cousins were increasingly legitimized through marriage, and thus encouraged, no such outlet existed for love between brothers and sisters.[71] However, sibling affection was accepted as a close attachment, and brothers would often draw on their sisters' support to consolidate their position. Sisters in particular—married or single—played an important role in integrating the new wife of a beloved brother into the family.[72]

The bourgeoisie in the nineteenth century expected marital unions to be successful on an emotional level—which meant that in a system in which patrilocality predominated, a positive experience of integration was extremely important. As a rule, this was actively supported both by the sisters-in-law and the mother-in-law of the young wife and, during the first years of marriage, by the wife's family of origin, even

from some distance away. Thus, the wife of a well-known textile manufacturer from the Zurich Oberland received visits from her family
almost continually for years, and she also met them for holidays or visits to spas.[73] Lina B. from Bern also married into this milieu. Her bridegroom was the cousin of a friend from her days at boarding school, and
Lina B. first met her husband-to-be at this school friend's wedding.
When her own family was ruined financially as a result of a brother's
unwise investment decisions, she volunteered to break off the relationship before the official engagement: "He (the manufacturer, E. J.) loves
his only son, wants him to spare him every difficulty and smooth his
path through life; in short, he wants him to have the very best. Such
love is touching! He wants you (the future bridegroom, E. J.) to succeed him, but this business involves money, I understand that very
well."[74] When the entrepreneur consented to the marriage nonetheless,
the bride's family regarded this as an immense concession. Despite her
lack of fortune, the bride's otherwise irreproachable background
favored the union. Her integration into her new family, which was geographically distant from her place of origin, Bern, was actively supported and managed by her own mother through regular letters, visits,
supplies of favorite foods and belongings from Bern, and the appointment of a Bernese maid. Given the inequalities in the bride's and
groom's fortunes, it was of crucial importance, from the mother's perspective, to ensure that her daughter's marriage was a success. However,
even when the financial positions were more or less equal, targeted
support from members of the bride's own family was generally provided in order to facilitate the young woman's emotional integration
into her new surroundings.[75]

The increasing emotional intensity of marriage contributed to its
"privatization" and is reflected in the changed importance of family history. Until the start of the nineteenth century, the writing of family
chronicles was almost exclusively a male domain.[76] Here, the priority
was to emphasize gender in a dynastic context, and the keeping of family chronicles was therefore a widespread practice in aristocratic families. In the 1840s, for example, Pastor Werdmüller, who came from an
old established Zurich family, would always rise at 3 A.M. in order to
work on the comprehensive history of the Werdmüller family.[77] In the
class-conscious Bernese aristocracy, it was the men who, even until
recently, wrote the history of their kinship.[78] In the bourgeoisie, on the
other hand, over the course of the nineteenth century, family chronicles increasingly became a genre which was also written by women,
with the focus shifting more and more to daily events and family relationships. They were also increasingly written for the family's own

children, with greater importance being attached to the emotional ties with the descendants rather than the more abstract notion of ascendancy. Fanny Sulzer-Bühler, who originated and married into Winterthur's industrialists' milieu, recounted daily events from her kinship and that of her husband in her family history, which she wrote for her children.[79] While men tended to reflect themselves in the company history, women became the repository of the family's memories. Whereas the private bequests which document the political and economic activities of men were presented to public archives, women were responsible for the safekeeping of letters and diaries which were deemed to be private. Thus, it was increasingly the women who, through their practices and interpretations, constituted the family and kinship. The problems associated with this gender-specific perception of family history are reflected in the archiving of materials. In the bequests of well-known families which were deposited in private archives, letters between family members and relatives are often missing, including very many letters from women, for unlike correspondence between men, they were regarded, and are still regarded, as private and therefore of no interest to academics. Even when the existence of private correspondence is documented, the convoluted paths by which letters were handed down within families mean that very often, they cannot be traced, or are traceable only with a great deal of hard work and especially luck. Moreover, with the separation of the supposedly private from the public sphere, the economic dimension of kinship has largely been ignored by academics as well.

Flexible Capital and Long-term Loans

By contrast, the telling statement, "but this business involves money," by the young Lina B., can hardly be bettered in terms of the clarity with which it describes the economic transfer function of a bride in the age of industrialization. Land lost its significance as a means of production and a basis for rental income. It merely became a location which could be changed or surrendered at any time. The primary form of dynamic business operations in the nineteenth century was the family firm which was reliant on private loans for its expansion and capital.[80] Flexible capital in the form of investments and loans became more important than the merger and expansion of land and estates. In many regions, women did not inherit land and property, but were paid out the equivalent value in cash. However, as early as the seventeenth and eighteenth centuries, if the women did not bring their money into a marriage, it was generally deposited with male relatives as a tied loan. Thus, in the nineteenth century, too, women tended to invest on a long-term basis and, due to their limited opportunities to take an active role in business, could not take much of an interest in short-term profits. They therefore handed over their money—often under moral pressure—to members of their family, to sisters as well as to brothers or sons. Very often, substantial fortunes owned by women, that is, wives, mothers, daughters, sisters, daughters-in-law, sisters-in-law, and so forth, were invested in companies as long-term loans, often forming a significant part of the basic equity, yet without conferring any rights of codetermination on the women as shareholders.[81] Husbands acting as trustees invested their wives' fortunes, while sons, nephews, brothers, and even brothers-in-law invested the funds belonging to single or widowed women. In families with business interests, a marriage always implied access to flexible capital, and thus the cultivation of kinship relations also implied the cultivation of potential business interests. Marriages resulted in partnerships, and by the same token, business partnerships also resulted in marriages, intensifying the relationship between families and firms. Capital was transferred, and so too were know-how, business connections, and creditworthiness.[82] In the De Bary silk manufacturing family, the marriages with women from the same social class frequently boosted the company's capital.[83] Although the formation of a joint stock company was considered as early as 1885 due to the increased demand for capital and the risk that a crisis would wipe out the assets, this step was not taken until 1920.[84] For Adolf Feller, a merchant specializing in tropical fruits who returned to Switzerland from Sicily, marriage to Emma Richi, daughter of the technical director and co-owner of the Hasler telegraphic workshop in Bern, provided not only the capital necessary to establish and expand his own firm, which manufactured switches and plugs; it also offered him extremely valuable connections to the fledgling electrical industry.[85] The entrepreneur Fritz Streiff, founder of the spinning company Spinnerei Streiff AG in the Zurich Oberland, traveled with his sister to the spa of Fideris specifically to look for a bride, finally settling on marriage to Rösli Mettler from a wealthy St. Gallen textile manufacturing family. It was only thanks to the funds provided by his wife, on the one hand, and his mother, on the other, that he was able to acquire the 1.3 million francs necessary to purchase land in Aathal in 1900 when it came up for sale.[86] Streiff originated from the textile manufacturing milieu in Glarus where the acquisition of equity was extremely important, but the base for such acquisition was very narrow. For example, it was only the marriage of Joachim Tschudi to the wealthy Rosa Jenny which ensured that the Tschudi company could avoid having to obtain capital from outside sources.[87] The importance of kinship relations for capital formation in the development of the new industrial complexes in textiles and, later, in the machine-building sector, is very clearly illustrated by the example of the Swiss town of Winterthur. Women brought money, land, and business connections to their marriage or averted bankruptcy. For example, Elisabeth Sulzer-Ziegler agreed in 1833 to make her fortune of 176,000 florins available to settle the debts of the textile printing company, Sulzer & Steiner, except for a reserve of 40,000 florins. This enabled the young Heinrich Sulzer to make a fresh start in the neighboring town of Aadorf, where a factory owner who was related by marriage to both Sulzer and Steiner had already established a company.[88] The table of alliances among these families is an interesting illustration of the multiple intermarriages cultivated in Winterthur's bourgeoisie.[89] Women's fortunes were not only the basis for capital injection; intermarriages also ensured that their fortunes remained tied into the same entrepreneurial families over the long term and did not have to be paid out as dowries for daughters. The twenty-five thousand examples of family relationships in Winterthur which I examined are most informative in this context, but little historical evaluation has been carried out on them to date.[90] By contrast, Nadja Stulz-Herrnstadt evaluated thirty-five thousand examples of individuals' biographical data for her recently published study of Berlin's bourgeoisie in the eighteenth and nineteenth centuries, which—albeit on a major urban dimension—reveals the same close kinship ties among entrepreneurs.[91] Finally, Sarasin's findings based on the evaluation of statistical data held by the City of Basel is also informative, revealing close kinship ties between the old-established, bourgeois, high-income taxpayers of the city.[92] As in Basel, for the Bernese aristocracy, too, it was not merit and profession but the marriage market which crucially influenced the continuation of power for the old influential and wealthy groups.[93]

Kinship and Survival

Throughout the long nineteenth century, the family retained its function as a social safety net, but only women, through their cultivation of the kinship network, guaranteed the family cohesion that was necessary for this purpose.[94] The exchange of letters, visits, and gifts was based on reciprocity. The element of obligation involved in reciprocity was also the basis for women's willingness to intervene as necessary and help out family members in a variety of ways. Due to its supposedly private

character and gender-specific connotation, this support, despite its economic significance, was neither recognized publicly nor recorded in statistics until very recently.

Men generally joined with other men to form business partnerships,
but did not do so with women. Although in terms of their labor and
financial contributions, women were their husbands' partners in daily
life, this status was not sanctioned by law. Implicitly, such partnership
was only formally recognized when the widow of a deceased entrepreneur took over the reins of his company. The work performed by wives,
sisters, and even daughters retained the character of service. This was
evident, above all, from the characterization of work performed by single women. It was defined in familiar and kinship terms, even in the
names of occupations, especially in German: "nursing sister" (*Kranken-
Schwester*) is a notable example. In contrast to the trend towards the
professionalization of male work, women's work continued to be
regarded as an element of a personal relationship. In women's work,
individual achievement was not recognized, nor was there any acknowl-
edgement of any associated right to individual advancement. These
services were provided by single and married women, were accepted by
relatives as a matter of course, and varied widely according to the individual situation. They might involve the care of parents and parents-in-
law, housework for brothers and even sisters, caring for grandchildren,
nephews and nieces, or sewing a trousseau for female relatives. Thus, at
her mother's request, the eldest daughter of Franziska Dosenbach-
Buchmann—the owner of a chain of shoe shops mentioned above—did
not marry, but functioned as a "wealthy aunt" for her siblings, of whom
there were twelve in all.[95] Half a century earlier, for domestic rather
than business reasons, the oldest daughter of the widowed textile manufacturer, Heinrich Zangger, declined to marry in order to manage her
father's household and provide support for her three sisters. In another
textile manufacturing family, the women contributed much to the company's advancement with their flexible involvement. While the brothers acted as business partners and professional entrepreneurs, the
women helped to feed the workers, worked in the warehouse or office,
and organized the field work on the family farm. In the same region, the
founding of an educational institution for girls enabled Pastor Werdmüller's three unmarried daughters to provide each other with support,
pursue the Pietist creed of "awakening," and teach their nieces at the
same time.[96] Other educationists and teachers described, in long letters
to their mentor, Josephine Stadlin, their diverse work to support their
relatives and the often painful suppression of their own aspirations.[97]
The renowned educationist, for her part, employed her widowed mother

as a housekeeper in her girls' institution and employed a brother and three sisters as teachers, sometimes simultaneously, and at other times successively.[98] Emilie Paravicini-Blumer, who came from a similar milieu, cared not only for her husband, who had some degree of mental incapacity, but also her disabled sister, Agatha, until the latter's death.[99] In 1912, on the death of her sister-in-law, Luise Hürlimann-Wehrli from Zurich included, as a matter of course, her brother's three children in the daily activities of her children and grandchildren.[100] These patterns of flexible cooperation between female relatives were also common in the petite bourgeoisie and in workers' families. A former nurse, who was unmarried, managed the household of her unmarried sister who worked from home as a seamstress. The former nurse also helped her married sister, while the seamstress supervised the niece as part of her apprenticeship.[101] The factory worker, Luise Lattmann, when unemployed, always found accommodation with her sister, who was employed as a maid in a manufacturer's household.[102]

Thus, through kinship, women performed a wealth of services which contributed to the family's economic livelihood and served as a social or emotional safety net.[103] Mothers, mothers-in-law, and other female relatives supported female factory workers by caring for their children.[104] Married sisters raised their unmarried sisters' illegitimate children. Single women took in siblings whose enterprises had failed, provided board and lodging for nieces and nephews, or assisted brothers with their businesses. Others married their widowed brothers-in-law following their sisters' deaths out of a concern for the children.[105] Such marriage practices were widespread in a variety of milieus until the twentieth century, and—I assume—were far more common in this variant than a man's marriage to his deceased brother's widow. In other words, men entered into the kinship structure through business links or employment. Women were involved in kinship through direct work, not as employees in their own right, but as persons who were obliged to render service. As Davidoff and Hall have shown, nephews were the preferred business partners after brothers and sons, but sisters were the preferred source of labor in brothers' households. Grandsons found positions in grandfathers' companies, whereas granddaughters worked in their households. Women were expected to work on behalf of the family, whereas men were expected to take an active role in its business, and women were only assigned a passive role here as the providers of loans or pensions.[106]

To summarize, we can say that alliances play a central role in the interplay of free forces. Kinship not only facilitates the adoption of binding relations, given that it is already structured in this way, but it also enables energies and financial resources to be pooled in pursuit of advancement and the consolidation of social status. The same or similar experiences of life foster the emotional intensity of such relationships and lead to an expansion of relationship practices based on feelings, which are the foundation on which emotions and material interests are reconciled. If this harmonization of interests is to be proved academically, however, there is a need for studies on kinship relations which include an analysis of capital structures, an evaluation of private correspondence, and an exploration of the locations in which education and sociability are fostered. Like family bequests, company archives are viewed as private and are rarely available to the public. This type of research is therefore a complex undertaking for a variety of reasons.

(Translation: Hillary Crowe)

Notes

*   My thanks are due to the Swiss economist Mascha Madörin for key ideas on the economic aspects of gender relations which go beyond the legal standards, as well as to the feminist economists, especially from the Third World, for their multifaceted contributions on this issue at the NGO Forum in Houairou, Fourth United Nations World Conference on Women, Beijing 1995.

1. David Warren Sabean, *Property, Production, and Family in Neckarhausen, 1700–1800* (Cambridge, 1990), pp. 101–3, 121; reference to Thompson p. 17, n. 43; see Edward P. Thompson, "The Grid of Inheritance: A Comment." in *Family and Inheritance: Rural Society in Western Europe 1200–1800*, ed. Jack Goody, Joan Thirks, and E. P. Thompson (Cambridge, 1976), pp. 328–60; idem, Die Entstehung der englischen Arbeiterklasse, vol. 1, p. 7.
2. David Warren Sabean, *Kinship in Neckarhausen, 1700–1870* (Cambridge, New York, 1998). I will not make any further reference to this work, but the conclusions contained, inter alia, in chap. 22 on "Kinship and class formation," pp. 449–89, and in chap. 23 on "Kinship and gender," pp. 490–510, are informative in terms of the hypotheses presented here, and provide a wealth of examples from modern Germany.
3. See Hans Medick and Anne-Charlott Trepp, ed., *Geschlechtergeschichte und Allgemeine Geschichte, Herausforderungen und Perspektive* (Göttingen, 1998), pp. 15–55, here pp. 42–48: "Die Nicht-Einheit der Geschichte als historiographische Herausforderung. Zur historischen Relevanz und Anstössigkeit der Geschlechtergeschichte"; Lynn Hunt, "The Challenge of Gender. Deconstruction of Categories and Reconstruction of Narratives in Gender History," in ibid., pp. 57–97, here pp. 86–97; Gianna Pomata, "Close-Ups and Long Shots: Combining Particular and General in Writing the Histories of Women and Men," in ibid., pp. 99–124, here pp. 114–24.
4. See Elisabeth Joris and Heidi Witzig, *Brave Frauen—Aufmüpfige Weiber. Wie sich die Industrialisierung auf Alltag und Lebenszusammenhänge von Frauen auswirkte (1820-*

1940) (Zurich, 1992); Elisabeth Joris, "Die geteilte Moderne: Individuelle Rechtsansprüche für Männer, ständische Abhängigkeit für Frauen," *Schweizerische Zeitschrift für Geschichte* 46 (1996): pp. 306–31; eadem, "Im Vertrauen, reden Staatsmänner auch etwa vom Weibe? Partizipation oder Dissidenz—zur Konstituierung eines weiblichen Handlungsraumes," in *Revolution und Innovation, Die konfliktreiche Entstehung des schweizerischen Bundesstaates von 1848,* ed. Andreas Ernst, Albert Tanner, and Mathias Weishaupt (Zurich, 1998), pp. 173–88. At present, I am using correspondence to analyze the relationship networks of the educationist Josephine Stadlin and the homeopath Emilie Paravicini-Blumer, two women from German-speaking Switzerland at the time of the founding and development of the Swiss Confederation in the nineteenth century.

5. Jon Mathieu, "Verwandtschaft als historischer Faktor. Schweizer Fallstudien und Trends, 1500–1900," *Historische Anthropologie* 2 (2002): pp. 225–44, here p. 225, and note 1; on Huber, see also Elena Ramelli, "Eugen Huber als Rechtshistoriker," in *Eugen Huber (1849-1923), Akten des im Sommersemester 1992 durchgeführten Seminars,* ed. Pio Caroni, Rechtshistorisches Seminar Universität Bern (Bern, 1993), pp. 243–59, here p. 254.

6. Philipp Sarasin, *Stadt der Bürger. Bürgerliche Macht und städtische Gesellschaft, Basel 1846-1914,* rev. ed. (Göttingen, 1997); Albert Tanner, *Arbeitsame Patrioten— wohlanständige Damen. Bürgertum und Bürgerlichkeit in der Schweiz 1830–1940* (Zurich, 1995). On kinship relations in Switzerland in the early modern era, see Simon Teuscher, *Bekannte—Klienten—Verwandte. Soziabilität und Politik in der Stadt um 1500* (Cologne, Weimar, Vienna, 1998); Albert Schnyder-Burghartz, *Alltag und Lebensformen auf der Basler Landschaft um 1700* (Liestal, 1992).

7. Joris and Witzig, *Brave Frauen;* Elisabeth Joris and Heidi Witzig, "Konstituierung einer spezifischen Frauenöffentlichkeit zwischen Familie und Männeröffentlichkeit im 19. und beginnenden 20. Jahrhundert," in *Frauen und Öffentlichkeit. Beiträge der 6. Schweizerischen Historikerinnentagung,* ed. Mireille Othenin-Girard, Anna Gossenreiter, and Sabine Tautweiler (Zurich, 1991), pp. 143–60; Elisabeth Joris and Heidi Witzig, "Die Pflege des Beziehungsnetztes als frauenspezifische Form von 'Sociabilité'," in *Geselligkeit, Sozietäten und Vereine,* ed. Hans-Ulrich Jost and Albert Tanner (Zurich, 1991), pp. 139–59; Elisabeth Joris and Heidi Witzig, "Frauen und Männer im Kampf um Macht und Einfluss in Uster," in *Vom Luxus des Geistes. Festgabe zum 60. Geburtstag von Bruno Schmid,* ed. Christoph Mörgeli (Zurich, 1994), pp. 293–309.

8. Heide Wunder, "Herrschaft und öffentliches Handeln von Frauen in der Gesellschaft der Frühen Neuzeit," in *Frauen in der Geschichte des Rechts. Von der Frühen Neuzeit bis zur Gegenwart,* ed. Ute Gerhard (Munich, 1997), pp. 27–54; Gerhard Dilcher, "Die Ordnung der Ungleichheit. Haus, Stand und Geschlecht," in ibid, pp. 55–73.

9. Sandro Guzzi-Heeb, "Marie-Julienne de Nucé (1725-1791): le pouvoir d'une veuve," in *Valaisannes d'hier et d'aujourd'hui, Walliserinnen gestern und heute,* ed. Marie-France Vouilloz Burnier and Barbara Guntern Anthamatten (Sierre, Visp, 2003), pp. 19–23.

10. Claudia Ulbrich, *Shulamit und Margarete. Macht, Geschlecht und Religion in einer ländlichen Gesellschaft des 18. Jahrhunderts* (Vienna, Cologne, Weimar, 1999).

11. See, inter alia, Jürgen Kocka, ed., *Bürgertum im 19. Jahrhundert. Deutschland im europäischen Vergleich* (Munich, 1988), vol. 3; Rebekka Habermas, *Frauen und Männer des Bürgertums, Eine Familiengeschichte (1750-1850)* (Göttingen, 2000), pp.

1–23; Leonore Davidoff and Catherine Hall, *Family Fortunes: Men and Women of the English Middle Class 1780–1850* (London, 1987).

12. Habermas, *Frauen und Männer*, pp. 301–5.

13. Tanner, *Arbeitsame Patrioten*, p. 95.

14. See the detailed discussion in Katrin Rieder, "Netzwerke des Konservatismus— Burgergemeinde und Patriziat im Neuen Bern 19./20. Jh." (unpublished diss., university of Bern, 2004), chap. 2, pp. 12–15.

15. For France, see, for example, Cécile Dauphin, Pierrette Lebrun-Pézerat, and Danièle Poublan, *Ces bonnes lettres. Une correspondance familiale au XIXe siècle*. Préface de Roger Chartier (Paris, 1995); for Switzerland, Joris and Witzig, *Brave Frauen*, p. 116; Tanner, *Arbeitsame Patrioten*, pp. 120–57.

16. Davidoff and Hall, *Family and Fortunes*, pp.193–270.

17. Mathieu, "Verwandtschaft als historischer Faktor," pp. 238–42; Max Baumann, *Kleine Leute. Schicksale einer Bauernfamilie 1670-1970* (Zurich, 1990), pp. 241–43; Heinz Albers-Schönberg, ed., *Die Geschichte der Hürlimann von Fluntern* (Zurich, 1993), p. 55; Dore Heim, "'Hier schicke ich Ihnen sechs Eier und den Brunnen meiner Frau'—Marie Heim-Vögtlin," in *Chratz & Quer, Sieben Frauenstadtrundgänge in Zürich*, ed. Verein Frauenstadtrundgang Zürich (Zurich, 1995), p. 189; Heidi Witzig, *Polenta und Paradeplatz. Regionales Alltagsleben auf dem Weg zur modernen Schweiz, 1880-1914* (Zurich, 2000), pp. 196–97.

18. Sabean, *Kinship in Neckarhausen*, pp. 12, 427, 466.

19. Tanner, *Arbeitsame Patrioten*, p. 154.

20. Ibid., p. 154.

21. Heinz Albers-Schönberg, ed., *Die Geschichte der Familie Hürlimann von Fluntern* (Zurich, 1993), pp. 77.

22. Schönberg, *Die Geschichte der Hürlimann*, p. 77–81.

23. See Irene Amstutz and Sabine Strebel, *Seidenbande: die Familie De Bary und die Basler Seidenbandproduktion* (Aarau, 2002), p. 35.

24. Ibid., pp. 126–29.

25. Sarasin, *Stadt der Bürger*, p. 191.

26. Ibid. pp. 191–92.

27. Under the influence of "federal baron" Escher, Heinrich Grunholzer subsumed his education policy ideals and socially critical views—which he had expressed during his time as a student in Berlin in a social report on the living conditions of 2,500 people in a Hamburg suburb (one of the earliest social reports in German literature) for Bettina von Arnim's work, *Dies Buch gehört dem König*—to his entrepreneurial interests. See Johann Heinrich Grunholzer, "Erfahrungen eines jungen Schweizers im Voigtlande. (Als Beilage zur Sokratie der Frau Rath)," in Bettina von Arnim, *Dies Buch gehört dem König*, Sämtliche Werke (Berlin, 1921), vol. 6, pp. 453–505; Traugott Koller, *Heinrich Grunholzer, Lebensbild eines Republikaners im Rahmen der Zeitgeschichte* (Zurich, 1876), vol. 2; *Geschichte des Kantons Zürich* (Zurich, 1994), vol. 3, pp. 74, 135, 141; Joris and Witzig, "Frauen und Männer im Kampf.", pp. 293–309.

28. Joris and Witzig, "Frauen und Männer im Kampf," p. 307.

29. Elisabeth Joris, *Die Pädagogin Josephine Stadlin–die Homöopathin Emilie Paravicini- -Blumer, Interaktionen Zwischen Franen und Kännern aus dem Bügertum, des 19. Jahrhunderts in der Schweiz*, unpublished, Part II, chap. 1, p. 31.

30. Tanner, *Arbeitsame Patrioten*, pp. 155-7, 266.

31. Roland Gysin, "Lina liest und korrigiert. Eugen Huber, seine Frau und das Zivilgesetzbuch," in *96 Jahre ZGB. Eine Festschrift*, ed. Roland Gysin, René Schuhmacher,

and Dominique Streben (Zurich, 2003), pp. 29–40, here p. 34. Eugen Huber outlived his wife by several decades. He wrote a letter to his deceased wife every day until his later remarriage.

32. Davidoff and Hall, *Family Fortunes*, pp. 13, 32–34.
33. Davidoff and Hall, *Family Fortunes*, p. 179. On this issue, see also Rebekka Habermas's criticism of the concept of the bourgeoisie put forward by Jürgen Kocka and by Manfred Hettling, Habermas, *Frauen und Männer*, p. 10. For an overview of the research debate on the legal impacts, see Ellinor Forster and Margareth Lanzinger, "Stationen einer Ehe. Forschungsüberblick," *L'Homme, Zeitschrift für Feministische Geschichtswissenschaft* 14 (2003): pp. 141–55. See also "Bürgertum als Konstrukt" in Tanner, *Arbeitsame Patrioten*, pp. 75–91.
34. Cited in Urs Fasel, "Eugen Huber und die soziale Frage," in Caroni, *Eugen Huber*, pp. 3–21, here p. 9.
35. See Ursula Vogel, "Gleichheit und Herrschaft in der ehelichen Vertragsgesellschaft—Widersprüche der Aufklärung," in Gerhard, *Frauen*, pp. 265–92, here pp. 267, 278.
36. Gerhard, *Frauen*; for Switzerland, see Annamarie Ryter, *Als Weibsbild bevogtet. Zum Alltag von Frauen im 19. Jahrhundert* (Liestal,1994), p. 74.
37. Regula Gerber Jenni and Claudia Kaufmann, "Frauenforderungen an das Schweizerische Zivilgesetzbuch," in Caroni, *Eugen Huber*, pp. 178–220, here pp. 183–87
38. For a good overview, see Nicole Arnaud-Duc, "Die Widersprüche des Gesetzes," in *Geschichte der Frauen. Band 4: 19. Jahrhundert*, ed. Geneviève Fraisse and Michelle Perrot (Frankfurt a.M., New York, 1994), pp. 97–132; see also *Feministische Geschichtswissenschaft* 14 (2003); Eleni Varikas, "Genre et démocratie historique ou le paradoxe de l'égalité par le privilège," in *Democratie et représentation*, ed. Michèle Riot Sarcey (Paris, 1995), pp. 145–62. For Switzerland, see Jenni and Kaufmann, "Frauenforderungen," pp. 178–220; Christian Simon, ed., *Dossier Helvetik 2, Sozioökonomische Strukturen, Frauengeschichte/Geschlechtergeschichte* (Basel/Frankfurt a. M., 1997); Anne-Lise Head-König, "Les femmes et la Justice matrimoniale dans les cantons suisses, XVIIe–XIXe siècles. Crédibilité et protection de la femme lors de contentieux matrimoniaux," in *weiblich—männlich. Geschlechterverhältnisse in der Schweiz: Rechtsprechung, Diskurs, Praktiken*, ed. Rudolf Jaun and Brigitte Studer (Zurich, 1995), pp. 59–70.
39. Max Gmür, cited in Jenni and Kaufmann, "Frauenforderungen," p. 212.
40. Ernst Holthöfer, "Die Geschlechtsvormundschaft. Ein Überblick von der Antike bis ins 19. Jahrhundert, " in Gerhard, *Frauen*, pp. 390–451, here p. 451.
41. Supplementary contractual provisions were negotiated in an attempt to safeguard the claims of the family of origin. Thus, contrary to the provisions of the Swiss Civil Code, parts of the special assets of a female member of the Usteri family from Zurich reverted to her family of origin as late as the twentieth century.
42. See Amstutz and Strebel, *Seidenbande*, pp. 27–28.
43. Letter to son, cited by Joris, "Geteilte Moderne," p. 315.
44. Sandro Guzzi-Heeb, "Marie-Catherine de Preux (1789-1871): la liberté d'aimer," in Burnier and Anthamatten, *Valaisannes d'hier et d'aujourd'hui*, pp. 51–55.
45. Kathrin Ueltschi, "Frauen kommen ins Geschäft. Erste Unternehmerinnen," in Verein Thurgauerinnen Gestern—Heute—Morgen, eds., *Bodenständig und grenzenlos: 200 Jahre Thurgauer Frauengeschichte(n)* (Frauenfeld 1998), p. 51–53.
46. Conzett, *Erstrebtes und Erlebtes* (Zurich, 1929).

47. Martina Ramming, "'Finken-Fränzi,'" in *Chratz & Quer, Sieben Frauenstadtrund-gänge in Zürich*, ed. Verein Frauenstadtrundgang Zürich (Zurich, 1995), pp. 33–37, here p. 36.

48. *Neue Zürcher Kantonsgeschichte, 19. und 20. Jahrhundert* (Zurich, 1994), vol. 3, p. 146.

49. Forster and Lanzinger, "Stationen einer Ehe," p. 145.

50. Barbara Hess-Wegmann, "Inländische Unruhen 1794 und 1795," in *Quellen zu Schweizer Geschichte* (Basel 1897), vol. 17.

51. Helene von Lerber, *Oben bleiben! Die Lebens–geschichte der tapferen Glarnerin Emilie Paravicini-Blumer, 1808-1885* (Glarus, 1961), pp. 245–48.

52. Amstutz and Strebel, *Seidenbande*, p. 48.

53. Joris and Witzig, *Brave Frauen*, pp. 295–301.

54. Ueltschi, "Frauen kommen ins Geschäft," p. 51. On the importance of matrilineage and the "son-in-law cases," see also Rieder, *Netzwerke des Konservativismus*, chap. 4, pp. 56–57, 80–81.

55. Joris and Witzig, *Brave Frauen*, pp. 239–44, 272–83; Joris and Witzig, "Pflege des Beziehungsnetzes," pp. 139–59.

56. For Germany and Switzerland, see Ulrike Weckel, Claudia Opitz, Olivia Hochstrasser, and Brigitte Tolkemitt, eds., *Ordnung, Politik und Geselligkeit der Geschlechter im 18. Jahrhundert* (Göttingen, 1998); Brigitte Schnegg, "Gleichgestimmte Seelen. Empfindsame Inszenierung und intellektueller Wettstreit von Männern und Frauen in der Freundsschaftskultur der Aufklärung," in *Werkstatt Geschichte 28* (2001), pp. 23–42. On the importance of kinship relations in the formation of a dissident public, see Erika Hebeisen, *Leidenschaflich fromm. Die pietistische Bewegung in Basel (1750-1830)* (Cologne, Vienna, Weimar, 2005).

57 Habermas, *Frauen und Männer*, pp. 398–401.

58. See also Tanner, *Arbeitsame Patrioten*, pp. 275–76.

59. Joris and Witzig, "Pflege des Beziehungsnetzes"; Joris and Witzig, *Brave Frauen*, pp. 239–83. See also Gerhard Schmied, *Schenken. Über eine Form sozialen Handelns* (Opladen,1996).

60. See Christa Hämmerle and Edith Saurer, ed., *Briefkulturen und ihr Geschlecht. Zur Geschichte der privaten Korrespondenz vom 16. Jahrhundert bis heute* (Vienna, Cologne, Weimar, 2003); Dauphin, Lebrun-Pézerat, and Poublan, *Ces bonnes lettres*; Friederike Budde, *Auf dem Weg ins Bürgerleben: Kindheit und Erziehung in deutschen und englischen Bürgerfamilien 1840-1914* (Göttingen, 1994).

61. Tanner, *Arbeitsame Patrioten*, p. 269.

62. See also Elisabeth Joris, "'der Himmel hat uns dagegen mit Gütern entschädigt:' Geschlechter- und Familienkonzeptionen in der Korrespondenz einer Schweizer Pfarrfamilie (1. Häfte des 19. Jahrhunderts)," in Hämmerle and Saurer, *Briefkulturen*, pp. 89–113, here pp.108–9.

63. Rieder, *Netzwerke des Konservatismus*, chap. 3, pp. 39–41.

64. Joris and Witzig, *Brave Frauen*, p. 249.

65. Letters from and to Emilie Paravicini-Blumer, de Quervain private bequest, Bern.

66. Albers-Schönberg, *Geschichte der Familie Hürlimann*, p. 94.

67. Tanner, *Arbeitsame Patrioten*, pp. 271–75.

68. Joris and Witzig, *Brave Frauen*, pp. 208, 249.

69. Habermas, *Frauen und Männer*, p. 399. Hans Medick and David Sabean, "Interest and Emotion in Family and Kinship Studies: A Critique of Social History and Anthropology," in *Interest and Emotion: Essays on the Study of Family and Kinship*, ed. Hans Medick and David Sabean (Cambridge 1984), pp. 9–27.

70. Habermas, *Frauen und Männer*, p. 293.
71. See *Die Liebe der Geschwister, L'Homme. Zeitschrift für Feministische Geschichtswissenschaft* 13 (2002).
72. Leonore Davidoff, "'Eins sein zu zweit': Geschwisterinzest in der englischen Mittelschicht des späten 18. und frühen 19. Jahrhunderts," *L'Homme* 13 (2002): pp. 29–49, here pp. 37–39.
73. Joris and Witzig, *Brave Frauen*, p. 252.
74. Private bequest of Lina A.-B., 20 January 1902.
75. Joris and Witzig, *Brave Frauen*, p. 117.
76. See Sabean, *Kinship in Neckarhausen*, p. 452.
77. Joris and Witzig, *Brave Frauen*, pp. 62–67; see the unpublished history in the Werdmüller bequest in the Zurich State Archives. The history by the historian Leo Weisz, which was commissioned by the Werdmüller family and entitled *Die Werdmüller. Schicksale eines alten Zürcher Geschlechtes* (Zurich, 1949), is based largely on the papers of Pastor Otto Anton Werdmüller.
78. Rieder, *Netzwerke des Konservatismus*.
79. Fanny Sulzer-Bühler, "Erinnerungen," Manuscript, (Winterthur, 1973).
80. Davidoff and Hall, *Family Fortunes*, pp. 32–34.
81. See Silvia Oberhänsli, *Die Glarner Unternehmer im 19. Jahrhundert* (Zurich, 1982), pp. 166–67.
82. Tanner, *Arbeitsame Patrioten*, pp. 177–202. Tanner provides a wealth of extremely informative examples.
83. Amstutz and Strebel, *Seidenbande*, pp. 28, 56–57, 75–77.
84. Amstutz and Strebel, *Seidenbande*, p. 80.
85. Elisabeth Joris und Adrian Knoepfli, *Eine Frau prägt eine Firma. Zur Geschichte von Firma und Familie Feller* (Zurich, 1996), p. 8.
86. Hans-Peter Bärtschi, *100 Jahre Spinnerei Streiff AG Aathal* (Aathal, 2001).
87. Oberhänsli, *Glarner Unternehmer*, p. 48. The Glarus-based companies were soon closely linked by kinship with the manufacturers from the Zurich Oberland; see Joris and Witzig, *Brave Frauen*, p. 117.
88. Klaus Sulzer, *Vom Zeugdruck zur Rotfärberei, Heinrich Sulzer (1800-1876) und die Türkischrot-Färberei Aadorf* (Zurich, 1991), app. 2, table of alliances of the Sulzer, Ziegler, Greuter, Rieter and Steiner families, pp. 284–86.
89. Sulzer, *Zeugdruck*, p. 51.
90. I am grateful to the former mayor of Zurich and passionate amateur historian, Urs Widmer, for examples from his database. See also the publication produced by Winterthur Municipal Library by Hans-Peter Bärtschi, ed., *Basis: Produktion, Industriekultur in Winterthur* (Zurich, 2002), especially the contributions by Urs Widmer, "Villen um 1895," pp. 194–204; Willi Wottreng, "Sulzer—eine Familiengeschichte," pp. 112–21; Gertraud und Rudolf Gamper, "Imitation and Innovation: Johann Sebastian Clais und die Winterthurer Frühindustrialisierung," pp. 60–66; and Christoph Keller, "Hard 1802-2002," pp. 67–83. The tables of names in the appendix to Sulzer, *Zeugdruck*, pp. 284–86, are also informative.
91. Nadja Stulz-Herrnstadt, *Berliner Bürgertum im 18. und 19. Jahrhundert, Unternehmenskarrieren und Migration, Familien und Verkehrskreise in der Hauptstadt Brandenburg-Preussens* (Berlin, 2002).
92. Sarasin, *Stadt der Bürger*, pp. 91–136, 198–215; Rieder, *Netzwerke des Konservatismus*, chap. 2, p. 12, chap. 3, pp. 29–34.
93. On the specific legally guaranteed form of the Bernese family trusts which granted support solely to kin, see Rieder, *Netzwerke des Konservatismus*, chap. 2, "Fami-

lienkisten als Zeichen der Verbundenheit, " pp. 34–37. Such trusts also existed in Zurich, for example, in the Werdmüller family. The conservative and patriarchal nature of these arrangements is illustrated by the annual family conferences, when the men met traditionally to discuss financial affairs before the ladies joined them for the family party. Rieder, *Netzwerke des Konservatismus*, p. 37.

94. See the examples cited above.

95. Martina Ramming, "'Finken-Fränzi,'" in *Verein Chratz & Quer, Sieben Frauenstadtrundgänge in Zürich*, rauenstadtrundgang Zürich, ed., (Zurich, 1995), pp. 33–37, here p. 36.

96. Joris and Witzig, *Brave Frauen*, pp. 200, 205, 250.

97. Josephine Zehnder-Stadlin bequest, letters to Josephine Stadlin, Manuscript Department of Zurich Central Library.

98. The Josephine Zehnder-Stadlin bequest held by the Manuscript Department of Zurich Central Library contains not only her extensive correspondence, but also, inter alia, the chronicle of her life, catalogued under Ms P 2198/3. On the flexibility of women in teaching, see also Gudrun Wedel, *Lehren zwischen Arbeit und Beruf. Einblicke in das Leben von Autobiographinnen aus dem 19. Jahrhundert* (Vienna, Cologne, Weimar, 2000), pp. 73–266.

98. Letters from and to Emilie Paravicini-Blumer, de Quervain private bequest.

100. Albers-Schönberg, *Geschichte der Familie Hürlimann*, p. 97.

101. Joris and Witzig, *Brave Frauen*, pp. 207–8.

102. Bequest of Luise Lattmann 1861–1953, Wald Town Archives. The chronicle of Luise Lattmann's life is an impressive example of the very unusual lyrical prose produced by a woman with little formal schooling.

103. Joris and Witzig, *Brave Frauen*, especially pp. 208, 248. Witzig, *Polenta*, p. 92.

104. Hermine Knapp, "Erinnerungen einer Arbeiterin aus dem Zürcher Oberland," in *Schweizer Volkskunde* 3 (1966), pp. 35–48, and 4 (1966), pp. 49–56; Otto Kunz, *Barbara die Feinweberin. Eine Lebensgeschichte aus dem Zürcher Oberland* (Lucerne, 1943).

105. See Dauphin, Lebrun-Pézerat, and Poublan, *Ces bonnes lettres*.

106. Davidoff and Hall, *Family Fortunes*, pp. 281–89.

Chapter XIII

Kinship, Civil Society, and Power in Nineteenth-Century Vannes

Christopher H. Johnson

Introduction

The very idea of coupling civil society and kinship may seem incongruous to many historians and political theorists of the modern age, in as
much as the first great voices proclaiming the notion of civil society (or
the public sphere), above all Hegel and Kant, effectively defined it as
antithetical to the family and kinship. Their civil society was an arena
in which free-floating individuals might reflect and act economically,
socially, artistically, and organizationally unimpeded by the prescriptions imposed by one's place in a kinship network or by the repressive
authority of the state. It would seem that participation in civil society
necessitated liberation from the family, and that the truly problematic
relationship was that between civil society and the state, which in
Hegel's view would be an ever-advancing integration of the two, culminating in the triumph of human freedom and the end of history. The
family would obviously not disappear, but it defined the private sphere
where women and children played an integral role on a field of sentiment, not reason, and thus were in need of shepherding (as well as
external representation) by rational male heads of household. Kant at

least maintained that familial relations were contractual, thus opening the theoretical possibility (which he did not pursue) for a connection with the larger social contract articulating the ties between civil society and the state. Jean Cohen and Andrew Arato, in the most comprehensive study to date of civil society in political theory, take Hegel to task for not including the family within civil society. If he had, the family, "if conceived in egalitarian terms [a requirement of civil society], could have provided an experience of horizontal solidarity, collective identity, and equal participation to the individuals comprising it—a task deemed fundamental for the other associations of civil society and for the ultimate development of civic virtue and responsibility with respect to the polity."[1]

What is striking about these lines is that they have some resonance with our new understanding of familial relationships at the turn of the nineteenth century. There had been an important shift in the nature of patriarchy during the era of the French Revolution, manifested most concretely in the end of primogeniture and the equalization of inheritance rights for legitimate children, male and female, but of much larger cultural significance. As argued by historians and political theorists such as Lynn Hunt and Carole Pateman, the authority of the father declines as the sons (Hunt's "band of brothers") declare a degree of independence, while daughters-sisters, later aunts, though remaining "dutiful," often play powerful roles on the interface between family, wider kin, and Hegel's civil society.[2] Although legally subordinated under the new "sexual contract" of "husband-right," the wife, better educated than in the past, corresponded with kin and friends, maintaining ties with circles of power, and oversaw an institution in the French notable world perhaps as important as the voluntary association, the soirée—the intimate dinner party. Unlike the male domain of the association, these events, always chez Madame so-and-so, amiably mixed polite conversation with family matters, especially the serious business of integrating potential in-laws and enhancing courtships, as well as discussions of civic and political affairs. The men might go off to the billiard room afterwards for cigars and cognacs, but the mixed conversations at the table, commanded by Madame, if not quite salons, were often "rational-critical debate" about public questions, even if formally situated in the "private sphere." In the enormous familial correspondence I have been privileged to work with, the sisters, wives, mothers, and aunts who write about six hundred of the letters are fully aware of the issues of the day and their relationship to their lives. Their men are deputies, mayors, deputy mayors, city councilmen, military and civil officers, judges, expert administrators, tax collectors, and notaries, as well as active members of voluntary associations and charitable boards. Dozens of letters indicate that the women knew what this work was all about and offered their advice on anything they wished.[3] I would like to suggest that family, kin, and the public sphere could not help but overlap, and while the latter seemed painted male, the place of women in this interaction was not insignificant.

Many contemporary writers on civil society see the family and kin connections as the first orbit of civil society. The revitalization of the concept over the past twenty years was strongly influenced by the overthrow of dictatorship in Eastern Europe, where kin often provided the first units of resistance and then flowed into wider clandestine organizations. It has also drawn strength, particularly in the United States, from the fear that the vibrancy of civil society is fast collapsing, replaced by a reclusive form of individualism wherein notions of public virtue have vanished. Anguish over the passing of close kin relations and the stable family accompanied this concern, leading theorists to consider the family a critical element of civil society. Michael Walzer perhaps best summed it up in 1997 when he described civil society as "the space of uncoerced human association" and "a set of relational networks—formed for the sake of family, faith, interest, and ideology—that fill this space."[4] The key word here is "uncoerced," and this is no doubt why theorists today generally feel comfortable with the inclusion of the family in civil society, while Kant and Hegel did not. They, of course, had in mind the prescriptive authority operating in aristocratic lineages, oligarchic powers of urban elites, arranged marriages, and an entire mode of behavior in which family and kin acted in a highly structured habitus in which choice was severely limited. Kant and Hegel were revolutionaries on behalf of freedom and thus railed against coercive institutions top and bottom. But historians of the family have mapped a sea change in the history of the family and kinship in the century between 1750 and 1850 during which most of the coercive attributes of the "old" (but hardly timeless) family were challenged from within and without. Is it an accident that this is precisely the era when civil society as concept and reality was also born? Are not the cries for freedom in one not precisely the same as the cries for freedom in the other? This is not to say that families and kin groups were "free associations"—far from it. But the discourse of the family ideal was changing, moving toward a site where love, a choice, outranked duty, an obligation.[5]

Linking civil society and kinship in France is further complicated by the relatively sparse body of research and theorization on the problem of civil society. Influenced no doubt by Tocqueville's powerful argument that the centralized state in France, unlike the weaker federal system in the United States, had overwhelmed local institutions and voluntary associations, historians in France have studied them less than in the German- and English-speaking West.[6] Part of the hesitation may have arisen from the fact that associations, for whatever purpose, had to be approved by the state until 1901, when full freedom of association was finally added to the French list of the rights of man. Still, selected French men had little trouble organizing voluntary associations, often, indeed, with official encouragement. In the earlier nineteenth century, the principal forms were Masonic lodges, learned societies, and social clubs known as *cercles*. Often conceived as alternatives to "aristocratic" salons, these groups rarely dipped below the social boundary of *la classe moyenne*. The moderate liberalism of the July Monarchy, specifically its conscious sponsorship of the "bourgeois citizen" by Guizot as Minister of Public Instruction, created fertile ground for the explosion of the newer forms of association, the circles and learned societies, at the expense of the Freemasonry.[7] Historians have also charted the extent of French enthusiasm for these institutions, celebrating their robust growth down to the Great War, though it seems clear that the circle lost luster in face of the more purposeful learned societies and Freemasonry, as well as the many other sorts of specialized groups, led by singing and sport societies, that also challenged the snobbism of these elite clubs.[8] Altogether, their work has stimulated a new focus on the significance of private associations in French history, now increasingly manifested in detailed local studies.[9]

What that significance constitutes, however, is problematic. The use of the word *sociabilité*, established by Agulhon in his massive work on popular forms of association in Provence and repeated by virtually all French historians thereafter, may have served inadvertently to lessen the stature of these "intermediary bodies" in the understanding of the ongoing history of French democracy.[10] As a basis for theoretical analysis, it is weak. The term "civil society" and its integral relation with the notion of the public sphere, rooted in the Scottish and German Enlightenment, elaborated largely by theorists, with the exception of Tocqueville, mostly writing in English and German and culminating in Talcott Parsons and Jürgen Habermas, provides a much richer theoretical vantage point.[11] Agulhon was thoroughly aware of these developments and wary of Michel Foucault's critique of them, but does not seem to have updated his concept of sociability into a theory of civil society.[12] Civil society describes an entire layer of participatory activity by private people in the public sphere serving at once as a framework for mobilization and for ideological orientation. In the contemporary world, in the form of transnational social movement organizations, it may serve as the last, best hope for a purchase of democracy on the new leviathan of global empire.[13] But we are still left with the conundrum that haunts all assessments of civil society, and seems particularly relevant for France: to what extent—or better, when and where—should the role of voluntary associations be seen as contributing to democratic practice rather than to the narrow influence of special interest groups? This is preeminently an historical question and lies at the heart of most debates over civil society today. Civil society's alleged passing is much bemoaned, but the ability of its most powerful elements to thwart broader democratic outcomes is equally so. In a time and place where state authorization was granted only to "citoyens ... jouissant d'un existance honorable et d'une moralité reconnue,"[14] the question is all the more relevant.

The unknown dimension in the study of civil society—the role of kinship in its articulation—should speak to both sides of the issue and perhaps clarify our assessment of it. On one hand, as we shall see, kinship can have a salutary effect on developing a common focus for civic action and bridging the barriers, political and fiscal, for realizing objectives. It can be particularly useful in building an organization. But on the other hand, few social formations are more suspect, especially in modern times, than those that seem cemented by family connections. No myth has been more abiding than the notion that France was really run by *les deux cents familles*.[15] But, beyond political sloganeering, the relationship among civil society, kinship, and power, even in the United States, Britain, and Germany, has in fact been little studied.[16] A solid beginning for France was the *colloque* at Rouen organized by Françoise Thélamon and entitled *Aux sources de la puissance: sociabilité et parenté*, but it seems to have failed to stimulate much further work, perhaps because of the conceptual disarray argued above.[17]

This chapter seeks to encourage debate about the place of kinship within associational and local political life during the first half of the nineteenth century through the careful examination of elite society in the Breton city of Vannes (Morbihan). The questions to be examined cut to the heart of French political mythology. Answers from one locality will hopefully stimulate comparative evaluations. To what extent did marriage and resulting kin networks bring together politically divergent groups, specifically royalists and revolutionaries, in a region riven with counterrevolutionary conflict? Can we begin to see the emergence of a center-left and center-right who largely agree on fundamental questions of social power? Can we also detect new patterns of marriage within this elite during the nineteenth century? Did

consanguineous marriage increase? Were outsiders nevertheless integrated through marriage and associational participation? Did Vannes
natives also marry "away" in significant numbers? Can one infer family
strategies in these regards? How did kinship networks correlate with
associational activities, and how did both connect with the local political power structure and influence programs for civic betterment? Is
kinship, then, the missing factor in the analysis of the elite formation
and the functioning of bourgeois civil society in the nineteenth century, a factor always suspected but rarely articulated within the reigning discourse of individual achievement?

In the course of the nineteenth century, Vannes, long the key port of
southern Brittany, lost its commercial significance to nearby Lorient. But
it had also played a prominent administrative, military, and religious role
in the past and relinquished none of these advantages in the nineteenth
century, becoming the capital of the Morbihan and a strategic garrison
town. It also retained its bishopric. Vannes's population remained stable
at around ten thousand souls from 1789 to 1831, then expanded by some
four thousand during the July Monarchy. The occupational character of
its non-noble elite population evolved away from the dominance of *négociants* in grain to a world of landed proprietors, lawyers, doctors, and other
professionals along with governmental personnel and military officers.
Industry, always weak, actually declined during the nineteenth century. In
these respects Vannes was probably more typical of France's urban life
than the nation's thriving industrial centers, but still a *ville bourgeoise* in
every sense of the word. Although the shortage of those enterprising
tigers of the Communist Manifesto in post-Revolutionary France has led
some historians to deny the very idea of bourgeois power, of a "bourgeois
revolution," and indeed, of class altogether, there can be no doubt that in
the minds of ordinary French people—men and women of non-noble
birth who possessed a certain education, had attained a certain level of
wealth, spoke a certain language, carried themselves in a certain manner,
raised their children in a certain way, understood that these children
would marry within a certain milieu based in a moral code with distinct
elements and boundaries—were clearly marked as "bourgeois," whatever
their occupations or sources of income as long as it did not involve working with one's hands. And with such status came the burden of leadership, which in the nineteenth century meant leading on behalf of
progress—better industrial and commercial production, to be sure, but
also better rendering of justice, better health for all, better and more general education, innovation in all the arts and sciences, administering with
efficiency and equity, and bringing to one's direct environment, one's city,
the fruits of one's education and talents: civic improvement seemed the

capstone of the bourgeois vocation and brought to its practitioners the best of all rewards—honor in the eyes of one's *concitoyens*.[18]

My documentation includes voluminous materials from the Société polymathique du Morbihan (SPM), founded in 1826, and sparser records concerning the Masonic Loge de la Philanthropie et des Arts, founded in 1803 and dissolved in 1841; the usual nominative lists and biographies of notables and public officials; and, above all, état civil records: *actes de mariage* for 118 marriages among the elite of the city concentrated in the period 1810 to 1852, along with birth and death records and notarial documents. I am also fortunate to have a mass of intimate correspondence, genealogies, and family memoirs relating to several of the principal families of the era, thus providing a depth rarely achieved in kinship studies.[19] Finally, this analysis would not be possible without the remarkable genealogical investigations of Bertrand Frélaut, whose book, *Les bleus de Vannes*, is a massive prosopography of the members of the city's Revolutionary club from 1791 to 1798.[20]

Elite Kinship in Post-Revolutionary Vannes

At the center of this analysis are three royalist families, the Galles, Jollivets, and Le Ridants, multiply intermarried, who survived the Revolution largely unscathed, improved their fortunes without rendering ardent support during the Empire, and came into their own during the Restoration, though explicitly rejecting the reactionary ideology of the Ultras. They were led by three men. René Jollivet, a notary and lawyer, was a Deputy, then *Procureur Général*, and the leader of moderate royalism in the city. Jean-Marie Galles, his nephew, ran a publishing house, served as first deputy mayor during the Restoration before his appointment with the July Revolution as *Conseiller de la Préfecture*, and founded the SPM. Jean-Marie Le Ridant, Jollivet's brother-in-law (doubly so), who had been a counterrevolutionary Chouan military hero, became a *Maréchal de Camp* under the Restoration and a leader of the Algerian invasion of 1830. Jollivet's children (he had nine by three wives) and Galles's and Le Ridant's siblings, nieces, and nephews were obviously desirable marriage partners during the Restoration and remained so after the families rallied to Louis-Philippe's July Monarchy.[21]

Besides marrying one another (more later), the main characteristic of their unions was political cross-pollination. Ridant's brother Alexis married a Danet, Galles's sister Fanny married into the Claret circle, Jollivet's sons wed a Kerviche and a Le Bouhéllec, while Galles himself married two women in succession who themselves were cousins from the Jamet-Jourdan family and his own cousins by marriage. Jollivet daughters wed a Le Montagner and a Thubé, thus linking with the Taslés and Boullés. And each of these was tied by marriage or blood to the Mahé de Villeneuve, Laumailler, Burgault, Bourdonnay, Lucas de Bourgarel, Jourdan, Glais, Thomas de Closmadeuc, Pradier, and Caradec families. What did these names have in common? All were prominent figures during the Revolution and Empire. All held elective and appointive offices, and some, like J. J. Danet, were renowned for their repression of the counterrevolutionary Chouannerie. Only two were marginally associated with the Terror, while the rest were jailed during the Jacobin era. Analysis of three other royalist families (Thomas-Ducordic, Marquer, Delorme) reveals similar intermixing with many of the same names and other "blue" families. They and our three families did marry royalists, too, while others married outsiders with less political baggage from the regional past. In examining the witnesses, usually relatives, as well as the signatures of privileged well-wishers on the marriage records, the universe of political connection expands exponentially, as does our understanding of the complex integration of the kinship networks of Vannes's elite.

One of the things that eased the potential tensions around politically divergent marriages is the fact that many brides and grooms were already related from pre-Revolutionary unions. So it was, for instance, that Virginie Danet and Alexis Le Ridant were second cousins. Moreover, several of the Galles-Jollivet group's direct relatives, for example, Joachim Oillic and Michel Lorvol, the family doctor, had been revolutionary sympathizers, even activists. Jollivet's third wife, a Thomas-Kercado, was related to the Thomas de Closmadeucs (revolutionaries) and the Thomas-Ducordics (royalists), all originating in La Roche-Bernard.[22]

But what unites them all, whether kin or not, is wealth and status in the community. The partners came from similar backgrounds and met in a social context where everyone knew everyone else. They married equals socially and economically.[23] Political differences could take a back seat. Young Adèle Jollivet summed up the milieu encouraging cross-political marriages in a letter to her husband-cousin Eugène Galles in 1820 about a dinner hosted by the Prefect for local notables, remarking: "There were a hundred persons, the seats had been assigned randomly at the beginning of the dinner, the *Libéral* and the *Ultra* rubbing shoulders; but being true Bretons , the wine brought them together and everything went gaily."[24] The social world of this departmental capital, its nearby towns, and multiple country houses that no aspiring notable could afford to be without made it certain that young people among the principal families had ample opportunity to meet

one another at balls, dinner parties, and the lazy days of summer vaca-
tion. Increasingly, country settings such as the beautiful enclave of
homes at nearby Arradon provided the perfect conditions for the
guided love that ended in appropriate marriage.[25]

If there is a unifying thread of political inclination that runs through
these families, whether royalist or revolutionary, it is to be found in the
adjectives "moderate" and "pragmatic." This also included religious attitudes, which may be the cement linking all. Although few felt any com-
punction about seeking a dispensation for close marriage, the elite of
Vannes were good Catholics. Some had supported the Constitutional
Church of the Revolution, while others participated in the clandestine
services of nonjuring priests. But the Concordat with Rome of 1801
brought most conflict to an end.[26] Moreover, the Freemasonry, which
locally was a bastion of Bonapartist nominal Catholics during the Empire,
opened easily to more observant Christian royalists, especially after 1815.
While the one might accept the views of Diderot or Condorcet and the
other the Jansenist interpretation of the Newtonian universe propounded
by Abbé Pluche, both sought the enlightenment (and the social prestige)
afforded by lodge membership.[27] If this elite were bound by ever more
intricate kinship in forms that protected its assets and consolidated its
social dominance, if it reconciled political and religious differences sufficiently to make "politics" for the rest of the century a matter of polite
interchange between moderate left and moderate right, the bonds of
intellectual camaraderie united it all the more strongly.

Further validating this interpretation is the fact that families of true
believers of the far right and left, ultra-royalists and neo-Jacobins,
though relatively few in number, did not intermarry with the moder-
ates on either side, though they did so within their own milieu. The ideological Ultras tended to be nobles, and while some married bourgeois,
they still chose partners within their own political camp. Neo-Jacobins
largely sprang from commerce and small manufacturing, many of their
leaders self-made professionals, such as Vannes's mayor appointed by
the Provisional Government in 1848, Toussaint Dantu, a physician.

Whatever the politics of these leading families, they all tended
strongly toward consanguineous marriage practices. That close relatives
should be attractive partners is hardly surprising, since, in the vibrantly
familial world of turn-of-the-century Europe, one saw more of them
than any other member of the opposite sex. Once the moral codes and
social values relating to marrying "blood" kin shifted in the later eighteenth century, cousins were increasingly desirable marriage partners
not only because such unions consolidated money, rank, and power, but
because, as sister Aimée Galles understood, cousins were "habituated to

each other almost in the manner of brother and sister."[28] The powerful attraction of the sibling/cousin bond has become increasingly well documented in literary and historical studies of the era, though its emotional characteristics (e.g., safe love versus incestuous passions) and its deeper causes have yet to be adequately analyzed.[29]

Beginning with Adèle Jollivet and Eugène Galles in 1818, who indeed sometimes called each other "*soeur*" and "*frère*" in their long correspondence, our three families and their satellites experienced five first-cousin marriages out of twenty-three that I have examined, and three more distant consanguine marriages.[30] They *were* unusual, but many others in Vannes's elite practiced close marriage. Of the one hundred eighteen marriages analyzed for this study, fourteen were between first cousins, twelve were between second cousins, and six were between step-cousins or half-cousins—altogether, 25 percent. Marriages between affines numbered nine: five were brother-sister=sister-brother marriages (e.g., Jollivet=Le Ridant, 1787, 1798) and four more reinforced previous alliances somewhat more distantly (e.g., uncle-nephew F. and L. Galles=Taslé sisters, 1848, 1856). If anything distinguishes these marriages from those of the past, it is that they reinforce alliances between families in the same or next generation rather than reattaching after two or more. Still unusual here, as elsewhere, until late in the century, is the long-tabooed marriage of the deceased wife's sister (only one Barré=Guery, 1848), though Jean-Marie Galles married Josephine Le Monnier's cousin.[31]

Just as interesting, however, is the proclivity of elite families to reserve at least one marriage to someone beyond the Vannes orbit, either an important new arrival (or, if a female, one whose recently installed father could aid the Vannes male) or one with a promising career elsewhere. Twenty-five marriages fit all categories, with ten women marrying men with careers in Paris (three), Rennes (three), Lodève (one), Versailles (one), Châteaulin (one), and Pontivy (one). Those welcoming in-migrants—connecting with career administrators and technical personnel or their daughters—accounted for the rest. In all cases except for the two sons of Judge Rialan, the spouse from Vannes was the only sibling in the family, usually a younger one, to enter an exogamous marriage. Thus, while reinforcing local connections, elite families went national as well.

Kinship and Civil Society

Let us now turn to the relationship between kinship and civic involvement, whether in voluntary associations, public agencies, or political and legal stewardship in elective and appointive office. The notability of Vannes, overwhelmingly bourgeois and more so after 1830, shared sociability, influence, and civic responsibility in their private associations and concrete power in the key institutions governing the life of the city and its department. The overlap between the Masonic Lodge and the Société Polymathique du Morbihan, on one hand, and the corridors of power, on the other, was significant, but by no means absolute. Still, access was usually as simple as a meal or a game of billiards, often between relatives, for those who did not possess official status. And when one examines the leadership of the voluntary associations, it was rare indeed for an officer not to be a public official. Nonnative appointees in the administrations as well as several professionals from elsewhere found a place in these associations as readily as they did in wedding parties.

Of the two associations, the SPM played a vastly more important role in the civic life of Vannes. It has lasted as an organization to this day, publishing a scholarly journal that dates to 1857, and still brings together—along with professional academics—Vannetais (and now, Vannetaises) concerned about their region and its history.[32] La Loge de la Philanthropie et des Arts dissolved in the midst of financial difficulties in 1841, though apparently a few people kept the flame alive until the revival of Freemasonry everywhere during the Third Republic. Its history is very poorly documented, in any case, though two studies have provided complete membership lists, some social analysis, and anecdotal information.[33]

Founded in 1803, the Imperial lodge reflected the favoritism shown to the Grand Orient by Napoleon, and few officials residing in Vannes failed to join.[34] It acted mainly as a social club for the city's elite, and so would it remain under the Restoration, which wisely reauthorized the Grand Orient and encouraged royalists to join. Though numbers declined from fifty-five to thirty-eight by 1829, the society slowly transformed into a group where former Bonapartists and royalists mixed happily, just as they did in the more serious business of marriage. Still, it tilted politically toward moderate royalism, and though it included a smaller proportion of public officials than was the case under the Empire, twelve members of the city council and seven Bourbon functionaries appeared on the reduced list of 1829. Its social prestige remained high, though Ultras demurred. All but five members were electors, meaning they paid 300 francs in taxes, mostly based in land. Ties of kinship grew dramatically during the Restoration. Whereas less than a quarter of the late Imperial membership appear to be kin of any sort, thirty-three of the thirty-nine members as of 1829 were related to at least one other, while most of the leaders were kin several times over. The lodge may be seen as the city's first *cousinage*, though whether it played much of a role as a force in its civil society during the Restoration seems questionable.[35]

Founded in 1826, the original fifteen-man nucleus of the SPM included only four who were also Francs-Maçons, though soon its attraction would send the masons into oblivion. Leaving aside the great archeologist-historian, Abbé Mahé, all were relatively young men, largely from the liberal professions and government service, character-istics that the society would retain.[36] The group first came together through a mutual interest in the natural history of the Morbihan, one of the most geologically and biologically diverse departments in France. Their field trips in search of specimens also led them to a fascination with its prehistoric and historic landscape of human habitation. At their meeting of 26 May 1826, after reports from several members on their observations, "What caught our attention above all, was the talk of Mis-ter Galles, in which our comrade presented the project of establishing a regional association specifically dedicated to bringing to flourish the sciences and the arts in the Morbihan."[37]

The SPM became Vannes' main private venue for civic action. Its statutes were typical of its era, as were its numbers: thirty-eight resident members during the July Monarchy.[38] To become a voting "resident" member, one had to be from the Vannes area, "to have demonstrated knowledge in the sciences and the arts," be nominated by a member and receive the support of two-thirds of the members present. *Associés libres*, Vannetais living elsewhere, or locals desiring to become members, could attend all sessions and comment on the papers, thus creating a much larger pool of intellectual comrades and community activists. The society quickly developed an impressive list of corresponding members nominated by *sociétés savantes* around the nation with status particularly in the natural sciences. The thirty-eight residents could thus function as an elite *cercle*, but enjoy a much wider range of participants. Politically, the SPM represented all elements of Vannes opinion, from hidebound legitimism to nineteenth-century republicanism. By statute, of course, actual political discussion at meetings was forbidden.[39]

Its principal purpose was to present research by members and asso-ciates on topics seeking to advance scientific knowledge both theoreti-cal and practical. To popularize these scholarly observations, the group taught public courses gratis to interested citizens. They published annual reports summarizing the key presentations of the year, which soon evolved into the *Annuaire du Morbihan*, a compendium of useful

information from agricultural and industrial statistics to lists of all officials and electors of the department as well as articles (*mémoires*), the
best of the society's papers. The Conseil Général subsidized this publication. Members also created a geological, natural history, and archeo-
logical museum, which became the special province of Jean-Marie
Galles and the foundation of the society's sponsorship of prehistorical
research culminating in the preservation and analysis of Brittany's proud-
est monuments, the ancient stones of Carnac, Locmariaquer, Crach, and
elsewhere. The society also founded what would become the Biblio-
thèque Municipal de Vannes and organized the initial collections of the
departmental archives.

The reports by members varied greatly in focus, but most foresaw
practical applications. Agricultural improvement and leasehold reform
rated high in a departmental economy increasingly dependent on it.
Geological reports, meteorological analysis, surveys of local flora and
fauna, public health recommendations, urban building and traffic projects, studies of Vannes's water supply, engineer Brégéon's exposé of the
inadequacy of the city fire department—the list of applied scientific
papers goes on and on.[40] Even history and literature papers had a pragmatic edge. Gaillard's study of the megaliths of Locmariaquer included
recommendations for using potential tourist revenue for agricultural
improvement. And at least three papers of the early thirties attacked
Breton traditions, establishing a theme that runs through the history of
the society and tells us a great deal about Vannes bourgeois elite, whatever their politics. Galles lamented the deterioration of the ancient
Celtic culture, now dominated by superstition locked in by a moribund
language, and urged education in French only, while others attacked
Breton literature and semi-pagan religious practices. And one subject
studiously avoided was the Chouannerie. The society welcomed aristocrats and clerics, but did not wax nostalgic about the sturdy Breton
peasant loyal to his bilingual priest and seigneur. As such, it divided
sharply with the rival Association Breton, dominated by legitimist aristocrats searching for their Celtic roots and glorifying resistance to the
imperialist French state. The SPM stood against this regional nationalism and later delivered the final blows to the myth that the great stone
monuments of Brittany were Celtic.[41] The Société Polymatique thus
emerges ideologically very much like its creator, Jean-Marie Galles, a
moderate and pragmatic royalist, an enlightened Catholic, and a man
imbued with civic virtue.

The internal cohesion of the SPM and its unity with officialdom was
cemented by a consanguineous kinship regime that nevertheless em-
braced talented and well-placed outsiders. Let us first profile its resi-

dent membership, from 1826 to 1852 (sixty-six men), with an emphasis on the leaders. Occupationally, professionals with university training, engineers, physicians, skilled administrators, and men of the law, dominated. But skill was usually accompanied by wealth, though younger scientific and medical professionals had only modest incomes and assets.[42] Altogether, thirty-six members (55%) were *censitaires* (paying more than 200 francs) according to the rolls of 1837 and 1845. The society's leaders, however, were almost unanimously from old, wealthy, and powerful local bourgeois families. Certainly outsiders participated, but they were a distinct minority and few originated beyond the borders of Brittany. It is true that two of the most active members, Mauricet and Cayot-Delandre, seem of modest means, but neither had yet come into his inheritance by 1845.

These two men served successively as Secretary and thus took responsibility for the organization's publications and internal paperwork, its most time-consuming tasks. Both are examples of how quickly talented non-Vannetais were integrated into its elite. Was their extra hard work also a function of their semi-outsider status and modest fortune?

Dr. Jean-Joseph Mauricet, along with Galles and Jean-Pierre Blutel, spearheaded the society's early development. He was born in nearby Port-Louis in 1799, where his father, Jean-François, was a pharmacist who moved his practice to Vannes during the early Empire. He flourished and sat on the city council from 1812 through the First Restoration but, like René Jollivet, refused Boullé's appointment to continue after Bonaparte's return from Elba. A principled royalist, he returned to the council in 1816. The son did his medical training in Bordeaux and helped to found a medical association there before coming to join Dr. Lorvol's practice in 1821. Mauricet succeeded his mentor as the Jollivet/Galles' doctor, and thus quickly entered that family's charmed circle. He married Athénée Bernard from Pont l'Abbé (Finistère) who produced a son for him in 1833.[43] Among the witnesses were his friends, Vincent Huchet and Paul Cheminant, themselves brothers-in-law whose families, respectively, tied with old Vannes lines of notaries and *négociants* and with relatives of the Galles from Auray.[44]

Marie-François Cayot-Delandre followed Mauricet as the spark of innovation in the group, starting the *Annuaire du Morbihan* in 1833. Born in Rennes in 1795, his father was an artillery captain assigned to Belle-Isle after 1815. In 1824, Marie-François married Julie Le Cointre, the daughter of a career tax official, as was he. Through his father, he had connected with Pierre-Louis Thubé, the financial officer for military supplies in Vannes and member of the city council, a witness at his wedding. Thubé was at the heart of a constellation of kin that included

Lorvol, Delorme, Jamet-Vial, and in the thirties extended to the Jollivets, Burgaults, Glais, and all their relations. Here, it would seem, the
SPM acted as much as a catalyst for kinship as a product of it.[45]

Both Mauricet and Cayot-Delandre were successful at garnering
public subsidies for the society's projects as well as promoting recommendations of its members for civic action. Let us now assess how the
SPM related to local officialdom. All prefects, deputies, and mayors
(save one) were active members, as were six judges. The deliberative
councils influenced government action with advice and budget decisions. Throughout the July Monarchy, three, then four of the five members of the Conseil de la Préfecture were SPM members. On the
subsidy-providing departmental Conseil Général, where Vannes only
held three seats, members and their relatives numbered eight out of
twenty-two, a formidable power bloc. Four of the nine members of the
district conseil d'arrondissement de Vannes, who signed off on regional
projects, were SPM activists, and two more were kin. In the administration of the municipality, Amand Taslé provided the premier SPM
influence first as *Secrétaire de la Mairie*, then as first Deputy Mayor,
and finally as Mayor after 1838. Overlapping membership with the
city council numbered around one-third (eight to ten) throughout the
entire period, reaching its maximum under mayor Jollivet-Castelot in
1852.[46] These numbers belie the potential influence of the SPM within
the council, however, since many of its leaders were exceptionally
active as well as repeatedly re-elected with high vote counts. And, as
usual, most councilmen were tied by blood and intimate friendship to
SPM leaders as well.[47] At all levels of power, SPM members and their
relatives were ready to act on behalf of civic improvement. Relations
among the various elements of this power mix were, not surprisingly,
harmonious, the only notes of serious contention arising during the
Second Republic.

The critical limitation in the realization of proposals emanating from
the society's research and visions was fiscal. The city budget had many
fixed costs that increased with the population, making most special
projects dependent on bond issues and state subventions. Nevertheless,
two major public health projects, based on SPM studies, an abattoir on
the city's outskirts and the first elements of securing an adequate water
supply, were accomplished under the leadership of Mayor Taslé
(1838–1846). The Comité central de Vaccine, chaired by SPM member
César Pradier, did fine work, in cooperation with the clergy, in spreading the message to the people. At Brégéon's urging, the fire department
was indeed better funded and reformed. Loss by fire in the city
dropped rapidly, especially as water supply improved. Departmental

agricultural production improved markedly after 1840 as all levels of government did everything in their power to rationalize land-tenure law and promote innovation. The very existence of the *Annuaire*, with its many articles and cantonal surveys, contributed to new ways of thinking. Primary education, whether lay or religious, made important forward strides, and the language of instruction was indeed French. The department became increasingly dotted with plaques marking historical monuments saved from the ravages of time, neglect, and the occasional stone-cutter. In Vannes, building projects such as the clearance of the *parvis* of the cathedral and a new main street connecting it with the lower city by the port multiplied—most, along with water and gas street illumination, only completed during the Second Empire, when central-state funding became adequate.[48] Initiated under mayor Jollivet-Costelot but completed by mayor Lallement (1854–1869), both ardent *sociétaires*, a mini-Hausmannization mirroring change elsewhere in France occurred.[49]

The kinship universe of Vannes, uniting civil society, administration, and elite society, was made up of a series of galaxies, though, unlike the natural universe, some of these galaxies attracted one another. At the same time, the galaxies themselves were not only contracting due to consanguineous marriage, but also reaching out to a parallel universe, not yet clearly charted, which was the national bourgeoisie. In these ways, we are observing how kinship informs class formation. Whether or not one can argue that the new kinship system of the nineteenth century served as a cause or as a manifestation of its unity, we can be certain that is was an element in the making of the modern bourgeoisie.[50]

The kin-galaxies of Vannes radiated around certain men, though in view of the relative equality of power and influence within this elite, it is rather arbitrary to select them. I have identified six, four among the dominant inner kindreds, two comprising the politically isolated Ultras and left-republicans: Jean-Marie Galles, Amand Jourdan, Emile Burgault, and César Pradier; Toussaint Dantu and Bon-Yves Jan de la Gillardaie. Space does not permit complete genealogies, but thumbnail sketches should be adequate for the purposes of this chapter.

Galles's (1789–1874) world has already been discussed. His own marriages and those of his parents, aunts and uncles, siblings, cousins, son, and nephews and nieces, besides modulating political differences, connected him with much of the civil society/political power structure of Vannes and the department. He was related to twenty-four of the sixty-six members of the SPM profiled for this study as well as half of its officers (1826–1852), connections multiplied further by son and nephew Louis and René Galles, prominent in the association after his death. The list of family names of relatives reads like a roster of the political leadership of the city and department: Jollivet, Le Ridant, Danet, Thomas-Ducordic, Bourdonnay, Taslé, Boullé, Jollivet-Castelot, Lallement, Muiron (prefect, deputies, or mayors); Claret, Glais, Kerviche, Le Bouhéllec, Pradier, Marquer, Morand, Tanguy, Gaillard, Charier, Jamet, Jourdan, Le Monnier, Le Montagner, Avrouin (all lesser office-holders). Amant Jourdan (1797–1888), a lawyer and then *juge de paix* who joined the SPM in 1828, besides being Galles's cousin by marriage and god-sibling via the Oillic family, connected more directly to the Jamet-Le Monnier-Glais constellation, which linked with the Thomas de Closmadeuc family, SPM stalwarts later on. His stepmother was a Thomas-Ducordic and his sister married a Burgault, tying him to the future republican mayor. His two marriages made him SPM founder (and outsider) Blutel's brother-in-law, then the father-in-law of the future royalist mayor, Charles Riou. His other brother-in-law was deputy Vincent Caradec, father of yet another deputy and kin by marriage to mayor Jean Lallement. He was also the uncle of Emile Jourdan, the Nabis painter. Emile Burgault (1808–1891), Vannes most famous politician, was the grandson of Imperial mayor Ambroise Laumailler; his many siblings linked him with a half-dozen SPM activists and their kin as well as the politically potent Claret, Thomas-Ducordic, Bourdonnay, De Hay de la Silz, Glais, Thubé, and Le Bouhéllec families. Finally, César Pradier (1786–1848), the only linchpin not born in Vannes, married mayor Mahé de Villeneuve's daughter virtually upon his arrival from Brest in 1806 (thus linking with a dozen families prominent in the Revolution), and went on to a variety of official posts, finally serving as the chair of the Prefect's Council (Galles's colleague) throughout the July Monarchy. His wealth was based in the purchase of church and emigré lands (as were many listed above), and he recemented his Bonapartist links by marrying a second time into the Boullé family of high Imperial officials, military officers, and, later, firm supporters of Louis-Philippe. His connections also included the illustrious Fabres, ennobled by Napoleon. Pradier was a major figure in both the masons and the SPM, as well as a constant presence on various charitable boards during all regimes before 1848. His son married into the royalist Marquer family, while he himself married Dr. Lorvol's daughter, thus, with both, entering the inner circle of the more conservative Galles and Jollivets. His history, this one of an outsider become the consummate insider, shows quite similar patterns to those of the Galles and our other examples: political reconciliation, socioeconomic homogeneity, the integration of stepfamilies, and increasing tendencies toward close marriage for most, with outreach and drawing in for a few.[51]

Similar stories may be told of the galaxies of Dantu and Jan de la Gillardaie, both physicians and major figures in the SPM and city politics, though, unlike the rest, their boundaries were clearly defined by social and political distance, with only rare connections with the others.[52] But all shared a commitment to the city, in the ancient sense. Civic duty, participation in a vibrant civil society, and kin cohesion, especially at the center-left/center-right haut-bourgeois heart of the universe, reinforced and reproduced each other at every turn. Within the SPM, thirty-three men held leadership positions from 1826 to 1852, and twenty-two were related by blood or marriage to at least one other officer, fifteen were related to two or more. Galles, Taslé, Jollivet, Jourdan, the Claret brothers, Thomas-Ducordic, Lallemand, Burgault, Glais, and Morand were all relatives of one another, eleven men whose connections could be configured in a hundred ways! As for the wider membership of this era (including active free-associates and correspondents who later became full members), twenty-seven in number, fourteen were related to at least one other member, twelve of these officers. We have already underlined the depth of connection of the SPM with the city's and department's political power structure, either in person or by kinship. Vannes's civil society, lively and effective, also amounted to an intricate *cousinage*.

Conclusion

Throughout this analysis, the goal has been to identify patterns of connection: between kinship and voluntary association participation; between kinship and the creation of a new politics of cooperation; between kinship, association, and power; between kinship and civic progress; between kinship and class formation. The engine of these connections was marriage. The patterns of marriage identified make it look very much as if a conscious strategy was afoot among the bourgeois notability of Vannes. Yet, as noted earlier and examined in detail elsewhere, young people grew up in a social and emotional *context* that was conducive to marrying the ways their elders seemed to desire. There are few stories of forced marriages here, although one Galles daughter, Aimée, married a man she knew little about because her aunt Marie pressured her to do so. But in fact, she seemed not to care much whom she married, for her true love was her brother. (Cousin Adèle married Eugène in her stead.)[53] Couples came together, shepherded by siblings, aunts, and cousins within a social world rather insulated from the outside, if politically diverse. A kind of guided love thus bloomed. Did

Virginie Danet and Alexis Le Ridant love each other when they married? I have no doubt about it, despite their age gap. And certainly those many later marriages that reinforced family position and power while saving on dowries arose in a delicious atmosphere of leisure and pleasure that made only the merest nod of approval from aunt Adèle the signal for a proposal. In the end, love and power simply intertwined.[54]

At stake here is a larger problem. To speak of "power," especially if tied to the word "elite," bears a negative connotation, at least within cultures, as our own, professing to be democratic. This chapter is about how kinship of the close-marriage type contributed to the consolidation of a local power elite. But it also purports to be about the flowering of civil society animated by this elite of cousins and contributes to a growing literature challenging Tocqueville's perception that the democratic potential in France was severely limited by the absence of voluntary associations, thus enhancing the dominance of the centralized state. Much of the current literature on the history and alleged crisis of civil society clearly marks its existence as a "good thing" for democracy. Yet what if its protagonists constituted an interrelated informal club, a veritable bourgeois *cousinage*, made all the more effective *because* of their kinship? In Vannes, this establishment accommodated diverse political opinions as long as they remained moderate, orderly, and socially conservative. But it did not accommodate men and women socially and, increasingly, genealogically beneath their circle. This circle's moment of consolidation in the next generation occurred largely during the July Monarchy. It was not simply closed, but sent its representatives out in marriage and public service to connect with the wider national bourgeoisie while absorbing intellectually, socially, and politically significant men and women from elsewhere. And as the regimes shifted with the trials of national politics, new generations from the same families maintained their power, keeping Vannetais politics located somewhere between moderate royalism and moderate republicanism (classically manifested by the in-law mayors who alternatively ran the city from 1870 to 1908, "republican" Emile Burgault and "monarchist" Charles Riou) and doing good works of all sorts in the SPM, the revived masonic lodge, and a half-dozen other voluntary service organizations, now including women's contributions directly.

These "*dynasties bourgeoises*," vilified by right and left alike, constituted civil society in its always interacting and overlapping relationship to actual political authority; they *made* Vannes, as they made countless cities in France and throughout the modernizing Atlantic world during the nineteenth century. The extent to which these elites were bound by kinship, as they were in Vannes, is of course a question yet to be explored. They established a vision of a social order, a set of expectations, a "way things are done" and modes of acceptable behavior that increasingly sought to shed the adjective "bourgeois," universalizing a framework of practices and values that had in fact originated in *le moment Guizot*, the elitist liberal political culture of the July Monarchy.[55]

We habitually couple "civil society" and "democracy" in an unproblematic way. But the elitist nature of nineteenth-century voluntary associations and the continued hounding of working-class formations by the bourgeois-dominated state, even after freedom of association was formally declared, not only may help explain many French historians' tepid response to theories of civil society and the public sphere, but also force us to think seriously about the implications of the French experience for our appreciation of democracy's meaning. Did not the great advances in French democracy arise largely from sources well beyond the orderly work of formal associations in the form of public demonstrations—indeed rebellion and revolution—in which the less organized masses (though perhaps stimulated by organized groups) provoked change in the uses and structures of power? Such demonstrative politics remains the bellwether of French democracy today, clearly overshadowing—at least within France—the work of voluntary associations.[56]

Notes

1. Jean L. Cohen and Andrew Arato, *Civil Society and Political Theory* (Cambridge, MA, 1992), p. 631, n. 48.
2. Lynn Hunt, *The Family Romance of the French Revolution* (Berkeley, CA, 1992); and Carole Pateman, *The Sexual Contract* (Stanford, 1988).
3. This is not a theme as yet emphasized in historical literature, though anyone familiar with nineteenth-century fiction knows it rings true. My comments here are based on my research into family correspondence, cited below, note 19. See also Anne Martin-Fugier, *Le vie élégante ou la formation du Tout-Paris, 1815-1848* (Paris, 1990), especially chapters III–V.
4. Michael Walzer, "The Idea of Civil Society," *Kettering Review* (Winter 1997): p. 8.
5. For a more extensive discussion of this fundamental shift, see Christopher H. Johnson, "Das Geschwister Archipel: Bruder-Schwester-Liebe und Klassenformation im Frankreich des 19. Jahrhunderts," *L'Homme. Zeitschrift für Feministische Geschichtswissenshaft* 13 (2002): pp. 50–67. See also the introduction to this volume by David Sabean and Simon Teuscher, and David Sabean, "Kinship and Issues of the Self in Europe around 1800" (paper presented at the American Historical Association meeting, Chicago, IL, 9 January 2003).

6. For an impressive overview and massive bibliography, see Stefan-Ludwig Hoff-mann, "Democracy and Associations in the Long Nineteenth Century: Toward a Transnational Perspective," *Journal of Modern History* 75 (June 2003): pp. 269–99.

7. The key general studies are Maurice Agulhon, *Le cercle dans la France bourgeoise, 1810-1848: étude d'une mutation de sociabilité* (Paris, 1977); Jean-Pierre Chaline, *Sociabilité et érudition: les sociétés savantes en France, XIXe-XXe siècle* (Paris, 1995); and Daniel Ligou, ed., *Histoire des francs-maçons en France de 1815 à nos jours* (Paris, 2000). See also Etienne François, ed., *Sociabilité et société bourgeoise en France, en Allemagne et en Suisse, 1750-1850* (Paris, 1986).

8. Marie-Véronique Gauthier, *Chanson, Sociabilité et Grivoiserie au XIXe siècle* (Paris, 1992). The excellent collection edited by Philip Nord and Nancy Bermeo, *Civil Society before Democracy: Lessons form Nineteenth-Century Europe* (Boston, 2000) emphasizes the problem of exclusivity in bourgeois civil society.

9. Jean-Pierre Chaline, *Les bourgeois de Rouen: Une élite urbaine au XIXe siècle* (Paris, 1982), chap. 7; Carol Harrison, *The Bourgeois Citizen in Nineteenth-Century France: Gender, Sociability, and the Uses of Emulation* (Oxford, 1999); Patricia Turner, *Class, Community, and Culture in Nineteenth-Century France: The Growth of Voluntary Associations in Roanne, 1860–1914* (Ph.D. diss., University of Michigan, 1994); Catherine Pellissier, *Loisirs et sociabilités lyonnais au XIXe siècle* (Lyon, 1996); Hervé Leuwers, ed., *Elites et sociabilité au XIXe siècle: heritages, identités* (Lille, 2001).

10. Maurice Agulhon, *Pénitents et Francs-maçons de l'ancienne Provence. Essai sur la sociabilité méridionale* (Paris, 1968).

11. On the history of the notion of civil society, see Cohen and Arato, *Civil Society*; Marvin B. Becker, *The Emergence of Civil Society in the Eighteenth Century* (Bloomington, IN, 1994); G.W.F. Hegel, *Philosophy of Right* (Oxford, 1967); 122–55; Charles Taylor, *Hegel* (Cambridge, 1975); idem, *Sources of the Self: The Making of Modern Identity* (Cambridge, MA, 1989); Adam B. Seligman, *The Idea of Civil Society* (New York, 1992); Frank Trentmann, ed., *Paradoxes of Civil Society: New Perspectives on Modern German and British History* (New York, 2000).

12. Pierre Nora, ed., *Essais d'ego-histoire* (Paris, 1987).

13. The classic statement was Ernesto Laclau and Chantal Mouffe, *Hegemony and Socialist Strategy* (London, 1985). The promise and limitations of non-governmental organizations are discussed in Michael Hardt and Antonio Negri, *Empire* (Cambridge, MA, 2000). For a balanced analysis and a good bibliography, see Jackie Smith, "Global Civil Society? Transnational Social Movement Organizations," in *Beyond Tocqueville: Civil Society and the Social Capital Debate in Comparative Perspective*, ed. B. Edwards, M. W. Foley, and M. Diani (Hanover, NH, 2001).

14. From the statutes of the Circle littéraire of Parthenay (Deux-Sèvres), 1840, reprinted in Agulhon, *Cercle*, p. 40.

15. E. Beau de Loménie, *Les responsibilités des dynasties bourgeoises*, 4 vols. (Paris, 1971).

16. A remarkable exception is Lynda Ann Ewen, *Corporate Power and Urban Crisis in Detroit* (Princeton, NJ, 1978).

17. Françoise Thélamon, ed., *Aux sources de la puissance: sociabilité et parenté* (Rouen, 1989).

18. Bernard André, "Ville rentière, ville de consommation: l'implosion (1815 à 1800)," in *Histoire de Vannes et de sa région*, dir. Jean-Pierre Leguay (Toulouse, 1988), chap. 9; Bernard André, *Bourgeoisie rentière et croissance urbaine, 1860-1910*, Thèse du 3ème cycle (Paris, 1980). On the old regime, see Timothy Le Goff, *Vannes and its Region: A Study of Town and Country in Eighteenth-Century France* (Oxford, 1981);

J. Allanic, "Histoire du Collège de Vannes," *Annales de Bretagne* 17 (1902–1903): pp. 59–105, 234–75. My thoughts on the French bourgeoisie are inspired by, among others, Pierre Bourdieu, *Distinction: A Social Critique of the Judgement of Taste* (Cambridge, MA, 1984) and idem, *Outline of a Theory of Practice* (Cambridge, 1977), chap. 2; Roland Barthes, "Myth Today," in *Mythologies* (New York, 1972), pp. 109–59; Edmond Goblot, *La barrière et le niveau: Etude sociologique sur la bourgeoisie française moderne* (Paris, 1925, 1967), an ignored classic of cultural analysis; Anne Martin-Fugier, *La bourgeoise: Femme au temps de Paul Bourget* (Paris, 1983); Béatrix Le Wita, *French Bourgeois Culture* (Cambridge, 1994); David Garrioch, *The Formation of the Parisian Bourgeoisie, 1690–1830* (Cambridge, MA, 1996); Christine Adams, *A Taste for Comfort and Status: A Bourgeois Family in Eighteenth-Century France* (University Park, PA, 2000). For the ideal of civic service, see Harrison, *Bourgeois Citizen*.

19. The last consists of the Fonds Galles, 2 J 1-262, Archives Départementale du Morbihan (ADM) (which includes over 1,600 letters, mainly from the first half of the nineteenth century, exchanged by members of the three multiply intermarried families; many genealogies; and a detailed manuscript autobiography concentrating on his early years by General René Galles, 1819–1889) and the Fonds Jollivet (which, though less extensive, includes earlier correspondence and the reminiscences of General René Jollivet, 1832–1895), and forms the foundation of my book, Christopher H. Johnson, *Becoming Bourgeois: Kinship and Class Formation in Vannes (1700–1850)*, in progress. *Actes de Mariage*, after the secularization of the état civil records in 1792, provide a remarkable source for social history, obviously critical for kinship study. Although there was some variation from regime to regime, they give the full names and titles of the groom and bride, their birth dates and places, their professions, and their residence; the same for the spouses' parents, except age and birth place (plus year and place of death); the same for the four witnesses—two for the bride, two for the groom, usually—except birthplace, plus the crucial indication of their relationship to the bride and groom. Overall, 83 percent of the witnesses in this social class were relatives. This figure runs higher than the national average and slightly higher than Brittany, generally. See Jacques Dupâquier, "Le choix des témoins dans les mariages civils au XIXe siècle," in *Aux sources de la puissance*, ed. Françoise Thélamon (Rouen, 1989), pp. 155–60. Signatures on marriage acts include relatives (a majority women) and friends. Although only the names appear, it is often fairly easy to identify them. Married women, happily, include their maiden names, another important source for understanding relationships. Unless otherwise noted, kin networks discussed below are constructed from these materials. The *Archives du Morbihan* has microfilmed all parish registers and communal *états civils* up to 1830 and manuscript registers for the rest of the century are available without restriction. ADM, 2E.

20. Bertrand Frélaut, *Les bleus de Vannes, 1791-1798: Une élite urbaine pendant la Révolution* (Vannes, 1991). As with the *actes de mariage*, unless otherwise noted, information on the politics and activities of pro-Revolutionaries is drawn from Frélaut's meticulous research. My own work on the anti- (or non-) Revolutionaries, when posed side by side with his work, leads to the conclusions of this paper.

21. Although the three are cited in René Kerviler, *Bio-bibliograpie bretonne*, 8 vols. (Rennes, 1886–1904) and 3 vols. (Mayenne, 1978–1985), most of this information is drawn from materials cited in note 19, above.

22. These paragraphs summarize a much longer section in my paper by the same title prepared for the *Kinship in Europe* conference, Monte Verità, Switzerland, 20–24 September 2002, pp. 8–24.
23. I have prepared profiles of all the principal actors and genealogies of their families (416 surnames, 1,042 individuals). Social status can best be appreciated, from 1804 to 1848, by the titles men and women are accorded by the presiding Juge du Tribunal civil and the Maire de Vannes or his adjoints on the official civil *actes de mariage*: 10 percent: Monsieur, Madame, Mademoiselle (the group under study); 30 percent: Le Sieur, La Dame, La Demoiselle; 60 percent: name only. The social homogeneity of all the assembled is the striking fact. Economic status and political prominence, measured by tax lists and a full set of appointive and elective office-holders, confirm the elite status of our protagonists. ADM 3 M 25 (1834 and 1837 cens lists for municipal elections) and the *Annuaire du Morbihan*, 1833–1848.
24. "Il y avait cent personnes, les places ont été données au hazard au commencement du repas, le Libéral et l'Ultra se fesaient l'épaule réunis; mais en vrais Bretons, le vin les a rapprochés et le tout a passé gaiement," Adèle Jollivet Galles to Eugène Galles, 23 July 1819, 2 J 79 (1), ADM.
25. General René Jollivet reminisces about the delights of summers in the country with all his cousins and family friends, identifying nine kin-connected houses in Arradon. "Mes souvenirs" (Fonds Jollivet), ADM.
26. On the religious history of Vannes and especially the Concordat, see Claude Langlois, *Un diocèse breton au début du XIXe siècle* (Rennes, 1974); Roger Dupuy et al., *Les Catholiques et la Révolution Française: autour de Pierre-René Rogue, Prêtre réfractaire vannetais, 1758-1796* (Vannes, 1998); and André Moisan, *Charles Le Masle, évêque constitutionnel du Morbihan, 1791-1801* (Vannes, 1993).
27. Abbé Pluche, *Le spectacle de la nature*, 8 vols. (Paris, 1750). Daniel Roche, in his *France in the Enlightenment* (Cambridge, MA, 1998), p. 509, notes that this book was a true best seller, going through twenty editions and reaching perhaps one hundred thousand readers. It figures prominently in the Galles's personal library and bookshop inventories, as do the works of La Harpe, before and after his disaffection with the French Revolution.
28. Although this is a general theme still requiring further research, the quantitative studies of Jean-Marie Gouesse and of André Burguière provide a solid foundation for its analysis: Jean-Marie Gouesse, "Mariages de proches parents (XVIe-XXe siècle): esquisse d'une conjoncture," in *Le modèle familial européen* (Rome, 1986), pp. 31–61; André Burguière, "Cher cousin: les usages matrimoniaux de la parenté proche dans la France du dix-huitième siècle," *Annales HSS 6* (1997), pp. 1339–60. See also Rudolph Trumbach, ed., *The Marriage Prohibition Controversy* (New York, 1985).
29. Aimée Galles to Eugène Galles, 29 August 1817, 2 J 79(5), ADM. For a discussion of the issue and a bibliography, see Johnson, "Geschwister Archipel," as well as the articles by David Sabean and Leonore Davidoff in the same collection.
30. 2 J 79 (2-4), 1816-1825; General René Galles, "Journal de ma vie," 5-24, 2 J 80, ADM. Cousins: E. Galles=A. Jollivet (1818); J. Le Ridant=C. Galles (1840); R. Galles=J. Le Montagner (1853); J. Le Ridant=M. Galles (1872); second cousins: A. Le Ridant=V. Danet (1811); Jean-Marie Galles=J. Le Monnier (1822); third cousin: A. Lallemand=L. Jollivet (1837).
31. The single instance of the soroate in my data was the classic case of a son-in-law married to the successive daughters of a restaurant owner without sons. The patterns noted above are generally similar to those observed by David Sabean, espe-

cially for the propertied elements of the population of Neckarhausen, as the nineteenth century unfolded. A separate and expanded study of the population of Vannes and its countryside will be necessary before one can argue with any assurance that consanguinity and close affinal reinforcement are mainly the characteristics of propertied families, though preliminary random looks at lower class urban and rural marriages make it appear to be the case. In Martine Segalen's famous case of the South Bigouden, rates of close consanguinity were low while those of affinal, relinking two or more generations down the line, were high, as were distant cousin marriage (beyond the Church's restrictions). The maps of Jean Sutter and Léon Tabah ("Fréquence et répartition des mariages consanguins," *Population* 3 [1948], pp. 481–98) for the twentieth century, and based on dispensation statistics, gives the Morbihan rather high rates, but makes no socioeconomic distinctions.

32. Jean-Pierre Chaline cites the SPM as one of the nation's most significant: Chaline, *Sociabilité*, p. 222. The *Bulletin* of the society and related printed materials are housed in the reading room of the ADM.

33. Michelle Le Fahler, *Recherche de documents maçonnique dans le Morbihan aux XVIIe et XIXe siècles*, Mémoire de Maitrise (Rennes, 1976); Yannic Rome, *La Franc-maçonnerie à Vannes, Auray, Belle-Isle, Ploërmel au XVIIIe et XIXe siècles* (Vannes, n.d. [1985?]).

34. His brother Joseph was the Grand Master. See Carol Harrison's incisive comment that the Imperial practice of encouraging regime-friendly associations and refusing to authorize possible dissidents held for all regimes throughout the nineteenth century (except the early Second Republic), *Bourgeois Citizen*, pp. 26–28.

35. In general, recent scholarship has stressed that past emphasis on the Freemasonry's political activism (as opposed to its social and fraternal aspects) seems considerably overdrawn. See, for a general assessment, Sudhir Hazareesingh and Vincent Wright, *Francs-Maçons sous le Second Empire* (Rennes, 2001), pp. 13–37.

36. In almost all respects, the SPM was typical of learned societies throughout the nation. Chaline, *Sociabilité*, passim.

37. "Ce que attira surtout notre attention, ce fut le discours de M. Galles, dans lequel notre confrère traça le plan d'une société départementale spécialement destinée à faire fleurir les sciences et les arts dans le Morbihan." M. Mauricet, *Compte rendue des travaux du Société polymathique du Morbihan* (Vannes, 1827), p. 1.

38. Most societies in France were limited to certain numbers during the first six decades of the century; the size of the city and the purpose of the organization were usually more important reasons for this than politics. Chaline, *Sociabilité*, chap. 2.

39. *Reglement de la Société polymathique du Morbihan etabli le 26 mai 1826* (Vannes, 1826). The society met the first Thursday of the month, with a *séance solonnelle* every 29 May, when the best papers of the year would be read (thus practicing Harrison's *émulation*). It rented houses at first, then occupied the Maison Lorvol (which the good doctor bequeathed to them after his death), on the place des Lices from 1851 to 1912, at which point it purchased the magnificent Château Gaillard. B. Frélaut, "L'Acquisition du Château Gaillard par la SPM," *Bullitin du SPM* (2001): p. 268.

40. These articles appeared in the annual *Comptes rendues* from 1827 to 1833 and in the *Annuaire* thereafter. See also Henry Marsille, "Les cent soixante ans de la Société Polymathique," *Bulletin de la SPM* (1986): pp.1-23.

41. They were in fact the work of a neolithic people whose origins and destiny remain shadowy. A summary of all this research, mostly presented in the society's *Bulletin*,

appears in Yannik Rollando, *La préhistoire du Morbihan: le vannetais littoral* (Vannes, 1971). See especially his comments on the "celtomanie" of the earlier nineteenth century, p. 5.

42. Among the wealthy, the four taxes comprising imposts due averaged about 5 percent of one's income, but the tax on real property (*immobilier*) normally comprised four-fifths of that amount, unless one derived a great deal of income from one's business. In general, the wealthier one was, the higher proportion of one's revenue derived from real property and therefore the higher one's percentage. Alexis Le Ridant, one of Vannes's richest *censitaires*, declared an annual income, mostly from land, of 20,000 francs when he stood for city council in the late thirties. His tax in 1837 was 1,110 francs. The vast majority of taxpayers paid quite small amounts because they owned little property; had small dwellings with few windows, if they did; possessed insignificant mobile assets; and even if they owned a business (e.g., a tailor's shop), the tax would be miniscule. The average annual income for a male wage earner was around 500 francs in this era, and since there was no actual income tax, workers paid virtually nothing in taxes.

43. Adèle Jollivet to Eugène Galles, 2 December 1820, 2 J 79, ADM.

44. Birth of 8 February 1833 (Alphonse Mauricet); Marriages of 2 July 1820 (Cheminant-Huchet [witnesses: Michel/Galles]); 17 November 1823 (Huchet-Hervieu [Caradec]); 6 August 1832 (Huchet-Bettany [Pitel].

45. Marriages of 15 May 1824 (Cayot Dalandre-Le Cointre [Thubé]; 27 January 1827 (Delorme-Thubé [Lorvol, Jamet]); 24 August 1830 (Jollivet-Thubé [Galles]); 7 May 1838 (Glais-Burgault [Jamet]); 6 January 1840 (Thubé-Burgault [Claret, Jollivet].

46. 2 M 149, ADM.

47. Bernard Frélaut, *Les maires de Vannes au XIXe Siècle* (Vannes, 2001), pp. 30–39.

48. There is no history of Vannes in the pre-Third Republic nineteenth century. Most of this information is drawn from Frélaut, *Les maires*, pp. 71–80, and from various reports in *L'annuaire du Morbihan*, 1833–1856.

49. Chaline, *Sociabilité*, chap. VII.

50. David Sabean's great chapter on kinship and bourgeois class formation in Germany has served as an inspiration for this analysis: *Kinship in Neckarhausen, 1700–1870* (Cambridge, 1998), pp. 449–89.

51. Pradier's story, like the rest, is pulled together from marriage records, tax lists, citations in SPM publications and *L'annuaire*, and the archival records of municipal affairs, especially ADM 2 M 118, 142, and 149 and 3 M 104 and 128.

52. The kinship circle of Dantu included fellow neo-Jacobins Pierre Richard and Hippolyte Judicis, as well as other less active families, also without connections to the moderate and wealthier elite. Jan de la Gillardaie was related to several other nobles in the Ultra camp, but also had right-wing bourgeois kin. He did witness two marriages in the Galles galaxy and, like Dantu, played a constructive role on the city council.

53. Johnson, "Das Geschwister Archipel."

54. See the excellent discussion of this issue by Philipp Sarasin, *La ville des bourgeois: Elites et société urbaine a Bâle dans la deuxième moitié du XIXe siècle* (Paris, 1998), pp. 115–16, which concludes his analysis of elite kinship in that city and resonates with the perspectives of my study of Vannes. Also, Gunilla-Fredericke Budde, *Auf dem Weg ins Bürgerleben: Kindheit und Erziehung in deutschen und englischen Bürgerfamilien, 1840-1914* (Göttingen, 1994).

55. Pierre Rosanvallon, *Le moment Guizot* (Paris, 1985), claims the moment passed after 1848. The study of typical cities such as Vannes makes one wonder. For this cultural conception of the bourgeoisie, see the studies listed in note 17 and Pierre Bourdieu, *La noblesse d'état: Grandes écoles et esprit de corps* (Paris, 1989).

56. On the concept of "demonstrative politics," see Christopher H. Johnson, *The Life and Death of Industrial Languedoc* (Oxford, 1995), chap. 6.

Chapter XIV

Middle-Class Kinship in Nineteenth-Century Hungary

Gábor Gyáni

Hungarian historians have only addressed kinship and the social history of the middle class during the last couple of decades. In this chapter, I will treat the two as closely related issues. First I will delineate the existing scholarship in the history of the family and kinship and the progress achieved in studying the middle classes of the nineteenth and early twentieth century. Special attention will later be paid to some of the ethnic and confessional characteristics of the middle and upper middle classes, defining both the extent and the ways in which kin structures could work at that level of society. Kinship ties served an essential function in fostering capital accumulation, because the late-nineteenth-century economy was still dominated by the family companies. Business-oriented marriage policies deserve a closer look. Marriage contracts concluded between middle class engaged couples in the early twentieth century, however, reveal that marrying meant more than just business, even for well-to-do men and women. At the same time, kin relations had a considerable role in shaping the public and semi-public sociability that will also be described in various contexts. The main point of the present chapter is that while consanguinity seems to have been indeed essential for establishing and strengthening a kind of middle and upper middle class status and identity, various forms of kin relations have always been used flexibly.

An Outline of the Historiography

In Hungary, kinship (family and household included) first emerged as a separate research problem within the framework of ethnography. With the passage of time, however, it began to attract the interest of historical demographers. Rudolf Andorka, who pioneered such research from the late 1960s onward, adapted the methods of family reconstitution created by French scholars of the 1950s and developed further by Peter Laslett and his research team under the aegis of the Cambridge Group for the History of Population and Social Structure. From the early 1970s, Andorka published a large number of case studies (twenty-seven) on rural families and households in the eighteenth and early nineteenth centuries, several of which are available in English.[1]

Andorka's research on the peasant family and household formations, using the Laslett-Hammel methods, established Hungary's structural position as being between those of Northwestern Europe and the Balkans. Both the populous and complex household formations (best exemplified by the Croatian *zadruga*) and the small and simple nuclear family of West Europe were to be found in the area of contemporary Hungary. Finally, Andorka also made an attempt to employ the dynamic approach advocated by demographers discontented with cross-sectional data. Examining only one village, he and his colleagues applied the method of record-linkage with the aim of describing the patterns of the developmental cycles of each of the peasant families and household forms.[2]

The topic, however, was not wholly monopolized by the social scientific approach to history. At the conference, "Historical Anthropology," held in 1984, the section entitled, "Family and Household Organization, Kinship," was opened with historians already advocating a fundamentally different approach. Erik Fügedi offers the best example. As a medievalist, he was among the first Hungarian historians to apply research methods similar to those applied by the *Annales* group. In a conference paper in 1984 and in his book published in English in 1992, Fügedi minutely reconstructed the kin of a medieval Hungarian nobleman, Elefánthy.[3] Fügedi focused on the customary laws defining noble status, inheritance, and marriage as they were summarized in the Tripartitum, the famous code of Stephen Werbőczy. Comparing these norms with actual practice, Fügedi concluded that practice diverged from the law in terms of both social mobility and kinship solidarity.

Research projects focusing on the bourgeoisie and the middle classes only began in the 1980s. One type related to the specific cultural profile commonly shared by the related groups. Péter Hanák was to inspire (and even in part to organize) research in that direction, the products of which were belatedly published only in the 1990s. In his seminal book, Hanák depicted the two fin de siécle metropolises of the Austro-Hungarian monarchy as two poles. Vienna and Viennese cultural modernism represented for him the hyperindividualistic, even atomized, subjective and wholly alienated sociocultural domain. Vienna was contrasted with Budapest, mainly characterized by social reformism, nationalism, and overabundant innovative energy. This duality was expressed by the metaphors of garden (describing Vienna) and workshop (identified with Budapest).[4] Another group of historians, gathered around Vera Bácskai, dealt especially with the evolving entrepreneurial middle and upper middle classes of the "long" nineteenth century.[5] The latter group hoped to clarify the various mobility patterns and business strategies of nineteenth-century entrepreneurial families.

A microhistorical approach was the sole common denominator of the two main lines of research; both wished to apply case study and prosopographic methods. The structuralist approach was also present in this area of historical research, the result of which was the publication of several synthetic monographs on various parts of the middle and upper middle classes. These focused either on the material base of the old-new elite (the great taxpayers) or discussed the mobility paths characterizing or even defining this or that segment of the middle classes.[6] As a result of these investigations, the understanding of the rise of the middle class and modernization (frequently branded as "embourgeoisement" in Hungary) has gradually been modified, thereby challenging the dominant historical syntheses. The conclusion was that the state bureaucrats, industrialists, merchants, and professionals stood much closer to each other than was earlier accepted within Hungarian historiography.[7]

Kinship in the Context of Ethnic and Confessional Specificities

The relevance of kinship to the development of Hungary's bourgeoisie is rooted in the fact that modernization was initiated and even politically led by the former nobility. Therefore, the survival of modes of behavior and a value system typical of the landed nobility characterized the formation of the middle class. The specific ethnic and confessional composition of the middle class also shaped it, meaning that a large part of the middle class was recruited from the rapidly assimilating Jews, domestic German urban groups, or other immigrant elements. Consequently, the importance of kinship relations in the establishment of the middle class had a great deal to do with several ethnic and denomina-tional characteristics. Because the ethnic and confessional backgrounds did not uniformly provide an easy and smooth assimilation for all those who fervently wanted to be assimilated, kin relations supplied the miss-ing integrative force. For example, the Germans who had already been living in Hungary for a longer period had far more favorable prospects of being fully accommodated than did the Jews, the greater part of whom only arrived in the country in the nineteenth century. Accord-ingly, the (entrepreneurial) career of the latter was dependent more upon the use of kinship structures than was the case for the Germans and other non-Magyars. The upward mobility of the Jews was initially made possible only by becoming wholesale merchants (during the first half of the nineteenth century). Later on, they also distinguished them-selves as bankers and industrial investors, but in all cases, it was neces-sary for them to rely heavily on available kinship networks to promote their own social advance. All this followed from overcoming several legal and many informal barriers on their way to becoming fully inte-grated. Concerning these legal restrictions, until a law on the emanci-pation of the "Israelite" denomination was passed in the mid 1890s, a mixed marriage between a Jew and a Christian was wholly impossible without the conversion of the former. Even thereafter, some latent sus-picion of Jews by Christians remained and constituted an obvious (although not an entirely insurmountable) obstacle to the structural assimilation of middle and upper middle class Jewish families. How-ever, the wealthiest of them, who had already been fairly acculturated and sometimes even ennobled, had much better prospects for being accepted as partners than did the average middle class families who were not yet assimilated and perhaps even ambivalent about full assim-ilation. For that reason, they were increasingly compelled to use kin relations intensively in stabilizing their new social status.

It would, however, be a mistake to suppose that all Jews utilized kin-ship links to the same degree. Converted Jews, especially, were far more accepted by the aristocracy and the Christian middle class of noble ori-gin than were their unconverted counterparts. Mór Wahrmann, who was one of the wealthiest (Jewish) Budapest haute-bourgeois bankers of the nineteenth century and quite politically prominent, seems to be an exception to this rule by insisting on his Jewish denominational identity. His descendants developed different familial strategies. Wahrmann's daughter Renée first married an ennobled Jewish entre-preneur who owned a large factory in a suburb of Budapest. When the marriage dissolved after twelve years, she married again, this time to an imperial and royal Chamberlain (and of course, to this end, she became a Christian). Finally, the last marriage she contracted was also with an aristocrat. Not too long after the death of their father, Wahrmann's two sons converted to Christianity, refused to continue the business, and in fact squandered their inheritance gambling.[8] It seems plausible to think of a kind of Buddenbrooks effect in Hungary, at least for this family.[9]

Paradoxically, Wahrmann did his best to weaken kin solidarity. He was rumored (which historians have confirmed) to have requested photographs from all his distant relatives. He then glued them in an album and gave it to his butler and instructed him to look the photographs over very carefully and memorize the faces, so that if one of them should ever knock at the door, he would identify and throw him or her out immediately. If he did not, he would be fired.[10]

The divide between the Neolog (Reformed) and Orthodox Jews, however, was no less important a factor.[11] For an Orthodox Jew to choose a Neolog for a marriage partner might often cause serious family tensions. The author of a family biography writes:

> After the honeymoon, the first journey the son took was to Nagyvárad to introduce his wife to his mother. I think my father—familiar as he was with the domestic atmosphere—was already afraid of this meeting. When as a bridegroom he had previously traveled there ... and showed the photograph of his bride to his mother and told her that the famous Goldzieher family, known in Nagyvárad as the paper kings, was a Neolog who would also expect him to join the Neolog parish, his mother simply said: "Are you thus ready to marry a faithless girl? Which language will my grandchildren use for praying?" "Hungarian, surely, since not even any of us understand Hebrew." Then she told him very gravely: "I won't intervene in anyone's life any more. Be very happy, but when you come here, please take lodging in a hotel. And if you like, bring your wife along with you once."[12]

Indeed, conversion might often lead to a partial or even a total loosening of family bonds, because Jewish identity was deeply rooted in a strong denominational commitment, loosened only after the mid 1890s.

The German (German-speaking) middle and upper middle classes, although also directly affected by the fundamental structural changes of the mid nineteenth century, had far fewer hardships in their assimilation efforts than did their Jewish counterparts. When they had recourse to kin relations in facilitating their social advance, they used them only to resolve specific mobility problems. For example, the Kölber and Kauser families both started as well-established urban master artisans and rose after some decades to the middle level of society as entrepreneurs. The process, however, was broken with the fourth generation in the early years of the twentieth century. While still in the ascendant phase, they tended to pursue an open marriage policy, but after beginning to decline, an inward-looking marriage practice came to dominate.[13]

A good example of this trend is the Zsolnay family, also of German origin, representing some of the most successful contemporary entrepreneurs outside of Budapest (living in Pécs in Transdanubia). Vilmos Zsolnay, founder of the internationally known ceramics factory, did not keep close business contacts with his brothers, although it is true that he had earlier made some failed attempts to establish such ties. As one of his daughters surmised, the tenuousness of family bonds derived from the strong wish of her father to acquire complete power over the management of the family company. This was enough to prevent the Zsolnay brothers from working together permanently, and resulted in very different mobility patterns shaping their lives.[14] Vilmos, the first born son who was to inherit the family company, rose into the upper bourgeoisie, while his brothers were stuck at the middle class level either as merchants, factory owners, army officers, or lawyers. Even through their marriages, they tended to leave the class of entrepreneurs. Vilmos Zsolnay's two daughters, however, remained faithful to the family company by serving it as painters and planners, and even their husbands were successfully integrated as permanent employees in the family enterprise. The kind of female emancipation shown by the Zsolnay daughters would have been wholly unimaginable a generation before, during the late nineteenth century.

Marriage Policy as Fostering Capital Accumulation

The difficulty of financing industrial capitalism was one of the most urgent problems to resolve in the age of the *Gründerzeit*, from the 1860s until the Great War. According to available case studies, setting up and running a family company (or even a joint stock company) by relying *exclusively* on family ties as a source of capital seems to have been a very common practice. Recent scholarship on the relationship between the banking sector and industry has underlined that, contrary to older historiography, there was no strong and positive link before the late 1860s between the two spheres of the economy. Subsequently, finance capital made inroads, but most investment of this kind was still in agriculture and urban tenement housing. Taking all the forms of bank investment in industry from credit to financial instruments, the role that banking played in the development of industry was very modest indeed. Not even the most dynamically growing industrial companies based their expansion on bank credit, the proportion of which always remained at a very low level and, in terms of fixed capital, even decreased over time. Accordingly, self-financing has to be considered even when discussing those enterprises requiring the largest capital investment.[15]

The unambiguously great importance that marriage strategy played in serving business interests derived from quite diverse sources. Would-be investors and modernizers of the economy faced striking shortages of both capital and specialists (both skilled workers and managers). It is true, however, that the relatively late industrialization of the country was built partly on existing commercial capitalism and took great advantage of foreign capital (mainly from Austria, Germany, and France) from the 1870s on. Still, so-called domestic commercial and industrial capitalism necessitated mobilizing all the accessible internal (private) sources. The absence, or weakness, of domestic public institutions (banks), which could assist them with the capital that they keenly needed, made this even more urgent.

The logical consequence of the situation is clearly shown by the bankruptcy proceedings in 1869 of a well-known Jewish merchant in Budapest, Ignác Kohen. They reveal that Kohen had far-reaching family connections extending from Vienna to Szeged. Kohen was related by marriage to a Viennese wool trader and related to the merchants of Pest through his brother-in-law and stepbrothers and sisters and to the merchants of Szeged through his cousin. Family relations were also business relationships, and family members held 43.5 percent of the bills of exchange in the bankruptcy proceedings of Kohen's firm. His relatives helped him to avoid bankruptcy, even setting their own liquidity at risk. In spite of all these efforts, however, the firm finally failed. Ironically, Kohen had not cooperated with his kin in the long-term investments: he had 52.3 percent of his active capital invested in securities. Kohen had used his family connections merely to mobilize capital in order to gain leading positions in establishing entrepreneurial consortiums and companies.[16]

Two fundamental types of consciously planned marriage policies seem to emerge: a strictly business-oriented and a more diversified one, whereby a family could expand its scope of activities to a wider social horizon. This is evidenced by the merchant family, Liedeman, in whose case not only the parental choice of marriage partners, but even the decision over the status careers of the sons were subordinated to the ends of a common family strategy.[17] Besides bringing children into the business, the senior members of the family selected careers for their sons or potential sons-in-law, ranging from the military to the university, Church, medicine, and bureau. Much the same can be said about the Wurm family's marriage strategy, where the single son continued the family business while the sisters married professionals or politicians.[18] It is noteworthy that the non-Jewish and/or swiftly feudalized entrepreneurs, who had quite often become landlords and were ennobled, were the first to adopt this strategy.

The business-centered family strategy was very widespread among emerging Jewish entrepreneurs of the mid nineteenth century. This practice went hand in hand with linking the sons to the family firm and recruitment of new members of the family from within the confines of their own social setting. One of the main incentives could have been that haute-bourgeois families endeavored to strictly control their vested interests and wanted to preserve the family wealth intact, as was exemplified by the eminent Jewish (although ennobled) wholesale merchant family of the nineteenth century, the Schosberger clan. The family even set up a legally institutionalized family council. A law passed in 1877 permitted setting up a family council for the purpose of tutelage and trusteeship in order to dispose of wealth valued at more than 100,000 forints. Such a council, made up of four kinsmen and chaired by an official, had the power to decide over the main issues of inheritance and of managing the entire wealth of the clan (including joint acquisitions by brothers-in-law). Additionally, the council might even claim the right to defend the common interest against the will of some of the individual descendants.[19] Establishment of registered family councils seems to have come rather late in Hungary, but the reasons for it are diverse. Late industrialization itself (starting only in the 1880s) required control of the flow of capital and the effective mobilization of what resources were available in the domestic economy. This sort of family council had already existed informally among the nobility. The family seat (*családülés* in Hungarian, difficult to translate into English), an organization associated especially with the Hungarian middle and lower nobility, was a private law institution, organized by the families themselves.[20] In the late nineteenth century, entrepreneurial haute bourgeois families took over this model, but we are uncertain about the extent of the practice, since the available data is weak.

Using kinship relations in recruiting the management personnel or raising capital persisted even after family companies were transformed into joint stock companies. A case in point is the enterprise led by the mill-owning Krausz family at the turn of the twentieth century. The shareholder registers between 1905 and 1916 present the image of a closely collaborating family and also reflect the wholly pragmatic marriage policy the Krausz family pursued during the previous decades. Among the families in the network created by marriages of the sons, there are representatives of the wealthiest wholesale merchant families of the late nineteenth century: the Wahrmanns, the Brülls, the Fürsts, and the Gutmanns. A member of the Gutmann family came to play a leading role alongside his father-in-law in the management of the company in the late 1910s. The three daughters of the family, however, apparently were freer to choose their partners—marrying a rentier, a lawyer, and an engineer—but they all still maintained business connections with the firm.[21]

That kind of marriage policy was very similar to the practice long exercised by the aristocracy and the middle nobility, who had also taken advantage of cousin marriages to retain their landholdings intact. The Gutmanns, an industrial family from Nagykanizsa (a provincial city in Transdanubia) who were rising into the ranks of the middle and upper middle class during the second half of the nineteenth century, were no exception to this rule. One of their members, belonging to the third generation of the highly successful entrepreneurial family (born in Vienna in 1874) married his *first* cousin in 1904.[22] Their case was not unique, although it might be considered a class-specific attribute, since similar practices did not characterize the lower social groups (not even the typical middle class). Much scattered data accessible on small town and village communities (populated mainly by agrarian populations) also suggest low rates of cousin marriage. Although a high rate of local endogamy prevailed, cousin marriage was rare at that time, especially among Catholics due to the rigorous prohibition policy of the Church. To mention one telling example, the marriage register of a Catholic village of four to five thousand people between the 1880s and the mid 1900s shows that not more than thirty-seven cousin marriages occurred throughout the whole period.[23] The same is true for the small Protestant town of Karcag (also located on the Great Plain) in the late nineteenth century (the research findings cited come from the data of the marriage register).[24] Unlike peasants in small towns and villages, several families of the haute bourgeoisie showed an obvious propensity toward "kinship endogamy" (cousin marriages) in the second half of the nineteenth century, as exemplified by the Kohners, among others. So the argument "that the most influential fifty families were more or less close relatives to each other" does not seem unfounded.[25]

Summing up, one can conclude that a marriage policy dictated by purposeful business considerations had strategic importance in the lives of the mobile, first-generation entrepreneurs, as well as on established families. Yet, such considerations did not characterize the well-established middle and upper middle classes as a whole. Some men in the middle ranks attempted to marry into wealthy bourgeois families (ambitious males marrying the daughters of their employers), which led them to cut ties with their families of origin. Among Orthodox Jewish families, a pattern of choosing a *sandak*, or godfather, developed, and between 1873 and 1895, immigrants almost always (95%) linked themselves to Budapest merchants. This evidence suggests a pattern of developing new ties while severing those from their places of origin and with their families.[26]

Interest and/or Emotion in Middle-Class Marriage

The delicate balance between economic consideration and personal emotion in middle-class marriages can be studied by looking at marriage contracts, which also provide some insight into the roles males and females were expected to play in the family. Since middle-class marriage was always based on an agreement regarding the possessions and material needs of each of the partners, these sources show us how men put an economic value on women, how couples dealt with financial security, and how they constructed devices to address their needs. In analyzing several marriage contracts, I will describe the possible variations of middle-class marriage patterns at the turn of the century. Alongside the continuation of classical bourgeois patriarchy, the emergence and rapid spread of family partnerships will be examined from three 1914 case studies.

A marriage contract between two professional librarians offers an instance where economic considerations played little role. Such a marriage seems to have been primarily based on emotional bonds. The written agreement was devoid of any patriarchal tone and might even have been disadvantageous to the husband, who took full material responsibility for his wife without claiming either her financial contribution to the marriage or his right to interfere in her budgetary practice.[27] As the text reads, the husband, wishing to provide a secure future for his fiancée, agrees to pay her a 6,000 crown life annuity—even in case of divorce initiated by the wife. Further, the final paragraph says that the wife will enjoy total freedom in spending this money towards whatever ends she chooses. It is worth mentioning that the amount of the annuity provided was as high as the salary of a well-paid municipal salaried employee.[28]

A somewhat different mentality shaped the behavior of another professional couple: the husband-to-be earned his living as a clerical worker at a private firm, while his spouse held a job as a municipal schoolmistress. In contrast to the first marriage contract discussed, this agreement spoke only about how the husband would dispose of the dowry brought in by the wife and, accordingly, did not contain any stipulation about obligations imposed upon the male head of the family.[29] This contract considered the marital relationship as a kind of unequal tie; the focal point solely concerned the method and the timing of transferring the control of these assets to the husband. Even the paragraphs, which at first glance suggest a concession made to the wife, turn out to perhaps favor the husband's primacy. This marriage contract established a property relationship between the husband and the wife, which gave each of them equal rights to what was acquired during the marriage, which, to say the least, implied highly ambiguous results for a middle-class woman. For a wife without a distinct source of income, such an agreement guaranteed her full rights to half the equity accrued during a marriage.[30] In this case, where the bride left her employment, the principle of common acquisition gave her a stake in the family assets and her husband's earnings. But, as many women (such as schoolmistresses) of the time were doing, if she did not give up work, her earnings helped build up the "acquisition."[31]

What might happen in the marriage under review? In keeping with the common acquisition relationship, both options available to the schoolmistress fiancée implied considerable loss in economic autonomy. If she decided to quit working to become a dependent wife for the rest of her life, she gave up her freedom and public status. But, if she insisted on continuing to work, the principle of common acquisition in the marriage contract restricted her liberty to dispose of all her income. This paradoxical situation operated like a trap and deprived middle-class professional women of personal autonomy, making them legally subordinate.

The third example comes from an upper-class merchant family. The husband-to-be was a timber merchant and director of a joint stock company, while the future wife came from a similar social milieu and did not exercise a profession. She came with a dowry of 100,000 crowns in cash, a trousseau valued at 10,000 crowns, and a completely furnished four-room dwelling. According to the agreement, all this, with the exception of the trousseau, was handed over to the husband, whose sole financial obligation was put into force in the case of divorce or upon his death.[32] The sum he was obliged to pay for his wife should they divorce and the amount he was ordered to bequeath to her expressed the value of the fiancée's social status. The higher social standing of her family is demonstrated by what was called the "compulsory female bequest," three times the amount in the previous example. These three samples provide a good picture of the range of middle-class practices for arranging material assets when founding a new family.

Kin-based Sociability

Although shifts in the intricate choreography in Hungary of public and private spaces cannot be dealt with in detail here, it is possible to point to a few moments in the nineteenth and early twentieth centuries to suggest some of the ways kinship considerations helped shape their configurations. The memoirs of the German wife of a Hungarian Christian wholesale merchant shed some light on the main characteristics of kinship considerations in the first half of the nineteenth century. The author tells us that the main creditors of the family firm were her brothers and assorted other relatives, illustrating the importance of kin for capital accumulation. But there were also cultural implications for what we could call "*Biedermeier* kinship solidarity consciousness."[33] *Biedermeier* characterizes the specific lifestyle and mentality throughout the German-speaking central European *Bürgertum* in the *Vormärz*.[34] The genuine *Biedermeier* atmosphere encompassing the daily life of the bourgeoisie living in Vienna or Pest and Buda (the unification of the Hungarian capital under the name Budapest only took place in 1873) during the first half of the nineteenth century gave a peculiar tone to private familial exchanges.[35] The example of the Liedemann family mentioned earlier demonstrates kin-based sociability following the *Biedermeier* ideals quite well. Kövér described it this way: "Not only the internal and external relations of the firm, but also the close social gatherings were defined by the family ..."[36] A fundamental institution of the family was the intense set of family receptions (*Winterkränzchen*) during the "season." Such assemblies bound families together through sentiment, social reciprocities, and cultural identity.

During the second half of the century, metropolitan development brought various changes. For one thing, denominational or ethnic groups became dispersed throughout a city like Budapest, breaking down the cohesion of neighborhoods. Yet there were remarkable instances of new ways in which relatives and kin could find themselves spatially concentrated. The luxurious apartment building standing on the Great Boulevard (no. 17 Lipót, now Szent István, körút) is a case in point. The tenants of this early-twentieth-century apartment house provide an excellent cross-section of contemporary middle and upper middle class—primarily Jewish—*Lipótváros*: mainly company directors, with some professionals, civil servants, and one or two landowners who used their apartments on a seasonal basis. What clearly distinguished this building from other average Pest apartment blocks was that so many of the tenants lived in a close family environment. Almost half of the tenants, although not forced to do so by material necessity, shared their homes with their adult children and their families. It is true, however, that in this city-owned apartment building, the reasonably priced apartments rented by middle and upper middle class elements were used only in the winter months, because the tenants spent the better part of the year in their country houses, in Buda summer residences, or in sanatoria. In these rented flats in the city center, every fourth tenant had some family member (sometimes as a sublessee) who used the apartment year-round, so it never stood empty. Another fifth of the tenants used their apartments to the maximum, subletting parts of them. These sublessees were frequently members of the immediate family, often the sons-in-law of the main tenant, who did not take on sublessees out of financial necessity, but so as not to have to live alone.[37]

Although the practice of leaving the parental home after marriage (neolocality) was rapidly spreading even in Budapest at the time, the role that kinship could play in reviving and strengthening some form of everyday sociability in the middle classes cannot be neglected altogether.[38] Even where there was obvious social differentiation among families linked together by ties of blood, the sense of internal solidarity manifested itself in the form of regular personal contacts. This pattern is plainly shown by a Budapest middle-class building contractor who kept a diary during the period between 1881 and the early 1930s. In assessing the entries, Vera Bácskai has contended:

> Members of this generation both in terms of their social standing and the measure of their wealth were dispersed in the social hierarchy. Notwithstanding, the Havel family kept up close connections with the relatives living all over Budapest and with those living abroad, and regularly met and corresponded with the widow and the son of Stefan Bartek. In addition, the family had up-to-date information about their relatives living in the countryside, at least concerning the relevant family events (illness, death, marriage, birth)."[39]

It is notable, however, that the family under review preferred to meet with their relatives mostly in public, not at home, most frequently in the form of having dinner together at a restaurant. Sociability of that sort became very important, especially for the daughters who, "beside the sociability available to them in spas under the close control of their mothers, had personal contacts in Budapest only with their relatives."[40]

A small provincial town like Veszprém (located in Transdanubia) made it much easier to maintain such personal contacts. The diary kept by a barber around the middle of the nineteenth century provides deep insight into local practice. By drawing distinctions between the intensity (the number of the references made in the text to the persons the diarist knew) and extension (the number of persons whom he actually met) of the barber's social connections, one can argue that relationships with his kin were more intense, while the relationships with his clientele and the creditors were more extended. Basically, the diary-keeping barber Francsics's closest relationships were with a very small circle of his relatives, but most of his meetings were with various strangers.[41]

The growing use of postal correspondence further facilitated maintaining contacts with one's own relatives. The "cult" of writing and reading letters, however, was specific only to the middle class during the nineteenth century. There is no room to discuss in detail the social practice of private correspondence—whose increasing popularity may also be discerned by the fact that the post in Pest and Buda handled 643,000 letters in 1846.[42] Considering that the population of the two towns combined was then around 150,000, the figure suggests that not more than a small minority of the urban dwellers made regular use of contemporary postal service. Another way of getting at the frequency of correspondence among the family members physically separated from each other is to look at diaries. A young lower-middle-class couple in mid-1870s Budapest, the Csorba family, wrote and sent one or more letters every third day, many of them dealing with public issues.[43]

Conclusion

Kinship played a central role in defining the economic and social profile of a newly emerging urban bourgeoisie, particularly within the entrepreneurial class. But kinship was flexible and open to being mobilized in quite a variety of ways. Certainly the use of kin persisted throughout the nineteenth century as a means for accumulating and concentrating capital. But kin were subject to selection, omission, transfer, or relocation. The use of kin as a resource, or the development of different familial strategies within the middle classes, shows that the dense kinship networks offered many chances for flexibility for some while hedging in options for others. While the nobility offered the middle classes certain models of kin-based organization, the latter constantly built and refashioned kinship relations according to economic, spatial, political, and cultural exigencies, offering new opportunities and posing novel problems with increasing speed as the century drew to a close.

Notes

1. Rudolf Andorka, "Family Reconstitution and Types of Household Structure," in J. Sundin and E. Söderlund, ed., *Time, Space and Man: Essays in Microdemography* (Stockholm, 1979), pp. 11–33.; Rudolf Andorka and Tamás Faragó, "Pre-industrial Household Structure in Hungary," in *Family Forms in Historic Europe*, ed. Richard Wall, (Cambridge, 1983), pp. 281–307.
2. Rudolf Andorka and Sándor Balázs-Kovács, "The Social Demography of Hungarian Villages in the Eighteenth and Nineteenth Centuries (With Special Attention to Sárpilis, 1792-1804)," *Journal of Family History* 11 (1986): pp. 162–92.
3. Erik Fügedi, "A középkori magyar nemesség rokonsági rendszerének két kérdése" (The Kinship System of the Medieval Hungarian Nobility: Two Research Problems), in *Történeti antropológia* (Historical Anthropology), ed. Tamás Hofer (Budapest, 1984), pp. 217–27; Erik Fügedi, *The Elefánthy: The Hungarian Nobleman and his Kindred* (Budapest, New York, 1998).
4. Péter Hanák, *Der Garten und die Werkstatt. Ein kulturgeschichtlicher Vergleich Wien und Budapest um 1900* (Wien, Köln, Weimar, 1992); idem, ed., *Bürgerliche Wohnkultur des Fin de siècle in Ungarn* (Wien, Köln, Weimar, 1994); idem, *The Garden and the Workshop: Essays on the Cultural History of Vienna and Budapest* (Princeton, N J, 1998); and some further publications of that kind: Gábor Gyáni, *Parlor and Kitchen: Housing and Domestic Culture in Budapest, 1870–1940* (Budapest, New York, 2002); idem, *Identity and the Urban Experience: Fin-de-Siécle Budapest* (New York, 2004)
5. Vera Bácskai, ed., *Bürgertum und bürgerliche Entwicklung in Mittel- und Osteuropa* (Budapest, 1986); idem, *A vállalkozók előfutárai. Nagykereskedők a reformkori Pesten* (Forerunners of Enterpreneurs: Wholesale Merchants in Pest in the Reform Age) (Budapest, 1989); idem, "Jewish Wholesale Merchants in Pest in the First Half of the Nineteenth Century," in *Jews in the Hungarian Economy 1760–1945*, ed. Michael. K. Silber (Jerusalem, 1992), pp. 40–53; György Kövér, "Liedemann und Wahrmann: Strategien von Kaufmann-Bankiersfamilien im 19. Jahrhundert," in *Eliten und Aussenseiter in Österreich und Ungarn*, ed. Waltraud Heindl et al. (Wien, Köln, Weimar, 2001), pp. 79–99; György Kövér, *A felhalmozás íve. Társadalom-és gazdaságtörténeti tanulmányok* (The Trajectory of Accumulation: Studies on Economic and Social History) (Budapest, 2002).
6. Károly Vörös, *Budapest legnagyobb adófizetői 1873-1917* (Budapest Biggest Tax Payers 1873–1917) (Budapest, 1979); János Mazsu, *The Social History of the Hungarian Intelligentsia, 1825–1914* (New York, 1997); Tibor Hajdu, *Tisztikar és középosztály 1850-1914* (Corps Officer and the Middle Class 1850–1914) (Budapest, 1999).
7. Cf. Gábor Gyáni, "Middle Class and *Bürgertum* in Hungary with Special Regard to Transylvania during the Period of Dualism," in *Minderheiten, Regionalbewusstsein and Zentralismus in Ostmitteleuropa*, ed. H-D. Löwe, G. H. Tontsch, and S. Troebst (Köln, Weimar, Wien, 2000), pp. 185–95; idem, "Key Problems of the Bourgeois Transformation in Hungary," in *The First Millennium of Hungary in Europe*, ed. Klára Papp and János Barta (Debrecen, 2002), pp. 430–38.
8. Károly Vörös, "Mór Wahrmann: A Jewish Banker in Hungarian Politics in the Era of the Dual Monarchy," in *Jews in the Hungarian Economy 1760–1945*, ed. Michael Silber (Jerusalem, 1992), pp. 187–96, here p. 195.

9. On the notion of the Buddenbrooks effect, see T. C. Barker and Maurice Lévy-Leboyer, "An Inquiry into the Buddenbrooks Effect in Europe," in *From Family Firm to Professional Management: Structure and Performance of Business Enterprise*, ed. Leslie Hannah (Budapest, 1982), pp. 9–26.

10. Kövér, "Liedemann und Wahrmann," p. 95.

11. The Jewish Congress held in 1867/1868 resulted in the split of the Israelite Church into a Reformed and an Orthodox wing, and this duality more or less corresponded to the antagonism between the assimilationist and the non-assimilationist Jews.

12. Hegedűs, Géza, *Elõjátékok egy önéletrajzhoz* (Preludes to an Autobiography) (Budapest, 1982), p. 76.

13. Károly Vörös, *Hétköznapok a polgári Magyarországon* (Everyday in Bourgeois Hungary) (Budapest, 1997), pp. 60–75.

14. Kata Jávor, *Életmód és életmód-stratégia a pécsi Zsolnay család történetében* (Way of Living and Life-style Strategy in the History of the Zsolnay Family in Pécs) (Budapest, 2000), pp. 46–47, 72–73.

15. Béla Tomka, *Érdek és érdekeltség. A bank-ipar viszony a századforduló Magyarországán, 1892-1913* (Interest and Disinterest: Bank-Industry Relations in Hungary at the Turn of the Century, 1892–1913) (Debrecen, 1999); idem, "Interlocking Directorates between Banks and Industrial Companies in Hungary at the Beginning of the Twentieth Century," *Business History* 43 (January 2001): pp. 25–42.

16. Kövér, *A felhalmozás íve*, p. 57.

17. Kövér, "Liedemann und Wahrmann," p. 84.

18. Vörös, *Hétköznapok a polgári Magyarországon*, pp. 80–82.

19. Kövér, *A felhalmozás íve*, p. 51.

20. László Kósa, *"Hét szilvafa árnyékában." A nemesség alsó rétegének élete és mentalitása a rendi társadalom utolsó évtizedeiben Magyarországon* ("In the Shade of the Seven Plum-Tree." The Life and Mentality of the Lower Strata of Nobility in the Last Decades of Estate Society in Hungary) (Budapest, 2001), p. 131.

21. Judit Klement, "Egy családi részvénytársaság a századelõn. Gizella Gõzmalom Rt. 1905-1917" (A Family Shareholding Company at the Dawn of the Century: The Gizella Steam Mill Share Company 1905–1917), *Korall*, no. 2 (Winter 2000): pp. 61–81, here pp. 68–69, 76.

22. Edit Kerecsényi, "A nagykanizsai Gutmann család felemelkedése a nagyburzsoáziába" (The Rise of the Gutmann Family of Nagykanizsa to the Upper-Bourgeoisie), *Zalai Gyûjtemény, no. 12* (1979): pp. 147–67, here pp. 159, 161.

23. Julianna Örsi, *Homokmégy társadalma* (Society of Homokmégy) (Homokmégy, 1998), pp. 489–91.

24. Julianna Örsi, *Karcag társadalomszervezete a 18-20. században* (Social Organization of Karcag in the Eighteenth and Twentieth Century) (Budapest, 1990), p. 160.

25. László Varga, "The Great Generation of the Hungarian Bourgeoisie," *Acta Historica Academiae Hungaricae* 30 (1984): pp. 353–79, here p. 361.

26. Anikó Prepuk, "Evidence of Residential Mobility Among the Orthodox Merchants of the Budapest Jewish Community 1873–1895," *History & Society in Central Europe 1* (1991): pp. 87-98, here p. 96.

27. Budapest Fõváros Levéltára (Budapest Capital Archives) VII 187. 1548/1914.

28. Budapest Fõváros Levéltára IV 1407 b. 4653/1911–VII.

29. Budapest Fõváros Levéltára VII 187. 1358/1914.

30. Andor Máday, *A magyar nõ jogai a múltban és jelenben* (The Rights of Hungarian Woman in the Past and the Present) (Budapest, 1913), p. 84.

31. See Gábor Gyáni, "Patterns of Women's Work in Hungary 1900–1930," *European Review of History* 5 (1998): pp. 25–36.
32. Budapest Fõváros Levéltára VII 187. 2040/1914.
33. Kövér, "Liedemann und Wahrmann," p. 87.
34. Béla Zolnai, *A magyar biedermeier* (The Hungarian Biedermeier) (Budapest, 1993), p. 9. The book was first published in the interwar period.
35. Cf. Hanák, *The Garden and the Workshop*, p. 8; and especially, Bácskai, *A vállalkozók elõfutárai*, pp. 174–216.
36. Kövér, "Liedemann und Wahrmann," p. 87.
37. More about both the house and the tenants in Gyáni, *Parlor and Kitchen*, pp. 43–56.
38. Cf. Tamás Faragó, "Housing and Households in Budapest 1850–1944," *History and Society in Central Europe* 1 (1991): p. 51.
39. Vera Bácskai, "'Csak saját erõmre és teljesítményemre utalva.' A 'self-made man'-ek világa" ("Relying on My Own Strength and Performance Only." The World of 'Self-Made Men'), *Aetas* 3-4 (2001): pp. 159–82, here p. 168.
40. Bácskai, "Csak saját erõmre és teljesítményemre utalva," p. 176.
41. G. Péter Tóth, "Otthon és külvilág, magánélet és nyilvánosság egy veszprémi polgár szemével" (Home and Outer World, Private and Public in the Eye of a Veszprém Bourgeois), in *Struktúra és városkép. A polgári társadalom a Dunántúlon a dualizmus korában* (Structure and Townscape: Bourgeois Society in Transdanubia in the Age of Dualism), ed. G. Péter Tóth (Veszprém, 2002), pp. 571–95, here p. 579–83.
42. See the dictionary entry "Post," in *Budapest lexikon* (Budapest Lexicon), ed. László Berza (Budapest, 1993), p. 332.
43. See Gábor Gyáni, *Identity and the Urban Experience*, pp. 62–83.

Chapter XV

Kinship and Class Dynamics in Nineteenth-Century Europe

David Warren Sabean

I want to begin my consideration of nineteenth-century kinship and class by a brief mention of two extraordinary novels of society and manners published during the last quarter of the nineteenth century. The first, Anthony Trollope's 1875 novel, *The Prime Minister*, is a tale of class milieu and family set in the context of Herefordshire proper-tied provincial life, while the second, Fontane's *Frau Jenny Treibel* of 1892, is placed within the context of social mobility and volatility of 1890s imperial Berlin.[1]

Trollope's novel, like almost everything he wrote, is a psychological portrait of money, property, and alliance. I do not want to use such a source directly as evidence for what I am going to argue, but rather as a point of departure—as evidence for what was on people's minds dur-ing the period. And further I want to extrapolate from this one repre-sented milieu to practices to be found throughout all property-holding classes throughout Europe during the nineteenth century. I find seven themes in the novel that neatly summarize bits and pieces from genealogies, letters, and autobiographies that together suggest a pecu-liar strategy to kinship in nineteenth-century Europe:

1. the reciprocal structuring of class and kin cultures;
2. endogamy within class milieus (like with like);

3. courtship within the context of family desires;
4. repeated exchanges among allied families (cousin marriage);
5. older women as gatekeepers and mediators of alliance (matrifocality);
6. marriage as a connection point for the flow of capital and access to property; and
7. erotic attraction between siblings and cousins.

Trollope's story involves courtship and marriage between two families already linked through marriage and innumerable social ties for many generations: the Fletchers and the Whartons. There had been a recent marriage between one branch of the Wharton family and the Fletchers, and—in the course of the novel—another of cousins between the two Wharton lines, and there was now the expectation of an alliance of Emily Wharton of the second branch and Arthur Fletcher. The two families—the Whartons and the Fletchers—had not only been allied together over many generations but in this particular generation also cemented ties through multiple, overlapping marriages. Cousinship was the dominant idiom through which social life was imagined and set into practice. Marriage and inheritance (or succession) provided the grid within which many forms of reciprocity developed and a cultural milieu was constructed. Everyone in the families concerned conspired to continue to arrange suitable marriages between the offspring, with "expectations" sorted out by rank order of birth, rights to succession in property, and professional and educational competence. The healthy social body was one where the veins through which capital and blood flowed were the same.

The Prime Minister is an argument about failed perceptions and mistaken choice. Rather than taking the predestined Arthur Fletcher, Emily Wharton falls in love with Ferdinand Lopez, a handsome man with all the external aspects of proper class behavior, the manners, and appearance of being a gentleman. Her mistake, as it turns out, was to trust her own judgment. Her father's objection goes to the heart of the issue, coming down to an often repeated refrain: "No one knows anything about him."[2] The theme is developed in two ways: the first, by setting up the lack of intimate knowledge about Lopez's family, profession, and milieu, suggesting that the proper route to a successful choice involved heeding the desires, implicit advice, and tacit understandings of the larger family; and the other, by exposing the falseness of appearance, the deception of surface manners, and the almost confidence-man characteristics of any gentleman missing roots in a publicly recognized family circle. Emily's father put the matter in this way: "When a man has connections, people that everyone knows about, then there is some guarantee of security."[3]

In this tale, the stranger, the man without family, the interloper out of whom mere education could not make a gentleman, was of course totally unsuitable as a spouse. The marriage began to fail as soon as it began—Lopez was seen as a kind of leech, sucking away the material substance, the lifeblood of the Wharton family. Emily's father had wanted the marriage to Arthur Fletcher because he was a "gentleman of the class to which I belong myself; because he works; because I know all about him, so that I can be sure of him; because he has a decent father and mother; because I am safe with him, being quite sure that he will say to me neither awkward things nor impertinent things … in all such matters … the great thing is like to like."[4] After the failed marriage, Emily reconfigures her emotions and, in the end, makes the proper alliance with Fletcher. In her self reflection, "gradually she had learned how frightful was the thing she had done in giving herself to a man of whom she had known nothing."[5] In the end, Arthur Fletcher, in wooing Emily, plays his trump card, telling her it was her duty to marry him: "I say it on behalf of all of us, that it is your duty....You are one of us, and should do as all of us wish you."[6]

I want to be briefer with Theodor Fontane's 1892 novel, *Frau Jenny Treibel*, which is subtitled, *Where Heart Finds its Way to Heart*. While Trollope painted a picture of landed provincial life, Fontane went to the heart of class relations in an urban society of extreme mobility, brashness, and calculation. The story here is simpler but similar. Rejecting the cousin she grew up with, Corinna Schmidt, the smart young daughter of a Gymnasium professor, sets her sights on the weak-willed, rather mediocre, son of a wealthy commercial family, whose matron, Jenny Treibel, finds the alliance quite unsuitable. As Professor Schmidt, who himself had once aspired to marrying Jenny, puts it—she is the "masterpiece of a bourgeoise."[7] Jenny Treibel plays the archetypical role of gatekeeper in the novel. Her son's duty is largely to obey, and under pressure from his mother, he finds himself unable to carry through on his engagement to Corinna. In the end, she finds her mate in her cousin, while Leopold Treibel finds himself engaged to his Hamburg sister-in-law's sister, unable to withstand the combined maneuvering of his mother and sister-in-law. All along, Professor Schmidt, who considers the two cousins as made for each other, encourages his nephew, colleague, and future son-in-law. From the beginning, he says that Jenny Treibel will only allow an alliance with a family of equal wealth, capable of paying a substantial dowry—which in the end resulted in a double alliance with the same Hamburg family. In some ways, the key concept in the novel is spoken by the Professor—*werde der du bist* (become what you are).[8]

I want to say little about the themes of courtship within the context of family desires, older women as gatekeepers and mediators of alliance, marriage as a connection point for the flow of capital and access to property, and the erotics of cousin/sibling interaction. Instead, I will concentrate on three central configurations: the reciprocal structuring of class and kin cultures; endogamy within class milieus (like with like); and repeated exchanges among allied families—the cousin or cousin-like marriages found here in the novels, sibling exchange (in *Frau Jenny Treibel*, the double alliance of two siblings marrying two siblings), and the repeated marriage of a person into the same family—deceased wife's sister, deceased brother's wife, or a near relative of a deceased spouse.

Reciprocal Structuring of Class and Kin Cultures

While I do not want to get into the arcane subject of conceptualizing class and operationalizing its use, I find it helpful to make a few observations. During the past several decades, class analysis and the use of the concept for even nineteenth-century social history has fallen on hard times. Part of the problem has had to do with the expectation that one could link class position to political activity in a more or less straightforward way and think of the connection as prompted by *interest*.[9] Scholarship on the French Revolution and the Revolutions of 1848 found great difficulty matching social structural features to political engagement, and research on parties, ideologies, and voting behavior found the concept of "interest" to be a dull tool. I certainly cannot straighten out very many of the issues here. But it does seem to me that we ought to look at class formation not so much in national terms or according to simple logics of property and labor, but as practices carried on at the local level—to examine the development of social milieus in which social distinctions, representations, and styles were worked out in everyday exchanges. "Milieu," I think, is the key concept here—and in using the concept, we need to look for the unspoken assumptions, practical ways of knowing and acting, the prejudices—in a sense—or perhaps, better, the *habitus* (Bourdieu) that structure and underlie the culture of political sentiment.[10]

What I want to suggest is that kinship practices, courtship, and marriage strategies were crucial for all kinds of things that have to do with class. Access to capital and property were not the least of the things which were controlled by kin ties, inheritance, and alliance. Another major activity of kin involved the education, training, and strategic support of individuals at key moments in their lives. I think of the innumerable examples of young men boarding with close or distant relatives while attending school or getting apprenticeship training in a business run by an uncle or second cousin. Marriage, godparentage, and guardianship were all fundamental for maintaining access points, entrances, and exits to social milieus. Families, frequently quite large kin groups, created and maintained cultural and social boundaries through extensive festive, ludic, competitive, and charitable activities. Within such kinship activities were worked out how the circuits would be hooked up—just how various subpopulations would be allied together through marriage, ritual coparenthood, or friendship. It was in the milieu of the extensive kinship interaction that style, manners, and character of specific types were developed.[11] Recent work by Christopher Johnson on a French provincial bourgeois family illustrates nicely how kinship milieus were the place for shaping desire and offering practice in code and symbol recognition.[12] Here in this early nineteenth-century example, a sister wrote to a brother about his impending marriage to their cousin: "Habituated from our childhood to your chérie as a sister and she loving you as a brother, you have developed an affection that can only end with life itself."[13] In this cousin example, where cousins were pulled ever more closely into the intimate sphere of the individual family (cousins becoming like siblings) and eroticized, we find a practice of integrating networks of culturally similar people. Through dances, parties, charades, games, sports, dinners, and vacations, rules and practices were trained into bodies.

I have gathered together many examples of the way interlocking families and close family friends created and maintained cultural and social milieus.[14] Festivals, birthdays, anniversaries, and family days provided many opportunities in the nineteenth century for family members near and far to come together, sometimes for weeks at a time. Families typically set a specific time in the year when they gathered in a particular place or at the home of a central person. Before the advent of the railroad, such travel was arduous enough to warrant relatively long stays. In Trollope's novel, Wharton and his daughter Emily typically spent a month in the country at his cousin's estate, where Emily came to share the values and style of her relatives and where the expectations of her alliance with Fletcher were worked out. In Germany, family associations formed from the 1870s onward tended to meet in groups of forty to fifty every two to five years. Christenings, confirmations, birthdays, anniversaries, and funerals more or less occasioned extended celebrations. Emil Lehmann, a Hamburg bourgeois, described how people came from Berlin, Paris, and London to Hamburg to celebrate the twenty-fifth anniversary of his parents.[15] For a full two weeks, the house was open in the evening for guests. Uncles and aunts and cousins danced, ate, and walked together during this time of intense family intercourse. But many families lived close to one another in complex overlapping kindreds. This allowed for a dense, elaborate winter season of balls, card playing, musical and literary evenings, or weekly get-togethers of aunts, uncles, and cousins for meals, walks, and conversation. Whenever a family was rich in cousins coming up to marriage age, social life intensified for a period of years. This intense family life—whether urban or rural, centered on clubs, houses, or casinos, or celebrated in the still of *Kaffeekränzchen* or the more rambunctious activities of sledding or balls—was central for the creation of cultural understanding and practice. Such social intercourse, as Zunkel points out, was crucial for the formation of stratified social consciousness. "Each self-conscious social stratum tended to consider its specific values and modes of behavior as superior and to raise claims for their general validity in society."[16] "In cities and industrial areas clans (*Sippenkreise*) formed out of entrepreneurial families of similar rank, which mostly belonged to the same economic branch, which agreed with each other in their social and practical opinions and cooperated in the pursuit of their economic interests."[17]

Over time, many families were dispersed across Germany or Europe or even across continents. Correspondence, visiting, and the exchange of children played central roles in knitting their extended families together. Visiting, often for long periods of time, was by no means a matter for business elites and the wealthy only. The children's book author, Ottilie Wildermuth, the wife of a Gymnasium teacher in Tübingen, described a constant stream of visitors, many of whom stayed for several months at a time.[18] But not just location in a central university town made this possible. Professor Bernhard Rogge described how his father's out-of-the-way parish in Silesia also was a magnet for visitors, his mother having to cook and care for as many as forty guests at a time.[19]

Cousins often were the first playmates young children had, and they often provided the chief circle of friends during the period of entering society and courtship. They were also frequently packed off to school and Gymnasium together or boarded with uncles and aunts. Summer vacations brought together cousins, uncles and aunts, adult siblings, and wider networks of family. Interaction in nineteenth-century middle-class families resulted in strong identification with family and schooling in specific forms of behavior and attitude.

There is an entertaining example of how the system worked even in the context of an exception to social endogamy. In the early 1840s, Jacob Henle, professor of anatomy in Zürich, picked up a seamstress on the street and, after a few months, decided he was in love with her.[20] After he accepted a call to Heidelberg, he dropped his plan to set her up as his mistress and decided to make her his wife. The problem was that she did not speak or move gracefully enough to represent him properly, so he devised a plan with his brother-in-law to send the 22-year-old woman to a finishing school for girls for a year and then integrate her into the brother-in-law's household so that Henle's sister could operate a kind of forced-action socialization in a short period (make her into a family member as it were). In fact, the family made up a story about her being a cousin who had come to live with them. Henle's brother-in-law, when he first met the woman, wrote that she moved awkwardly and conversed hesitantly, pointing to her lack of two attributes essential to middle-class culture, manners trained into the body and developed in crucial years through games, parties, dancing, and everyday family exchange. The brother-in-law said: "Mostly it is her manners, her way of carrying herself, of walking, of conversing, which betrays her earlier class..." Henle himself wrote that what he wanted was for her to be able to appear among friends and acquaintances without betraying her origins. There was also an inner part to her education (*Bildung*) that would not allow her to be bored as the men sit around and talk. Anyway, Henle's sister eventually "familized"/familiarized the fiancée to the point where the marriage could take place. The couple lived together in blissful matrimony until her death in childbirth three years later.

Endogamy within Class Milieus (Like with Like)

Two aspects of both class and kinship strike me as crucial. Both are lived and experienced "locally" and both give rise to practices that continually force choices on people. Social class is always constantly being generated and kinship ties are always constantly being negotiated. There are no hard and fast boundaries to either. Kathleen Canning puts it this way: the "boundaries of class are seldom fixed—class formations and the exclusions on which they were based were continually contested and transformed."[21] And if the boundaries are not fixed, neither is class unified at the core but rather is made up of a multiplicity of different milieus. Class in formation in the nineteenth century was a process of making connections across localities and regions, between more or less well-articulated milieus, neighborhoods, clans, and strata, and among occupational, professional, and craft groups with strong traditional practices of exclusion.

Until World War I, various groups were open or closed to one another depending on the way in which transfers of capital and property were directed—with distinct tendencies toward hypergamy. The details of how class was regulated through marriage are lost in the hundreds of unstated assumptions surrounding negotiations between individuals, their friends and peers, and their families. Whatever limitation one would want to put on Lorenz von Stein's generalization that property lay at the foundation of social existence and social difference, one cannot deny that marriage involved substantial property transfers and was too important in that regard to be left unattended. Dowry was one of the great social regulators in the nineteenth century. And it appears that dowries became ever more substantial for the middle class and played an ever greater role in determining which groups and individuals were open to each other at any particular time. There seems to have been a constant inflation throughout the nineteenth century, making the dowry ever more useful for underlining class differences and as a regulator for providing social access, integration, and differentiation.[22]

The Freiher von Schaezler from Augsburg (writing about events in the early nineteenth century) gave an instructive account of his marriage strategy and negotiations.[23] As a young merchant living far from home in Aachen, he wrote to a cousin (father's brother's son) to find him a suitable party. He was soon invited to join the firm of Baron Liebert, whose eldest daughter fell in love with him at first sight. Since the arrangement seemed suitable, the two men drew up a contract involving the exchange of a substantial dowry and the obligation of the young man to work for the firm for a set number of years.

As Zunkel pointed out, the emergence of capable young men of industry and trade in the early stages of industrial growth took precisely this route.[24] The new alliance system, which I will describe more fully later, developed step-by-step with the opening up of the economy and the shifts in the nature of government and state administration. There has been excellent spade work done on the development of family organized trade networks, for example, between Holland and the Rhineland after the mid eighteenth century.[25] The historian Zunkel argued for a great economic expansion during the last third of the eighteenth century and provided evidence to show that the systematic use of marriage to create trading networks, to bring together and concentrate capital, and to attract able young men from the right families to a firm expanded at the same time.[26] Biographies of such early nineteenth-century figures as the German entrepreneur Franz Haniel offer rich examples of the proliferation of economic activity and the intensified practices of the care of kin.[27] For the Hamburg merchant houses between 1780 and 1800, the period when they were established, part of the process involved the creation of a dense network of family connections through systematic and planned marital strategies.[28] It is hard to avoid the conclusion that the work that went into the new kinship system was related to a new kind of economy—this was the fundamental insight of Gérard Delille in his important work on the kingdom of Naples.[29] The old system was occupied in maintaining a patrimony, while the new acceded to a much more open and flexible way of managing and creating opportunity. This worked for the old nobility as well. Heinz Reif has contrasted a tight inheritance-driven system in the ecclesiastical territories of eighteenth-century Westphalia with the creation of a regional elite through marriage alliance and the cultivation of emotional social networks after secularization.[30] In the earlier period, the nobility monopolized office by virtue of their status and purity of blood. "Private" families exercised their right to "public" office. In the new conditions of the nineteenth century, office had to go to an incumbent through merit, and nepotism could no longer operate as an openly acknowledged system of recruitment to position. Nonetheless, office-holding families spawned office holders. With the growth of government, here too, like with the economy, was a growing field of opportunity. Rather than maintaining a particular right to a particular property or office, families gave up or were forced to give up such claims with the expectations that what they gave up in one place, they would receive in another. But such politics involved cultivating intensively and extensively both narrow and extended groups of kin. And the whole game had to be played differently with the family's relationship to institutions recast. It now became important for allied kin to see that their youth got proper educations, that daughters were provided with dowries, and that capable and enterprising young men were backed with capital. The circulation of goods and services was redirected in a new system of exchange.

People in the nineteenth century had to learn to manage quite different kinds of networks, and part of the issue in this delicately choreographed system involved the presentation of each family and its members according to the rules of the particular stratum and cultural sphere in which they wished to operate. The private house and its activities were intricately articulated with a larger network of social connections and aesthetic assumptions. The education of both men and women to open and fluid systems where couples had to cooperate in tasks of social representation required protracted drill in taste, morality, sentiment, and style. Love and sentiment and emotional response or their expected development were built into the very nature of familial circuitry. They were the software necessary to direct the course of all the hard-wired connectors. There were, of course, different ways of falling in love. Some people first chose a suitable family by visiting, dining, walking, and playing cards together in the evening, and others did it by correspondence. Some looked for a friendly face among relatives, while others latched onto families where their careers were directed. Some followed the wishes and advice of their parents and siblings, and some bravely struck off for themselves. But love always determined the flow of capital, access to office, the course of a career. Some people like Emily Wharton in Trollope's novel and Carl Friedrich Siemens who, in reality, came home with a quite unsuitable bride, failed to make the right choice.[31] In the Siemens case, the family hired detectives and presented him with evidence that his wife was not of the right station. His mother and sister declared him socially dead—like the relatives of Emily Wharton—and cut off all relations until he meekly followed their lead and never saw his wife again. After his divorce, his sister took over his household and entertainment duties, and she later played a key role in negotiating for him with family members who wanted to pull their capital from the family enterprise.[32]

Marital Exchanges between Allied Families

Beginning in the second half of the eighteenth century, among all property holding classes everywhere in Europe, a fundamental reconfiguration of kinship alliance took place. I just want to sketch in what I see as its fundamental features here, but the phenomenon needs to be studied in much greater depth.[33] Broadly speaking, by the seventeenth century, for all but a very small group of rulers, repeated alliances among allied families over several generations were not possible, and for many groups, not desirable. People could not and did not marry their first or second cousins and sometimes even their third or fourth cousins. Just as interesting, they did not marry close blood relatives of a deceased spouse. In France, in a celebrated seventeenth-century case, a man purchased a papal dispensation for "thirty thousand livres" to marry his deceased wife's sister, but when challenged in the civil courts, the marriage, despite producing progeny (or because) was annulled. In the 1680s, a German prince called an academic conference together to discuss his impending marriage with his deceased wife's sister. Progressively, after 1700, all states in Europe reduced the prohibitions against marrying cousins and in-laws either by changing the law or putting in a de jure or de facto liberal policy of dispensations. (England is the outrider by forbidding the deceased wife's sister in the 1830s.) Marriages previously thought incestuous or dangerous became quite normal in the nineteenth century. In France, for example, by the last decades of the century, 3 percent of all marriages were with the deceased wife's sister. It should be pointed out that in many states, the changes in the law or the system of dispensations often took place many decades before the population made use of them. It is also clear that certain kinds of marriages that did not violate canon, ecclesiastical, or state law, such as sibling exchange, are not found in many places before the sea change in kinship took place.

All of these new forms of marriage entailed multiple links between allied families over time. A marriage with a second cousin reties an alliance made in the generation of the grandparents, to first cousins, in that of the parents. The marriage of siblings to siblings or with the close relative of a deceased spouse reestablishes an alliance in the same generation. In other words, the shift was from a strongly exogamous system (symbolically, if not always in practice) to a highly endogamous one, from searching for a mate among "strangers" to searching among friends and familiar relations. The new system matched like with like culturally—as we have seen—and consanguineously. Two families could make persistent alliances even though tracing blood ties for individual marriages could be indirect. What frequently took place was a *set* of marriages between related lines in each generation, calling on several different principles at once; that is, two allied families could make a combination of first, second, and third cousin marriages, sibling exchanges, marriage to deceased wives' sisters, and other less direct linkages in the same generation. A marriage with a new family might call for a renewed alliance in the next generation. The rate of direct cousin marriages can only indicate higher levels of kin links. For example, in the village I studied closely, by the 1860s, 2.4 percent of marriages were with first cousins, while 49.4 percent were with close kin altogether.[34] There were, of course, some families whose strategies led to very high rates of first cousin marriages. The Rothschild family, while undertaking no cousin marriages in the eighteenth century, undertook 50 percent of their fifty-six marriages with first cousins in the nineteenth.[35] We should be clear that, in any one locality, different classes adopted different strategies of alliance. The overall morphology, however, seems to have been to create an overlapping, extensive, integrated, *horizontally* constructed set of kindreds, which provided at least one of the structural supports for the production and reproduction of class milieus. The first steps were taken around 1750, and the high point was reached between 1880 and 1920. After that, close kin alliances sloped off everywhere, to be gone in even the most remote Scandinavian villages by 1950. Perhaps missing one of its chief props, class milieus lost their cohesion over time, and observers lost faith in the salience of class as a tool for social analysis.

Notes

1. Anthony Trollope, *The Prime Minister*, ed. David Skilton (London, 1994); Theodor Fontane, *Frau Jenny Treibel, oder "Wo sich Herz zum Herzen find't"*, ed. Helmuth Nürnberger (Munich, 1997).
2. Trollope, *Prime Minister*, pp. 41–45.
3. Trollope, *Prime Minister*, p. 44.
4. Trollope, *Prime Minister*, p. 88.
5. Trollope, *Prime Minister*, p. 477.
6. Trollope, *Prime Minister*, p. 684.
7. Fontane, *Jenny Treibel*, p. 15.
8. Fontane, *Jenny Treibel*, p. 179.
9. William Reddy summarized all the objections in *Money and Liberty in Modern Europe: A Critique of Historical Understanding* (Cambridge, 1987).
10. The literature on class is enormous. Some helpful sources for working through the thicket are: Stefan Hradil, "System und Akteur: Eine empirische Kritik der soziologischen Kulturtheorie Pierre Bourdieus," in *Klassenlage, Lebensstil und kulturelle Praxis: Beiträge zur Auseinandersetzung mit Pierre Bourdieus Klassentheorie*, ed. Klaus Eder (Frankfurt, 1989); Pierre Bourdieu, "What Makes a Social Class? On the Theoretical and Practical Existence of Groups," *Berkeley Journal of Sociology* 32 (1987): pp. 1–17.
11. I have given many examples of these phenomena in *Kinship in Neckarhausen 1700–1870* (Cambridge, 1998), pp. 449–89.
12. See the remarkably detailed and suggestive paper in this volume.
13. Christopher H. Johnson, "Das 'Geschwister Archipel': Bruder-Schwester-Liebe und Klassenformation im Frankreich des 19. Jahrhunderts," *L'Homme. Zeitschrift für feministische Geschichtswissenschaft* 13 (2002): pp. 50–67, here pp. 63–64.
14. See Sabean, *Kinship*, chap. 22, 23.
15. Emil Lehmann, *Lebenserinnerungen*, 3 vols. (Kissingen, 1885–1895), vol. 1, p. 55.
16. Friedrich Zunkel, *Der Rheinisch-Westfälische Unternehmer 1834-1879: Ein Beitrag zur Geschichte des deutschen Bürgertums im 19. Jahrhundert* (Köln, 1962), p. 82.
17. Zunkel, *Unternehmer*, p. 82.
18. Bernhardine Schulze-Smidt, ed., *Ottilie Wildermuths Briefe an einen Freund. Mit einer Lebensskizze* (Bielefeld, Leipzig, 1910), p. 56.

19. Bernhard Rogge, *Aus sieben Jahrzehnten. Erinnerungen aus meinem Leben* (Hannover, 1897), p. 28.
20. Paula Rehberg, ed., *Elise Egloff: Die Geschichte einer Liebe in ihren Briefen* (Zurich, 1937). The episode was well enough known for Gottried Keller to write the novel "Regine" about it: Gottfried Keller, *Historisch-kritische Ausgabe*, ed. Walter Morgenthaler, et al., ed., (Zürich 1998), vol. 7, pp. 56–127.
21. Kathleen Canning, "Gender and the Politics of Class Formation: Rethinking German Labor History," *American Historical* Review 97 (1992): pp. 736–68, here p. 744.
22. Wolfgang Zorn, *Handels- und Industriegeschichte Bayerisch-Schwabens 1648-1870: Wirtschafts-, Sozial- und Kulturgeschichte des schwäbischen Unternehmertums* (Augsburg, 1961), p. 266.
23. His text is reprinted in Zorn, *Handels- und Industriegeschichte*, pp. 310–22.
24. Zunkel, *Unternehmer*, p. 20.
25. For example, Brigitte Schröder, "Der Weg zur Eisenbahnschiene. Geschichte der Familie Remy und ihre wirtschaftliche und kulturelle Bedeutung," in *Deutsches Familienarchiv: Ein genealogisches Sammelwerk* 91 (1986): pp. 3–158.
26. Zunkel, *Unternehmer*, pp. 9–23.
27. Hans Spethmann, *Franz Haniel, sein Leben und seine Werke* (Duisburg-Ruhrort, 1956).
28. Manfred Pohl, *Hamburger Bankengeschichte* (Mainz, 1986), p. 29.
29. Gérard Delille, *Famille et proprieté dans le royaume de Naples (xve-xixe siècle)* (Rome, 1985).
30. Heinz Reif, *Westfälischer Adel 1770-1860: Vom Herrschaftsstand zur regionalen Elite* (Göttingen, 1979).
31. Georg Siemens, *Carl Friedrich von Siemens: Ein grosser Unternehmer* (Freiburg, 1960), pp. 27–29.
32. Siemens, *Carl Friedrich*, p. 254.
33. The following is taken from Sabean, *Kinship*, pp. 63–91, 428–48.
34. Sabean, *Kinship*, pp. 435–36.
35. Frederic Morton, *The Rothschilds: Family Portrait* (New York, 1962), pp. 57-8.

Notes on Contributors

Giulia Calvi is professor of history at the European University Institute Florence in Italy. Her research fields are gender, medicine, culture, and society in Italy and Europe mainly during the early modern period. Currently, she is working on a comparative study of women of the European courts, on ego documents, letter writing, the construction of gender identities, and on family and kinship history. Her publications include: *Histories of a Plague Year* (Berkeley, 1989); *Il contratto morale. Madri e figli nella Toscana moderna* (Roma-Bari, 1994); *La mujer barroca* (Madrid, 1995); *Le ricchezze delle donne. Diritti patrimoniali e poteri familiari in Italia (XII-XIX)* (Torino, 1998); *Innesti. Donne e genere nella storia sociale* (Roma, 2004).

Gérard Delille has been professor at the European University Institute in Italy. Currently, he is *Directeur de recherche* at the Centre National de la Recherche Scientifique (CNRS) and *Directeur d'études* at the Ecole des Hautes Etudes en Sciences Sociales (EHESS) in Paris. He teaches in Paris and Rome. Being a specialist on early modern Italy, he has conducted research on family systems (*Famille et propriété dans le Royaume de Naples, XVe-XIXe siècle* [Rome, Paris, 1985]) and on the relationships between kinship, alliance, and political coalitions (*Le maire et le prieur. Pouvoir central et pouvoir local en Méditerranée Occidentale, XVe-XVIIIe siècle* [Rome, Paris, 2003]). He is engaged in an extensive study on the mechanisms of alliance construction in Western Europe from the Middle Ages to the modern period, from which he has already published certain results ("Echanges matrimoniaux entre lignées alternées et système européen de l'alliance: une première approche," in *En substances.*

Textes pour Françoise Héritier, ed. by Jean-Luc Jamard, Emmanuel Terray, and Margarita Xanthakou [Paris 2000].)

Bernard Derouet is member of the Centre National de la Recherche Scientifique (CNRS) and the Centre de Recherches Historiques at the Ecole des Hautes Etudes en Sciences Sociales (EHESS) in Paris. He is especially interested in issues of family, kinship, marriage, inheritance practices, and social reproduction in general in France and Europe (sixteenth–nineteenth centuries). His publications include: "Territoire et parenté. Pour une mise en perspective de la communauté rurale et des formes de reproduction familiale," *Annales. Histoire, Sciences Sociales* 50 (1995); "Nuptiality and family reproduction in male-inheritance systems: reflections on the example of Franche-Comté (17th-18th centuries)," *The History of the Family: An International Quarterly* 1 (1996); "Les pratiques familiales, le droit et la construction des différences (15e-19e siècles)," *Annales. Histoire, Sciences Sociales* 52 (1997); "Parenté et marché foncier à l'époque moderne: une réinterprétation," *Annales Histoire, Sciences Sociales* 56 (2001); "La terre, la personne et le contrat: exploitation et associations familiales en Bourbonnais (XVIIe-XVIIIe siècles)," *Revue d'Histoire Moderne et Contemporaine* 50 (2003).

Christophe Duhamelle, Ph.D., is director at the Mission Historique Française en Allemagne, a French research center for German history in Göttingen (Germany). He has research interests in the social history of the confessional identities in early modern Germany. He has worked on the Rhenish Catholic nobility, Christian names and conversions, and is currently investigating interrelations between space, community, and Catholic identity during the Enlightenment in a small rural region of East Germany, the Eichsfeld. Principal publications: *L'héritage collectif. La noblesse d'Église rhénane, 17e - 18e siècles* (Paris, 1998); *Die Eheschließungen im Europa des 18. und 19. Jahrhunderts: Muster und Strategien* (ed. with Jürgen Schlumbohm) (Göttingen, 2003); *Les espaces du Saint-Empire à l'époque moderne* (Paris, 2004).

Laurence Fontaine has been professor at the European University Institute in Italy. She is now *Directeur de recherche* at the Centre National de la Recherche Scientifique and at the Ecole des Hautes Etudes en Sciences Sociales. Her main research fields are migration and mountain societies, and poverty, credit, and economic cultures in seventeenth to nineteenth-century Europe. Her publications include: *Le Voyage et la mémoire. Colporteures de l'Oisans au XIXe siècle* (Lyon, 1984); *History of Pedlars in Europe* (Cambridge, 1996); *Pouvoir, identités et migrations dans* *les hautes vallées des Alpes occidentales (XVIIe-XVIIIe siècles)* (Grenoble, 2003). Her forthcoming book is called *Alternative Exchanges: Second-Hand Circulations from the Sixteenth Century to the Present.*

Gábor Gyáni graduated from the University of Debrecen and initially worked as an archivist. Since 1982, he is member of the Institute of History, Hungarian Academy of Sciences, now as a senior research fellow. He is a university professor at the social science faculty of the Eötvös Lóránd University, Budapest, and founding member of the History Doctoral School of the Central European University, Budapest. His work has focused on Hungary's social and urban history in the nineteenth and twentieth centuries and the theory of recent historical scholarship. His English language monographs include *Parlor and Kitchen: Housing and Domestic Culture in Budapest, 1870–1940* (Budapest, New York, 2002); *Social History of Hungary from the Age of Reform to 1998* (New York, 2004); *Identity and the Urban Experience: Fin-de-Siécle Budapest* (New York, 2004).

Michaela Hohkamp, Ph.D., is a lecturer at the Freie Universität Berlin (Germany), and has been a research assistant at the Max-Planck-Institut für Geschichte in Göttingen, and a fellow at the European University in Florence (Italy). She is interested in rural society, aristocratic power and kinship, and in gender issues in early modern Europe. Her main publications are: *Herrschaft in der Herrschaft. Die vorderösterreichische Obervogtei Triberg von 1737 bis 1780* (Göttingen, 1998); "La Dénonciation ou l'apprentissage de la docilité citoyenne," *Revue Européenne d'Histoire* (2000); "Grausamkeit blutet – Gerechtigkeit zwackt: Überlegungen zu Grenzziehungen zwischen legitimer und nicht-legitimer Gewalt," in *Streitkultur(en). Studien zu Gewalt, Konflikt und Kommunikation in der ländlichen Gesellschaft (16. bis 19. Jahrhundert)*, ed. Barbara Krug-Richter, Magnus Eriksson (Cologne, 2003); *Nonne, Königin und Kurtisane. Wissen, Bildung und Gelehrsamkeit von Frauen in der Frühen Neuzeit* (Königstein/Ts., 2004). Her habilitation thesis (summer 2006) is entitled *The transmission of power and kinship within the european noble societies between the 16th and the 18th centuries.*

Christopher H. Johnson is professor emeritus of history at Wayne State University in Detroit (USA). He is currently engaged in research on the history of kinship and the family. His book, based on a massive collection of letters and manuscripts of several related families and wider genealogical research on the town's ruling elite, is nearing completion and is tentatively entitled *Becoming Bourgeois: Family, Kinship, Love, and*

Power in Nineteenth-Century Vannes. A parallel interest is the history of siblings, discourses of incest, and sensibility from 1750 to 1850. An article, "Die Geschwister Archipel: Bruder-Schwester Liebe und Klassenformation im Frankreich des 19. Jahrhunderts," *L'Homme. Zeitschrift für feministische Geschichtwissenschaft* 13, no. 1 (2002), pp. 50–67, explored this theme. Johnson is also at work on a study of family conflict, ordinary women's search for rights, and the shifting perspectives of the law in Paris during the last decades of the Old Regime. His previous work, in working-class and economic history, includes *Utopian Communism in France: Cabet and the Icarians, 1839-1851* (Cornell, 1974) (nominated for the National Book Award in 1975); and *The Life and Death of Industrial Languedoc, 1700–1920: The Politics of De-Industrialization* (Oxford, 1995).

Elisabeth Joris graduated from the University of Zurich and is currently a member of the Interdisziplinäres Zentrum für Frauen- und Geschlechterforschung (IZFG) at the University of Bern. Her main research field is women's and gender history in the nineteenth and twentieth centuries. Selected publications: *Brave Frauen – Aufmüpfige Weiber. Wie sich die Industrialisierung auf Alltag und Lebenszusammenhänge von Frauen auswirkte (1820-1940)* (Zürich, 1992); *Frauengeschichte(n). Dokumente aus zwei Jahrhunderten zur Situation in der Schweiz,* new enlarged edition (Zürich, 2001); *Tiefenbohrungen in Raum und Zeit, Frauen und Männer rund um die grossen Tunnelbaustellen der Schweiz* (Baden, 2005).

Jon Mathieu is professor of history at the University of Lucerne. He has been teaching in different universities in Switzerland and in other countries, and he is the founding director of the Istituto di Storia delle Alpi at the Università della Svizzera italiana. His main interests in research and research management concern the agrarian, social, and cultural history of the early modern period and the nineteenth century, especially in mountain areas. Currently, he is working on a comparative mountain history in the modern period. His latest book is: *Die Alpen! Zur europäischen Wahrnehmungsgeschichte seit der Renaissance/Les Alpes! Pour une histoire de la perception européenne depuis la Renaissance* (Berne et al., 2005). His latest publications in family and kinship history are: "Verwandtschaft als historischer Faktor. Schweizer Fallstudien und Trends, 1500–1900," *Historische Anthropologie* 10 (2002); "Ein Cousin an jeder Zaunlücke. Überlegungen zum Wandel von Verwandtschaft und ländlicher Gemeinde, 1700–1900," in *Politiken der Verwandtschaft,* ed. Margareth Lanzinger, Edith Saurer (Göttingen 2007).

David Warren Sabean is Henry J. Bruman Professor of German History at the University of California at Los Angeles. A graduate of the University of Wisconsin where he studied under George Mosse, Sabean has taught at the University of East Anglia, University of Pittsburgh, and Cornell, and he has been a fellow at the Max Planck Institute for History in Göttingen, the Maison des Science de l'Homme, and the Wissenschaftskolleg zu Berlin. He is a fellow of the American Academy of Arts and Sciences. His publications include: *Power in the Blood: Popular Culture and Village Discourse in Early Modern Germany* (Cambridge, 1984); *Property, Production, and Family in Neckarhausen, 1700–1870* (Cambridge, 1990); *Kinship in Neckarhausen, 1700–1870* (Cambridge, 1998). Currently, he is engaged in an extensive study on the history of incest discourse and other fields of European cultural history.

Karl-Heinz Spiess is professor for *Allgemeine Geschichte des Mittelalters und Historische Hilfswissenschaften* at the Ernst-Moritz-Arndt-Universität Greifswald in Germany. He is a member of several academies and of the Konstanzer Arbeitskreis für Mittelalterliche Geschichte, and he is an advisor for the Deutsche Forschungsgemeinschaft. Selected books include: *Lehnsrecht, Lehnspolitik und Lehnsverwaltung der Pfalzgrafen bei Rhein im Spätmittelalter* (Wiesbaden, 1978); *Familie und Verwandtschaft im deutschen Hochadel des Spätmittelalters (13. bis Anfang des 16. Jahrhunderts)* (Stuttgart, 1993); *Prozesse der Normbildung und Normveränderung im mittelalterlichen Europa* (Stuttgart, 2000); *Das Lehnswesen in Deutschland im hohen und späten Mittelalter* (Idstein, 2002); *Principes. Dynastien und Höfe im späten Mittelalter* (Stuttgart, 2002); *Medien der Kommunikation im Mittelalter* (Stuttgart, 2003).

Simon Teuscher is professor of medieval history at the University of Zurich. He earned his doctoral degree at the University of Zurich, where he taught between 1996 and 1999. Since then, he has been teaching at University of California at Los Angeles and several Swiss universities while doing research with a grant from the Swiss National Foundation. He was a *professeur invité* at the Ecole des Hautes Etudes en Sciences Sociales in Paris in 2001, and member of the Institute for Advanced Study, School of Historical Studies in Princeton, 2004–2005. Besides the history of personal relationships, his research interests are urban and rural society and administrative culture of the late Middle Ages in Western and Northern Europe. His publications include *Bekannte—Verwandte—Klienten. Soziabilität und Politik in Bern um 1500* (Cologne, Weimar, Vienna 1998). He is currently in the process of finishing a book on the codification of local customs in Switzerland between 1200 and 1500.

Sylvia J. Yanagisako is professor of cultural and social anthropology at Stanford University. She has served as chair of the Department of Cultural and Social Anthropology, and she is a past president of the Society for Cultural Anthropology. Professor Yanagisako's scholarship has focused on the comparative study of kinship, gender, and capitalism. Her most recent monograph, *Producing Culture and Capital: Family Firms in Italy* (Princeton University Press, 2002) traces the processes through which family sentiments and commitments shape the Italian silk industry. A volume she coedited with Dan Segal, *Unwrapping the Sacred Bundle: Reflections on the Disciplining of Anthropology* (Duke University Press, 2005), critically examines the conventional configuration of the discipline of anthropology in the United States. Other books include *Transforming the Past: Kinship and Tradition among Japanese Americans* (Stanford University Press, 1985); *Gender and Kinship: Essays Toward a Unified Analysis*, coedited with Jane Collier (Stanford University Press, 1987); and *Naturalizing Power: Essays in Feminist Cultural Analysis* (Routledge, 1995), coedited with Carol Delaney. She is currently conducting research on joint ventures between Italian and Chinese textile and garment manufacturing firms.

Index

blood relation, relative, 2, 5, 34, 56, 135,
157, 172, 178, 181, 213, 222, 310
Blumer, Agatha, 250
Blumer, Emilie, 237, 241, 243, 250,
252n4
Blumer, Johann Jakob, 236
Blumer, Katharina, 237
Blumer, Susanne, see Heer (née),
Susanne
Blutel, Jean-Pierre, 271, 274
Boche (family), 173
Bohemia, 94
Bonaparte, Joseph, see Joseph I
Bonaparte, Napoléon, see Napoléon I
Bonapartist, 266, 268
bookseller, 198-199
Bordeaux, 112, 271
Boullé (family), 265, 271, 274
Bourbon (family), 268
Bourdieu, Pierre, 25, 89n27, 283n55,
304
Bourdonnay (family), 265, 274
bourgeoisie, 17, 20, 22, 26, 45, 208,
115, 121n7, 123n18, 123n23, 165,
180, 188, 190-191, 197-198, 223,
229n15, 232-238, 241, 243-245, 248,
250, 254n33, 261, 263-264, 266,
268, 270-271, 273, 275-277, 278n8,
279n18, 282n50, 282n52, 283n55,
285-287, 289, 291-293, 295, 297,
303, 305-306
Boveri (family), 243
Boveri, Walter, 243
branch, 9, 11, 56, 62, 64, 67, 116, 118-
119, 131-132, 140n4, 143n26, 145,
153, 166-167, 172, 198, 209n10,
220, 302, 306
Brandenburg (family), 131
Brandenburg (margrave), 94
Brégéon (engineer), 270, 272
Brentano (family), 197-198, 209n10
Brentano, Carl, 197
Brentano, Domenico, 198
Brentano, Martino, 197
Brentano, Peter Anthony, 198
Brentano-Cimaroli (family), 197
Brentano-Gnosso (family), 197
Brentano-Toccia (family), 197
Brentano-Tremezzo (family), 197
Brest, 274

Breton, 164, 190, 262, 265, 270,
280n24
Briançon, 198, 203
Britain, 25-26, 141n14, 262-263, 270-
271, 279, See also England
Broglias (family), 166
Bromley (family), 22
brother, viii-ix, 9, 15, 18, 25, 54, 57, 59,
62, 64, 66, 69-70, 75n69, 78, 81, 84-
85, 93-98, 100-101, 103n19, 103n25,
103n27, 103n28, 103n29, 104n30,
107, 116-119, 120n4, 121n6, 126,
129-130, 132-134, 136, 138, 143n29,
144n36, 147-151, 155-157, 164-166,
170-171, 173, 181, 182n7, 206, 243-
245, 247, 249-250, 259, 264, 267,
275, 281n34, 289, 295, 304-305, 322
brotherhood, 1
brother-in-law, 18, 20, 22, 98-100, 126,
147-149, 152-158, 198, 206, 236-
237, 247, 250, 264, 271, 274, 290-
291, 307
stepbrother, 290
Brüll (family), 292
Brunacci, Alesandro, 155
Brunacci, Lucrezia, 154-156
Brunets (family), 173
Brussel, 198
Buchmann, Franziska, 240, 249
Budapest, 286-287, 290, 293, 295-297
Bühler, Fanny, 246
Burgault (family), 265, 272, 274-275
Burgault, Emile, 273-274, 276
Burgundy, 122n13, 168, 170, 197
businessman, -men, 204-205

C

Caceràs, 182n14
Caceres, 174
Calvi, Giulia, 52-53, 55, 314
Calvin, John, 131, 214
Cambridge, 285
Canary Islands, 104n35
Canning, Kathleen, 307
canon, canonical, 12, 55-56, 125-130,
132-133, 135-136, 138-139, 140n3,
142n17, 143n29, 165, 214-216, 220-
221, 223, 227, 311
family, 55, 128, 132-133

canon, 20, 66, 69, 100, 127, 182n6, 213
civil, 181, 215, 223, 239
inheritance, 88n10, 160n2, 233, 238, 242
marriage, 70, 212-213, 216, 223-224
Roman, 97, 107, 120n2, 147, 161n5
written, 120, 201
Le Bouhéllec (family), 264, 274
Le Cointre, Julie, 271
Lectoure, 121n6
Lehmann, Emil, 306
Le Monnier (family), 274
Le Monnier, Josephine, 267
Le Montagner (family), 265, 274
Leopold I, Holy Roman Emperor, 98-100
Le Pas de Sécheval (family), 172
Le Play, Frédéric, 54
Le Ridant (family), 264, 274
Le Ridant, Alexis, 264-265, 276, 282n42
Le Ridant, Jean-Marie, 264
L'Estang-Parade (family), 172-173
letter, 13, 16, 68, 77, 79, 81-83, 89n18, 89n21, 95, 138, 144n41, 152, 155, 163, 232, 243, 245-246, 248-249, 254n31, 154n43, 255n65, 257n97, 257n98, 259-260, 265, 279, 301, 314, 316
Levi, Giovanni, 199, 208n3
Lévi-Strauss, Claude, 36, 220, 229n26
Leyen, von der (family), 137
Liebert von Liebenhofen, Benedikt Adam, 308
Liedemann (family), 290
Limburg, 130
Limoges, 168
Linth-Escher (family), 240
Locmariaquer, 270
Lodève, 267
Logrono, 176
Loire River, 107
Lombardy, 19
London, 306
Lorraine, 122n13
Lorvol (family), 272, 281n39
Lorvol, Michel, 265, 271, 274
Louis XI, King of France, 84

Louis XIII, King of France, 99
Louis XIV, the Sun King, King of France, 98-100, 164
Louis-Philippe, King of France, 274
Lucas de Bourgarel (family), 265
Ludwig I, Landgrave of Hesse, 103n25
Ludwig I, the Pious, Roman Emperor, 59
Ludwig II, Landgrave of Hesse-Kassel, 103n25
Luther, Martin, 233
Lüttich, 66
Luxemburg (family), 72n7
Luxemburg (territory), 141n14
Luzern, 218-219, 229n17, 240
Lyon, 197-198

M

McKinnon, Susan, 36, 38
magistrate, 146-147, 151, 153-156, 158
Mahé de Villneuve (family), 265
Mahé, Abbé, 269
Maine, Henry James Sumner, 43
Mainz, 55, 126, 131, 134-135, 143n35, 198
Malthus, Thomas, 131
Manduria, 167-168, 172-174, 176, 179, 182n14
Mannheim, 198
Margarete of Austria, Governor in the Netherlands, 97-98
Margarete of Austria, Electress of Saxony, 103n28
Margareta Theresia, Infanta of Spain, Holy Roman Empress, 99-100
Maria of Austria, Queen of Hungary and Bohemia, 98
Maria Anna, Duchess of Bavaria, 101
Maria Anna of Palatinate-Neuburg, Queen of Spain, 98
Maria Anna, Infanta of Spain, Holy Roman Empress, 99-100
Maria Antonia of Austria, Electress of Bavaria, 99
Maria Louisa, Duchess of Orléans, Queen of Spain, 98
Maria Maddalena of Austria, Grand Duchess of Venezia, 155
Maria Theresia, Infanta of Spain, Queen of France, 100, 164